Criminology at the Crossroads

READINGS IN CRIME AND PUNISHMENT
Michael Tonry, *General Editor*

What Works in Policing
David H. Bayley

Criminology at the Crossroads:
Feminist Readings in Crime and Justice
Kathleen Daly and Lisa Maher

Incarcerating Criminals:
Prisons and Jails in Social and Organizational Context
Timothy J. Flanagan, James W. Marquart, and Kenneth G. Adams

Community Corrections:
Probation, Parole, and Intermediate Sanctions
Joan Petersilia

Criminology at the Crossroads

Feminist Readings in Crime and Justice

Edited by

Kathleen Daly and Lisa Maher

New York   Oxford

OXFORD UNIVERSITY PRESS

1998

Oxford University Press

Oxford   New York
Athens   Auckland   Bangkok   Bogota
Bombay   Buenos Aires   Calcutta   Cape Town
Dar es Salaam   Delhi   Florence   Hong Kong
Istanbul   Karachi   Kuala Lumpur   Madras
Madrid   Melbourne   Mexico City   Nairobi
Paris   Singapore   Taipei   Tokyo
Toronto   Warsaw

and associated companies in
Berlin   Ibadan

Published by Oxford University Press, Inc.
198 Madison Avenue, New York, NY 10016

Oxford is a registered trademark of Oxford University Press

Library of Congress Cataloging-in-Publication Data
Criminology at the crossroads : feminist readings in crime and justice
/ edited by Kathleen Daly and Lisa Maher.
p.   cm.—(Readings in crime and punishment)
Includes bibliographical references.
ISBN 0-19-511343-8 (cl).—ISBN 0-19-511344-6 (paper)
1. Feminist criminology.   I. Daly, Kathleen, 1948–
II. Maher, Lisa.   III. Series
HV6030.C746 1998
364′.082—dc21   97-18731
CIP

Printing (last digit): 9 8 7 6 5 4 3 2 1

Printed in the United States of America
on acid-free paper

Contents

Criminology at the Crossroads

CHAPTER 1

Crossroads and Intersections
Building from Feminist Critique

KATHLEEN DALY AND LISA MAHER

Crossroads and intersections are common metaphors for feminist thinking in the 1990s. Crossroads highlight the different directions that feminist and allied social theories began to take in the 1980s concerning knowledge and representation (di Leonardo 1991). Intersections characterize the diverse subjectivities and positions of "women" and "men" arising from cross-cutting, rather than additive understandings of inequality and identity (Collins 1993; Crenshaw 1989, 1991). While we live in a period of political and economic conservatism and global retrenchment, the 1990s are an energetic, creative time for feminist thought across the disciplines.

This collection reflects the vitality and maturing of nearly three decades of feminist work in criminology. In this introduction, we first sketch historical shifts in feminist thought to orient the reader's understanding of contemporary developments. Next we describe our aims for the volume and our concerns in selecting the articles. Then we turn to our central focus: a discussion of the four themes that structure the volume and the articles (and other work) that illustrate those themes.

In the final section, we discuss familiar, if unresolved, problems inhering in feminist efforts to engage with law and criminology. Do we begin with theories of crime (or law) or theories of gender? Do we devote our creative energies to critiques of androcentric and poorly conceived theories or to developing feminist theoretical approaches? Do we focus attention on gender, crime, and justice as socially constructed, or do we conduct closely textured studies of the particularities and diversity of women's (and men's) lives? Like other areas of feminist inquiry, the answer surely is "both." And yet, like gender divisions of paid and unpaid labor, men and male-centered theories do not typically contend with this intellectual "double shift." They may be the poorer for it. An intellectual double shift—of working across discursive and disciplinary

1

boundaries and of analyzing "real people" and "texts"—holds great promise for theory, research, and social change.

HISTORY

Feminist contributions to criminology can be divided into two phases, a first or early phase, and a second more recent phase. Although it is difficult to fix precise dates, the early phase began in the late 1960s and the second, in the late 1980s. If we were to poll feminist scholars in criminology today, we would find that one portion—perhaps a majority in the United States—remain committed to the concerns and issues raised in the early phase, whereas another is working with recent ideas about the limits of knowledge and truth claims, including those associated with feminist inquiry. The first and second phases of feminist work in criminology have been described and reviewed elsewhere (see, e.g., Daly and Chesney-Lind 1988; Gelsthorpe and Morris 1987: chap. 1; Naffine 1994: chap. 1; Naffine 1997: chaps. 1–3; Rafter and Heidensohn 1995: chap. 1; Smart 1995: chaps. 1 and 13; Young 1996: chap. 2). Our essay builds on and extends this body of work.

In the *first or early phase* of feminist contributions to criminology, the major academic activities were (1) to critique criminological theories for failing to consider gender difference or for characterizing women in sexist ways; and (2) to conduct careful empirical studies of women's experiences as lawbreakers, victims, and workers in the justice system. A common question running through this work was *where* are the women and women's experiences? Often characterized as forgotten offenders and silenced victims, women emerged as a "popular subject" in the 1970s (Bowker 1978: xiii).

We might pause to consider this question: what explains this interest in women as lawbreakers, victims, and prisoners in the 1970s? Some reasons are obvious: there was a critical mass of feminist scholars and activists interested to understand and to improve the lives of girls and women whose experiences and worldviews were not registered in criminology, law, or institutions of formal and informal social control. But then and today, there are other reasons why women are popular subjects in criminology and mass culture—reasons that are less obvious and less frequently recognized.

Smart (1995: 221) observes that "the law is like [a] room full of men. . . . When it notices women, it inevitably sexes them and embodies them (us)." If we replace "law" with criminology or with media characterizations of victims and victimizers, we can see that one reason women become "popular subjects" is that they are "sexy" to viewers and consumers. If furthermore, as Smart (1995: 222) suggests, women's "bodies are deemed problematic and disruptive of the modern (masculine?) social order," viewers and readers may enjoy being surprised and shocked to learn that it was a woman, not the expected man, who turned out to be the slasher. At the same time, women's place as "eternal" and "deserving" victims (Smart 1990b: 207) in the socio-legal order, while punctuated with moments of transgression, is secured. As criminological subjects and as producers of criminological knowledge about women, women cannot avoid being "sexed" (Chancer 1993). Thus we suspect that there was (and is) more than the desire to fill "knowledge gaps" that attracted academic entrepreneurs in the 1970s and that continues to attract interest in women, crime, and victimization in the popular media.

The *second or more recent* phase of feminist work in criminology parallels major shifts that took place in feminist theory during the 1980s. In the 1970s, feminist scholars referred to *women* or to *women's experiences* in an unreflective way. They stressed the importance of distinguishing biological sex from socio-cultural gender, and of developing a comprehensive feminist theory that might replace liberal, Marxist, or psychoanalytic theories. These efforts became untenable in the 1980s with critique and challenge from two sources: women marginalized by feminist theory (e.g., women of color and lesbians) and postmodern/poststructuralist texts and theorists. Although springing from distinctive political and theoretical concerns, these critiques raised fundamental questions about how feminist knowledge is (and should be) produced and evaluated.

A brief definition of the terms *postmodern* and *poststructuralism* may be useful. Following Seidman (1994: 2) we use the terms *modern* and *postmodern* "to refer to broad social and cultural patterns and sensibilities that can be analytically distinguished for the purpose of highlighting social trends." Elements of each may be embedded in the other, but among those associated with *modern* are "the claim of the exclusive truth-producing capacity of science," centered and transcendental subjects, and causal relations; for *postmodern*, a rejection of Enlightenment theories of knowledge, decentered subjects or multiple subject positions, and noncausal relations. Most scholars working with a postmodern sensibility term their analyses *poststructuralist,* which signals an interest to deconstruct hierarchical binary oppositions in language and to analyze the role of discourse in "shaping subjectivity, social institutions, and politics" (Seidman 1994: 18). We shall use postmodern and poststructuralist loosely and interchangeably, although others have suggested ways of distinguishing them (see Smart 1995: 1–15; see also Schwartz and Freidrichs 1994).

In the second or more recent phase of feminist work in criminology, the major academic activities have been (1) to problematize the term *women* as a unified category; (2) to acknowledge that *women's experiences* are, in part, constructed by legal and criminological discourses; (3) to revisit the relationship between sex and gender; and (4) to reflect on the strengths and limits of constructing feminist "truths" and knowledge. Compared to the first phase, this second phase is more attentive to differences among women (and men); to problems of "essentialism" in theoretical categories; to racism and heterosexism in feminist and criminological thought; and to the construction of men and masculinities. (Note that the term *essentialism* has come to stand for many things [see deLauretis 1990; Spelman 1988]. Analyses that are essentialist may assume that categories such as "black" or "women" or "black women" have a fixed, natural, or homogeneous character or "essence"; this is in contrast to assuming that such categories are unstable, socially produced, and heterogeneous.) Second phase scholarship is interested in the significance of the partiality of knowledges (that is, both incomplete and grounded in specific social relations and worldviews) and to the ways in which legal and criminological discourses are constitutive of sex and gender, race and ethnicity, class, age, and sexuality.

In the first phase, feminists sought to document women's lives, lawbreaking, and victimization. We berated criminology for forgetting half the population, and we attempted to rectify this original sin by conducting research "on women." It was an understandable reaction to a field that had distorted and forgotten women. And it was an obvious first move: to replace older, prejudicial, and "sexist" images with newer, more accurate ones. Drawing from broader currents in feminist theory (e.g., Butler and Scott 1992; Nicholson 1990), second phase feminist work has emphasized the diversity of women's experiences as lawbreakers, victims, and justice system workers, and it has attempted to analyze how women are constructed in and by particular cultural or discursive formations.

In this second phase, we see two apparently contradictory developments. One trajectory of feminist scholarship remains interested in the "real women" of feminist social science (e.g., Carlen 1988; Maher 1997), whereas another is more concerned with "the Woman" [or women] of legal and criminological discourses (e.g., Smart 1990a; Young 1996: chap. 2). We use the terms *real women* and *women of discourse* as metaphors to contrast two ways of theorizing about women (and men) in the social world. Although these trajectories need not be viewed as incompatible, they reflect differences in the intellectual positions that scholars take toward their subjects.

By "real women" we refer to studies that explore women as agents in constructing their life worlds, including their lawbreaking and victimization. By "women of discourse" we refer to studies that explore how women are constructed in and by particular discourses, including those of criminal law, medicine, criminology, and even feminism itself. Whereas the first tends to characterize women as subjects of their own lives, the second more often characterizes women as effects of discourse. We are aware that as soon as a contrast like this is made, it will be met with objection; and we recognize the difficulties in categorizing scholars and their work neatly into one of these categories.

We imagine that many might say, "I am interested in both." But taking a position of *interest in both* is different from taking a position of *interest to connect both* in theory and research. Each position comes with its own set of theoretical referents and specialized vocabularies; hence the connections can be hard to make. We shall not canvass the epistemological and political debates about the strengths of working with either intellectual position. Our stance is that neither alone is sufficient, and that strong versions of either should be avoided (see, e.g., Carlen's 1992 critique of theoreticism and empiricist realism). One cannot analyze "real women" without reference to the discursive fields by which women are constructed or construct themselves. And one cannot assume that analyses of "women of discourse" necessarily reflect women's identities and the lives women lead. Thus the problem is *not* that these two positions exist, but that making connections between them can be difficult for theory, research, and politics.

By the 1990s, scholars had become aware that terms such as *women* (or *men* or *blacks* or *lesbians*) should reflect a nonessentialist, socially constructed, and varied character. And at the same time, many of us decided that it was possible to do empirical work without becoming entrapped by forms of discursive determinism. Moreover, as Scheper-Hughes (1992: 23) suggests, we need not "get into a tortured discussion of facticity, empiricism, positivism, and so on." She argues that

> Some events are "factual." Either 150 or 350 children died of hunger and dehydration [in an area in the Brazilian Northeast] in 1965. . . . [T]he ethnographer has a professional and a moral obligation to get the "facts" as accurately as possible. This is not even debatable. But all the facts are necessarily selected and interpreted from the moment we decide to count one thing and ignore another . . . so that anthropological understanding is necessarily partial and is always hermeneutic.

Her point, one that has been lost on some feminist philosophers (e.g., Flax 1990) and sociologists embracing poststructuralist analyses of texts and discourses (e.g., Lemert 1994), is that "empirical work need not be empiricist," . . . that is, it need not "entail a philosophical commitment to Enlightenment notions of reason and truth" (Scheper-Hughes 1992: 23).

Testifying to the unevenness with which new ideas reach and challenge disciplines, criminology lags well behind law and socio-legal analyses in taking seriously the idea of multiple inequalities or *intersectionalities*. The joining of feminist and critical race analyses of criminal law and justice system practices has blossomed in American legal and socio-legal scholarship (for reviews, see Coombs 1996; Crenshaw 1991; Daly and Stephens 1995; Harris 1990, 1996). In criminology, by contrast, scholars have been constrained by essentialist understandings of race (e.g., Russell 1992 on a "black criminology"), or they rely on male-centered notions of multiculturalism (Barak 1991; Thornberry 1990; Young and Greene 1995).

Criminology as a discipline continues to think of race in ungendered terms (see critique by Renzetti 1993/94). This problem is occurring at the same time that a research study announces that criminology textbooks in the United States give more coverage "to women than to racial and ethnic minorities" (Walker and Brown 1995: 75). Surely, this sort of gender vs. race scorekeeping stymies the building of feminist antiracist knowledges. Would it not be better to examine how race, ethnicity, and gender structure criminological assumptions, theories, and interpretations? And would it not be better to think of race and ethnicity in less fixed terms?

White criminology avoids "the race issue" because of racism both in the discipline and the wider society, a lack of theoretical grounding in what racial-ethnic relations and identities are, and too few scholars of color in criminology who are in a position to take on white criminology. Our concern is that as minority and majority group scholars challenge the field, we use nonessentialist understandings of racial-ethnic relations and identities, and draw from other allied literatures. In addition to the critical race scholarship in law (see, e.g., Delgado 1995), sociologists have started with racial and ethnic categories, expanding them and making them more complex by including other divisions such as gender, color, and sexuality (Anthias and Yuval-Davis 1992; see also Omi and Winant 1994). Nuanced and contingent analyses of race have featured for some time in literary works and cultural commentaries (e.g., Carby 1987; hooks 1984; Lorde 1984). There is no excuse for mainstream criminology's delinquency in the matter.

Today, when scanning those journals and books in criminology, sociology, and socio-legal studies that attend to questions of sex/gender, we find a mix of first and second phase contributions, although the former remains prevalent. That is, feminist analysts are still criticizing androcentric theories and presenting careful empirical studies of gender, crime, and justice. This work is important because, from a feminist perspective, the field of criminology acts like a recalcitrant student. It seems to require constant reminding that its subjects are gendered and racialized, and that its simplified folk theories of gender and race cannot begin to account for the complexities of multiple, cross-cutting social relations. Second phase feminist work is present, however, and it is capturing an increasing share of academic airtime.

AIMS

Three aims guided us in selecting the contributions to this volume. First, we wanted to move beyond the familiar critiques (though well deserved) of androcentrism, racism, and ethnocentrism in the field. Rather than asking *where* are the women? or *where* is sex/gender in criminology? we are saying, *here* are women (and men) and *here* is sex/gender in criminal law, lawbreaking, and state responses to harm. That assertion is made, cognizant of the varied and partial knowledges about women (and men), including feminist knowledges. It is also made with an awareness of, indeed with an interest to expose, the varied debates in feminist scholarship on terms and assumptions used. Second, we wanted selections not only from the United States but also from England, Canada, and Australia. That decision reflects our biographies and international interests: Daly, an American citizen now based in Australia, and Maher, an Australian citizen who studied and lived in New York City for several years while completing her Ph.D. It also reflects the need to draw from feminist and related theoretical developments in countries other than the United States. Third, we wanted selections from the social science and law literatures. This choice reflects our concern that the disciplinary contributions of law and social science should be utilized together. Socio-legal studies continues to make important theoretical contributions and challenges to criminology, and, in part, this is because its practitioners have been working across disciplinary boundaries. Ultimately, our selection criteria were those articles that have stimulated us and our students, and that have raised unresolved problems for the field.

THEMES

One unresolved problem is how to connect "real women" with "women of discourse." Some argue that women (or men) can only ever be apprehended or known through discourses and that an epistemology of realism is misplaced (compare Smart 1990a with Cain 1990, 1995). Earlier feminist analyses assumed it was possible not only to expose but also to overcome "stereotypes" of women in theories of crime or criminal justice officials' responses. More recent feminist work has analyzed the ways in which women are constrained within and by legal and criminological discourses *and* some feminist discourses, as well (see, e.g., Schulhofer 1995; Worrall 1990). For example, whereas Smart's article (this volume) illustrates a position that emphasizes "women of discourse," those by Joe and Chesney-Lind, and Polk (this volume) illustrate a position that emphasizes "real women" (and men). None of the volume's contributors focus single-mindedly on "women of discourse" or "real women." All draw from empirical studies (or historical records and texts) of "real women," and all raise questions about how women (or men) are represented in feminist, legal, and criminological discourses. However, the authors do vary in their start points and the degree to which they emphasize "real women" and "women of discourse."

Women of Feminist, Legal, and Criminological Discourses

Carol Smart's article opens by noting problems that confront feminist socio-legal theory, together with the critics associated with black letter law, liberal theory, and feminist activism. Her analysis of problems in law has its analog in criminology. Many criminologists do not see the value of working outside the confines of the discipline of criminology; many do not see the value of bringing feminist theories of sex/gender to bear on the discipline; and some feminists may not see the value of theoretical work, wishing instead to focus on practical change. Smart's article maps developmental shifts in feminist socio-legal theories before turning to her argument that Woman is a "subject position which legal discourse brings into being." She discusses two elements that construct women: types of women (including criminal and victimized women) and Woman in distinction to Man. And she provides an example of the historical emergence in Europe of the category of "bad mother" through law and material circumstances.

Kristin Bumiller examines the legal construction and containment of the "raped woman" as this unfolds in a gang rape trial in Massachusetts. She argues that contrary to the hopes of some feminist reformers that celebrated trials could educate the public about sexual victimization, the trial testimony may reinscribe traditional notions of "reasonable" and "unreliable" women. Bumiller also suggests that it would be naive to think that women can describe their experiences of rape in the courtroom: their words are framed and contained by dominant legal discourse and procedure. Her analysis raises questions about what "real women" are able to say when they speak, whether in the courtroom or elsewhere.

Hilary Allen analyzes the commonalities in how accused and convicted women are represented in court reports (presentence investigations) and feminist discourse. Working with materials from the 1980s, she argues that both court and feminist analyses tend to downgrade women's actions as "not serious" and to neutralize women's responsibility for crime. Allen was a pioneer in suggesting that feminist discourse looked no different from dominant court discourse in denying "the responsibility, culpability and even the agency of female offenders" (Allen 1987: 92). Her critique is similar to that put forward by Daly (this volume) on the limits of explaining lawbreaking by reference to victimization.

Kerry Carrington considers current developments in feminist work in criminology in relation to social theory, and especially the influences of postmodern thought. She discusses the meanings of terms such as modernity, postmodernity, and postmodernism; and she provides examples of essentialism in criminological analyses. On balance, Carrington sees value to feminist engagement with postmodernism, but, at the same time, she sees no reason to privilege postmodern theoretical insights over those that had already been developing in feminist theory.

Blurred Boundaries of Victimization and Criminalization

Traditional criminology, both of the past and present, has been unduly focused on distinguishing "them" (the lawbreakers) from "us" (the law abiding). Furthermore, there is a statistical and theoretical division of labor in counting and explaining the experiences of "victims" and "offenders." A prominent theme in feminist theorizing in the 1980s and early 1990s was of blurred boundaries between victimization and criminalization. There are several ways this theme has been used. First, in Britain, it could explain the movement of girls, whose families were too poor to support them or whose familial circumstances were bad, from institutionalized foster care to juvenile/adult custody (Carlen 1987). Second, in the United States, it could explain the experiences of girls who ran away from abusive households and whose street survival strategies were criminalized (Chesney-Lind 1989; Gilfus 1992). Third, it was used to politicize and problematize the categories of "offender" and "prisoner." If offenders and prisoners were also victims, they could then be viewed as only partly "criminal" and hence in a more positive light. These rhetorical moves were strong in grassroots and academic feminist campaigns to raise awareness of imprisoned women who had killed abusive mates; they continue to be evident in analyses of women who are used as drug "mules" (Huling 1995) or who enter the sex-work industry (Bell 1987). Victimization-criminalization arguments for male lawbreakers who had been abused as children also reached mainstream cultural currents, although pejoratively, in the form of the "abuse excuse" (Dershowitz 1994).

The articles in Part II illuminate and challenge the victimization-criminalization thesis for women and for men. They also explore how racial-ethnic identities and categories among women may (and may not) differentiate their pathways to common crime and their experiences of lawbreaking. We have learned that there is some empirical support for a developmental sequencing of lawbreaking as spawned, in part, by abuse in families and the survival strategies of "running" to the streets (e.g., Widom 1989). Yet many children and adolescents who have been sexually and physically abused do not run away nor do they become criminalized. Moreover, for many adolescents "the street" is not something to "run" to, but one's neighborhood, where one lives. Pathways to lawbreaking are many and varied.

Karen Joe and Meda Chesney-Lind analyze Samoan, Filipino, and Native Hawaiian girls' and boys' reasons for joining gangs. Most of the girls they interviewed had been physically and sexually abused by family members (just over half the boys had been physically abused), and the authors tend to explain the girls' uses of violence as caused by their victimization in families. Joe and Chesney-Lind find that gangs serve as sites for social activity and as surrogate families. We may wonder whether gangs may also reproduce some of the same power dynamics in families that gang members are attempting to escape.

Lisa Maher and Richard Curtis reveal the situational dynamics of victimization and lawbreaking for African-American, Latina, and European-American women in economically distressed New York City neighborhoods. They find that women drug users who are forced to rely on the declining cash value of their sexual services may use violence against male dates as a form of resistance to their own subordinated status. In an ironic inversion, the women term the actions they take against their dates as "viccing": shifting their own identities as "victims" to their male clients. Maher and Curtis argue that an analysis of women's victimization in the informal economy helps to contextualize their agency.

The psychological developmental processes and the situational dynamics of crime render the metaphor of blurred boundaries of victimization-criminalization a useful one. At the same time, it may gloss over crucial questions of agency and responsibility in women's (and men's) lawbreaking. Kathleen Daly suggests that in feminist analyses, there is a "black box" between structured oppression and experiences of victimization, on the one side, and actions that harm others and become subject to state intervention as crime, on the other. From an examination of the biographies of black and white women and Latinas in New Haven, Daly asks, where does victimization end and responsibility for acts that harm others begin? How do we characterize women when they do things that are wrong? Daly anticipates that feminist analysts may find it more difficult to accept the blurred boundaries theme in explanations of men's lawbreaking.

Masculinities and Violence

To some, it might initially seem odd that feminist scholars would be interested in men and crime. After all, as early works by Smart (1976) and Leonard (1982) showed, criminological theory and research have centered on boys' and men's lawbreaking to the neglect of girls and women. But, upon reflection, we find that since the early 1970s, a good deal of feminist attention has been given to men and crime with analyses of men's violence against women. Feminist explanations of men's violence did not come from criminological theories or vocabularies, but rather from activists and ideas that had been developing outside academic criminology (Dobash and Dobash 1992). Indeed, for over a century, practitioners of both mainstream and radical criminology overlooked a large portion of men's harms, i.e., assaults and rapes, and attempts to do so, on partners or ex- partners. This lack of attention began to change in the 1980s when both mainstream and radical criminologists started to notice and to rely upon feminist studies of violence against women.

In addition to enlarging the field of behavior to be analyzed under "men and crime," the task for feminist scholars in the 1990s is to move beyond mainstream criminology's folk theories of men, as for example, in "the simple association of masculinity with . . . 'machismo'" (Newburn and Stanko 1994: 1). The task is also to move beyond radical feminist analyses of the 1970s and 1980s that characterized men's violence toward women in mechanical and hydraulic terms as reflective of men's "needs" to control women.

One-dimensional and deterministic understandings of men have been criticized by scholars interested in masculinities and crime. They are discovering that the same problems confronting feminist analyses of women in crime are present in their analyses of men. As enumerated by Jefferson (1996), they include a desire to deal with the challenges of postmodern social theory *and* the exigencies of devising sound policy; wanting to analyze men or masculinity in discourse but not to be limited by discursive determinism; and seeking ways of linking structure and agency in explaining human behavior. Key theoretical contributions to the masculinities and crime literatures have been made by Connell (1987, 1995), Messerschmidt (1993), and Jefferson (1994). We cannot give a full discussion of the arguments here (see Daly 1997; Jefferson 1996; Newburn and Stanko 1994), but we would note that different theoretical trends are emerging. For example, whereas Messerschmidt (drawing from Connell 1987; West and Zimmerman 1987) views gender as a set of practices, and crime as a resource in "doing masculinity," Jefferson (1996: 341) wonders why it is that only some men "identify with crime as an option . . . to accomplish . . . masculinity." To address that question would necessitate, in Jefferson's view, a theory of subjectivity, i.e., of the formation and meaning of masculine identity. Toward that end, Jefferson wants to use a mixture of psychoanalytical theories, which may show "how subjects position themselves in relation to the discursive choices facing them, how they come to adopt certain positions and not others" (p. 341).

The articles in Part III present different forms, contexts, and meanings of boys' and men's violence. Men's violence against women is learned and practiced in many sites: not just in familial domestic settings but also in organizations such as the military and all-male social clubs such as college fraternities in the United States. Patricia Martin and Robert Hummer's piece tries to make sense of a gang rape that occurred in a fraternity house in Florida and the subsequent cover-up by the larger "brotherhood." They argue that we need to stop thinking of gang rape as caused by individual men's pathologies or even "peer pressure," as so often occurs. Rather, such incidents arise from the norms and dynamics of fraternities as organizations that (re)produce hegemonic conceptions of masculinity.

Joyce Canaan explores the variable constructions of masculinity among working class (mostly white) British boys who differentiate themselves and other boys through categories of "acting hard" and "being hard." Merged in the idiom of masculine "hardness" is an ability to fight other boys and to have sex with girls, although strength for some boys lay in their heads, not in their hands or genitals. Like Martin and Hummer and other scholars (Sanday 1990), Canaan finds that most boys relate to young women as "sexual commodities" in competing with other men, in forming alliances with them, and in affirming the superiority of heterosexuality.

Kenneth Polk explores patterns of a particular form of homicide, "confrontations [that] began as a contest over honour or reputation," using coroner's records from the state of Victoria (Australia). Like other scholars, he finds these contests largely involve economically marginal men. And, preempting Jefferson's (1996) point, Polk wonders "why some males pursue violence to secure . . . reputation or status, while others avoid such challenges." Thus general claims of masculine physical violence in a competitive, hostile, and misogynist environment in which men lack economic resources, may initially seem useful. However, such claims would appear to massively overpredict the frequency of men's violence.

Crossroads and Intersections

Feminist work in criminology stands at three related crossroads. First are the crossroads created by the impact of poststructuralist thought on the social sciences, that is, the crossroads of discourse and realism, of "words" and "things" (Barrett 1992). Second are the crossroads of narrative and logico-scientific modes of reasoning (see Bruner 1986; Ewick and Silbey 1995; Richardson 1990). Specifically, what kinds of texts will we write and read? What form and conventions will we employ to present evidence, argue, and persuade? Third are the crossroads of academic and activist knowledges that can "make a sociopolitical difference" (Klein 1995: 217). Specifically, how can research, writing, and speaking influence the larger world? None of these crossroads is unique to feminist work in criminology; they feature generally in efforts to link social theory and research to social change.

What is unique to feminist work in criminology is the dilemmas of engaging in the political and policy world of crime and its control. The stakes are high in this world: it is concerned with core questions about freedom, security, and democratic order. The dilemmas of engagement are exacerbated when considering multiple inequalities (of class, race, gender, age, sexualities) and lives lived in multicultural contexts. The articles in Part IV address some of these dilemmas.

Kathleen Ferraro analyzes what happens when new policies are introduced in the criminal justice system, in this case a presumptive arrest policy for domestic violence. The policy, endorsed by the Phoenix chief of police, was not implemented uniformly by the rank and file. Ferraro gives a critical and sympathetic reading of how officers exercised discretion in responding to "family fights," and she explores the impact of language and cultural differences on the officers and the communities they police.

Sherene Razack considers several feminist dilemmas when cultural defense arguments are used to explain and excuse minority men's violence against women. Drawing from legal cases involving Canadian First Nation male defendants, Razack is concerned that "culture" not be used against women. Her article edges near, but does not directly address, the difficulties that can arise in building feminist and antiracist coalitions in shaping crime and justice policies. Such coalitional building should, in our view, be placed at the top of the feminist agenda. Otherwise, a false separation of "race politics" and "gender politics" in public life will divide those groups who share a common vision for the future.

Razack raises questions, taken up by Laureen Snider, about what is a "too lenient" sentence for a First Nations man convicted of rape. Following Smart (1989), Snider sees criminal law and justice system institutions as inhospitable, inappropriate sites for feminist struggles for social change. In particular, she argues that what appear to be symbolic victories in passing tougher laws to control men's violence will only be hollow gains, and, in fact, may worsen women's situations. Other feminist scholars challenge Snider's position. Among them are Ferraro (this volume), Stubbs (1995), and Dobash and Dobash (1992), who argue for maintaining a strong criminal law presence and who stress that some criminal justice interventions can in fact work.

Regina Austin examines the intersections of class, race, and gender in challenging the mythic ideal of the "black community" in the United States. She considers the difficulties for members of the black middle class (and conventional working class) in identifying with black lawbreakers, particularly women. She discusses the important role that "bridge people" can make: to "work the line between street and straight" by bringing to light the meanings and practices of lawbreaking. Like other feminist and critical race scholars who have written on crime (e.g., Greene 1990; Roberts 1991), Austin neither romanticizes nor stigmatizes black lawbreakers. Her analysis goes beyond questions of feminist engagement with law: she pushes us to consider questions of community, identity, and economy.

CONCLUSION

As Smart (1989) suggests, feminist scholars cannot ignore law, but equally, we cannot make law and legal reform the center of our activism and scholarship. So too for criminology: we cannot ignore the field, but we need not permit its preoccupations to circumscribe feminist inquiry. Feminist work in and against criminology must move on two fronts: building feminist knowledges and continuing to challenge and correct a nonfeminist field for its gender blindnesses, ethnocentrisms, and theoretical rigidities. In criminology, getting spent ideas out of the literature remains a recurrent task. There is a persistent need for feminists to participate in what Geertz (1973: 27) calls "intellectual weed control" or "hastening the demise of moribund notions." Such weed control can be a full-time job because old theories continue to reappear in new forms, to wit, the varied ways in which women's "emancipation" is linked to increases in female arrest rates. To be sure, women today do not face the same set of cultural, economic, and social conditions, nor modes of legal and medical regulation, as they did, say, in the 1950s. Theories of lawbreaking and victimization will, of necessity, reflect these changing social realities. But whenever we hear criminologists or media commentators claim that there are "new female criminals" of one sort or another, we assume that *what is really new* is not the character of women's lawbreaking per se, but rather the study of women lawbreakers for that particular criminologist or commentator.

We noted that the early phase of feminist work in criminology was devoted to discovery and recovery of women as crime victims and victimizers. Today, feminist scholars no longer need to ask *where* are the women? We have produced research and theories that assert the gendered, racialized, classed, and aged presence of women and men in crime and justice system institutions, both as producers and subjects of knowledge. We have moved from noting that women in crime are "popular subjects" toward effecting change in the ways that victimization data are gathered (Bachman and Taylor 1994), to having a journal devoted to these questions (*Women and Criminal Justice*), and to separate spaces in criminology texts and readers devoted to "feminist perspectives."

Increasingly, feminist contributions to criminology start outside criminology. We start by asking questions about women (and gender), rather than questions about crime (Cain 1990: 10). Such a position does not mean that elements of current criminological theories may not be relevant, as some assert (Baskin and Sommers 1993: 561). Nor that gender is the sole (or primary) consideration in criminal justice response, as others infer (Akers 1994: 43). Rather, it is to say that feminist analyses of sex/gender relations open up a window on the worlds of deviance, conformity, and social control that traditional masculinist theories of crime and justice do not. Analyses that begin with race/ethnicity or with age may also open up new windows of understanding. An example by analogy can help. Recall from our discussion of Bumiller's article that rape victims may not be able to convey the harm of sexual victimization in their trial testimony because of the law's framing of what is considered permissible and relevant to disclose. This also occurs in criminology: its concepts and metaphors may not be able to register the ways in which gender organizes deviance and social control (Bottcher 1995), nor the ordinary ways in which "what happens to girls and women in courts and prisons connects with what happens in the playground, in the family, and at work" (Cain 1990: 6).

In the late 1990s, we detect a shift away from some of the problems that seemed to haunt feminist scholarship in the 1980s, which put us at an impasse. These problems centered on postmodern challenges to feminist truth claims and on the significance of discourse analysis for the social sciences. One way to move forward is to connect studies of "real women" with "women of discourse." Another is to develop more sophisticated and imaginative understandings of "intersectionality"—of the multiple influences of gender, race, age, class, and other social relations—as sources of inequality and identity in social life, and as constitutive of social institutions like law. And ultimately, to connect that work with political struggles for social change.

Acknowledgments

We appreciate the comments by Wendy Chan, Lynn Chancer, Emma Ogilvie, and Sally Simpson on earlier versions of this introduction. Thanks also to Carol Ronken for research assistance.

Ed. note: Readers will see different referencing, punctuation, and spelling styles in the chapters. Rather than imposing a uniform scheme, we decided to preserve these differences.

REFERENCES

Akers, Ronald L. (1994) *Criminological Theories: Introduction and Evaluation.* Los Angeles: Roxbury Publishing Company.

Anthias, Floya and Nira Yuval-Davis (1992) *Racialized Boundaries: Race, Nation, Gender, Colour and Class and the Anti-Racist Struggle.* New York: Routledge.

Allen, Hilary (1987) *Justice Unbalanced.* Philadelphia: Open University Press.

Bachman, Ronet and Bruce M. Taylor (1994) "The measurement of family violence and rape by the redesigned national crime victimization survey," *Justice Quarterly* 11(3): 499–512.

Barak, Gregg (1991) "Cultural literacy and a multicultural inquiry into the study of crime and justice," *Journal of Criminal Justice Education* 2: 173–92.

Barrett, Michele (1992) "Words and things: materialism and method in contemporary feminist analysis," in Michele Barrett and Anne Phillips (eds) *Destabilizing Theory,* pp. 201–19. Stanford: Stanford University Press.

Baskin, Deborah and Ira Sommers (1993) "Females' initiation into violent street crime," *Justice Quarterly* 10(4): 559–83.

Bell, Laurie (ed) (1987) *Good Girls/Bad Girls.* Seattle: Seal Press.

Bottcher, Jean (1995) "Gender as social control," *Justice Quarterly* 12(1): 33–57.

Bowker, Lee H. (1978) *Women, Crime, and the Criminal Justice System.* Lexington: Lexington Books.

Bruner, Jerome (1986) *Actual Minds, Possible Worlds.* Cambridge: Harvard University Press.

Butler, Judith and Joan W. Scott (eds) (1992) *Feminists Theorize the Political.* New York: Routledge.

Cain, Maureen (1990) "Realist philosophy and standpoint epistemologies or feminist criminology as a successor Science," in Loraine Gelsthorpe and Allison Morris (eds) *Feminist Perspectives in Criminology,* pp. 124–40. Philadelphia: Open University Press.

Cain, Maureen (1995) "Horatio's mistake: notes on some spaces in an old text," *Journal of Law and Society* 22(1): 68–77.

Carby, Hazel V. (1987) *Reconstructing Womanhood: The Emergence of the Afro-American Woman Novelist.* New York: Oxford University Press.

Carlen, Pat (1987) "Out of care, into custody: dimensions and deconstructions of the state's regulation of twenty-two young working-class women," in Pat Carlen and Anne Worrall (eds) *Gender, Crime and Justice,* pp. 126–60. Philadelphia: Open University Press.

Carlen, Pat (1988) *Women, Crime and Poverty.* Philadelphia: Open University Press.

Carlen, Pat (1992) "Criminal women and criminal justice: the limits to, and potential of, feminist and left realist perspectives," in Roger Matthews and Jock Young (eds) *Issues in Realist Criminology,* pp. 51–69. Newbury Park, CA: Sage.

Chancer, Lynn Sharon (1993) "Prostitution, feminist theory, and ambivalence: notes from the sociological underground," *Social Text* 37: 143–71.

Chesney-Lind, M. (1989) "Girls' crime and woman's place: toward a feminist model of female delinquency," *Crime and Delinquency* 35(1): 5–29.

Collins, Patricia Hill (1993) "Toward a new vision: race, class, and gender as categories of analysis and connection," *Race, Sex, and Class* 1(1): 25–45.

Connell, R. W. (1987) *Gender and Power*. Stanford: Stanford University Press.

Connell, R. W. (1995) *Masculinities*. St Leonards, NSW: Allen & Unwin.

Coombs, Mary (1996) "Interrogating identity," *Berkeley Women's Law Journal and African-American Law and Policy Report* Joint Issue 11: 222–49.

Crenshaw, Kimberele (1989) "Demarginalizing the intersection of race and sex: a black feminist critique of antidiscrimination doctrine, feminist theory, and antiracist politics," *University of Chicago Legal Forum* 1989: 139–67.

Crenshaw, Kimberele (1991) "Mapping the margins: intersectionality, identity politics, and violence against women of color," *Stanford Law Review* 43: 1241–99.

Daly, Kathleen (1997) "Different ways of conceptualizing sex/gender in feminist theory and their implications for criminology," *Theoretical Criminology* 1(1): 25–51.

Daly, Kathleen and Meda Chesney-Lind (1988) "Feminism and criminology," *Justice Quarterly* 5(4): 497–538.

Daly, Kathleen and Deborah Stephens (1995) "The 'dark figure' of criminology: toward a black and multi-ethnic feminist agenda for theory and research," in Nicole Hahn Rafter and Frances Heidensohn (eds) *International Feminist Perspectives in Criminology*, pp. 189–215. Philadelphia: Open University Press.

de Lauretis, Teresa (1990) "Upping the anti (sic) in feminist theory," in Marianne Hirsch and Evelyn Fox Keller (eds) *Conflicts in Feminism*, pp. 255–70. New York: Routledge.

Delgado, Richard (ed) (1995) *Critical Race Theory: The Cutting Edge*. Philadelphia: Temple University Press.

Dershowitz, Alan M. (1994) *The Abuse Excuse: And Other Cop Outs, Sob Stories, and Evasions of Responsibility*. Boston: Little Brown & Co.

di Leonardo, Micaela (1991) "Introduction," in Micaela di Leonardo (ed) *Gender at the Crossroads of Knowledge: Feminist Anthropology in the Postmodern Era*, pp. 1–48. Berkeley: University of California Press.

Dobash, R. Emerson and Russell Dobash (1992) *Women, Violence, and Social Change*. New York: Routledge.

Ewick, Patricia and Susan S. Silbey (1995) "Subversive stories and hegemonic tales: toward a sociology of narrative," *Law & Society Review* 29(2): 197–226.

Flax, Jane (1990) "Postmodernism and gender relations in feminist theory," in Linda Nicholson (ed) *Feminism/Postmodernism*, pp. 39–62. New York: Routledge.

Geertz, Clifford (1973) *The Interpretation of Cultures*. New York: Basic Books.

Gelsthorpe, Loraine and Allison Morris (1987) "Introduction: transforming and transgressing criminology," in Loraine Gelsthorpe and Allison Morris (eds) *Feminist Perspectives in Criminology*, pp. 1–9. Buckingham: Open University Press.

Gilfus, Mary E. (1992) "From victims to survivors to offenders: women's routes of entry and immersion into street crime," *Women & Criminal Justice* 4: 63–89.

Greene, Dwight L. (1990) "Drug decriminalization: a chorus in need of Masterrap's voice," *Hofstra Law Review* 18: 457–500.

Harris, Angela P. (1990) "Race and essentialism in feminist legal theory," *Stanford Law Review* 42: 581–616.

Harris, Angela P. (1996) "Foreward: the unbearable lightness of identity," *Berkeley Women's Law Journal and African-American Law and Policy Report* Joint Issue 11: 207–21.

hooks, bell (1984) *Black Feminist Theory: From Margin to Center.* Boston: South End Press.

Huling, Tracy (1995) "Women drug couriers," *Criminal Justice* 9(4): 14–19, 58–62.

Jefferson, Tony (1994) "Theorizing masculine subjectivity," in Tim Newburn and Elizabeth A. Stanko (eds) *Just Boys Doing Business? Men, Masculinities and Crime*, pp. 10–31. New York: Routledge.

Jefferson, Tony (1996) "Introduction," *British Journal of Criminology* 36(3): 337–47 (special issue on "Masculinities, Social Relations and Crime").

Klein, Dorie (1995) "Crime through gender's prism: feminist criminology in the United States," in Nicole Hahn Rafter and Frances Heidensohn (eds) *International Feminist Perspectives in Criminology*, pp. 216–40. Philadelphia: Open University Press.

Lemert, Charles C. (1994) "Post-structuralism and sociology," in Steven Seidman (ed) *The Postmodern Turn: New Perspectives on Social Theory*, pp. 265–81. New York: Cambridge University Press.

Leonard, Eileen (1982) *Women, Crime, and Society.* New York: Longman.

Lorde, Audre (1984) *Sister Outsider.* Trumansburg, NY: The Crossing Press.

Maher, Lisa (1997) *Sexed Work: Gender, Race, and Resistance in a Brooklyn Drug Market.* Oxford: Oxford University Press.

Messerschmidt, James W. (1993) *Masculinities and Crime: Critique and Reconceptualization of Theory.* Lanham, MD: Rowman & Littlefield Publishers.

Naffine, Ngaire (1994) "Introduction," in Ngaire Naffine (ed) *Gender, Crime and Feminism*, pp. xi–xxx. Brookfield, VT: Dartmouth Publishing Company.

Naffine, Ngaire (1997) *Feminism and Criminology.* St Leonards, NSW: Allen and Unwin.

Newburn, Tim and Elizabeth A. Stanko (1994) "Introduction: men, masculinities and crime," in Tim Newburn and Elizabeth A. Stanko (eds) *Just Boys Doing Business? Men, Masculinities and Crime*, pp. 1–9. New York: Routledge.

Nicholson, Linda (ed) (1990) *Feminism/Postmodernism.* New York: Routledge.

Omi, Michael and Howard Winant (1994) *Racial Formation in the United States*, 2nd edition. New York: Routledge.

Rafter, Nicole Hahn and Frances Heidensohn (eds) (1995) *International Feminist Perspectives in Criminology.* Philadelphia: Open University Press.

Renzetti, Claire (1993/94) "Feminism and criminology: criminal justice education," *Socio-Legal Bulletin* 11: 10–15.

Richardson, Laurel (1990) "Narrative and sociology," *Journal of Contemporary Ethnography* 19(1): 116–35.

Roberts, Dorothy E. (1991) "Punishing drug addicts who have babies: women of color, equality, and the right of privacy," *Harvard Law Review* 104: 1419–82.

Russell, Katheryn K. (1992) "Development of a black criminology and role of the black criminologist," *Justice Quarterly* 9: 667–83.

Sanday, Peggy Reeves (1990) *Fraternity Gang Rape*. New York: New York University Press.

Scheper-Hughes, Nancy (1992) *Death Without Weeping: The Violence of Everyday Life in Brazil*. Berkeley: University of California Press.

Schulhofer, Stephen J. (1995) "The feminist challenge in criminal law," *University of Pennsylvania Law Review* 143: 2151–2207.

Schwartz, Martin D. and David O. Freidrichs (1994) "Postmodern thought and criminological discontents: new metaphors for understanding violence," *Criminology* 32(2): 221–46.

Seidman, Steven (1994) "Introduction," in Steven Seidman (ed) *The Postmodern Turn: New Perspectives on Social Theory*, pp. 1–23. New York: Cambridge University Press.

Smart, Carol (1976) *Women, Crime and Criminology: A Feminist Critique*. Boston: Routledge and Kegan Paul.

Smart, Carol (1989) *Feminism and the Power of Law*. New York: Routledge.

Smart, Carol (1990a) "Feminist approaches to criminology, or postmodern woman meets atavistic man," in Loraine Gelsthorpe and Allison Morris (eds) *Feminist Perspectives in Criminology*, pp. 70–84. Philadelphia: Open University Press.

Smart, Carol (1990b) "Law's power, the sexed body, and feminist discourse," *Journal of Law and Society* 17: 194–210.

Smart, Carol (1995) *Law, Crime and Sexuality: Essays in Feminism*. London: Sage.

Spelman, Elizabeth V. (1988) *Inessential Woman*. Boston: Beacon Press.

Stubbs, Julie (1995) " 'Communitarian' conferencing and violence against women: a cautionary note," in Mariana Valverde, Linda MacLeod, and Kirsten Johnson (eds) *Wife Assault and the Canadian Criminal Justice System*, pp. 260–89. Toronto: Centre of Criminology, University of Toronto.

Thornberry, Terrence P. (1990) "Cultural literacy in criminology," *Journal of Criminal Justice Education* 3(2): 331–40.

Walker, Samuel and Molly Brown (1995) "A pale reflection of reality: the neglect of racial and ethnic minorities in introductory criminal justice textbooks," *Journal of Criminal Justice Education* 6(1): 61–83.

West, Candace and Don H. Zimmerman (1987) "Doing gender," *Gender & Society* 1(2): 125–51.

Widom, Cathy Spatz (1989) "Child abuse, neglect, and violent criminal behavior," *Criminology* 27(2): 251–71.

Worrall, Anne (1990) *Offending Women*. New York: Routledge.

Young, Alison (1996) *Imagining Crime*. London: Sage.

Young, Vernetta D. and Helen Taylor Greene (1995) "Pedagogical reconstruction: incorporating African-American perspectives into the curriculum," *Journal of Criminal Justice Education* 6(1): 85–104.

PART I

WOMEN OF FEMINIST, LEGAL, AND CRIMINOLOGICAL DISCOURSES

CHAPTER 2

The Woman of
Legal Discourse

Carol Smart

INTRODUCTION

Feminist socio-legal theory has been developing in exciting and (happily) controversial ways over the last twenty years. The developments that we can see
almost certainly parallel developments in feminist thought elsewhere. This
should hardly surprise us, yet the field of law poses quite specific intellectual
and political problems for feminist theory which may not be found in other
fields.[1] These problems are threefold and, surprisingly, cumulative, considering that they originate from quite different constituencies. The first constituency voices a resistance to the idea that theoretical analysis is relevant to
law outside the narrow confines of courses on jurisprudence. This could be said
to be the "black letter" constituency. The second voices a resistance to the idea
that specifically *feminist* theory is relevant to law because it is argued that law
(at least in most developed countries) has transcended "sexual bias." This is
the liberal constituency. The third voices a form of resistance to all theory and
is based on the argument that, because law is a practice which has actual material consequences for women, what is needed in response is counter-practice
not theory. This constituency demands "practical" engagement and continually
renders (mere?) theoretical practice inadequate. This argument comes from
certain feminist constituencies which may define "doing" theory as male. These
three elements present a major obstacle to proponents of feminist legal theory
as they (we) meet with the frustrations of being ignored or seen as outmoded
in and by law and are simultaneously moved to renounce theory by the moral
imperative of doing something through or in law.

But feminist socio-legal theory faces another difficulty in as much as the

Reprinted from Carol Smart, "The Woman of Legal Discourse," *Social and Legal Studies*, Vol. 1,
pp. 29–44, © 1992. Reprinted by permission of Sage Publications Ltd.

tension that has always existed around the issue of whether to try to "use" law for "women" has taken on a new shape. This tension traditionally used to take the form of an assertion that law, being an epiphenomenal effect of patriarchy, could hardly be used to dismantle the said patriarchy. Attractive and succinct as this may sound, we now recognize that it is both an oversimplification and a recipe for despair, given that theorizing everything as an effect of a monolithic patriarchy rendered feminism itself little more than a false consciousness at best, or a device for sustaining patriarchy at worst.

Our theories of gender and of law have moved on, but there has been another important development. The entry of feminists into law has turned law into a *site* of struggle rather than being taken only as a *tool* of struggle. Yet the increase in numbers of feminist legal scholars and practising lawyers has (ironically) led to what I regard as contradictory consequences. The first, which I applaud, is a refinement of our theories of law, especially in relation to legal method and logic. The second, which is perhaps more problematic, is a renewed vigour in attempting to deploy law in the cause of women.[2] My concern over the latter move is not an attempt to resurrect the old argument I have just rejected above but rather reflects my concern that this renewed strategy continues to give law a special place in the resolution of social problems. This tendency, which is perhaps most clearly evident in North America, fails to challenge not only law's inflated vision of itself and thus empowers law (Smart, 1989), but it also enhances law's imperialist reach.[3] The move to use law for "women" also collides with the recent and profound recognition in feminist theory deriving from other disciplines, that to invoke an unproblematic category of Woman, while presuming that this represents all women, is an exclusionary strategy (see, for example, Spelman, 1988). But I now find myself in advance of my argument and so I wish to return to an earlier stage in the mapping of feminist socio-legal theory. In order to do this I shall concentrate on two related arguments. The first will address the question of how law is gendered, the second examines law itself as a gendering strategy.

HOW LAW IS GENDERED

There are three phases we can identify in the development of the idea that law is gendered. These are basically stages of reflection in feminist theory which have provided a foundation of understanding and have been largely, but not entirely, superseded (see also Naffine, 1990).[4] The first stage is epitomized by the phrase "law is sexist," the second by the phrase "law is male," and finally we reach the point of arguing that "law is gendered." These three levels of argument may be found to be deployed simultaneously in some feminist work on law, however, it is useful to differentiate between them in order to see what analytical promise each approach has.

Law Is Sexist

The starting point of the "law is sexist"[5] approach was the argument that in differentiating between men and women, law actively disadvantaged women by allocating to them fewer material resources (for example, in marriage and on divorce), or by judging them by different and inappropriate standards (for example, as sexually promiscuous), or by denying them equal opportunities (for example, the "persons" cases, Sachs and Wilson, 1978), or by failing to recognize the harms done to women because these very harms advantaged men (for example, prostitution and rape laws). These were (and remain) important insights, but the attribution "sexist" really operated more as a strategy of redefinition than as a mode of analysis. Thus the attribution of the label "sexist" was a means of challenging the normative order in law and reinterpreting such practices as undesirable and unacceptable.

Law is undoubtedly sexist at one level. However, this attribution did not really begin to tap the problem that law poses and does, I would suggest, slightly misrepresent the problem. The argument that law is sexist suggests that a corrective could be made to a biased vision of a given subject who stands before law in reality as competent and rational as a man, but who is *mis*taken for being incompetent and irrational. This corrective suggests that law suffers from a problem of perception which can be put right such that all legal subjects are treated equally. This form of argument is by no means a simplistic one. It is framed with different degrees of sophistication from those who suggest that the introduction of gender neutral language into law rids us of the problem of differentiation and hence discrimination (e.g., spouse instead of wife, parent instead of mother) to those who appreciate that discrimination is part of a system of power relations which needs to be addressed before the sexism can be "extracted." For the former, sexism is a surface problem to be tackled by re-education programmes and a rigorous policy of hiding visible signs of difference. For the latter, law is embedded in politics and culture and the route to fairer treatment for women lies in changes which will allow women to occupy different positions in society so that differentiation will become redundant.[6]

The problem with these approaches is that the meaning of differentiation tends to become collapsed into the meaning of discrimination and the fulcrum of the argument rests with the idea that women are treated badly in law because they are differentiated from men. It is often remarked that this means that men are retained as the standard by which women must be judged.[7] Irksome and nonsensical as this may seem, pointing it out only leads us to imagine that judging women by the standard of women is the solution. This may not be a great leap forward if those women who set the standard are white and middle class. If they are, we are left with an equally problematic legal system in which sexism is apparently eradicated but other forms of oppression remain. But this fallacy of substitution is not the core problem of a perspective which invokes the concept of sexism rather than gendering. The concept of sexism implies that we can override sexual difference as if it were epiphenomenal rather than embedded in how we comprehend and negotiate the social order. Stating it more boldly, sexual difference—whether we see it as constructed or not (Fuss, 1989)—is part of the binary structure of language and meaning. If eradicating discrimination is dependent on the eradication of differentiation, we have to be able to think of a culture without gender. Thus what seems like a relatively easy solution such as the incorporation of gender-neutral terminology into law, masks a much deeper problem. Moreover, as many feminists have argued, it is not at all certain that the desired outcome of feminism is some form of androgyny.

Law Is Male

The idea that "law is male" arises from the empirical observation that most lawmakers and lawyers are indeed male. It transcends this starting point, however, because of the realization that maleness or masculinity, once embedded in values and practices, need not be exhaustively anchored to the male biological referent, i.e., men. Thus MacKinnon (1987) has made the point most eloquently when she argues that ideals of objectivity and neutrality which are celebrated in law are actually masculine values which have come to be taken as universal values. Thus, in comparison to the "law is sexist" approach, this analysis suggests that when a man and woman stand before the law, it is not that law fails to apply objective criteria when faced with the feminine subject, but precisely that it does apply objective criteria and these criteria are masculine. To insist on equality, neutrality and objectivity is thus, ironically, to insist on being judged by the values of masculinity.

As with the "law is sexist" approach, the "law is male" perspective covers a range of more or less sophisticated positions. From the early work of Gilligan (1982) which *seemed* to attach male or masculine values to the biological referent and thus appeared biologically reductionist,[8] to more recent work (Young, 1990; Tronto, 1989; Mossman, 1986) which details the exclusion of values of caring in preference for "uncaring" (i.e., impartiality), or the actual rules and methods for arriving at the legal (and hence impartial) decision by systematic exclusion of other perspectives.

Yet, important as these insights are, they perpetuate a number of specific problems. Firstly, this approach perpetuates the idea of law as a unity rather than problematizing law and dealing with its internal contradictions. Secondly, and without necessarily being explicit, this approach presumes that any system founded on supposedly universal values and impartial decision making (but which is now revealed to be particular and partial) serves in a systematic way the interests of men as a unitary category.[9] We can see, therefore, that while great care is taken in these arguments to effect a distance from a biological determinism, there lingers an unstated presumption that men as a biological referent either benefit or are somehow celebrated in the rehearsal of values and practices which claim universality while (in reality) reflecting a partial position or world view.[10] Yet we know that law does not serve the interests of *men* as a homogeneous category any more than it serves the interests of *women* as a category. It might, of course, be argued that these authors do not make this connection between male value systems and the interests of men and that I am forcing their argument to the sort of limits where any argument would start to look absurd. But there is a reason for stretching this argument, perhaps unfairly, which does not lie in the rather futile desire to show that no feminist argument transcends biological reductionism.

Any argument that starts with ceding priority to the binary division of male/female or masculine/feminine walks into the trap of demoting other forms of differentiation, particularly differences within these binary opposites. Thus the third problem with this sort of approach is that divisions such as class, age, race, religion tend to become mere additives or afterthoughts. This process of adding "variables" which appears on the face of it to overcome the criticism of racism and classism levelled against feminist theory, in fact merely compounds the problem by obscuring it. As Spelman (1988) has stated,

> ... according to an additive analysis of sexism and racism, all women are oppressed by sexism; some women are further oppressed by racism. Such an analysis distorts Black women's experiences of oppression by failing to note important differences between the contexts in which Black women and white women experience sexism. The additive analysis also suggests that a woman's racial identity can be "subtracted" from her combined sexual and racial identity: "We are all women." (Spelman, 1988: 125)

Or, as Denise Riley has stated more succinctly, "Below the newly pluralised surfaces the old problems still linger" (1988: 99).

Law as Gendered

The shift between taking "law as male" and taking "law as gendered" is fairly subtle, and the transition does not entail a total rejection of all the insights of the former. But while the assertion that "law is male" effects a closure in how we think about law, the idea of it as gendered allows us to think of it in terms of processes which will work in a variety of ways and in which there is no relentless assumption that whatever it does exploits women and serves men. Thus we can argue that "[t]he same practices signify differently for men and women because they are read through different discourses" (Hollway, 1984: 237). So we do not have to consider that a practice is harmful to women because it is applied differently in relation to men. Rather, we can assess practices like, for example, imprisonment without being forced to say that the problem of women's prisons is that they are not like men's. But further, the idea of "law as gendered" does not require us to have a fixed category or empirical referent of Man and Woman. We can now allow for the more fluid notion of a gendered subject position which is not fixed by either biological psychological or social determinants to sex.[11] Within this analysis we can turn our focus to those strategies which attempt to do the "fixing" of gender to rigid systems of meaning rather than falling into this practice ourselves.

This means we can begin to see the way in which law insists on a specific version of gender differentiation, without having to posit our own form of differentiation as some kind of starting or finishing point. We can therefore avoid the pitfall of asserting a pre-cultural Woman against which to measure patriarchal distortions (i.e., a starting point), as well as avoiding a Utopianism which envisions what women will be once we overcome patriarchy (i.e., the finishing point). Thus we can take on board the sort of argument made by Allen (1987) in relation to the way in which law can only see and think a gendered subject without invoking the same form of differentiation ourselves. Her argument is worth rehearsing here. She examines the use of the concept the "reasonable man" in criminal law. It has always been taken to be an "objective test" of *mens rea* (guilty intent) but Allen demonstrates the sheer impossibility of this proposition. She states:

> Legal discourse thus incorporates a sexual division not only into what the law can legitimately "do," in terms of particular provisions and procedures, but also, more profoundly, into what it can reasonably *argue*. Yet beneath even this we can trace a third and yet deeper level of sexual division in legal discourse—at the level of what the law can intelligibly *think*. What is revealed in these arguments is that ultimately legal discourse simply cannot *conceive* of a subject in whom gender is not a determining attribute: it cannot *think* such a subject. (Allen, 1987: 30)

With this approach we can deconstruct law as gendered in its vision and practices, but we can also see how law operates as a technology of gender (de Lauretis, 1987).[12] That is to say we can begin to analyse law as a process of producing fixed gender identities rather than simply as the application of law to previously gendered subjects.

The revised understanding of "law as gendered" rather than as sexist or male has led to a modified form of enquiry. Instead of asking "How law can transcend gender?" the more fruitful question has become, "How does gender work in law and how does law work to produce gender?" What is important about these enquiries is that they have abandoned the goal of gender neutrality.[13] Moreover, law is now redefined away from being that system which can impose gender neutrality towards being one of the systems (discourses) that is productive not only of gender difference, but quite specific forms of polarized difference. Law is seen as bringing into being both gendered subject positions as well as (more controversially?) subjectivities or identities to which the individual becomes tied or associated. It is therefore appropriate, at this stage in the argument, to turn to the concept of law as a gendering strategy which needs to be read in conjunction with the idea of "law as gendered."

LAW AS A GENDERING STRATEGY

In this section my argument will develop the point that Woman is a gendered subject position which legal discourse brings into being.[14] This is of course a sweeping statement; one that will invoke the cry that women have always existed, they did not have to wait for law to give them entry into the Social, that law is hardly so powerful, that women are the product of natural, biological processes and so on. I can concede some of these points for certainly law alone does not constitute what Woman is, but it is perhaps necessary to consider what is meant by Woman and by "gendering strategy" before looking in more detail at the parts played by law and legal discourse.

Woman is no longer self-evident (Riley, 1988; Hekman, 1990; Spelman, 1988; Butler, 1990; Fuss, 1989).[15] Such a statement is, of course, an affront to common sense which knows perfectly well what women are and reacts keenly should anyone try to blur the naturally given boundaries between the two (also naturally given) sexes. Yet first we must concede a distinction between Woman and women. This is familiar to feminists who have for some centuries argued that the *idea* of Woman (sometimes the *ideal* of Woman) is far removed from real women. Moreover, feminism has typically claimed an access to real women denied those who perceive the world through patriarchal visions. So the distinction between Woman and women is not new but it has become more complex. For example, we have begun to appreciate that Woman is not simply a patriarchal ideal and that the women that feminism(s) invoke(s) are perhaps the Woman of/constructed by feminist discourse(s) rather than an unmediated reality simply brought to light. In other words, the claim to an absolute reality located in the body of women against which the excesses of patriarchy can be measured has become less tenable. Feminism does not "represent" women. Indeed as Butler has argued,

> [T]here is the political problem that feminism encounters in the assumption that the term *women* denotes a common identity. Rather than a stable signifier that commands the assent of those whom it purports to describe and represent, *women*, even in the plural, has become a troublesome term, a site of contest, a cause for anxiety. (Butler, 1990: 3)

Some have argued that this form of thinking removes feminism's constituency and thus threatens feminism as a political and social movement. However, this assumes that both intellectual innovation and political work must have an absolute, unmediated object of knowledge on which to ground itself. This requirement seems to be set stringently for any forms of poststructuralist feminism, while many other feminisms are allowed to operate on the basis of "as if."[16] Indeed, feminism has long taken issue with common sense and its counterpart the "unmediated real"; recognizing the cultural and historical elements of knowledge and rejecting the claim to a transcendental authority. So if we accept that Woman and women are not reducible to biological categories or—at the very least—that biological signs are not essences which give rise to a homogeneous category of women, we can begin to acknowledge that there are strategies by which Woman/women are brought into being. These strategies (in which I include law as well as discipline[17]) vary according to history and culture, they are also contradictory and even ambivalent. They may also be strategies without authors in as much as we should not imagine that strategy here implies a plan, masterminded in advance by extra-cultural (Cartesian) actors.

There is, of course, a distinction to be made between the discursive production of a type of Woman and the discursive construction of Woman. I want to invoke both of these meanings because it is my argument that they work symbiotically. Put briefly the (legal) discursive construction of a *type* of Woman might refer to the female criminal, the prostitute, the unmarried mother, the infanticidal mother and so on. The discursive construction of Woman, on the other hand, invokes the idea of Woman in contradistinction to Man. This move always collapses or ignores differences within categories of Woman and Man in order to give weight to a supposedly prior differentiation—that between the sexes. Thus this prior differentiation acts as a foundationalist move on which other differentiations can be grounded. Thus the female criminal is a type who can be differentiated from other women but, at the same time, what she is is abstracted from the prior category of Woman always already opposed to Man.

Thus she may be an abnormal woman because of her distance from other women, yet simultaneously she celebrates the natural difference between Woman and Man. Only by understanding this double move can we comprehend what we might otherwise mistake for inconsistency or oversight. Rather than taking it as a contradiction which can be resolved by the application of a little logic, we should recognize that the very foundation of the discursive construct of modern Woman is mired in this double strategy.

Thus Woman has always been *both* kind and killing, active and aggressive, virtuous and evil, cherishable and abominable, not *either* virtuous *or* evil.[18] Woman therefore represents a dualism, as well as being one side of a prior binary distinction. Thus in legal discourse the prostitute is constructed as the bad woman, but at the same time she epitomizes Woman in contradistinction to Man because she is what any woman could be and because she represents a deviousness and a licentiousness arising from her (supposedly naturally given) bodily form, while the man remains innocuous.[19]

While these strategies which produce gender are many and varied, I want to tell a straightforward story so that I can reach my topic of law without too much further delay. It has been argued that the end of the eighteenth century and the nineteenth century in Britain marked an important moment in the history of gender. What was witnessed was a polarization of genders in which difference became increasingly fixed and rigid, and at the same time was naturalized (Davidoff and Hall, 1987; Jordonova, 1989; Laqueur, 1990). Scientific discourses were central to this process, giving new vigour to traditional religious and philosophical beliefs about the inferiority of women. Women became more and more closely associated with their bodies, and their bodies became both overdetermining and pathological. It becomes possible to argue that scientific, medical and later psychoanalytic discourses operated to create the very gender differences we have come to take for granted as natural but, more importantly, these discourses have rendered natural the ideal of natural differences. At the same moment, of course, feminism was constructing a very different Woman, one who was not a semi-invalid (if middle class) nor sexually licentious and vicious (if working class). Yet even this feminist discourse fixed difference in the realm of the natural.

For my analysis of law, the nineteenth century is also particularly significant. This century marks both the pinnacle of law's exclusion of women from civil society (e.g., the denial of the legal personality of married women) and the moment when written law began to inscribe in finer and finer detail the legal disabilities of Woman. (Put another way, we can say that gender became increasingly fixed in terms of its attributes and in terms of being increasingly polarized.) At the most basic of levels we can see that legislation dating from the eighteenth century and before was sketchy in its terms and succinct to a fault (at least to twentieth-century eyes). But the nineteenth century marks a moment in which there grows a greater refinement and a "pinning down" of relevant categories and legal subjects.

We could therefore claim that nineteenth-century law brought a more tightly defined range of gendered subject positions into place. We can also see how law and discipline "encouraged" women to assume these identities or subjectivities. This idea is perhaps best pursued with an example and the one I wish to trace concerns motherhood, but not the good mother, or even the "good enough" mother—I am interested in the bad mother.

AN EXAMPLE OF LAW AS A GENDERING STRATEGY: SPECIFYING THE CATEGORY OF THE BAD MOTHER

Although I have specified the nineteenth century as a particularly significant moment in the fixing of gendered identities, I shall start my story earlier than this in order to identify how the nineteenth-century engagement of law and discipline, as two different forms of regulation, marks a break with earlier periods.

Thus my story begins in 1623 in England. In that year a new statute was introduced, creating a new crime and criminal. The statute made it a penal offence for a mother to kill her bastard infant on pain of death. The point about this new law was that the mother was to be presumed guilty if her infant died, and it was for her to provide evidence of her innocence. A presumption of guilt was extremely rare in English law and so the unmarried mother was brought into being in law as a culpable murderer. It should be stressed that at this time the state did not regulate marriage or even insist on formal marriage and so the condition of being married or not married was in some ways more fluid, especially as some people did not marry until they had several children together.

Thus we have the problematization of a specific form of motherhood. Its regulation was to take the form identified by Foucault (1977) as the power of the sovereign to inflict death. This woman is perhaps one of the first to enter into statute specifically as Woman.[20] Her entry marks a number of associations which are implicit yet must be understood for the legislation to make any sense. Not only is she unmarried and hence without protection, she occupies a specific class position (i.e., poor), she is deprived of the material conditions to raise a child, yet she is to be put to death for seeking to escape her plight—even if the child died of natural causes (or the effects of poverty on pregnancy and childbirth).

This piece of legislation was so draconian that it was rarely enforced because juries failed to convict. We can, however, map how the strategy of inflicting harsh punishment on the few became translated into modes of discipline and surveillance of the many. The penalties became less harsh, but fewer women could escape the reach of the revised forms of legal categorization.

In 1753, Lord Hardwick's Marriage Act began the process of regulating marriage such that there no longer existed indeterminate states of semi-matrimony—women were either married or unmarried. In 1803, the draconian Infanticide Act of 1623 was transformed into legislation against the concealment of birth. A presumption of innocence was restored and the penalty much reduced. However, its aim was to bring more women into the reach of the law because there was no requirement to establish murder. In the same year (1803), the first criminal statute on abortion was introduced. Abortion at any stage of pregnancy was criminalized and, although there was a distinction made between the pre- and post-quickening stages, this was later removed. English law never criminalized the production and sale of information on birth control (as, for example, Canadian law did), but the spread of such information was effectively controlled by the use of private prosecutions against blasphemous or obscene libel. In 1882 the age of consent was raised to 13 and in 1885 to 16. Thus marriage could not take place before these ages and this exposed young women who became pregnant, but could not marry, to legal and philanthropic scrutiny. In 1913 the Mental Defective Act facilitated the incarceration of unmarried mothers on the grounds of moral imbecility or feeble-mindedness.

My point is not just that these different forms of law constructed a category of dangerous motherhood, but that the net of law widened at precisely the same time as it made it increasingly difficult to avoid unmarried pregnancy and childbirth. The end of the nineteenth and early part of the twentieth century also coincides with the problem of the surplus woman, who had no chance of marrying anyway because of the export of men to the colonies or their slaughter in various wars.

The penalties (especially for infanticide) became less harsh, but more women were caught in the net of inescapable motherhood. If they attempted to escape through the use of contraception or abortion they were condemned as prostitutes or (virtual) murderers, if they failed they were subject to newer forms of discipline in the shape of philanthropy and mental health legislation/provision. We can see, therefore, how motherhood was actually materially constructed as a "natural," hence unavoidable, consequence of heterosex. Means of avoiding motherhood were denied to women, and the inevitability of the link between sex and reproduction was established through the harsh repression of those deploying traditional means of rupturing this link. We see the rise of compulsory motherhood for any woman who was heterosexually active. But by compulsory motherhood I do not simply mean the imposition of pregnancy and birth, but also entry into the nexus of meanings and behaviours which are deemed to constitute proper mothering. Moreover, as the nineteenth century turned into the twentieth, we witnessed the growth of surveillance and institutionalized intervention into women's lives through the establishment and spread of health visitors and social workers (Davin, 1978; Donzelot, 1980).

The unmarried mother obviously served (and still serves) to reinforce our cultural understanding of what "proper" motherhood means. In this sense she is a *type* of woman rather than Woman. Yet she simultaneously operates in the discourse as Woman because she always invokes the proper place of Man. She is the problem (supposedly) because she does not have a man. Therefore Man is the solution, he signifies the stability, legitimacy and mastery which is not only absent in her but inverted. The unmarried mother is therefore also quintessential Woman because she represents all those values which invert the desirable characteristics of Man.

At this point it may appear that my concerns are with the symbolic. However, my interests extend beyond this because my purpose in mapping the development of the legal subject "unmarried mother" is to throw light on the dominant regime of meaning which always already treats this woman as problematic and destabilizing. Just as Foucault has shown that categories such as the criminal or the homosexual are not pre-existing entities to be investigated and understood by science, so we can also see that the unmarried mother comes into being as a consequence of specific strategies and knowledges. While she is not a fixed or unchanging category she enters into an established web of meanings which make instability and dangerousness virtually self-evident and matters of common sense.

The significance of this for the contemporary situation is that more and more women can be fitted into this category. The Act of 1623 that I started with affected relatively few women. Now the category includes the never married and the divorced lone mother. (The widow is rarely included because she is thought to keep the symbolic father alive, and so is hardly a lone mother.) More recently this category has extended further to include the "surrogate" mother and the woman seeking infertility treatment. I should therefore like to close with a contemporary example. In 1990 the British Parliament passed a piece of legislation entitled the Human Fertilisation and Embryology Act. Section 13(5) reads,

> A woman shall not be provided with treatment services unless account has been taken of the welfare of any child who may be born as a result of the treatment (including the need of that child for a father) . . .

This legislation also continues the fiction that a woman's husband is the father of her children even if he is not biologically related to them and creates a new form of illegitimacy by insisting that the husband and biological father of a child will not be treated as the legal father if his sperm was used or if an embryo of his was implanted after his death.

These measures are nonsensical unless you already know that the mother without a husband is a danger. These measures may seem quite different to the measures passed in 1623 or later on in the nineteenth century, but they build upon an understanding of the category Woman of which law is a partial author. It is this Woman of legal discourse that feminism must continue to deconstruct but without creating a normative Woman who reimposes a homogeneity which is all too often cast in our own privileged, white likeness.

CONCLUDING REMARKS

It is of course almost impossible to conclude. In any case I do not want to impose a false closure where we are just beginning to ask more and more challenging questions. From where I stand, feminist socio-legal scholarship faces two main tasks at the beginning of the 1990s. The first is to grasp the nettle that law is not simply law, by which I mean it is not a set of tools or rules which we can bend into a more favourable shape. Although we have known this for a long time, I am not sure we have done enough with this knowledge. The desire to be political has been confused with the desire to be practical, and thus law has continued to occupy a conceptual space in our thinking which encourages us to collude with the legalization of everyday life. We must therefore remain critical of this tendency without abandoning law as a *site* of struggle. The second is to recognize the power of law as a technology of gender, but not to be silenced by this realization. Thus we should see the power of law as more than that negative sanction that holds women down. Law is also productive of gender difference and identity, yet this law is not monolithic and unitary.

Moreover, much more work needs to be done in tracing how women have resisted and negotiated constructions of gender, since we should not slip into a new form of determinism which suggests that, because power constructs, it produces women in some predetermined, calculated, powerless form. I am suggesting therefore that law remains a valid focus of feminist theoretical and political scrutiny, but that we need to recast our understanding of the relationship between "law" and "gender." Recognizing that law is a more complex problem than might once have been thought need not, however, lead to despair since we can quite clearly see that feminist scholarship and enquiry are also much more tenacious and insightful than might once have been imagined.

NOTES

This paper was originally presented on 16 May 1991 as an Inaugural Lecture on the (temporary) assumption of the Belle van Zuylen Chair, in the School of Women's Studies at the University of Utrecht. The oral style of the presentation has been preserved.

1. It is important to define what I mean by the field of law. Although the term "law" implies a singularity or unity, law is many things. At one level it is what is passed into statute as a result of a political process. Statute law is open to interpretation, of course, although not a "free" interpretation. A range of conventions apply which we can refer to as legal methodology. We cannot understand law without a critical appraisal of this methodology. At another level there is the practice of law. While legal method conforms to conventions which can be (arguably) revealed, legal practice is far less visible. I refer to how solicitors and other legal actors like the police use the law (and interpret it with less scrutiny) in everyday practice. This kind of law is known to be a long way away from law "in books" or in case law, but it is not unrelated to it of course.

   But law is also more than the summation of these elements. It is also what people believe it to be, in as much as they may guide their actions by it. Indeed, we could go further to suggest that law creates subjectivities as well as subject positions. Take, for example, the category of bastardy, which became the category of illegitimacy in the twentieth century. This was both a mere legal category, but it also became an economic positioning and a psychological condition. We created disadvantaged children and disinherited adults through this legal category.

2. The work of Catharine MacKinnon is perhaps most instructive in this respect. For while analysing law and legal method as irrefutably male, she pursues a litigation strategy which celebrates law as a solution to the very problems it epitomizes. (This is not to suggest, however, that she is unaware of this contradiction.)

3. In using the term "imperialist reach" I am referring to the process of legalization of everyday life which has become increasingly visible in the Western developed countries in the past century, but which has gathered pace in the last forty years. Hence the idea that every social problem has a legal solution has become more widely held, and when law fails the solution is often posited as more law to cover the inadequacies of existing law. Within this general framework, litigation has come to play a special role either through developing "test case" strategies (proactive) or through more defensive measures like exploiting the judicial review procedure. My point is not that nothing can be achieved by these strategies, nor that there

are self-evidently available alternatives waiting to be deployed, but that this legalization of everyday life transforms (and changes) the problems it encounters, it gives the impression that there are procedures that are emancipatory rather than disempowering, it gives decision making to legal and quasi-legal tribunals and courts (i.e., to judges) and hence empowers law further. It also requires a growing dependency on a legal elite who are the only persons who can interpret and negotiate the increasingly complex system of law.

4. Ngaire Naffine (1990) has also mapped the development of feminist legal theory in a similar way in her extremely useful book *Law and the Sexes*. She refers to three phases of feminism: the male monopoly, the male culture of law, and legal rhetoric and the patriarchal social order. Her first two phases correspond closely to my "Law as Sexist" and "Law as Male," but a different focus emerges with our analysis of the third phase and subsequent ideas for directions of theoretical endeavour.

5. I must acknowledge that sexism is not a term we hear a great deal any more. It was current in the 1970s and early 1980s, but it has been abandoned somewhere along the way except in fairly polemical texts. Yet I have chosen to revive it here because, although the term itself has fallen out of fashion, the form of analysis it represents has not. Moreover, this form of analysis transcends old boundaries between socialist, liberal and radical feminists since all have deployed some version of it with greater or lesser degrees of sophistication. I am therefore using it as a kind of shorthand, not as a straw woman that I can easily knock down. The concept of sexism is the base line of feminism, and I know I have often been reduced to this line when I begin the story of feminism for the "uninitiated."

6. Katherine O'Donovan's (1985) work might be said to represent this sophisticated end of the "law is sexist" argument. Her argument calls for the abolition of the private/public distinction in the ordering of everyday life. It is this distinction which, she argues, is the stumbling block to the usefulness of even a reformed legal system. Thus abolishing the system which differentiates between men and women (i.e., the private/public divide) would create the conditions under which law could cease to disadvantage women.

7. The argument that men set the standard by which women are judged (i.e., equality = being treated the same as men; difference = being treated differently from men) should not be taken as the same argument that suggests that standards in law are based on a masculine imperative. The former takes as its object an unproblematic empirical referent called men. The latter invokes the concept of gendered values which are not linked to any assumptions of a biologically given category of men (or women). While the former invites us simply to substitute women for men, the latter invokes ideas about how values, standards and principles are never free of their cultural context but how in a phallocentric culture some values come to be taken as universal and gender-free.

8. I would argue that it is incorrect to take Gilligan's work as biologically reductionist. She bases her analysis on a psycho-social process of gender identification which in turn produces different moral standpoints which can be typified as masculine and feminine. If her work is reductionist it is in specifying a psychological process in childhood as being so overdetermining that it produces masculine and feminine ways of reasoning.

9. Kingdom (1991) would also add that any analysis of law which treats it as a "front" for something else like patriarchy or male values, adopts an essentialist view of

law. In such an approach law is always understood by reference to something else and this diverts attention from an analysis of the specific workings of law.

10. I wish to make it clear that I do not absolve myself from this criticism. It is all too easy when criticizing others to give the impression that one would never have made such an obvious "mistake" oneself. Not only have I done so, I almost certainly continue to do so. In any case an "error" is usually only apparent after ideas have been worked on for a while. And perhaps it is misleading to speak in terms of errors when we know that each development of feminist thought depends on the ground work that has gone on before, even if this groundwork is superseded.

11. Note I am using the term "fixed" here. I am not sure that I concede to Butler (1990) that gender is mere performance and that there need be no relationship between sex and gender. However, I do accept Fuss's (1989) argument that constructionist arguments are just as over-determining as biological essentialist arguments. As I have no answer to these problems I prefer to leave the issue open.

12. Whilst I am borrowing de Lauretis's concept of technology of gender here I am aware that I may be forcing the category somewhat. Law cannot be analysed in exactly the same way as film or television or other media yet her concept invokes the activity of producing gender differentiation which I wish to capture here.

13. What is perhaps unfortunate is that the perception of feminist legal scholarship held in many quarters is that the idea of gender neutrality and equality remains the pinnacle of feminist aspiration.

14. The term legal discourse is now, of course, quite familiar in writing influenced by Michel Foucault. However, it may be worthwhile for me to clarify my usage of the term. I take discourse to refer to a body of texts, not necessarily drawn from one discipline, which are productive of a given type or subject. The classic examples in Foucault's work are the lunatic, the criminal and the homosexual. These types or subjects, he argues, were brought into being by specific discourses of the late eighteenth and nineteenth centuries. Walkowitz (1982) makes a similar argument on how laws on Contagious Diseases in the second half of the nineteenth century were productive of the category or subject prostitute.

    This approach turns materialism on its head, although it does allow for consideration of what is referred to as non-discursive elements. Thus there is no denial of the material but the conceptual dominance of materialism and "realism" is revoked.

15. Indeed there are those who would argue that Woman has always been problematic to feminism, for example de Lauretis (1987). I am not sure that I agree with this as a general statement because feminism as a political movement seemed to be untroubled by the question of "What is a woman?" even if these philosophical discussions were then ongoing.

16. By "as if" I am using the shorthand terminology which acknowledges that, for example, pure communication is impossible but we act in the everyday world "as if" it were. Thus, while we doubt the foundations of knowledge we nonetheless act. My point about poststructuralism is that it is more open about acting "as if" than forms of epistemology which invoke the "real."

17. I make this point because I differ from Foucault in seeing law as part of the ancient regime which operates in different ways from the mechanisms of discipline. While acknowledging that there are differences, I would argue that law has come

to deploy many of discipline's mechanisms. See Smart (1989) for a fuller discussion of this.

18. Unlike the concept Woman, the term femininity has never allowed these multiple meanings. The concept of femininity has always been contingently related to Woman, introducing both class and race dimensions rather than being a final or closing statement on the nature of womanhood. When I suggest that femininity invokes class and race, rather than being a quintessential statement on gender difference, I mean that only white, middle-class women were allowed entry into the feminine. Women of African descent "were" never feminine, Asian women "were" always passive and obsequious, Jewish women "were" aggressive, white, working-class women "were" uncouth, and so on.

19. There is only one exception to this that I can think of and that is the situation in which divorce law came to recognize the undesirability of men "consorting" with prostitutes, by giving the wife a right to a separation where her husband had knowingly communicated a venereal disease to her. It should also be noted that in the UK we have legislation against "kerb crawling." However, this does not create a category of licentious men in the way that legislation on soliciting creates the category of prostitute.

20. Of course the Common Law tradition of English law means we cannot identify a moment in which other categories of woman (e.g., the wife) entered into legal discourse. Ecclesiastical law also has origins which are not easily traceable, yet Woman is clearly to be found there in the regulation of divorce *a mensa et thoro* and in relation to abortion. She also entered as a specific category of offender for whom certain sorts of punishment were deemed inappropriate.

REFERENCES

Allen, H. (1987) *Justice Unbalanced*. Milton Keynes: Open University Press.

Butler, J. (1990) *Gender Trouble*. London: Routledge.

Davidoff, L. and C. Hall (1987) *Family Fortunes*. London: Hutchinson.

Davin, A. (1978) "Imperialism and Motherhood," *History Workshop Journal* 5, (Spring).

de Lauretis, T. (1987) *Technologies of Gender*. Bloomington, IN: Indiana University Press.

Donzelot, J. (1980) *The Policing of Families*. London: Hutchinson.

Foucault, M. (1977) *Discipline and Punish*. London: Allen Lane.

Fuss, D. (1989) *Essentially Speaking*. London: Routledge.

Gilligan, C. (1982) *In a Different Voice*. London: Harvard University Press.

Hekman, S. (1990) *Gender and Knowledge*. Boston, MA: Northeastern University Press.

Hollway, W. (1984) "Gender Difference and the Production of Subjectivity," in J. Henriques et al. (eds), *Changing the Subject*. London: Methuen.

Jordonova, L. (1989) *Sexual Visions*. London: Harvester.

Kingdom, E. (1991) *What's Wrong With Rights*? Edinburgh: Edinburgh University Press.

Laqueur, T. (1990) *Making Sex*. Boston, MA: Harvard University Press.

MacKinnon, C. (1987) *Feminism Unmodified*. London: Harvard University Press.

Mossman, M. J. (1986) "Feminism and Legal Method: The Difference It Makes," *Australian Journal of Law and Society* 3: 30–52.

Naffine, N. (1990) *Law and the Sexes*. Sydney: Allen & Unwin.

O'Donovan, K. (1985) *Sexual Divisions in Law*. London: Weidenfeld & Nicolson.

Riley, D. (1988) *Am I That Name?* London: Macmillan.

Sachs, A. and J. H. Wilson (1978) *Sexism and the Law*. Oxford: Martin Robertson.

Smart, C. (1989) *Feminism and the Power of Law*. London: Routledge.

Spelman, E. (1988) *Inessential Woman*. Boston, MA: Beacon Press.

Tronto, J. (1989) "Women and Caring: What Can Feminists Learn about Morality from Caring?" in A. Jaggar and S. Bordo (eds), *Gender/Body/Knowledge*. London: Rutgers University Press.

Walkowitz, J. (1982) *Prostitution and Victorian Society*. Cambridge: Cambridge University Press.

Young, I. M. (1990) *Justice and the Politics of Difference*. Princeton, NJ: Princeton University Press.

CHAPTER 3

Fallen Angels
The Representation of Violence Against Women in Legal Culture

KRISTIN BUMILLER

INTRODUCTION

One of the most frequent sources of contact by individuals with legal ideas is through the reporting of trials about notorious crimes and persons. For the casual observer, these trials are worthy of attention because they capture the imagination or generate uncertainty about the law's ability to deal with human tragedy and depravity. Yet avid interest in media reports spawned by notable criminal cases is more than a spectator sport, these reports are the means by which symbolic representation of victims and criminals are produced for consumption in popular culture. The messages that are disseminated in democratic societies by the media about the causes and consequences of crime and the behavior of the principal actors in courtroom dramas are a prolific source of powerful legal symbols. This essay examines the ways in which symbolic trials concerning sexual violence, despite ostensibly promoting justice in individual cases, may actually reinforce dominant preconceptions about women, men, and crimes of sexual violence.

This perspective is sharply different from the legal realists, who attributed significance to forms of symbolic justice in their efforts to demonstrate the influence of legal thinking outside formal institutional structures. For legal realists, the symbolic function of the trial was to affirm the morality of government: the criminal trial was considered the "great stabilizing institution" embarked upon to reconcile contradictory ideas or to prevent popular hysteria (Arnold, 1962; see also, Frank, 1949). The realists' vision of symbolic justice

Reprinted from Kristin Bumiller, "Fallen Angels: The Representation of Violence Against Women in Legal Culture," *International Journal of the Sociology of Law*, Vol. 18, pp. 125–142, © 1990. Reprinted by permission of the publisher Academic Press Ltd. London.

placed faith in the rectitude, certainty, and humaneness of the trial. In so doing, it failed to look beyond procedural functions to the trial's legitimating role.

Many feminist reformers shared the realists' vision and therefore assumed that they could employ the symbolic trial as means to make public the historical silence about rape. Their hope was that rape trials' re-enactment of the victimization process would create a focal point for consciousness-raising strategies. Since these trials employed the traditional definition of rape and framed the issues in terms of legal discourse, the reformers' strategies may have reinforced dominant cultural stereotypes as well as provided limited opportunity to transform political consciousness about rape (Pitch, 1985; Bumiller, 1987).

The subject of this inquiry is a major symbolic trial that focused attention in its community and the wider world on the American justice system's treatment of sexual violence and ethnic prejudice.[1] The symbolic trial is viewed as a signifier within the dominant legal culture: it is a forum that projects authoritative messages through language and legal form about identity and social relationships in a struggle between the antagonistic world views of the defense and the prosecution (Bourdieu, 1987). The symbolic power of the law is projected through linguistic attributions concerning the character and motives of defendants, victims, and legal professionals (see Santos, 1982). Because dominant modes of constituting the self (as a woman, criminal, or victim, for example) are maintained through the conventions of legal language, symbolic trials are moments when the rejection of those categories may come about through resistance to legal discourse (Bourdieu, 1987; see also Foucault, 1977).

From the perspective of the mass audience, all criminal trials are symbolic, since defendants and victims come to represent social roles. Each trial has within it a message about the way to reconcile the social vision of a good society with justice in the individual case (Kirchheimer, 1961). Yet these public morality plays, often about disturbing and incomprehensible acts of brutality against isolated victims, evoke in the mass consciousness conflicted emotions: genuine soul-searching for a more humane society mixed with superficial evaluations of dangerous stereotypes and misconceptions about criminals and victims (see Enzensberger, 1974; Lazere, 1987). Even though the stories are controversial, they serve to portray the event as a tragedy and thus relieve anxieties about the sources of violence and the legal system's ability to control them (Edelman, 1977).

Drawing on political and feminist theory (see Spivak, 1987; Moi, 1985), the following passages interpret messages about sexual violence that originate from sources outside and within a controversial rape trial. Interpretations are presented from three vantage points. First, one form of communication that mediates legal issues for the mass public, the newspaper stories that report the initial incident and the legal proceedings, generates accounts that structure perceptions of the crime. Second, accounts are provided from the principal lawyers that reflect their professional identity and their assumptions about the scope and purpose of criminal law. A third dimension is presented through the interpretation of the trial proceedings, and in particular the victim's testimony. This discourse reveals how her speech in a courtroom both conforms to legal ways of understanding violence and yet embodies resistance to accepted modes of expression. The analysis will show how multiple levels of discourse in a symbolic trial, in particular the public and professional language, frame public perceptions and constitute barriers to the articulation of the victim's perspective.

This essay presents a story about women and violence that is rarely written about or discussed in the context of a legal case. Generally, the story line that captures the public interest involves the curious circumstances of the individuals brought into the drama as well as evaluations of their moral character. The public audience plays the role of a jury of one's peers; each person evaluates the credibility of the charges based upon incomplete and fallible renditions of the facts. The themes developed here, however, do not turn on the factual premises of the case. The symbolic import of the trial depends less on the witnesses' adherence to or betrayal of the truth, and more on the way the stories told resonate with images of victims and thus form the context for interpretation.

This rape trial displays the multiple meanings implied in a woman's image of innocence. Simply stated, when the claim that a woman has been sexually assaulted is made, it is often based upon her blamelessness in contributing to her own harm. Thus, the claim to innocence is not easily made, for the shadow of guilt lingers (as with the defendants). More significantly, the multifaceted meanings of innocence widen the scope of judgment about a woman's worth. The "innocence" of a female accuser is lost with her initial charge that she has been touched by sexual violence, and is further eroded as her moral purity becomes an issue in court.

The trial turns on her "innocence of experience" or "freedom from guilt"; this has powerful symbolic consequences, for it reinforces the presumption that punishing violent men is justified to the extent that women are worthy of trust and protection. This presumption is symbolically as threatening as the actual violence of rape, for it exposes a woman's intimate life in the courtroom. The accuser is forced into the role of an "angel" who must defend her heavenly qualities after her fall from grace. The symbolic message is, in some degree, an expression of the legal system's high tolerance for violence against women and its low threshold for the measure of her unworthiness. The various meanings attached to the concept of a woman's innocence in the following interpretations of a major rape trial illustrate the vulnerability of the woman as an accuser in contemporary legal culture.

THE PUBLIC TRIAL

The 1984 rape trial of six Portuguese immigrant men in New Bedford, Massachusetts, was a celebrated moment of media attention to issues of sex and violence.[2] The political language of the media reporting of the New Bedford incident encouraged the public audience to vicariously imagine and draw judgments about the sequence of events in the bar called Big Dan's. The media constructed the story in a way that intensified and polarized issues for purposes of the alternative agendas of the feminist and Portuguese communities (e.g., Edelman, 1977, 1988; see also Smart and Smart, 1978: 91, 101–2). Rather than inscribing these acts of violence with meaning, the newspapers reported a lurid "spectacle" in which a "gang" of Portuguese men engaged in "senseless brutality" against a lone woman pinned down on a pool table. Although violent sexual assaults occur frequently in New Bedford and other communities across the country, this case was the subject of immense publicity because it was depicted as an inconceivably brutal gang rape cheered on by pitiless bystanders.

Six Portuguese immigrants were tried for aggravated sexual assault and sexual assault in a Fall River, Massachusetts courtroom about one year after the incident in Big Dan's. Because it received massive local and international newspaper coverage, the rape became an important symbol in popular culture and a focal point for the mobilization of feminist groups. The extensive publicity surrounding the Big Dan's incident's disputability may have arisen from the uniqueness of the circumstances, yet by subjecting the issue of gang rape to public scrutiny, the media constructed powerful images of the case through selective reporting of information and structuring of perceptions for the popular audience. While the power of the media to set agendas and to mobilize interest groups is often regarded with suspicion, the media's role in the creation of dominant images is ignored by skeptics unaware of the more subtle role of news accounts in constructing the conceptual framework within which conflictual events are interpreted and understood.[3]

In the *New Bedford Standard-Time*'s characterization of the incident, the implied motives and intentions of the victim and defendants moved in and out of focus within a larger picture which included legal authorities and community organizations. Although a considerable amount of reporting space was allotted to the defendants (their arrest, court hearings, personal information, and statements by their attorneys), the language employed by the press, at least superficially,[4] placed the spotlight on the victim. One news story, for example, described the rape as the "victim's ordeal," in which "ordeal" broadly referred to the acts of violent sexual aggression, the trial, and the publicity surrounding the trial. For the most part, references to the victim ignored her as an individual who had her own specific responses to rape. Either the victim was named by her formal legal status and demographic qualities (e.g., the "complainant," "young woman," "21 year old city woman"), or more elaborate discussion of the victim was carried out through references to "generic" victims of rape (e.g., antirape activists' statements of solidarity with the victim and special reporting features about rape crisis centers' efforts to respond to the psychological trauma of victims).

The majority of stories were unqualified in their description of the brutality of the crime and full of general sympathy for the victim and hostility toward the perpetrators. The newspapers told of a mob scene: "[according to police and witness reports] the bar was whipped into a lurid, cheering frenzy, as they watched the sexual assault." A rape reform activist is reported to have said: "The rapists knew exactly what they were doing. It went on so long, they obviously had a chance to consider what they were undertaking. The bail is ridiculously low." Her words are one example of the panoply of law-and-order demands that gain their intensity from the symbolic invocation of enemies. Thus, the Portuguese defendants metaphorically took on the instinctive qualities and look of uncivilized people; for example, one news report quoted a Portuguese man in the neighborhood referring to the accused as "barbarians."

Although the references to the victim tended to be sympathetic, there were ambivalent undercurrents in her portrayal. A New Bedford reporter attributed a heavenly innocence to the victim through the rhetorical questioning of an investigating police officer: "Where will she go from here? She'll probably have to leave New Bedford. . . . She won't be able to handle the memories. Look at her angelic face. It's *almost* full of innocence. She'll never be innocent again." She is not attributed earthly innocence, but the innocence of an angel fallen from grace.

The most conspicuous aspect of the event in terms of its symbolic representation in popular legal culture is not the portrayal of either the victim or the defendants, but the emphasis on the setting of the crime. The tone was set by the first major local newspaper story about the rape, which included a large photograph of Big Dan's Tavern. Thus, attention was drawn to the incompatibility of the setting with expected norms of human behavior. The fact that the incident occurred in a *public* place, in a barroom and on a pool table, is discordant with the social conception of consensual sex as a private and intimate act. The public nature of the crime has significance beyond its location; the image of a gang, yelling, mocking, and humiliating the woman, jars common sensibilities about personal dignity in social interactions. The early coverage employed the shock of these circumstances as a rhetorical device to establish that illegitimate sex occurred. The effect was to inhibit further speculation about the woman's responsibility for the violence. Reporting about the scene of the crime implied that "no woman" would want "that" to happen. In such cases, the woman's private intentions regarding her intimate behavior are considered irrelevant as long as the news reporting focuses on a bar portrayed as a "sore spot" where only the "riff-raff go."

The language describing the setting of the crime creates a picture of the personalities of the actors and sets the framework for popular interpretations. The structuring of public perceptions about this particular incident intensified hostilities over the description of the social setting of the rape, which in this case involved immigrant defendants from a primarily ethnic community. Because popular cultural interpretations emphasized setting, the terms of political discourse were polarized between the response of the Portuguese community that New Bedford is a decent place to live and the demand of advocates of women's rights that women must have the freedom to associate safely in public places. For the "Take Back the Night" protesters, the setting of the crime clarified the underlying moral issue, that regardless of this woman's character and circumstances, *any* woman should have the freedom of movement to enter a public bar without the fear of being gang raped. Supporters of the Portuguese defendants objected to newspaper reporting that, in their view, employed inappropriate references to the ethnic origins of the defendants. Moreover, concerns were raised that characterizations of Big Dan's as a bad establishment in a marginal neighborhood in the city were responsible for creating the impression that New Bedford was the Portuguese "rape capital" of the country.

At the level of the public trial, the news media both linguistically and visually created a story about brutal and public sexual violence and narrowed the interpretative framework for understanding the crime. In the actual trial, the setting of the rape was also re-created, but often by testimony that recast the scene in terms of precise movements indicated by pointing to a scaled down replica of Big Dan's in front of the witness stand. For the defense attorneys, once the case was brought to trial, their stated objective was to reconstruct the image of the bar so that a plausible story about human behaviour would account for and justify the men's actions.

THE COURTROOM TRIAL

My ethnographic observations, obtained from interviews three years after the trial, offer an interpretation of the events that differs from the symbolically constructed accounts by the media.[5] From the perspective of the principal legal actors in the trial, the professional discourse of the law protects defendants from unbridled public hostility. The attorneys chose to analyze events by employing a language of equilibrium that employed commonsense personifications of good and evil, as well as of commendable and unworthy character.

From the defense attorneys' standpoint, the case was notable for its mundane nature rather than its notoriety; the case was nothing other than "a routine sexual assault case," "a dull, dull case," or "a classic case based on the mistrust of government witnesses." For these professional participants, the trial was similar to other rape trials and operated according to a predictable set of norms and procedures. The most perceptive of the defense attorneys recognized (similar to the social scientist) that social reality is reconstructed for the purposes of any trial. Several of the attorneys involved readily admitted that the reality of what happened in Big Dan's was unclear and were willing to entertain three possibilities: (1) that a brutal rape occurred; (2) that "something consensual" happened in the bar that night; or (3) that "something consensual" crossed the line into a criminal act. As a group, they openly discussed which image of the bar fit their reading of the facts and would best serve the interests of the defendants. As good criminal defense lawyers, their objective became to turn this incredible scenario into a story that made sense to a jury.

These lawyers confronted the ambiguity of the case but not without acknowledging the life-and-death consequences for a "lone defendant fighting for freedom" or experiencing the sheer scariness of one's heart pounding in making one's way through the mob on the courthouse steps. The defense attorneys identified with what they saw as the human side of the case. For one lawyer, the defendant was "gentle" Joseph Viera and the victim was a survivor: "she is no weeping willow or shrinking violet. She is a tough woman defending something. She has a big interest in the trial—her most important relationships are at stake. That is her public position, not what the people in L.A. think about her, but what the people around her and closest to her think of her." For the advocate, intuition about the victim is necessary to convince the jury that she was both consciously and unconsciously self-protective; that is, not to create the pretense that there was no rape, but to convince the jury that since the first experience of the victim after the attack was a confrontation with an accusatory grandmother, then she should no longer be seen as capable of expressing unadulterated truth. As the lawyer explains, "Why should I subordinate my perceptions about what the battle is about in the courtroom to [feminists'] demands that society devalues the victim because her boyfriend is a schmuck, because she is not married, or had a child out of wedlock—when the fellow next to me has his life on the line?" The bottom line for this defense attorney is that society cannot put its faith in the victim because she "has no commitment to justice."

The moral passion of the defense attorneys both recognizes and buries one truth. As actors in these roles they live with the dilemma that no language is able to express all aspects of the truth—yet all language carries the force and power of the word—and these words that may be employed to condone violence against women carry the force of the law.

THE VICTIM'S TRIAL

The victim's testimony in the courtroom, reviewed from the videotaped record of the proceedings,[6] provides another kind of symbolic interpretation that connects the presentation of events inside the courtroom with the social construction of sexual relationships. The victim's accounts give authority to the perspectives of women and other excluded voices that are revealed neither by controversies generated by legal analysis nor by public speculation about personalities and circumstances. Yet these accounts confront barriers to a full understanding of the person, or self, as an actor in the social world (Cassirer, 1985; Merleau-Ponty, 1964; Taylor, 1985). The move to ground understanding in discourse, in particular the discourse of women and other victimized groups, can be seen as a straightforward strategy to give authority to their speech. But their perceptions of social reality, and our ability to reflect upon and understand their reality, are bounded by their capacities to express themselves in language. The political implication of this epistomological problem is that the discourse of excluded groups provide us with socially constructed "ways of knowing" that are partial and as a result can be employed to undermine their interests (Belenky et al., 1986). As my reading of the trial will show, however, these interpretations give utterance to the strengths as well as the vulnerability and duplicity of victims. These expressions, therefore, must be reconciled within a political context and ultimately evaluated in the larger scheme of institutional life.

The predominant theme of the trial was the inquiry into the "innocence" of the victim, whom I call Diana. Both the prosecution and the defense produced theories to account for her motivations in going to the bar and the appropriateness of her behavior. As defense attorney Lindahl questioned: "At first your only intention was to buy cigarettes . . . ; at some point you decided to stay. . . . *That's the decision* you regret most about that night?" Defense attorney Edward Harrington posed the question: "If you're living with a man, what are you doing running around the streets getting raped?" (see MacKinnon, 1987: 80). This frame of reference inevitably flows from the definition of rape that forces the prosecution to show nonconsent in order to prove that a sexual assault has been committed. The state of mind of the victim is the window to the *mens rea* that establishes the culpability of the defendant. Since the social construction of rape in the courtroom or in society ignores the victim's perception of the attack, she becomes the object of a theory about nonconsent that uses information not only about her behavior on the day of the rape but also about the moral choices she has made throughout her lifetime.

The best defense in a rape trial, therefore, is often the indictment of the victim. That is why the defense attorneys attempted to incriminate Diana by posing a series of questions intended to raise doubts about the sincerity of her charge of rape: Was she desperate to have sex that night? So desperate that she would agree to sex in a public place? Was her behavior irresponsible or inviting? Was she too drunk to know what was happening?

The testimony of witnesses who actually heard and saw Diana that night, along with her own testimony, provides us with an account of her motives, words, and actions. Each element of evidence, however, derives its authority from the source and form of communication. For example, Diana's own accounts were different immediately after the rape from what she said at the trial and were given in the form of recollections, written police reports, and reports of witnessed confrontations in the bar or police station. Even as stories unfold in the courtroom, the value of the "facts" the court will call evidence has been predetermined by the social mechanisms that privilege certain forms of communication. In this case, it means that the simple and direct recollection of the facts she gave in court would stand against the enormous collection of documents already recording the events of the crime and her life.

As she testified in a calm monotone, she tried to present herself in society's image of an innocent victim rather than revealing weakness and anger. Adopting the pose of the innocent victim required her to show that her actions conformed to what is expected of a person of good character: consistency, sobriety, and responsibility. While the defense attorney's questions constrained her ability to explain her actions, her responses were also limited by the prosecution which was concerned that her testimony would contradict the police officers' official version and the testimony of witnesses who were in the tavern during the rape (see McBarnet, 1984). The defense attempted to question her credibility by pointing out inconsistencies in the accounts she gave to the police; even her private conferences with a rape counselor were introduced into evidence. Faced with such constraints, her strategy was not to reveal the "whole" story, but to construct a narrative that she felt would best establish her innocence. In a firm voice she recounted what she believed to be the truth about her victimization.

Given the focus on her innocence, the task was to convince the court of her capability to be cognizant of and explain all that had happened to her. This meant she had to draw a line in her description of her own emotional distress that preserved the credibility of her statements. When subjected to an extensive cross-examination that disputed the version of the facts she gave immediately after the rape, she defended her ability to perceive and report events in a state of mind that was (in her words) *near* hysterical and *slightly* confused.

The major challenge to her credibility rested on the record of her "exaggerations" in the police report written the night of the attack. In subsequent police reports she retracted the claim that there were fifteen men involved, including six who had sexual intercourse with her, and said she "lost count." She also modified the statement that "the men had knives" to "one man held a knife in front of her face" (then again, she "admits" he did not *say* anything threatening to her). She was continually questioned by the defense attorneys about these inconsistencies, to which her response was frequently that she "doesn't know" how to account for them.

Ultimately, none of her explanations captured the shock or trauma she had experienced. Instead, she offered admissions that she was tired and slightly confused. She said, "the events are clearer now than then"; and about the first police report, "I don't remember anything I said"; "I was tired, I didn't want to talk to anybody and I wanted to be left alone." Defense attorney Lindahl's effort to get her to justify her statement to the police produced this moment in the trial:

Lindahl: Did you tell [officer Sacramento] 12 or 15 men were involved?

Diana: Every man there was involved.

Lindahl: Did you say six men had sexual intercourse with you; when in fact two men had intercourse?

Diana: Yes.

Lindahl: Is this your testimony to the jury today? If you said 12 or 15; if you said 16 or more; if you said—

Diana: *I believe everybody that was there was guilty!*

Lindahl: Objection!

[At this point the jury was asked to disregard the witness's statement.]

At the same time she spontaneously blurted out that everyone was guilty, she was able to characterize her "exaggerations" as a product of the horror she experienced in the bar that night. Yet Lindahl's next question was, "Maybe you were so upset you exaggerated." Diana's response was, "no." Her denial indicates both that she felt uncomfortable about the manner in which the attorneys were using the law to try to place blame on her and that she was willing to defend her own view of moral responsibility that accounted for her rage against all of the men in the tavern.

Incriminating statements about Diana were not only used to undermine her credibility, they were also developed into theories about consent by comparing the victim's character with the moral position of other women who were principal actors in the retelling of the story. These comparisons are poignantly brought forth in the testimony of the women who were with Diana during the day she was raped. The first witness called by the defense was Rosetta, who testified about their activities during the afternoon before Diana went to Big Dan's. Rosetta was asked a series of questions about their consumption of drinks at the Knotty Pine, an Italian restaurant and bar, where they stopped to get soup for their boyfriends. Defense attorney Harrington appeared disappointed with her testimony, as if he expected her to provide a more definitive answer to whether or not Diana had any alcoholic drinks that afternoon.

However, the defense was able to establish that Diana had asked Rosetta if she would like to go out with her for a drink. The defense attorney initiated the following exchange on cross-examination:

Waxler: [Diana] wanted more to drink?

Rosetta: Yes.

Waxler: What did you say?

Rosetta: I told her she should *just* go home.

Waxler: Did she respond?

Rosetta: No.

Waxler: Did she say anything further?

Rosetta: No.

The purpose of this exchange was to attempt to establish that Diana intended to go out drinking when she left the house at dusk, but Rosetta insinuated that she disapproved of Diana's desire to get out of the house and, in so doing, implied that Diana's own restlessness was responsible for her being raped at Big Dan's. Her testimony also enabled the defense to draw a contrast between Rosetta, who had recently married her boyfriend and made the wise decision of staying home, and Diana, who lived with the father of her two children and made the fateful decision to go out that night.

Another incriminating voice came from the other woman who had been in Big Dan's. Marie was introduced to the court as a reliable person with professional credentials: she is employed as a nurse and is much older than Diana (probably in her forties). (She was referred to as the "fat lady" in the testimony by the men in the bar who did not know her name.) She went out that night to get something to eat, but when she discovered the restaurant across the street was closed, she decided to see if she could get a sandwich at Big Dan's. Marie was a regular in the bar, and in fact, knew several of the men quite well. Previously, she had helped the defendant Victor Rapozo get a job. Marie gave the following description of Diana's actions in the tavern:

Harrington: What did you see her do?

Marie: She went to the bar to get a drink.

Harrington: Were you seated at the table?

Marie: Yes.

Harrington: Did she come to the table?

Marie: Next thing she did is, [she] came over and asked if [she] could sit down.

Harrington: Then?

Marie: I said you can sit down, but I am leaving shortly.

Harrington: What observations did you make about the young lady?

Marie: She was bubbly; she was bouncing 'round the chair; she never stood still, her pupils were very large and her eyes were glassy.

A few moments later, Marie added that during their ten minute conversation Diana had told her that "she didn't have sex for several months, I think nine months," and that her "boyfriend or ex-husband [suggested that she] should get out and meet people because she is a lonely person."

A third confrontation with the morality of other women came from her closest relative and substitute parent, her grandmother. This confrontation was also recorded for the official record because it was overheard by the police officer accompanying her to the hospital and by the nurse. Her grandmother, when she first saw Diana in the hospital, called her a drunk, accused her of shaming the family, and asked her why she was not at home with her children. Diana was reluctant to talk about her grandmother's denouncements, and at one point insisted that they were irrelevant:

Lindahl: Do you remember the conversation with your grandmother?

· · ·

Diana: I don't want my grandmother brought into this.

Lindahl: The reason you didn't remember is because you didn't want to talk about your grandmother?

Diana: Yes, it is.

Lindahl: It was true you didn't remember?

Diana: It wasn't a lie. I don't think it should have been brought up.

Lindahl: Isn't it true, whenever you don't want anything brought up, you say I don't remember?

Diana obviously cared deeply about her grandmother's opinion of her, yet she explained her grandmother's reaction by asserting that she must have been so upset that she did not realize her words were harmful. Diana tried to present the story as if there had been no direct conversation, as if her grandmother had been screaming and as if most of the actual conversation had been directed at her grandfather. The re-enactment in the trial of her grandmother's assault on her character not only revealed the powerful forces of condemnation at work in her private life, but brought these painful experiences into the realm of public judgment.

Using the morality of other women to incriminate Diana exemplifies how the social conception of rape finds authority in the woman's duty to protect herself. The defendants, however, relied on more overt challenges based on their ordinary treatment of women. As defendant John Cordeiro told the court, in his testimony on his own behalf, he was surprised to hear the next morning that the police were looking for him because there had been a rape in Big Dan's Tavern. He said, "A rape? Nobody raped anybody." When asked in the trial if he knew what rape was, Cordeiro responded, "It is when you tear off their clothes. . . ." In Cordeiro's account of that night, he left Big Dan's for a short while, and when he came back he saw Diana on the pool table with defendant Joe Viera on top of her. He watched defendant Rapozo put his penis in her mouth and then did the same thing, while Diana was "smiling and laughing at them." Cordeiro was relatively unconcerned about talking to the police the next morning, because all he believed he had to do was to "tell the truth . . . *the truth never hurts*." His confidence turned out to be misplaced, but his lack of concern reflects the unproblematic state of mind of the rapist. There was initially no reason for him to doubt his own opinion about what the woman wanted to have happen to her that night.

Defendant Daniel Silva's story was less frank and based upon more complicated assumptions about how Diana had communicated her desire to be raped. Silva claimed that he had met Diana a few months before and had had a short conversation with her in a cafe named Pals Four. By his account, Diana approached him and asked if he had any drugs. After a few more words, she asked, "Do you want to play, fool around?" He reportedly responded "yes" and claimed she "looked very happy." He explained to her that he could not take her home, however, because he lived with his mother. As they continued to fool around with each other, the only thing that concerned Silva was that he "thought she was holding me too tight; like a hysterical woman; like she wanted something." Daniel Silva portrayed the situation in Big Dan's as an ordinary "pick-up" in a bar, at least until the other men started making fun of him and then participated in the attack.

The challenges from the women and the defendants were based upon assumptions about how men and women communicate sexual aggression and desire. The proceedings became a search for facts that would explain a cause and effect sequence in which the defendant makes "reasonable" judgments about her desires and the victim either rebukes him or acquiesces in his actions. In this construction of the social interaction, there are "spaces" opened for speculation about typical behavior that allows the defense to draw upon images in society that hold women responsible for their own victimization.

The reconstructed story of that night took place in the context of Diana's life as retold for the purposes of the trial. Sometimes the effort to make sense of her motives and actions in terms of her life suited the purposes of the prosecution and the defense, while at other times the context was ignored. The defense characterized her life as filled with hardships, but suggested that she responded to those conditions in immoral and desperate ways. The formulation of a credible set of reasons why she caused or deserved her attack depended on the depiction of her as unloved and forsaken by those who should have cared about her. The defense wanted to know: where was her boyfriend Michael during the night of the attack? Why didn't he call the police when she didn't come home? Did they have a fight before she left the house? Why didn't the police officer see Michael when Diana was brought back to her home? Once this line of questioning was introduced, part of her intimate life was made relevant to the judgment about her nonconsent. She was seen as a woman whose value is determined by the judgment of men. Her culpability was suggested by the fact that the rape did not upset (and thus violate his interests) the man she lived with and the fact that she was seeking to escape from her environment at home.

Since Diana had received public assistance during her life, the defense attorneys had access to information that could only be obtained from government records. In her Medicaid records, there was a report of a previous trip to the hospital in 1981 for medical treatment after a rape. She denied having made a previous report, and argued with the defense attorneys about the verifiability of her Medicaid number. The entire discussion of the prior rape was pursued in the context of whether or not the use of this number confirmed her identity as the person who made the visit to the hospital in 1981 (e.g., Do you check over your yearly public assistance reports? Do you give out your Medicaid number "willy-nilly" to other persons?).

The prosecution, in contrast, tried to evoke a sympathetic understanding of Diana's life situation by relying on her role as a mother. In the District Attorney's opening statement, he noted that she gave her child medication before she put her to bed. In direct examination of Diana, the District Attorney allowed her to mention that while in Big Dan's she showed Marie pictures of her children. This look into her personal life was orchestrated by the prosecution, but there were other, more unexpected moments in the trial in which she revealed herself. When questioned about her grandmother, she became so upset that the judge had to intervene. She also refused to use her grandmother's name in the courtroom and was granted permission by the judge to use a nonidentifying reference. While guarding against public exposure of her grandmother, she revealed the same courage it took to make the charge of rape and possibly subject both herself and her family to public harassment. It was at these moments that the victim struggled to protect her integrity and prevent the exposure of her intimate life. Yet in the moments in which she broke out of her monotonic response pattern, she was best able to express her feelings of violation and offer alternative theories of responsibility and blame.

IMPLICATIONS FOR FEMINIST STRATEGIES

Feminist reformers have tried to use the trial forum to raise public awareness about the prevalence of rape and other violent crimes affecting women. The rhetorical stance of these reformers, however, has accepted the presumption of legal realists that trials have an educative function. As a result, the publicity generated by organized courtwatchers and statements of outrage about particular cases are intended to educate an insensitive audience that violence against women had become commonplace both on the streets and in the courtroom (see Pitch, 1985; Fineman, 1983). This analysis, however, demonstrates that publicity encouraged by rape reform advocates may have failed to focus discontent, while generating ambiguous messages about the motivations of victims and the nature of feminine "innocence."

The legal realist's vision of the symbolic trial is adhered to by the professionals in the courtroom, despite realism's arguable inability to capture the social meaning of controversial events. Both the physical setting of the courtroom scene and the procedures and language of the trial created the image of law as separating out the truth from the hysteria of the victim. The prosecutors and defense attorneys act as guardians of this order and are resistant to any form of dialogue that attempts to make sense of the violence in a way that does not fit the legal models of guilt or innocence. For example, in the New Bedford rape trial, a motion for mistrial arose from District Attorney Kane's reference to police officer Carol Sacramento's statement, "How did this happen?" Kane repeated it several times during his opening statement, as if this was the question he wanted to leave foremost in the jury's mind. Defense attorney Coffin argued that this inappropriate statement was inadmissible as evidence and therefore should not have been included in his opening statement. Moreover, he claimed that "How did it happen?" is an ambiguous question because it could have meant either "How could this rape have happened? or "How could these consensual acts have happened?"

Kane's response to the motion for mistrial was that the court should recognize that Sacramento's amazement was part of the proof that the rape occurred: since the rape was an extraordinary event, it was important to note that those who first heard the complaint that night would have responded to it in an extraordinary manner. Yet the prosecution's willingness to stimulate our bewilderment was limited. As participants in professional legal discourse, the prosecutors tried to discourage speculation about how society's approval of violence against women created the conditions for the rape at Big Dan's. From the prosecution's perspective, the case was simply about a tragedy that involved a confused young woman. In fact, the District Attorney attempted to explain the inconsistencies in his case by arguing, in his closing statement, that this was a story without "heroes." Diana was portrayed as a character in a human tragedy who must confront, like all tragic figures, her own faults and vulnerabilities.

But to call this trial a tragedy is to individualize Diana's misfortune and ignore the way that the ordinary has been given larger than life significance. It is a tragedy only if one believes that the event is otherwise inexplicable and that the cause of the attack did not grow out of the group dynamic in the tavern but arose instead from an evil that lurked within the victim. The District Attorney's analogy to a tragedy was meant to reassure the jury that the trial is the best method to bring forth the truth, and that these truths must self-evidently account for the rape.

Yet the legal system is itself implicated in the tragedy unless one is willing to agree with defendant John Cordeiro that the "truth never hurts." As the trial is interpreted in its symbolic context, one sees how truths that are partial may become powerful instruments that can assign blame and absolve guilt. From the perspective of legal professionals, partial truths are defensible as part of a larger battle in the pursuit of justice. Defense attorney Lindahl, for example, defended the trial to the press because, "in our attempts to protect those who are truly victims, we better take care that we don't victimize not only the men accused, but all of us if we give up the confrontation inherent in a trial." But the symbolism of this trial involved more than rituals of confrontation; the trial produced messages which served to disempower women both inside and outside of the courtroom. Lindahl's concerns focused on the search for justice in the individual case, and were warranted if the only threat to justice is the excessive power of the state and the unbridled vengeance that stems from victimization. Otherwise, she has ignored the way that law has unleashed metaphors that attack basic notions of human decency. The celebrated trial has an impact far greater, and a message more complicated, than the realists envisioned. Their claim that these contests affirm a legalistic society's reliance on procedure can be made only at the risk of ignoring these trials' cultural significance and meaning.

The narrative constructed in this essay suggests that those who purposely desire to use the trial forum to send a message condemning sexual violence confront a dilemma-ridden strategy. The more vehemently reformers maintain that "objective" evidence can be provided to prove the abuse of victims, the more necessary it becomes to establish the victim's innocence according to commonly held notions of verifiability (Griffin, 1986). The reliance on objective evidence, therefore, forces the defenders of victims' rights to resort to tactics that narrow or limit the telling of the woman's story. The claim of objectivity may also have the effect of making it more difficult to establish the woman's "innocence" in more ambiguous situations where rape differs from the overt violence of "real rape" (Estrich, 1987), which is marked by a relationship of strangers, the use of a weapon, and a public scene. The forms of communication that are appropriate in a courtroom and that are disseminated by the media conform to conventions of the "public" discourse of news reporting and the "professional" discourse of criminal procedure. If reformers strive toward transforming the social construction of rape, even abandoning the model of consent, then changes in the public understanding of the crime may only come about with challenges to the dominance of legal discourse.

CONCLUSION

In this essay, the New Bedford trial was analyzed as a spectacle that projected symbolic messages about sexual violence: it presented a story, reconstructed in different media, about a woman's life and her responses to a violent sexual assault. The trial was a moment in which the violation of women's sexuality was reproduced for mass public consumption in a manner to satisfy the internal logic of the legal system.

Although the ultimate convictions of four of the defendants might be seen as symbolic vindication of the victim's innocence, my reading of the trial suggested that even in a situation of multiple acts of violence (in the presence of witnesses) the victim was subject to the vulnerabilities of a woman as an accusor. From the initial media presentation of the case, it appeared that the "public" nature of the violent act served to affirm the assumption of the victim's "innocence" while vilifying the Portuguese defendants and their conduct in the community. As the "facts" became public knowledge, however, the unnamed complaining witness was portrayed as a confused young woman of unreliable character. The public persona of the victim was transformed by a reconstructed account that scrutinized her behavior in the tavern by comparing it to "reasonable" standards of women's propriety. Within the legal forum, her fearful assertion of violation was obscured by questioning that implied personal irresponsibility in protecting herself from male aggression while raising suspicion about her sexual motivations as a woman: she was forced to defend the propriety of her actions while being held suspect for female capriciousness.

The woman as a courtroom witness to sexual violence was unable to speak from her own terrain. Although the trial posed the questions relevant to the legal determination of guilt and innocence, the victim of the attack, however, was able to reveal little about her suffering. In the words of French feminist Luce Irigaray: ". . .[S]he comes to be unable to say what her body is suffering. *Stripped even of the words that are expected of her upon that stage invented to listen to her. . . .* But hysteria . . . *now has nothing to say*" (1985: 140). The ambiguity and uncertainty in her accounts of violent sexual experiences are appropriated in a field of language that interprets these responses as self-doubt created by her repression of sexual desire. Like a pornographic show her "hysterical" cries of violation were received as duplicitous utterances of wantonness and denial. Yet the fantasy may be all the more dangerous when the public portrayal of the fallen angel is fulfilled within the symbolic forum of law.

NOTES

1. The New Bedford trial was loosely the subject of the 1988 American movie "The Accused". The movie does not draw from the media or court presentations of events, and most conspicuously does not represent the ethnic dimension of the case.

2. Four of the six defendants were convicted, see *Commonwealth* v. *Rapozo, Cordeiro, Silva, and Viera* (Mass. Super. Ct., Mar. 17, 1984).

3. The following analysis is based upon contents analysis of national and local newspaper reports on the incident and the trial, including the *New York Times*, the *Boston Globe*, and the *New Bedford Standard-Times*.

4. The greater the fixation on her individual qualities (i.e., her name, ethnic identity, and social background), the more frequently the reporters attributed blame and responsibility to the "alleged victim." Sympathy was drawn by alluding to the "any person" victim who suffers sexual violence.

5. Interviews were conducted with five defense attorneys, one prosecutor, and the presiding judge.

6. The entire trial was videotaped and televised by a local New Bedford public television station. The research was conducted from the videotape archives at the Harvard Law Library.

REFERENCES

Arnold, T. (1962) *The Symbols of Government*. Harcourt: New York.

Belenky, M. F. et al. (1986) *Women's Ways of Knowing: The Development of Self, Voice, and Mind*. Basic Books: New York.

Bourdieu, P. (1987) The force of law: towards a sociology of the juridical field. *The Hastings Law Journal* **38**, 805–853.

Bumiller, K. (1987) Rape as a legal symbol: an essay on sexual violence and racism. *University of Miami Law Review* **42**, 75–91.

Cassirer, E. (1985) *Symbol, Myth, and Culture: Essays and Lectures of Ernst Cassirer*. (D. P. Verne, Ed.). Yale University Press: New Haven.

Edelman, M. (1977) *Political Language: Words That Succeed and Policies That Fail*. Academic Press: New York.

Edelman, M. (1988) *Constructing the Political Spectacle*. University of Chicago Press: Chicago.

Enzensberger, H. M. (1974) *The Consciousness Industry: On Literature, Politics and the Media*. Seabury Press: New York.

Estrich, S. (1987) *Real Rape*. Harvard University Press: Cambridge.

Fineman, M. (1983) Implementing Equality: Ideology, Contradiction and Social Change. *The Wisconsin Law Review* **1983**, 789–886.

Foucault, M. (1997) *Discipline and Punish: The Birth of the Prison*. Vintage Books: New York.

Frank, J. (1949) *Courts on Trial*. Princeton University Press: Princeton.

Griffin, S. (1986) *Rape: The Politics of Consciousness*. Harper and Row: New York.

Irigaray, L. (1985) *Speculum of the Other Woman*. Cornell University Press: Ithaca.

Kirchheimer, O. (1961) *Political Justice: The Use of Legal Procedure for Political Ends*. Princeton University Press: Princeton.

Lazere, D. (Ed.) (1987) *American Media and Mass Culture: Left Perspectives*. University of California Press: Berkeley.

Merleau-Ponty, M. (1964) *Signs*. Northwestern University Press: Evanston.

McBarnet, D. (1984) Victim in the witness box-confronting victimology's stereotype. In *Criminal Law in Action*, 2nd Edn. (Chambliss, W., Ed.). Wiley: New York.

MacKinnon, C. A. (1987) *Feminism Unmodified: Discourses on Life and Law*. Harvard University Press: Cambridge.

Moi, T. (1985) *Sexual/Textual Politics*. Methuen: London.

Pitch, T. (1985) Critical criminology, the construction of social problems and the question of rape. *International Journal of the Sociology of Law* **13**, 35–46.

Santos, B. (1982) Law and revolution in Portugal: the experiences of popular justice after the 25th of April 1974. In *The Politics of Informal Justice* Vol. 2 (Abel, R., Ed.). Academic Press: New York.

Smart, C. & Smart, B. (1978) Accounting for rape: reality and myth in press reporting. In *Women, Sexuality, and Social Control* (Smart, C. & Smart, B., Eds). Routledge and Kegan Paul: London.

Spivak, G. C. (1987) *In Other Worlds: Essays in Cultural Politics*. Methuen: London.

Taylor, C. (1985) *Human Agency and Language*. Cambridge University Press: Cambridge.

CHAPTER 4

Rendering Them Harmless

*The Professional Portrayal of
Women Charged with Serious
Violent Crimes*

HILARY ALLEN

Marco Jones is dead.[1] A violent death—stabbed through the heart on a Saturday night in a fight over a fifty-pence debt. He was 24 years old, a father and a husband. He was always, his widow maintains, a faithful partner and a good provider. He was also the only man she ever loved. It is with his widow that the social-worker's report is primarily concerned. She is described in this report as a sensitive and tender person, physically frail and emotionally devastated by his death. The older of their children is just 2 years old; the younger still a babe at her breast. She does not know how she will face the future without him, or how she will ever find words to explain to her children what has happened. Even though she is now living in a caring and supportive hostel, she still feels utterly alone. The report recommends that she be given psychiatric counselling to help her through this period of bereavement, public assistance with her housing and finances, and the support of a social-worker to help her rebuild her shattered life. Two independent psychiatrists concur with this recommendation, as do each of the various officials who promptly agree to put the proposals into action. By all accounts, Marco's widow is a tragic and pitiful figure. Were it not for the fact that it is she who has thrust the fatal knife into his heart, and that the occasion for these reports is her formal trial for his homicide, these compassionate arrangements might seem entirely uncontroversial.

In its own context there is little that is unique and almost nothing that is particularly remarkable about this case. At the outset of the trial, the woman is an alleged murderer who has admitted killing her husband, and thus risks a sentence of life imprisonment. By the trial's conclusion, however (by which time the offence has been reconstituted as no more than manslaughter),[2] she ap-

Reprinted from Hilary Allen, "Rendering Them Harmless: The Professional Portrayal of Women Charged with Serious Violent Crimes," in *Gender, Crime and Justice*, edited by Pat Carlen and Anne Worrall, Open University Press, pp. 81–94 (1987). Reprinted by permission.

pears as a helpless and pitiful victim, to whom society owes all manner of compensatory benefits. In the portrayal of women charged with serious violent crimes, such transformations are so recurrent to be almost standard. And they are transformations that are systematically reflected in the treatment that is actually meted out to these women by the courts. Successive Home Secretaries and numerous pronouncements by senior judges have emphasised the need for severe custodial sentences in cases of serious violence against the person (Thomas 1979), and in the case of male offenders this policy is routinely followed.[3] In the case of *women* convicted of such crimes, however, the commonest practice is to impose noncustodial sentences, and in the severest cases—notably those involving homicide—it is common for such sentences to be accompanied by quite elaborate arrangements for medical and social support.

This chapter is concerned with the terms whereby this transformation is achieved and sustained. It takes as its material the depiction of female offenders and their offences in court reports by psychiatrists and probation officers.[4] And it illustrates the various ways in which, during the deliberations as to the proper disposal of these cases, the meanings attributed to both offenders and offences are typically manipulated, modified and reconstructed. As I shall illustrate in the main body of the discussion, professional reports can provide the court with an alternative "frame" for the judgment of criminal cases. Like the concluding speech in mitigation (Shapland 1981), they are outside the restrictive discourse of the formal trial. As such they are free not only to introduce many considerations that would properly be excluded from the trial itself, but also to provide an alternative (and sometimes ironic or contradictory) perspective on the very issues of action and responsibility that the trial has in principle resolved.

The central assertion of this chapter is that within these reports the portrayal of female violence follows a distinct and sexually specific pattern which tends towards the exoneration of the offender and deploys discursive manoeuvres that are either absent or untypical in cases involving males. Against the bald facts of the criminal allegation or conviction, these reports counterpose a subtler and more compromising version of the case, which systematically neutralises the assertion of the woman's guilt, responsibility and dangerousness, and thus undercuts any demand for punitive or custodial sanctions. As I discuss in the final section, such treatment of violent female offenders is somewhat uncomfortable to feminist analysis. On one hand, the notions of female subjectivity that underpin this treatment are in many ways offensive to feminism; on the other hand, they sustain a logic of denial and exculpation of female crime which many feminist discussions are also engaged in promoting.

THE SUPPRESSION OF THE CRIME

Given that the occasion for the professional report is a prosecution or conviction for a serious criminal offence, it goes without saying that the unpleasant "facts" of the case will be amply present to the court. The initial baldness of those facts may be illustrated by such documents as the offence summaries that are appended to the official court records of each case.[5] The following is a typical example:

> Victim drinking with girlfriend in pub. At closing time his jealous ex-wife comes over and stabs him in the back with knife. Defendant admits and tells police she had wanted to kill him. Victim in intensive care for 9 weeks; continuing invalid. (Court file, defendant charged with attempted murder.)

In suggesting that the reports on female cases may function to suppress or erase such "facts," I am not suggesting that they typically engage in any material *dispute* with them. On the contrary, by the time the report is prepared, it is rare for the material facts to be a matter of any argument, and indeed it is common for the report to include a brief description of the commission of the crime. What these accounts typically achieve, however, is a suppression or erasure of a rather subtler kind: they acknowledge the trajectory of objects in space—the knife in the hand, the thrust of the blade into the heart—but progressively delete from that trajectory all that would mark it as an action by an intentional and culpable subject.

An important component of this suppression is the routine problematisation of the psychological aspects of female cases. Reports on female offenders almost invariably address themselves to the issue of the mental state of their subjects, and throughout these reports the discussion of both the offence and the appropriate judicial response to it is interwoven with complex observations about the female offender's mentality and inner experiences. Overall, an average of 20 per cent of the total length of reports on female offenders is occupied by statements which in some way refer to the subject's psychology (Allen 1986). This is in sharp contrast to reports on male offenders, which instead tend to focus on the more external and material aspects of the offender's behaviour, biography and life-style. Quantitatively, psychological statements occur only half as frequently in reports on males; qualitatively, such psychological observations as *are* made about male offenders tend to be perfunctory and formulaic. The following, for example, is an extract from a psychiatric report on a man who has clubbed and hacked to death a casual friend, stolen his electric kettle and a shopping bag, and then set fire to the body. The major part of the report, as is typical in male cases, has confined itself to the flat recounting of the external details of the offender's history and behaviour. The following is all that the psychiatrist has to say about the psychological background to the offence:

> The defendant is of average intelligence. I could elicit no evidence of mental disorder and he is fit to plead. He had consumed a good deal of alcohol on the day of the alleged offence, but he was an habitual drinker and there is no evidence of psychosis. (Psychiatric report, male accused of murder and arson)

Such desultory observations make no attempt to mitigate the material meanings of the offence, and suggest no particular reason for the offender's moral exoneration. By contrast, the attention to psychological questions which is typical of female cases allows both material and moral significances to be systematically reconstructed. Most conspicuously, the psychologisation of the case allows the question of the criminal intentions of the female offender (even if formally undisputed for the purpose of the conviction) to be reinvoked at the point of sentencing—and to be reinvoked in terms which both displace the material significance of the offence and attenuate the offender's moral responsibility for it.

The manoeuvre depends upon undercutting the formal acknowledgment of the offender's action with the assertion that at the moment of the deed she was acting without conscious volition, without comprehension or without meaning. In a few cases (as, for example, in the well-publicised cases involving pre-menstrual tension), sophisticated medical explanations are given for this curious state of mind (Allen 1984). More commonly, however, no such explication seems to be regarded as necessary; instead, there is a simple denial of the woman's mental engagement with her behaviour, as if such an unreasoning and unreasonable condition were a quite natural state of womankind, for which no exceptional cause need be sought. Thus, in the case of a woman who has strangled and suffocated a girlfriend in the course of an argument (and who is not assessed as in any way mentally ill), we are suddenly informed,

> It may well be that she was not aware that by putting a plastic bag over [the victim's] head and tying a flex around her neck that she was thereby killing her. (Psychiatric report, female accused of murder)

Of another, who has stabbed her common-law husband through the heart, again in the course of an argument, we are told,

> Whatever happened on the night in question causing the death of [the victim] I do not believe that [the defendant] acted with any intent to cause him harm. (Psychiatric report, female accused of murder)

At the very moment where these narratives seem most to require a definitive moral subject, as the responsible author of the crime, these women's status as such subjects is emphatically revoked. The psychological commentary presents them as not intending the deed, as not knowing or understanding that they are committing it, as experiencing nothing in relation to it. The following narrative expresses these ideas more explicitly and at more length. It is drawn from a psychiatric report on a woman who has gone to her lover's house, fought with his wife and killed her, then started a fire which has killed his two children.

> Olive remembers the early parts of the fight except that she does not remember having her hair pulled out. Her mind is then quite blank until she realised that Jenny had stopped fighting and was seriously wounded. This fact can easily be explained by Olive becoming totally involved in the battle and oblivious to everything around her. She was brought back to her senses, she states, by the sound of one of the children crying. She noticed that a fire had been started in the room, but does not remember starting it. In a daze she fed the child and left the house . . . Her lack of memory for the events can be explained by her natural defences in protecting herself. I do not think it at all likely that she planned to commit this crime. The crime, in all probability, developed from the original fight, and the tragic events which followed were caused by the defendant's dissociation from her

own feelings, so that she was in an emotionless trance and unable to appreciate what she had done or take steps to prevent a further tragedy from occurring. At this point she could not make responsible decisions. This too was her natural defence against extreme stress. It is a well-known and typical hysterical reaction. (Psychiatric report, woman charged with murder, manslaughter and arson).

At the heart of the crime we are offered a characteristic series of mental disjunctions, absences, dissociations. The woman is oblivious to everything around her, does not perceive even the injuries she is causing and sustaining. She is not "in her senses," does not understand or recognise the work of her own hands. She is in a daze, dissociated, cannot appreciate what she has done. Across the whole drama there is an absence of intention, of will, of responsibility for action. The crime "develops," the "tragic events" "follow," she can do nothing "to prevent a further tragedy from occurring."

The initial psychologisation of female behaviour thus provides the conditions for a further characteristic manoeuvre—that of the *naturalisation* of the crime. Through the suppression or denial of criminal intention, the violent deed which provides the occasion for judgment is progressively erased or redefined. Having first been displaced from a domain of *culpable* human actions, for which the subject can be held morally responsible, the crime may then, by extension, come to be displaced from the domain of human actions altogether. Instead, it is rewritten as a mere event in nature, a natural disaster in whose devastation the offender has simply been swept away, without either volition or responsibility. Conspicuously, this naturalisation of female crime will have the effect of blunting whatever moral discredit would otherwise attach to its author, and will thereby reduce the apparent need for any punitive sanction against her. And in the more extreme cases, it may even allow the offence to enter the moral calculus paradoxically. Instead of counting *against* the offender, as a morally reprehensible action for which she must be punished, the "tragic event" of the crime may actually come to be added to the sum of her involuntary and undeserved troubles, for which, if anything, she deserves public compensation. This tendency is strikingly illustrated in the following case. The defendant's lodger has irritated her by refusing to turn off the television and come for his supper. In response she has killed him, by tossing a gallon of paraffin over him in his chair, followed by a lighted match.

It would be hard to over-estimate the effect which these events have had upon her. She is naturally, I think, a somewhat nervous and anxious person, and at times has felt quite overwhelmed by her feelings of guilt. As she has told me her history, I have felt the stage being set for this tragedy by her parents. Unloved and repressed by them, she has found herself in relationships which seem to have reinforced her feelings of worthlessness and uselessness. From her description the victim appears to have been a violent borderline alcoholic, and for much of her life she seems to have been the one who has been put upon and generally exploited, until this violent retaliation took place. (Social inquiry report, woman charged with murder)

The terms of this presentation interrupt the attribution of personal blame. The woman has not *formed* the difficult relationship with her lodger but merely "found herself" in it. She is not the author of her unsatisfactory life and circumstances but simply the puppet of others who have "set the stage" for her "tragedy." And even the crime itself is not an act that she has perpetrated but only a series of "events" and a "retaliation" that has "taken place." The loss of the victim's life, under conditions of unthinkable suffering, seems morally incidental to this scenario and is accorded no place in the calculation of the offender's due deserts. Instead this calculation focuses only on the woman's own suffering, of which these events are significant only as symptom or cause.

DAMAGE AND DANGEROUSNESS

The same discursive manoeuvres that thus neutralise the demands for a *punitive* custodial sentences may also serve to neutralise the demands for a *protective or preventive* one. To the extent that these reports tend to obscure the past and current violence of the offender, they often allow any question of her *future* dangerousness to be simply passed over, as of no pertinence. In reports of violent males, the need for public protection is almost always taken seriously, and any recommendation of a noncustodial sentence is a matter that will require explicit justification. In female cases, on the other hand, the possibility that the offender may pose a continuing threat to those around her is seldom even addressed, and a recommendation of a noncustodial sentence is treated as unremarkable. The following, for example, is drawn from a report on a young woman with a long criminal record, now convicted of causing actual bodily harm:

> [Whilst in a unit for difficult adolescents] Gail was destructive, obstructive, aggressive, malevolent. She stole, absconded, bullied and in general absorbed an enormous amount of attention and had to be supervised constantly. Her mother died in 1971, when Gail's behaviour began to deteriorate. The violence she had shown within the Unit was extended to people outside, and there are 4 recorded examples of attacks on girls in the local area. Following these incidents it was decided that she could only leave the Unit with an adult. This did not prevent her hitting two other girls. She . . . attacked her sister's 9 year old son who narrowly escaped serious eye injury. She totally lacked remorse when she hurt anyone . . .
>
> [Over the next 3 years] her violent behaviour continued and in 1975 she is reported to have attacked her social worker, pulling her hair out and kicking her. Later that year outbursts of violence at her lodgings led to her emergency admission to LM Hospital, as the Social Services had nowhere for her to go. A month later she was charged with assault . . . and she was remanded to T Remand Centre. A week later she is reported to have attacked 2 members of staff and was charged with assault. Later that year she appeared before S Court and was convicted of wounding. (Psychiatric report, woman convicted of causing actual bodily harm.)

After such a catalogue of nastiness (which continues unabated through several more episodes of attacks and woundings), one might suppose that the dangerousness of this offender could hardly be ignored. When we arrive at the summary of the case, however, these uncomfortable details seem suddenly to evaporate:

> When interviewed she gave a background history somewhat at variance with our documents and there was an understandable tendency for confabulation and retrospective adjustment. None the less, the essential ingredients of her past life story remain unchanged, with a clear evocation of severe parental deprivation, inconsistent handling, in multiplicity of institutions, a gravitation towards petty criminality, release being sought in drug taking, impulsive and irresponsible behaviour leading to victimisation by sexual predators and a frenetic search for comfort, security and affection. She has a determined and volatile personality, and her general background, taken in conjunction with the last 4 years of institutionalisation, have left her as a severely damaged personality. As the interview progressed, she became more animated, and one was able to detect the combination of profound insecurity and defiance. Eventually she was able to talk of her fundamental striving to find some kind of a father figure, her dislike of women and her need to be cared for in terms of security. Understandably her self-image was distorted, with considerable guilt and self-denigration. She aspired to a home, husband and children, and a conventional family life, but when questioned had little concept of how to achieve such a goal. (*ibid.*)

These "essential ingredients of her past life "do not seem to include her persistent aggression towards everyone around her. What is emphasised instead are the various privations and unhappinesses which she has herself endured. Her violent behaviours now appear only nonspecifically as a gravitation towards petty criminality and impulsive and irresponsible behaviour—and even these are only accorded significance to the extent that they led to her "victimisation by sexual predators and a frenetic search for comfort, security and affection." Similarly, her "volatile and determined personality" is given significance not as the origin of her repeated acts of violence, but as evidence of the damage that she has suffered at the hands of others, and as a factor disguising her inner security and "need to be cared for." With the more concrete and less savoury aspects of her biography thus displaced, even the woman's (arguably quite appropriate) feelings of guilt and self-denigration can then be sympathetically pathologised as merely the product of a "distorted self-image." So this, accordingly, is the point where the report can invoke the orthopaedic image of all that this poor creature lacks and will ultimately aspire to: a conventional home, husband, children and family life.

IN HER OWN PLACE

This fantasy of the domestication of the violent female offender provides the final link in the process whereby she is discursively tamed, sanitised, rendered harmless. The invocation of the domestic and "feminine" positions of these women serves two complementary purposes in these documents. First, as has been discussed by Krutschnitt (1982), it gestures towards a domain of alternative social controls, which may render the formal controls of judicial sanctions redundant. A typical example is that of a mentally disordered female offender who has repeatedly threatened to kill her husband and is now convicted of setting light to the family home with intent to endanger his life. Both medical and social inquiry reports agree that penal detention would be undesirable, as it might exacerbate her psychiatric condition. But they also maintain that even the *medical* detention of the offender is unnecessary, since she can be suitably contained within the family setting:

> I would not feel that her admission to [a secure hospital] is justified. For many years she seems to have coped reasonably well when living with her family and having out-patient treatment. She is not imminently dangerous to others at present and . . . I think she could be satisfactorily looked after in the community. (Psychiatric report, woman convicted of arson with intent to endanger life)

This assumption that the demands of public protection can be adequately met by placing a violent offender under familial supervision seems restricted almost exclusively to cases involving women. The sexual distinction is particularly clear in cases where the violence is directed at the offender's children. In cases of serious paternal violence, the protection of the children from further violence is often treated as an automatic priority, self-evidently justifying the removal of the offender through the imposition of a custodial sentence. In cases of maternal violence, by contrast, the possibility of further danger is rarely even raised, and instead, the "home and family" continue to be constituted as the ideal site for the offender's containment and surveillance—an arrangement that preempts the demand for formal custodial detention.

A second and related effect of the invocation of home and family is to place the female offender in statuses which not only entail privileged responsibilities (that would be gravely disrupted by imprisoning her as a dangerous criminal), but which also seem fundamentally incompatible with the *perception* of her as a dangerous criminal. As is illustrated graphically in the following case, the activation of the woman's alternative statuses, as housewife, mother, and spouse, seem sometimes to undermine the very *possibility* of treating her as dangerous. In this case, the woman has been convicted of causing grievous bodily harm to her baby daughter, whom she has stabbed in the back. Ever since the birth the mother has shown hostility to the child and has been under close medical supervision, with a diagnosis of puerperal depression. What is being proposed in the report is that the woman should be briefly hospitalised as a voluntary patient in a local hospital, and should then be returned to her home under the general supervision of social-workers, visiting nurses and members of her family. This is essentially a continuation of the prior and existing regime of treatment, unmodified by the fact of the attack on the child or the subsequent criminal conviction.

> [From the birth onwards] Pamela Groves clearly constituted a serious risk to her child. My department was extremely concerned that Pamela might commit suicide or infanticide. Our obvious aim was to cement as much as possible the mother–child relationship from an early stage for the sakes of both Pamela and baby Emma, for we have always had the view that the depressive disorder would resolve itself in due course and allow Pamela to re-

turn home to care for baby Emma and her husband. This is, indeed, what happened when she was eventually discharged. She continued to receive support from her husband, her mother, and a health visitor and from my community nurse colleague Mr. Woods; also her medication continued through my out-patient clinic. Throughout the first half of that year she was leading a normal life, caring for her husband, child and home. In early August unfortunately she became depressed again.

[Following the attack] baby Emma, understandably, still shows some anxiety in the presence of her mother. Mr. Groves understandably is under great stress, and although he is living in the family home, he is also showing evidence of excessive anxiety when faced with coping with his new job, his child in care and his wife mentally ill in hospital. Given this very difficult situation, it is obviously important to have a clear view of the future management. Firstly our aim here is to treat Mrs. Groves. One would usually then expect her to return home to care again for her family. It is still important that she should be able to reestablish her relationship with her child. It is equally important for the child that this should occur . . .

Now that Mrs. Groves has suffered from at least two severe episodes of psychotic depression, then the risk that she may suffer in the future must be higher than for the average woman. I believe that the risks to Emma will be minimal once the child can communicate clearly verbally, and in particular once she is attending school. (Psychiatric report, woman convicted of causing grievous bodily harm)

From a strictly criminological perspective, this report and its recommendations are really quite remarkable. Here is a subject who for more than a year has been officially regarded as likely to commit homicide. The officials responsible for her management have decided that she should none the less remain in constant and close proximity to her predicted victim, and they have knowingly arranged for her to do so in a situation where for the larger part of every day she will be alone with this person, who is utterly defenceless. Such social and medical measures as have been arranged in the hope of averting the risk have then manifestly failed: the subject has fulfilled the original expectation, by stabbing the predicted victim in the back. The offender is now judged liable to make further such attacks, and as likely to remain so for a period of years. Yet the officials concerned still insist that the desirable course of action is to restore the original situation where the offender will be alone with the (still helpless) victim and made responsible for her safety and well-being. This is regarded as the optimal situation for the offender, for the victim and for all concerned.

Although all these uncomfortable criminological details are present in the report, the coherence of its recommendations is nowhere founded on any construction of the woman as a violent and continuingly dangerous criminal. Instead, what grounds the coherence of the report is the apparently overriding construction of its subject *as a woman, as a mother and as a wife*. Home and family are her proper place. Looking after her husband and child is her normal life. Tenderness towards her family is her natural emotion. The possibility of disrupting this domestic idyll by the preventive detention of the offender is simply never raised—and the recommendations of the report are accepted without demurrer by the court.

NORMAL LIVES

Throughout, the credibility and the coherence of these documents depends on their resonance with certain taken-for-granted images of female lives and subjectivity. In the insistence on the domestic statuses of these women, this appeal to the familiar and the "normal" is relatively unambiguous. What my discussion may have obscured, however, is the degree of normalisation that is also involved in the other manoeuvres of these reports. In my attempt to expose these manoeuvres, I sought to construct a sense of their "strangeness"—the strangeness of presenting their crimes as impersonal misfortunes rather than personal misdeeds; of claiming that even at the decisive moment of their crimes, these adult and averagely intelligent individuals were behaving without volition, intention, understanding or consciousness. But this sense of strangeness is exterior to the texts themselves. *Within* the texts, these portrayals are treated unproblematically, as if reflecting a taken-for-granted and uncontentious perspective on the everyday reality of female existence.

Thus the "absence of agency" that characterises the description of women's crimes is not presented in these texts as any sudden or aberrant departure from their female normality: instead, it appears continuous with even the most unremarkable moments of their existence. In the brief biographies that routinely form part of these texts, it is not simply in relation to *crimes* that there appears a reluctance to describe these subjects as intentional or active: there appears a striking paucity of references to these women doing anything intentional *at all*. The lives of *male* offenders are regularly described in simple statements in the active voice, detailing the succession of things that the offender has "done" in his life. By contrast, the description of women's lives is everywhere hedged about with circumlocutions and grammatical inversions that constantly obscure the subjects' active responsibility and agency.[6] There is a conspicuous concern with the women's emotional responses to the material events of their lives, but little expectation that they will normally be the active authors of these events—and every readiness to conclude that they are *not*.

Rather similarly, the frequent suggestion of mental irresponsibility in relation to the commission of the crime is rarely treated as indicating an *aberration* from female normality, and at times seems to be taken as virtually *evidence* of such normality. Earlier on, for example, I discussed a case in which the offender has killed her lover's wife in a fight, and has then caused the death of his children by setting light to his house. She is described as doing so in a state of dissociation, amnesia, emotionless trance, unconsciousness of her actions and unawareness of their consequences. Even in the course of this account, this state of mind is referred to as a "natural" and "easily explainable" one, and as a "well-known and typical" reaction. These hints, however, only lightly prefigure the striking statement of normality with which the report concludes:

A pleasant straightforward girl . . . Open with good social skills and normal emotions. I could detect no sign of any mental illness or any abnormal thought process [and she] could not be described as having a personality disorder . . . *She is a perfectly normal young woman in every respect.* (Psychiatric report, woman accused of murder, manslaughter and arson; emphasis added)

PASSING JUDGMENTS

From a feminist perspective it is easy to take objection to such a conception of perfectly normal young womanhood. The image of the female sex as passive, ineffectual, unstable and irresponsible is a familiar target for criticism by feminists, as indeed is the expectation that women's social and legal existence will be governed by the restraints of domesticity and the family. Feminist analyses of the law have long recognised that the privileges and exemptions that such conceptions may allow are bought at the expense of making legal invalids of women, of excluding them from their full status as legal subjects, and of perpetuating their social and legal subordination (Edwards 1985). And in the specific field of criminal justice, feminist authors have been uniformly suspicious of the judicial "lenience" towards female offenders which such conceptions of female incapacity can help to sustain (Anderson 1976).

On one hand, this judicial lenience can be theorised as merely compounding the initial invalidation of women's action and responsibility. The imposition of a modest or nugatory sentence, as is common in cases of violence by women, carries the public implication that the crime itself need not be taken particularly seriously. From this perspective, the lenient sentencing of violent women can be interpreted as a more or less calculated tactic of patriarchal oppression, whereby the potential power of women's action can be censored from public recognition, and the politically sedative myth of women's compliance and harmlessness can be conveniently preserved (e.g., Squire 1981). On the other hand, the accompanying preference for "rehabilitation" of deviant women routinely involves the reinforcement of conventional sexist expectations about the "proper" domains of feminine activity (Rowett and Vaughan 1981: 149; Rafter and Natalizia 1981) and often implies no more than the women's supervised attachment or reattachment to the informal controls of the family (Krutschnitt, 1982). From a radical perspective, any apparent gains of this approach may be dismissed as illusory: they are won only by exchanging overt coercion for a "privileged" and "voluntary" submission to patriarchal authority, which neither relieves women from the normal constraints of sexual oppression, nor removes the threat of explicitly coercive sanctions in the event of further dissidence.

At the level of a general critique of the law, such arguments and objections have an obvious appeal. They offer the possibility of countering any suggestion of female advantage in the operation of the law, and of assimilating the judicial treatment of female offenders to a uniform theory of women's oppression. But aside from the rhetoric and the overarching theories, there remains an obvious dilemma. The logical implication of objecting to the existing paternalism is that these violent women—reconstituted in the full dignity of responsibility, culpability and dangerousness—should be exposed to the full rigours of penal sanctions. In short, they should be punished, and in serious cases they should (as is typical with males) be imprisoned for a very long time. This is not a position that feminists find easy to espouse.

The dilemma exemplifies the fallacy of assuming that women's interests can in principle be treated as homogeneous and universal. In a general sense, the kinds of portrayal of women that I have discussed in this text may quite easily be theorised as "contrary to women's interests." Certainly, they reproduce and elaborate a number of unwelcome conceptions of femininity, and in relation to a "general" field of women's interests one may reasonably object to the pattern of differential treatment of women that such conceptions underpin. But at a lower level of analysis, and in relation to the particular women concerned, the avoidance or reduction of punitive sanctions cannot easily be seen as anything but advantageous—and if the activation of these otherwise problematic notions of femininity can be of advantage to particular women, then it may seem unduly puritanical to allow generalised ideological scruples to rule them out of court.

A conspicuous feature of feminist discussions that focus directly on the interests of female offenders is thus their tendency to reproduce rather than challenge the manoeuvres that I have discussed in this chapter. In some cases this reproduction is self-conscious and more or less cynical: without ignoring the darker side of such portrayals, it is quite possible to urge their calculated exploitation, as offering both a limited opportunity for particular women to avoid the full rigours of punishment, and a point of leverage from which the general bias *against* women may to some small extent be redressed (e.g., Luckhaus 1985).

Perhaps more interesting, however, are those feminist discussions where the reproduction of these tactics is more uncritical and wholehearted. Feminist analyses are often just as ready as the reports discussed above to deny the responsibility, culpability and even the agency of female offenders, and even where the political valency of these arguments is very different from those of the court reports, their content and structure are often much the same. Thus, for example, feminist discussions are often quick to invoke the notion that the individual female offender is not herself the true agent of the offence, or at least is not to blame for it. Much like the court reports, feminist discussions are often ready to explain female offending by reference to social or economic forces, or to attribute it to the oppressive domestic and familial situations in which these women involuntarily "find themselves" (Leonard 1982; Rafter and Natalizia 1981). Likewise, certain feminist discussions participate in the "normalisation" of the female criminal—refusing any notion of the female criminal as in any way more irresponsible or antisocial than other women, and instead asserting that "any woman" might react with such behaviour in comparable circumstances. Feminist arguments may also parallel the court reports in the priority they accord to the maternal roles of women offenders (Haley 1980), and in extreme cases there is the implication that a mother's right to look after her children should be given almost automatic priority over her responsibility to the law, and that the imprisonment of mothers should therefore be avoided at all costs (Lockwood 1980).

Beneath all these arguments, feminist discussions share with the court reports the underlying predisposition to view criminal women as more victims than aggressors, more sinned against than sinning, more to be pitied than blamed. The positioning of female subjects as victims rather than aggressors is to some extent a structural characteristic of *all* feminist discourse, as is the refusal to allow female subjects to appear as morally guilty or personally discreditable. The maintenance of this reassuring and sympathetic perspective tends to motivate a rather selective attention to the field. In discussions of homicide, for example, the feminist literature routinely stresses those cases of battered women who finally resort to homicide after years of their own victimisation (Edwards 1985)—something of a veil tends to be drawn over those more uncomfortable cases where the victim is a child or another woman, or where the circumstances of the offence seem more unambiguously discreditable.

The woman who commits violent crime is a disturbing figure. She cuts across many of the expectations of the judicial system, and much of the idealism of feminism also. From either perspective it is therefore tempting to detach her from the unwelcome position of violent criminal and reposition her in some other less uncomfortable status. This repositioning is all the more attractive in that the statuses typically invoked will in many cases be quite "correct." The violent female offender may indeed be a victim of circumstances, of social or economic pressures, of violent men or violent emotions; she may indeed be much like other women, and have similarly pressing responsibilities in such feminine domains as motherhood and the family; she may indeed be a generally harmless creature who poses little threat outside the immediate—and perhaps exceptional—circumstances of a single crime. Furthermore, the recognition of these factors may quite genuinely enlighten many aspects of the case, and their acknowledgment is by no means necessarily oppressive or illegitimate. If anything, one might argue that there is greater oppression in the general exclusion of such considerations from the deliberations concerning males—who may also be subject to personal frailties, family pressures and external disadvantages, even though in male cases the prevailing images of criminality make it more difficult for such factors to be acceptably or effectively emphasised. The disturbing aspect of the professional depiction of female offenders is thus not that these alternative statuses are invoked *at all*, but that their invocation is so sexually specific, so deeply implicated in a general judicial sexism (of potential disadvantage to offenders of *either* sex), and so often deployed to preempt rather than enlighten the serious examination of criminal women's actions and responsibilities. For what *is* potentially oppressive to women—criminal or otherwise—is for the frailties and disadvantages that do tend to characterise their position in society to be treated as exhaustive of their condition as social or legal subjects. There is every reason for feminist analysis to retain an awareness of those personal vulnerabilities of criminal women that are so insistently portrayed in the professional reports. The delicate task is to do so without also following these reports into suppressing the recognition that these women can also—even at the very moment of their victimisation and coercion—be conscious, intentional, responsible, and potentially dangerous and culpable subjects of the law.

NOTES

This discussion is based on findings from a research project funded by the Economic and Social Research Council (Allen 1986). I am grateful to the Lord Chancellor's Department, the Inner London Probation Service and the Metropolitan Police for their help in making available the documentary material.

1. All the illustrations discussed in this text relate to cases heard in English Crown courts during the 1980s. In order to preserve confidentiality, all names have been changed, and personal details likely to identify the offenders have been omitted.

2. Under English law there are a number of circumstances in which an offence initially charged as murder can be reduced to that of manslaughter—namely, provocation, diminished responsibility and lack of "specific intent" to cause "really serious harm" to the victim. The last of these is the most commonly invoked, and is the ground for the reduction of the charge in the case under discussion here.

3. In male homicide cases, for example, custodial sentences are almost invariably imposed, and long custodial sentences are the rule rather than the exception. The probationary treatment that is often ordered in female cases of homicide is almost never adopted in male cases. See Home Office, *Criminal Statistics for England and Wales*.

4. Medical and social inquiry reports are not read out in open court, but form part of the confidential material available to the judge or magistrate at the point of sentencing. They are almost invariably prepared in cases of homicide, and are commonly sought in any case involving serious violence—especially where a female offender is involved. The assumption that these reports both reflect and contribute to the general construction of these cases is borne out by the high correlation between their recommendations and the final decisions of the court.

5. These summaries are prepared by clerks of court at the opening of the trial usually on the basis of information provided by the police.

6. A quaint example of such circumlocution is the comment with which a report on an elderly female tramp refers to the point in her early twenties when she first left home and took to the road: "At this point an instability developed in her living situation."

REFERENCES

Allen, H. (1984). "At the Mercy of Her Hormones: Premenstrual Tension and the Law," *m/f* 9, 19–44.

———. (1986). "Psychiatric Sentencing and the Logic of Gender," unpublished PhD thesis, Department of Human Sciences, Brunel University.

Anderson, E. (1976). 'The "Chivalrous" Treatment of the Female Offender in the Arms of the Criminal Justice System: A Review of the Literature,' *Social Problems* 23 (3), 49–57.

Edwards, S.S.M. (ed.) (1985). *Gender, Sex and the Law*. London, Croom Helm.

Haley, K. (1980). "Mothers Behind Bars: A Look at the Parental Rights of Incarcerated Women," in S. Datesman and F. Scarpitti (eds.) (1980) *Women, Crime, and Justice*. New York, Oxford University Press.

Kruttschnitt, K. (1982). "Women, Crime and Dependency," *Criminology* 19 (4), 495–513.

Leonard, E. B. (1982). *A Critique of Criminology Theory: Women, Crime and Society.* New York and London, Longman.

Lockwood, K. (1980). "Mothers as Criminals," *Women's Law Review* 9, 78–86.

Luckhaus, L. (1985). "A Plea for PMT in the Criminal Law," in S. Edwards (1985).

Rafter, N. and Natalizia, E. (1981). "Marxist Feminism: Implications for Criminal Justice," *Crime and Delinquency* 27, 81–91.

Rowett, C. and Vaughan, P. (1981). "Women and Broadmoor: Treatment and Control in a Special Hospital," in B. Hutter and G. Williams (eds) (1981) *Controlling Women.* London, Croom Helm.

Shapland, J. (1981). *Between Conviction and Sentence.* London, Routledge and Kegan Paul.

Squire, C. (1981). "Indescribable Tension," *The Leveller*, 11 December, 16–18.

Thomas, D. (1979). *Principles of Sentencing.* 2nd edn, London, Heinemann.

CHAPTER **5**

Postmodernism and Feminist Criminologies
Disconnecting Discourses?

KERRY CARRINGTON

The genre of postmodernism has contributed to an increasing scepticism about essentialism in feminist theory and research. This paper considers the implications of postmodernism for feminist criminological research. Arguments about essentialism have been a major area of contention in feminist criminology as they are in feminist theory and social theory more generally. This paper attempts to link the debates about postmodernism and the fragmentation of the subject to debates in feminist discourses about essentialism and the criminological subject. My argument neither romanticises nor hysterises postmodernism, but seeks to locate the emergence of this discourse in a genealogical field in which the subject is understood as fluid and fractured, and not the fixed transcendental subject of history. I argue that it is important to recognise that a variety of intellectual currents have been crucial in the genealogical development of nonuniversalist ways of thinking about issues like gender, crime and criminal justice. Research in feminist criminology has made a substantial contribution to the intellectual project of disconnecting essentialist discourses about crime and gender. Only more recently has postmodernism become one of these.

POSTMODERNIST GENRES

Postmodernism has become a buzz word used to describe a wide range of objects, conditions, and experiences, including a style of architecture, painting, or performance, the development of global information technologies and the di-

Reprinted from Kerry Carrington, "Postmodern and Feminist Criminologies: Disconnecting Discourses?" *International Journal of the Sociology of Law*, Vol. 22, pp. 261–277, © 1994. Reprinted by permission of Academic Press Ltd. London.

versification of forms of work, sexuality and living in contemporary societies (Hebdige 1988: 182). The genre of postmodernism suggests that modernity has undergone a rapid succession of transformations with the emergence of the mechanical and electronic means of reproduction. These transformations in production, consumption and signification have cut across an elitist aesthetics based on authorship and excellence. In postmodernity there is no authenticity, just renditions of former representations. This is why Baudrillard (1983, 1992) describes the postmodern as the replacement of the real by a hyper-reality of simulation (simulacra). Nothing is new. The artist, the pop star, the criminologist, the poet, the novelist do not create a song, poem, a book, or an image out of nothing—but through a constant reworking of the antecedent. The cycle of reflection, nostalgia, deconstruction and reconstruction is always incomplete. Madonna's shifting persona and seductive style, for example, bear all the hallmarks of a postmodern consumer culture where notions of authenticity surrender to postmodern fabrication and replication (Schwichtenberg 1993: 130). Nor is there any past or future—but a never-ending present shadowed by the past—as Chambers describes:

> With electronic reproduction offering the spectacle of gestures, images, styles and cultures in a perpetual collage of disintegration and reintegration, the "new"—a concept connected to linearity, to the serial prospects of "progress," to "modernism"—we move into perpetual recycling of quotations, styles and fashions: as uninterrupted montage of the "now." (Chambers 1986: 190)

The postmodern condition has been variously described as an epoch characterised by simultaneous continuity and discontinuity; the profusion of cultural diversity; the implosion of meaning, the collapse of cultural hierarchies; the dominance of the image, the text, the preference for the popular, the end of grand narratives, certainties or stable referents (Frow 1991; Smart 1992). Lyotard (1986) refers to this list of postmodern conditions as "the derealisation of society." He elaborates:

> The postmodern would be that which, in the modern, puts forward the unpresentable in presentation itself . . . that which searches for new presentations, not in order to enjoy them but in order to impart a stronger sense of the unpresentable. (Lyotard 1986: 81)

One of the major difficulties with the genre of postmodernism is that it has been "stretched across different debates, different disciplinary and discursive boundaries" (Hebdige 1988: 181). It allows you to associate it with any political position whatsoever (Frow 1991: 7). Such vagueness and elasticity can become a licence for schematisation. Consider for example Bauman's sweeping generalisation about the emergence of a new kind of political technology wholly unreliant on legitimation because: "The twin techniques of panoptical power and seduction (. . .) were increasingly put in charge of the reproduction of the social order" (Bauman 1992: 14).

Curiously, what is said about postmodernity, as a set of conditions transcendent of some antecedent, was said about modernity. So the postmodern is not necessarily a condition, or epoch, or style *decisively* distinguishable from the past, as commonly suggested, but a discursive rupture in the conditions of possibility, which is very much genealogical. There is nothing at all *new* about this, as the genealogical excavations in Foucault's (1980, 1991) many works indicate.

Nevertheless the currency of postmodernism as an intellectual genre, and particularly its critique of the discourses of modernism, is something sufficiently important to argue about. As Huyssen puts it, "The postmodern must be salvaged from its champions and its detractors" (Huyssen 1990: 234). The postmodernist critique of modernity has been wide-ranging; taking issue with the modern sense of self and subjectivity, the progress view of history as linear and evolutionary and the modernist separation of art and popular culture (Nicholson 1990: 3). The postmodernist project of deconstruction has sought to deconstruct three key aspects of modernism (sometimes called the enlightenment project)—its essentialising conception of history, politics, society and the transcendental subject, its teleological search for origins or causes, and its utopian solutions to the problems of modernism (Hebdige 1988).[1]

The postmodernist critique of modernism has had an uneven reception in feminist discourses. A postfeminist discourse has used postmodernist genre to deconstruct the notion of an essentialist category of women's culture, writing or discourse. Women's identities are conceptualised as fragmented and multiple and not unified by some fictive female essence (Flax 1987; Weedon 1987; Nicholson 1990; Swichtenberg 1993). This feminist encounter with postmodernism has been considered a liability for feminist essentialism, precisely because it challenges the notion of a unified single experience based on sex. The following attempts to link the debates about postmodernism and the fragmentation of the subject to debates in feminist discourses about essentialism and the criminological subject.

ESSENTIALISM AND FEMINIST CRIMINOLOGIES

Feminist discourses have rightly and repeatedly expressed concerns about victims of crime—of rape, domestic violence and sexual assault and about the wholesale neglect of these issues within the discipline of criminology (i.e., Smart 1976; MacKinnon 1983; Heidensohn 1985; Cain 1986; Naffine 1987; Allen 1988). Feminist discourses have also been strident in their critique of the treatment of female offenders by the criminal and juvenile justice systems (Campbell 1981; Mukherjee & Scutt 1981; Carlen et al. 1985; Chesney-Lind 1974; Hancock & Chesney-Lind 1985; Carlen 1988; Daly 1989; Smart 1989; Allen 1990).

It is important to note that there is no one feminist position on any of these issues. The development of these positions has followed similar developments in feminist theory more generally (Grosz 1986). The initial critiques of criminology emerged out of the radical discourses of woman-centred second-wave feminist discourses of the 1960s and 1970s. From the mid-1980s to the present, feminist discourses have developed out of a more diverse range of genealogical positions. Some of these have been explicitly committed to the enterprise of deconstructing phallogocentricism (i.e., Smart 1989: 86) others to de-essentialising women's criminality with a view to engaging in the politics of social

justice (Carlen 1992: 65–67) and others with the opposite project to essentialising women as a unified subject of a masculinised social order (Allen 1990:
86–88). After reviewing some of these shifts in feminist discourses about crime,
criminal justice and law, I want to address an issue other feminist scholars (cf.
Nicholson 1990) have felt compelled to address in relation to their own areas
of research. How has the feminist interrogation of crime, the operation of the
law and criminal justice gained from an encounter with postmodernism?

A feminist discourse emerged in the 1960s which inserted the analysis of
gender into the disciplines which had hitherto ignored or misrepresented half
of humanity. Some have called this "liberal feminism" (Grosz 1989). Irrespec-
tive of what you want to call it, this is exactly what feminist scholars did with
criminology in the 1970s, and what a few still do today. This feminist discourse
criticised both the omission of women from the discipline as well as the misogynist representation of women with it. They thought that existing criminological theories could be remedied by simply correcting the many false images of
women constructed in them (cf. Naffine 1987: 2–5). The great value of this work
has been the mass of critical attention directed to the misrepresentation of
women within criminological discourse and the folly of biologically reductionist accounts of female crime which assign to the female population fixed sex-
related characteristics (for example, the Lombrosian notion that women's criminality is innately related to their reproductive capacities or sexual organs, as
deconstructed by Smart (1976: 27–30); Campbell (1981: 36) and Heidensohn
(1985: 111).

However the invocation of social explanations of female criminality (for example, that women's criminality can be explained as the product of male oppression, gender inequality, their confinement to the domestic sphere and the
female role etc.) have simply replaced one set of reductionisms with another
(Cousins 1980). The female offender has emerged in this feminist discourse as
a unitary subject. She is a hapless victim of a patriarchal legal system which,
according to MacKinnon "sees and treats women the way men see and treat
women" (MacKinnon 1983: 644). So while most of the feminist challenges to
criminology in the 1970s and early 1980s developed rigorous critiques of its
misogynous content, rarely were these accounts critical enough of the concept
of criminality or the discipline of criminology itself. The central failing of criminology was simply its failure to adequately address the female sex (Cousins
1980: 111). This critique of feminist criminology has been pursued in different
ways by other feminist scholars across the globe (cf. Brown 1986: 367; Smart
1989; Cain 1990; Carlen 1992). It is to these different feminist critiques I now
turn.

Defending and challenging the force of essentialism has become a major
area of contention in feminist criminology[2] as it has in feminist theory and social theory more generally. Gender essentialism projects onto all men and
women capacities or attributes which are historically and culturally specific
(Nicholson & Fraser 1990: 28). It assumes "that a unitary, 'essential' women's
experience can be isolated and described independently of race, class, sexual
orientation, and other realities of experience" (Harris 1990: 585). The commonalities of sex subordination are said to make it meaningful to adopt essentialist positions and to speak trans-historically and cross-culturally about

women's experiences. Gender essentialism can be detected in accounts of universal female oppression, as well as in appeals to a female essence, because both impose a unity upon its object of inquiry—women (Fuss 1989: 2). The flip side of this is the attribution of a shared masculinist interest to all men, or to certain institutions such as the state or the law which are regarded as patriarchal, phallogocentric or masculinist in essence, effect or nature.

A major problem with essentialism for feminist criminology, as Cousins suggested over a decade ago, is that neither the category law nor the category women are homogeneous entities capable of supporting a singular relation between them (Cousins 1980). Carol Smart too has argued that the law is no simple tool of either patriarchy or capitalism (Smart 1986: 117). As she suggests, to assume so is to assume that law has a unified object, no autonomy from other state instrumentalities and a singular essential relation with the female sex. An essentialist position also assumes that the affectivity of sexual differences acts upon the minutiae of specific discourses and penal practices from the vantage point of some exterior sovereign power. Sometimes sexual differences may be effective within the operation of the law, as it is in certain restricted respects in the processing of delinquent girls (cf. Carrington 1993: 28–35). For example, discourses of sexual difference are active in the means instituted to control socially undesirable male sexuality through the government of girl's bodies.[3] But there is no pre-given unity to such relations (Cousins 1980: 114–115). The criminological subject, like the legal subject has no fixed status associated with gender or sex.

In defence of gender essentialism it has been argued that while women's experiences differ according to race and class position, their position in relation to the men of their own class or race has been one of subordination (Allen 1990: 5). Hence the shared experiences of subordination are said to make it meaningful to adopt essentialist positions and to speak with authority about "women as a group." Others have argued more cynically that essentialist positions, while problematic, are inescapable (Fuss 1989; 3–6) and that feminists need to retain the idea of women as a group if for no other reason than for rhetorical purposes (Fuss 1989: 36). The major problem with these defences is the rather dubious assumption that women's experiences are monotonously similar, regardless of their endlessly varied cultural, spatial and historical specificity. In any case the rhetorical effect of talking about "women as a group" can be used either way, positively or negatively (i.e., women are good drivers, women are bad drivers; women are less criminal, women are more devious). Essentialism whatever form it takes cannot cut across the reductionism of binary opposites such as these.

Nevertheless more intellectually sophisticated defences of gender essentialism have multiplied and developed which are not easily dismissed. A feminist discourse emerged in Australia during the 1980s, strongly influenced by what were called "French Feminisms." It took male theory or phallocentricism as its object "using the perspective of women's experience" to produce feminist ways of knowing (Grosz 1989: 97). One particularly interesting development was the rejection of behaviourist and rationalist conceptions of the body which conceptualise it as neutral in the formation of consciousness (Gatens 1983). Gatens argues that the feminine imaginary body and the masculine imaginary body correspond with the female body and male body respectively (Gatens 1983: 155). Thus the relation between masculinity and the male body, and femininity and the female body is not arbitrary. She supposes that since the body cannot be neutral with regard to the formation of consciousness then there are only two sexed bodies, one male the other female. While Gatens insists that this assertion does not imply a fixed essence to the masculine or feminine, it is difficult to see how there can be any historical specificity or variation in female or male sexed bodies if their correspondence to an imaginary body is always historically fixed.

These more sophisticated defences of essentialism in feminist theory have had a commensurate impact on the development of feminist criminologies. Most significantly they have inverted the essentialist formulae. The central failing of criminology is now its inherent phallocentricism; its failure to confront its sex question with regard to men (Allen 1989: 20–21; Van Swaaningen 1989: 288; Cain 1990: 11). These critiques have in Cain's terms transgressed the discipline of criminology (Cain 1990: 6), and fit loosely into Carlen's typification of an anti-criminology position (Carlen 1992: 53). The concept of the sexed body has entered into the discursive field of feminist discourses about the law (cf. Smart 1990). Feminist scholars have begun to take issue with "the law" as a phallogocentric culture (Smart 1990: 201). They have also begun to interrogate criminology as a form of masculinist thinking about women. Criminology is now regarded not just as sexist discourse but a phallocentric one (Allen 1988, 1989: 20; Van Swaaningen 1989: 288; Cain 1990: 11), because: "Criminological theory is written largely by men and about men, whilst a universal validity is simply taken for granted" (Van Swaaningen 1989: 288).

It is difficult to disagree with these seemingly plausible assertions. On the basis of recorded statistical sex differences maleness does appear to be the strongest predictor of crime and delinquency. The fact that boys far outnumber girls coming before the Children's Courts is empirically well founded and clearly supported by Australian and international collections of juvenile crime statistics (see Carrington 1993: 18). In 1991 six times as many men as women were convicted of a criminal offence in the State of NSW (81 715 men compared to 13 751 women) (NSW Bureau of Crime Statistics 1992: 301). Thus the criticism that criminology has left untheorised the relationship between masculinity and crime is a forceful one.

The difficulty begins when this general *description* of recorded sex differentials becomes the *end* of the analysis and when feminist politics is read off from these over-interpreted statistical sex discrepancies. The criminal then emerges in this feminist discourse as a phallocentric phenomenon—as nearly always male whose victim is nearly always female (cf. Allen 1990: 252). While this is true of certain crimes, such as sexual and domestic violence, men, not women, are the vast majority of victims of violence, including nonreported assaults (National Committee on Violence 1990: 33). In any case the formulation of "the problem" as a product of phallocentricism has led to demands for the law to be much more vigilantly enforced on men "as men." A major flaw in this argument as Hogg and Brown suggest, "is that it rests on an idealised conception of the way the criminal justice system, in particular the police, operate with respect to the so called 'public' sphere" (Hogg & Brown 1992: 8–9). They explain:

The argument that police should simply enforce the law in the case of domestic assault (and other forms of violence against women) by arresting and charging offenders, as they would in any other assault, ignores the particularism and selectivity that characterise policing outside, as well as within the domestic sphere. It therefore oversimplifies the problems entailed in getting the police to behave differently, by reducing them to the problem of police sexism. However, many men as well as women are vulnerable to both violence and the tendency for such violence to be officially and popularly denied and disregarded. An example can be found in the most public of male domains, the pub. (Hogg & Brown 1992: 8–9)

Several empirical studies, two statistical and one ethnographic, have suggested that the levels of unreported victimisation of intra-male violence are as high as the levels of unreported domestic violence (Homel, Thommeny, & Tomsen 1989; Victorian Community Council Against Violence 1990; Deverey 1992). The National Committee on Violence, established in 1987 by the Prime Minister in association with the States concluded that

the vast majority of those who commit crimes of violence are males . . . With the important exceptions of sexual assault and domestic violence, men are also more likely to become victims of violence. Males comprise approximately two-thirds of Australian homicide victims, and 75 percent of victims of serious assault recorded by police." (National Committee on Violence 1990: 33)

The committee also concluded that the victims, like their perpetrators, come from relatively disadvantaged backgrounds, that infants up to one-year-old are the age group at greatest risk of homicide (the female sex is the most likely offender here), and that Aboriginal Australians have a much higher risk of victimisation, up to 10 times greater in the case of homicide (National Committee on Violence 1990: xxiii). Rather than dismiss these empirical details as unwelcome nuisances to the continuum of male violence argument, feminist criminologies would do better to construct genealogies of intra-sex, intra-familial, and inter-sexual violence, and to interrogate the sites and means of their production, before assuming any universal significance about the sex of the victim or offender.

There is one major practical advantage with essentialism. Essentialist explanations of sex differences are convenient because that which is assumed universal, singular and deterministic hardly warrants any attention to empirical detail. All those nuisances and discrepancies, like those above, can be relegated to status of irrelevance. In other words teleological feminist truths, "that the law is the law of patriarchy," and that violence is simply the product of a "hyper-masculine male," can be exempt from any thorough genealogical investigation. These "truths" are polemics "encased in privileges" that ensure they will never be questioned (Foucault 1984: p. 382). In any case, where the theoretical construct of universal gender oppression does not fit the facts, it seems the facts can be sacrificed anyway.

One particular example is the recurring claim that the criminal justice system is masculinist. A major problem with this argument, at least in an Australian context, is that dramatic over-representation of Aboriginal girls and women (and their men) in the justice system contradicts an insistence on an essential relation between it and sex. I am not suggesting that discourses about sexuality are not authoritative in contexts where court action is taken against Aboriginal girls or women. Sometimes Aboriginal girls are criminalised because of their sexual encounters with white boys. But discourses of racial hygiene cannot be easily separated from such instances (cf. Carrington 1993: 44). Nor am I suggesting that there is an essential relation between race and criminal justice which simply displaces an essential relation between criminal justice and sex. Rather that despite the immense genealogical relevance of colonialism in positioning Aboriginal women very *differently* from non-Aboriginal women in relation to criminal justice, this glaring relevance has been persistently absent from feminist research on female crime and delinquency in this country.

The only feminist text to explore a history of crimes "involving Australian women," for example, concentrated exclusively on crimes involving non-Aboriginal women (Allen 1990). Yet Aboriginal women comprise nearly 50 percent of all female custodies and almost 14 percent of all female prisoners in Australia although they account for less than two percent of the Australian female population (Biles 1989: 10; McDonald 1990: 9). Aboriginal girls constitute the single most over-represented group of girls who regularly appear before the New South Wales Children's Courts (Carrington 1993: 37–38). There is hardly an Aboriginal woman in Australia untouched by the operation of criminal justice in her life, either directly or through the repeated criminalisation of her children, her kin, her men or through her own victimisation from various crimes. Very few non-Aboriginal women are subject to anything resembling this extensive management of their lives, families and communities by the criminal justice system, with the exception of a few who live in areas connected to families identified as police targets (i.e., some housing commission communities). The massive rate of criminalisation among Aboriginal women contradicts the dogmatic insistence that the criminal is a phallocentric phenomenon, as well as the assertion that women are positioned as a unified group before the law.[4] It seems, however, that the specificity of Aboriginal women's experiences with the law *must* remain submerged within essentialist feminist discourses to maintain the credibility of the general claim that the criminal justice system is masculinist in that it generally operates in interests on one sex, men.

Hilary Allen (1987) in *Justice Unbalanced* has also taken issue with attempts to explain the treatment of women in the criminal justice system by reference to some general force of sexual oppression. She argues

> Such an explanation demands as its initial premise the assertion of "the patriarchy," as an all-embracing, all-powerful system of male dictatorship, which determines, more or less violently, all the forms and outcomes of social relations, including those of psychiatry and the law. This is certainly a convenient way to explain away all the discrepancies in the treatment of men and women . . . At a substantive level, it blurs the edges of all the specific questions that might otherwise be asked about the nature and extent and form of this discrepancy in sentencing, by unifying it with all the other social divisions of gender, wherever and however they occur . . . This is a

form of analysis which lends a surface of intelligibility to everything in general—behind which everything in particular seems suddenly indistinct. (Allen 1987: 12)

The major problem with the assumption that the female sex is singular in its relation to a masculinist legal system is that too little attention has been paid to the striking *differences* among those of the same sex. The vast majority of the female population rarely come into contact with the criminal justice agencies. Those who do have very little in common with the vast majority of women insulated from the effects of criminal justice, as the specific empirical detail of feminist inquiries like Pat Carlen's have documented (Carlen et al. 1985: Carlen 1988). Maybe what is important is not some seamless web of women's oppression, but the variation in levels of criminalisation and victimisation among them. This obviously calls for a feminist politics of alliances rather than a false unity of sisterhood premised on a utopian overthrow of the masculinisation of the social order. It also demands a genuine recognition of the diversity of women's experiences and a recognition that there is no single problem or solution but a tapestry of commonalities by no means universal, interlaced with difference and even conflict (Nicholson & Fraser 1990: 35). These political realisations are precisely those being promoted in postmodernist feminist discourse (cf. Flax 1987: Nicholson 1990).

After two decades of developments in feminist criminologies we have an internally inconsistent feminist discursive territory. One trajectory has reduced criminality and violence to the effects of masculinity (or a male sexed body); another deconstructed women's crimes as understandable responses to their oppression by men. So on one hand Lomboroso is denounced as a misogynist monster and on the other the shadow of Lomboroso is invoked to explain the innate criminality of the male sex. There are some major exceptions of course (for example, Allen 1987; Carlen 1988; Smart 1989; Cain 1990; Howe 1991). I have three major difficulties with these kinds of arguments. They are essentialist in that they insist on a singular relation between sex and the law. Such an insistence is then Anglocentric in its application as it has produced profound silences within feminist research about Aboriginal girls and women whose lives are mostly affected by the operation of criminal justice in Australia. Finally such insistence has led to a simplistic feminist politics demanding the criminal justice system institute the rule of law over men. This position rests on a popular misconception that the criminal justice system actually divests most of its resources into the investigation of serious crime. The bulk of the resources of the mundane daily functioning of the criminal justice system are directed at the management of social marginality and particularly its social visibility (see Carrington et al. 1991; Hogg 1991; Carrington 1993). Power operates not through some juridicial mechanism of sovereignty (be it patriarchal or some other totalising structure of domination) which has as its central point of application law, but by techniques of normalisation (Foucault 1980: 89–91) and technologies of governmentalisation (Foucault 1991). The types of feminist discourses I have been criticising have not only failed to grasp the politics of the criminal justice process and its mechanisms of power, but have actively silenced major discrepancies in the patterns of victimisation, violence and criminality in and among the female sex. A little more attention to the specificity of the margins and less devotion to the unexamined claims about universal female oppression would make feminist criminologies at least a little more relevant to a few more women—rather than "relevant" to all and specific to none.

POSTMODERNISM AND FEMINIST CRIMINOLOGIES: DISCONNECTING DISCOURSES?

The genre of postmodernism, among many things, has promoted an antiessentialist thinking deeply sceptical of the kind of claims to universality which have strongly influenced the development of feminist criminologies. Totalising discourses construct grand narratives which depend on subjects having fixed essences. These discourses assume the existence of a unitary or transcendental subject and are referred to variously as essentialist, monocausal, teleological, enlightenment or universalist meta-narratives.

Postmodernism suggests that it is no longer possible to posit general or universalistic solutions or answers to problems concerning contemporary life, because ". . . human order is vulnerable, contingent and devoid of reliable foundations" (Bauman 1992: xi). A corollary of this is that we can no longer find comfort in explanations of social phenomena based on essentialisms, grand narratives, secure foundations or fixed subjects. The production of subjectivity, like the production of truth, is contingent, fragmentary and multifarious. It is not possible to impose a unity upon the diversity of subjectivities, nor on the processes of their production. Thus in postdiscourses the subject is fragmented, fluid and diverse. The following implications of this for a postmodern feminism have been suggested.

> Thus, the categories of postmodern-feminist theory would be inflected by temporality, with historically specific institutional categories like the modern restricted, male-headed, nuclear family taking preference over ahistorical, functionalist categories like reproduction and mothering. Where categories of the latter sort were not eschewed altogether, they would be genealogised, that is, framed by a historical narrative and rendered temporally and culturally specific. Moreover, postmodern-feminist theory would be nonuniversalist . . . Finally, postmodern-feminist theory would dispense with the idea of a subject of history. It would replace unitary notions of woman and feminine gender identity with plural and complexly constructed conceptions of social identity, treating gender as one relevant strand among others, attending also to class, race ethnicity, age and sexual orientation. (Nicholson & Fraser 1990: 34)

The question remains does the feminist interrogation of crime, the operation of the law and criminal justice stand to gain from such an encounter with postmodernism? In limited, but vital, respects, I would say yes. It could be argued that the postmodernist critique of subjectivity has had a considerable impact on the conceptualisation of law and the criminal subject as complex, fragmented and diverse thus avoiding many of the difficulties associated with essentialism. But why should postmodernism be privileged as the sole source of this critique? The argument that legal personality is fragmented, that is attached to statuses and not fixed sexed subjects, is not new. For example, in 1980 Cousins wrote:

> The heterogenous collection of statuses and capacities in law, which mostly seem to bear upon the organisation of sexual differences, cannot be made commensurate with the categories "men" and "women." (Cousins 1980: 119)

There have been a whole series of critiques of the essentialism of second wave feminism from other feminist positions, not necessarily associated with the genre of postmodernism. For example, Maureen Cain has consistently argued that the structures of gender, race and class are not reducible to each other in feminist forms of knowledge or any other (Cain 1986). Other significant critiques from within feminism have come from those seeking to de-essentialise the criminal, the victim and the criminal justice system. Notable texts in this critical genre include Carlen's edited collection *Criminal Women* (1985) and subsequent book *Women, Crime and Poverty* (1988), and Smart's *Feminism and the Power of Law* (1989).

Pat Carlen has consistently urged the abandonment of reductionist accounts of women and crime and tried to dispel the myth of the "essential criminal woman" (Carlen et al. 1985: 10). She says that much of feminist criminology has pursued "global, a-historical, monocausal and essentialist explanations" of women's offending (Carlen et al. 1985: 9) and has since embarked on an ambitious project of politically engaged deconstructionism (Carlen 1992: 59–60). She argues convincingly that "The essential criminal woman does not exist" (Carlen et al. 1985: 10). Rather that the heterogeneous effects of sex and gender combine with the differential effects of other statuses (i.e., class and race) to produce a constellation around which women's offending occurs, is understood and punished (Carlen et al. 1985: 9). She has since pointed to the following limits of feminism as an explanation of female offending:

> No single theory (feminist or otherwise) can adequately explain three major features of women's lawbreaking and imprisonment, that women's crimes are, in the main, the crimes of the powerless; that women in prison are disproportionately from ethnic minority groups, and that a majority of women in prison have been in poverty for the greater part of their lives. (Carlen 1992: 53)

Carol Smart's project of deconstructionism has also made a substantial, if somewhat ambivalent,[5] contribution to the sustained critique of a unified subject in both law and feminism. In particular, her book *Feminism and the Power of Law* (1989) criticises the quest for a feminist jurisprudence for its essentialism and determinism. In this important text Smart demonstrates how male power is constructed in this grand theory as omnipotent and how "women are completely over-determined," as if they are constructed by men (Smart 1989: 76–77). The quest for a feminist jurisprudence elevates the law's claim to truth and may simply lead to the replacement of one truth claim with another equally as totalising. She suggests that:

the last thing we need is a feminist jurisprudence on a grand scale which will set up general principles based on abstractions as opposed to the realities of women's (and men's) lives. It is not just that it would be a difficult task to achieve but it would run counter to the main direction of feminist thinking which is moving away from universalizing strategies. (Smart 1989: p. 69)

The critique of essentialism has certainly had a major impact on feminist modes of analysis, in criminology as elsewhere. But how much of this reconstruction is the product of the self-reflexive character of discourse rather than the currency of postmodernism and its encounter with feminism is impossible to gauge. The status of women as a unified category has long been the subject of contestation within feminist discourses. Black feminists, for example, have not needed postmodernism to tell them that women are not a unified subject of history and culture (cf. Harris 1990).

The production of discourses is contingent and variable—self referential and reformulating. They have no single source, ownership or authenticity, and their power effects are just as inescapable for feminist discourses as they are for any other, including postmodernism. So there is no reason to privilege the genre of postmodernism as the sole source of reconstruction in feminist discourses in criminology or elsewhere. But nor can it be relegated to a status of insignificance. Postmodernism has occupied an important place in the geneaology of anti-essentialism. For this reason, if no other, it is likely to continue to exert a strategic, albeit limited, influence over the production of specific feminist knowledges about gender, crime and criminal justice. Well at least for those wishing to analyse "power within the concrete and historical framework of its operation" (Foucault 1980: 90).

NOTES

1. (i) Essentialism is a form of analysis in which social phenomena are understood not in terms of the specific conditions of their existence, but in terms of some presumed essence or interest (Hindess 1977: 95). Thus membership of a social category (i.e., women, working-class) is understood to produce certain shared interests even if these are not recognised by the members themselves. Essentialism therefore imposes a unity upon its object of inquiry by assuming that members of a social group have similar interests or essence (i.e., women, blacks, workers). The postmodernist critique argues that because the subject is fragmented, contingent and variable, the insistence on a fixed transcendental subject or essence is fictive and unnecessarily totalising.

(ii) Teleological discourses search for functionalist determinations, causes or origins of social, historical and political phenomena. Postmodernist critique instead insists on the arbitrary and mediated nature of the contemporary life and its diverse representation in text and discourse. Postmodernism abandons the search for teleological truths.

(iii) Utopian solutions to the problems of contemporary life posit a misplaced faith in the transcendental subject of history on the inevitable march toward enlightenment. Postmodernisms seek solutions in much more local and limited ways through invention in the present, rather than revolutionary transcendence from the past.

2. See, for example, the debates in and between: MacKinnon 1983; Carlen et al. 1985; Brown 1986; Cain 1986; Dahl 1986; Gelsthorpe 1986; Smart 1986; Allen 1987; Daly 1989; Van Swaaningen 1989; Harris 1990.

3. Feminist readings of female delinquency have tended not only to overstate the centrality of discourses authorised around sex, but in so doing have actually *misread* their effects. By positing the effectivity of discourses about sex in some sovereign form of patriarchal power which operates from the outside upon the field of juvenile justice and its specific mechanisms for processing delinquent girls, the opportunity to analyse their production within this particular site of government is forgone. Obviously the latter is what I attempted to do with readings of specific case studies of delinquent girls (see Carrington 1993).

There is no doubt that the justice authorities sometimes develop an intense and moralistic concern with the sexual behaviour of girls, and sometimes their criminal behaviour is sexualised. However to see this concern simply as a form of social control which only seeks to repress adolescent *female* sexuality, while turning a blind eye to the sexual transgressions of boys, is to miss the crucial point that the regulation of socially injurious forms of *male* sexuality, such as incest, rape and carnal knowledge, also operate through technologies of government centred on the corporeality of young women. Let me explain. Because male sexuality is understood in masculinist discourses as instinctive, his sexual urges are regarded as hydraulic or biologically driven. Hence it is incumbent on the female sex to govern her body and conduct in such a way as to not arouse the instinctive sex-striving of the male sex (Tyler 1986: 55–58). This means that the only strategic mechanisms of governance conceivable for dealing with undesirable forms of male sexuality actually operate through the bodies of the female sex. While the effect of these technologies of government may limit and order the corporeal positions legitimately available to girls, they are primarily intended to control *male* not female sexual deviance through the prevention of arousal. Whilst this is all dreadfully misguided, it also has repressive effects on undesirable forms of *male* sexuality, such as incest and rape, which in vital respects disrupt discourses about family life, manhood and nationhood. The issue is therefore not as simple as saying that a masculinist criminal justice system systematically and wilfully neglects the sexual transgressions of boys.

4. For example, Judith Allen asserts: "sexual difference made women of whatever class a unity, a group whose interests might seriously imperil the liberty of men" (Allen 1990: 88).

5. The arguments in Smart's book (1989) and other recent writings (1990) tend to oscillate between a deconstructionism and an essentialism. On one hand feminist jurisprudence is criticised for its essentialising discourses about male power, while on the other "the law" is continuously referred to as phallogocentric, masculine and so on. So the problem with the quest for a feminist jurisprudence is not so much its essentialism, but the crudity of that essentialism and its privileging of law in the hierarchy of knowledges. The general argument advanced by Smart that law is phallogocentric in that it is a knowledge and practice commensurate with masculinity (Smart 1989: 86) reconstructs the feminist essentialism she so superbly deconstructs as nonsense.

REFERENCES

Allen, H. (1987) *Justice Unbalanced: Gender, Psychiatry and Judicial Decisions.* Open University Press: Milton Keynes.

Allen, J. (1988) The masculinity of criminality and criminology: interrogating some impasses. In: *Understanding Crime and Criminal Justice* (Findlay, M. & Hogg, R. Eds). Law Book Co.: Sydney.

Allen, J. (1989) Men, crime and criminology: recasting the questions. *International Journal of the Sociology of Law* **17**, 19–39.

Allen, J. (1990) *Sex and Secrets: Crimes Involving Australian Women since 1770.* Oxford University Press: Oxford.

Baudrillard, J. (1983) *Simulations*, Semiotext(e): New York.

Baudrillard, J. (1992) Simulations. In *A Critical and Cultural Theory Reader* (Easthorpe, A. & McGowan K. (Eds). Allen & Unwin: Sydney.

Bauman, Z. (1992) *Intimations of Postmodernity.* Routledge: London.

Biles, D. (1989) *Aboriginal Imprisonment—A Statistical Analysis.* Research paper No. 6, Royal Commission into Aboriginal Deaths in Custody, Research Unit, AGPS, Canberra.

Brown, B. (1986) Women and crime: the dark figures of criminology. *Economy and Society* **15**, 355–402.

Cain, M. (1986) Realism, feminism, methodology, and law. *International Journal of the Sociology of Law* **14**, 255–267.

Cain, M. (1990) Towards transgression: new directions in feminist criminology. *International Journal of the Sociology of Law* **18**, 1–18.

Campbell, A. (1981) *Girl Delinquents.* Basil Blackwell: Oxford.

Carlen, P. (1988) *Women, Crime and Poverty.* Open University Press: Milton Keynes.

Carlen, P. (1992) Criminal women and criminal justice, the limits to, and potential of, feminist and left realist perspectives. In *Issues in Realist Criminology* (Matthews, R. & Young, J. Eds). Sage: London.

Carlen, P., Hicks, J., O'Dwyer, J., Christina, D. & Tchaikovsky, C. (1985) *Criminal Women.* Polity Press: Cambridge.

Carrington, K. (1993) *Offending Girls: Sex, Youth & Justice.* Allen & Unwin: Sydney.

Carrington, K., Dever, M., Hogg, R., Bargen, J. & Lohrey, A. (1991) *Travesty! Miscarriages of Justice.* Pluto Press: Sydney.

Chambers, I. (1986) *Popular Culture*, Methuen: London, pp. 3–13.

Chesney-Lind, M. (1974) Juvenile delinquency and the sexualisation of female crime. *Psychology Today* July, 4–7.

Cousins, M. (1980) Men's rea: a note on sexual difference, criminology and the law. *Radical Issues in Criminology* (Carlen, P. & Collison, M. Eds). Martin Robinson: Oxford.

Dahl, T. (1986) Taking women as a starting point: building women's law. *International Journal of the Sociology of Law* **14**, 239–247.

Daly, K. (1989) Criminal justice ideologies and practices in different voices: some feminist questions about justice. *International Journal of the Sociology of Law* **17**, 1–18.

Deverey, C. (1992) *Mapping Crime in Local Government Areas*, NSW Bureau of Crime Statistics & Research, Sydney.

Flax, J. (1987) Postmodernism and gender relations in feminist theory. *Signs* **12**, 621–633.

Foucault, M. (1980) *The History of Sexuality: Volume 1*, Vintage Books: New York.

Foucault, M. (1984) *The Foucault Reader* (Rabinow, P., Ed.). Pantheon Books: New York.

Foucault, M. (1991) Governmentality. In *The Foucault Effect: Studies in Governmentality* (Burchell, G., Gordon, C., Miller, P., Eds). Harvester Wheatsheaf: London.

Frow, J. (1991) *What Was Postmodernism?* Local Consumption Publications: Sydney.

Fuss, D. (1989) *Essentially Speaking Feminism, Nature and Difference*. Routledge: London.

Gatens, M. (1983) The critique of the sex/gender distinction. In *Beyond Marxism* (Patton, P., Allen, J., Eds). Intervention: Sydney.

Gelsthorpe, L. (1986) Towards a skeptical look at sexism. *International Journal of the Sociology of Law* **14**, 125–152.

Grosz, E. (1986) Conclusion: what is feminist theory. In *Feminist Challenges* (Pateman, C. & Gross, E. Eds.) Allen & Unwin: Sydney.

Grosz, E. (1989) The in(ter)vention of feminist knowledges. In *Crossing Boundaries: Feminisms and the Critique of Knowledges* (Caine, B., Grosz, E., de Leperuanche, M., Eds). Allen & Unwin: Sydney.

Hancock, L. & Chesney-Lind, M. (1985) "Juvenile justice legislation and gender discrimination. In *Juvenile Delinquency in Australia* (Murray, J. & Borowski, A. Eds.) Methuen: Australia.

Harris, A. P. (1990) Race and essentialism in feminist legal theory. *Stanford Legal Review* **42**, 581–616.

Hebdige, D. (1988) *Hiding in the Light*. Routledge: London.

Heidensohn, F. (1985) *Women & Crime*. Macmillan: London.

Hindess, B. (1977) The concept of class in Marxist theory and Marxist politics. In *The Communist University of London* (Bloomfield, J., Ed.). Lawrence & Wishart: London.

Hogg, R. (1991) Policing and penalty. *Journal for Social Justice Studies* **4**, 1–26.

Hogg, R. & Brown, D. (1992) Policing patriarchy: unwelcomed facts on domestic violence. *Australian Left Review*, **144**, 8–9.

Homel, R., Thommeny, J. & Tomsen, S. (1989) Causes of public violence: situational versus other factors. Paper presented at the National Conference on Violence, Canberra.

Howe, A. (1991) Postmodern penal politics. *Journal for Social Justice Studies* **4**, 61–72.

Huyssen, A. (1990) Mapping the Postmodern. In *Feminism/Postmodernism* (Nicholson, L., Ed.). Routledge: New York.

Lyotard, J. (1986) *The Postmodern Condition: A Report on Knowledge*. Manchester University Press: Manchester.

MacKinnon, C. A. (1983) Feminism, marxism, method and the state: toward a feminist jurisprudence. *Signs* **8**, 635–658.

McDonald, D. (1990) *National Police Custody Survey August 1988*. Research Paper No.

13, Royal Commission into Aboriginal Deaths in Custody, Research Unit, AGPS, Canberra.

Mukherjee, S. & Scutt, J. (Eds) (1981) *Women and Crime*. Allen & Unwin: Sydney.

Naffine, N. (1987) *Female Crime: The Construction of Women in Criminology*. Allen & Unwin: Sydney.

National Committee on Violence (1990) *Violence: Directions for Australia*. Australian Institute of Criminology: Canberra.

Nicholson, L. J. (Ed.) (1990) *Feminism/Postmodernism*. Routledge: New York.

Nicholson, L. J. & Fraser, N. (1990) Social criticism without philosophy: an encounter between feminism and postmodernism. *Feminism/Postmodernism* (Nicholson, L. J., Ed.). Routledge: New York.

NSW Bureau of Crime Statistics (1992) *New South Wales Lower Criminal Courts*. (Statistical Report Series) Australian Government Printing Service: Sydney.

Schwichtenberg, C. (1993) Madonna's postmodern feminism: bringing the margins to the center. In *The Madonna Connection*. (Schwichtenberg, C., Ed.). Allen & Unwin: Sydney.

Smart, B. (1992) *Modern Conditions, Postmodern Controversies*. Routledge: London.

Smart, C. (1976) *Women, Crime & Criminology*. Routledge & Kegan Paul: London.

Smart, C. (1986) Feminism and law: some problems of analysis and strategy *International Journal of the Sociology of Law* **14**, 109–123.

Smart, C. (1989) *Feminism and the Power of Law*. Routledge: London.

Smart, C. (1990) Law's power, the sexed body, and feminist discourse. *Journal of Law & Society* **17**, 194–210.

Tyler, D. (1986) The case of Irene Tuckerman: understanding sexual violence and the protection of women and girls, Victoria 1890–1925. *History of Education Review* **15**, 52–67.

Van Swaaningen, R. (1989) Feminism and abolitionism as critiques of criminology. *International Journal of the Sociology of Law* **17**, 287–306.

Victorian Community Council Against Violence (1990) *Violence In and Around Licensed Premises*. Victorian Community Council Against Violence: Melbourne.

Weedon, C. (1987) *Feminist Practice and Post-structuralist Theory*. Basil Blackwell: Oxford.

PART II

BLURRED BOUNDARIES OF VICTIMIZATION AND CRIMINALIZATION

CHAPTER 6

"Just Every Mother's Angel"

An Analysis of Gender and Ethnic Variations in Youth Gang Membership

KAREN A. JOE
MEDA CHESNEY-LIND

Official estimates of the number of youth involved in gangs have increased dramatically over the past decade. Currently, more than 90 percent of the nation's largest cities report youth gang problems, up from about half in 1983. Police estimates now put the number of gangs at 4,881 and the number of gang members at approximately 249,324 (Curry et al. 1992). As a result, public concern about the involvement of young men in gang activity, and the perceived violence associated with this lifestyle, has soared. The role of young men of color in these official estimates of gang activity, to say nothing of the public stereotypes of gangs, can hardly be overstated. Indeed, with nearly half (47 percent) of African American males between the ages of 21 and 24 finding their way into the police gang database in Los Angeles (Reiner 1992), *gang* has become a code word for race in the United States (Muwakkil 1993).

But what of girls and young women? The stereotype of the delinquent is so indisputably male that the police, the general public, and even those in criminology who study delinquency, rarely, if ever, consider girls and their problems with the law. Connell (1987) describes this process as the "cognitive purification" of social cleavages. Moore (1991), writing about the impact of this process on the public perception of gang activity, notes that media images of gangs "sharpen and simplify" middle-class notions of what constitutes lower-class maleness (p. 137).

Occasionally, girls and women do surface in media discussions of gangs and delinquency, but only when their acts are defined as either very bad or profoundly evil. The media's intense interest in "girls in gangs" (see Chesney-Lind 1993), which actually revisits earlier efforts to discover the liberated "female

Reprinted from Karen A. Joe and Meda Chesney-Lind, "Just Every Mother's Angel: An Analysis of Gender and Ethnic Variations in Youth Gang Membership," *Gender and Society*, Vol. 9, No. 2, pp. 408–430, © 1995. Reprinted by Permission of Sage Publications, Inc.

crook" (Adler 1975, 42), is lodged within the larger silence about the situation of young women of color on the economic, political, and judicial margins. The absence of any sustained research on these girls means there is often little with which to refute sensationalistic claims about their involvement in violence and gangs, as well as very little understanding of why they are in gangs.

There is a clear need, then, to balance, sharpen, and focus our analytical lenses on gender and ethnic variations in youth gang participation. Toward this end, this article first examines the place of gender in theoretical discussions on gangs and delinquency, and suggests that the most immediate task is to understand the role of masculinities and femininities in gang involvement. We then provide a general overview of the geographical setting of our current gang study, particularly in relation to ethnicity, economy, and crime. Next we report the findings from our in-depth interviews with 48 boys and girls from a number of ethnic gangs in Hawaii. We found that although boy and girl members faced common problems, they dealt with these in ways that are uniquely informed by both gender and ethnicity; moreover, consistent with previous ethnographic research, we found that delinquent and criminal activities in boys' gangs have been so exaggerated that it has prevented an understanding of the many ways that the gang assists young women and men in coping with their lives in chaotic, violent, and economically marginalized communities.

MASCULINITY AND GANGS

Historically, the gang phenomenon and its association with youth violence has been defined and understood as a quintessentially male problem. This analytical focus first emerged in the pioneering work of Thrasher (1927) and continued in the same fashion with subsequent generations of gang researchers. During the second wave of research on gangs in the 1950s and early 1960s, the "gang problems" as "male" was even more clearly articulated (Cloward and Ohlin 1960; Cohen 1955; Miller 1958). The only point of difference among these researchers was found in their explanation as to why such delinquent peer groups and their distinctive subculture emerged among boys living in poor communities.

According to Cohen (1955), boys in lower-class communities suffer from "status frustration" because of their inability to succeed by middle-class standards. Ill-equipped to compete in school with their middle-class counterparts, they reject middle-class values and develop a delinquent subculture that emphasizes nonutilitarianism, malice, and negativism. These alternative values justify their manly aggression and hostility and become the basis for group solidarity. Miller (1958) contends, however, that the value gang boys place on "toughness, smartness, excitement, and conning" is part of lower-class culture where boys and men are constantly struggling to maintain their autonomy in households dominated by women. Cloward and Ohlin (1960) counter this "culture of poverty" explanation and adopt a structural framework for understanding gang subculture in lower-class communities. Lower-class boys are blocked from legitimate, and in some cases, illegitimate opportunities, and as a result, rationally choose from among their limited options to engage in particular types of crime. Again, though, all these researchers assume gangs to be a uniquely young men's response to the pressures and strains of poverty.

After this work, research on the gang phenomena fell out of fashion, even though the few studies done during that period document the fact that gangs continued to be a feature of life in poor, minority communities (Moore 1978; Quicker 1983). The economic dislocation of these communities during those decades of silence meant that gang cliques gradually found a place in the underclass (Hagedorn 1988; Moore 1991). In this context, a number of researchers attribute the involvement of young men in gangs and crime (as in organized drug sales) primarily to the material advantages a collective can bring in an environment with fewer and fewer legitimate options (Jankowski 1991; Skolnick et al. 1989; Taylor 1990). Others (Hagedorn 1988; Moore 1991; Waldorf 1993), however, have found little evidence to support the notion that gangs are lucrative business enterprises. In other words, the reasons for membership are far more complex and varied, because gangs flourish while clearly failing to provide their members with a ticket out of poverty.

In this connection, how are we to interpret the role of violence and the subcultural emphasis on toughness and bravado in boys' gangs described by earlier as well as later generations of researchers? Jankowski (1991) believes that gang violence and the defiant attitude of these young men is connected with the competitive struggle in poor communities.

> The violence associated with members of gangs emerges from low income communities where limited resources are aggressively sought by all, and where the residents view violence as a natural state of affairs. There the defiant individualist gang member, being a product of his environment, adopts a Hobbesian view of life in which violence is an integral part of the state of nature (p. 139).

In the end, Jankowski's argument is actually little more than a revisiting of the culture of poverty arguments of the late 1950s, with all of the flaws associated with that perspective (Ryan 1972). Of greater concern, though, is the fact that such characterizations "totalize" a range of orientations toward violence found among gang youth (Hagedorn 1992). Such generalizations are not only insensitive to the critical differences among individuals and groups, but they also result in a one-sided, unidimensional understanding of the lives of gang members; moreover, policymakers, the police, and the media are likely to interpret these findings precisely in that way, and the notion that "one bad ass is just like the next" becomes a justification for repressive, and ultimately racist, social control policies.

A far more promising theoretical avenue is found in recent discussions about masculinities and crime that examine the "varieties of real men" in relation to their differential access to power and resources (Connell 1987; Messerschmidt 1986, 1993). These authors move beyond the culture of poverty thesis, recognizing that manly displays of toughness are not a rebellious reaction to "the female-headed household" nor an inherent value of lower-class culture (Miller 1958). Instead, they have widened the lenses by adopting a structural approach, which locates such acts of manliness within the broader economic and social class context. Specifically, Messerschmidt (1993) argues that social structures situate young men in relation to similar others so that collectively they experience the world from a specific position and differentially construct cultural ideas of hegemonic masculinity—that is, dominance, control, and independence. Young minority males living in economically dislocated communities "are typically denied masculine status in the educational and occupational spheres, which are the major sources of masculine status available to men in white middle class communities and white working class communities" (Messerschmidt 1993, 112). This denial of access to legitimate resources creates the context for heightened public and private forms of aggressive masculinity.

As Katz (1988) calls it, "street elite posturing" (e.g., displays of essential toughness, parading) represents one cultural form of public aggressiveness and is a gender resource for young minority men to accomplish masculinity. Similarly, acts of intimidation and gang violence by marginalized young men are not simply an expression of the competitive struggle in dislocated neighborhoods, but a means for affirming self-respect and status. These are cultural forms that celebrate manhood and "solve the gender problem of accountability" in increasingly isolated poor communities (Messerschmidt 1993, 111). The "street," then, becomes both a battleground and a theater dominated by young minority men doing gender (Connell 1987).

GIRLS, FEMININITY, AND GANGS

Gang research generally has assumed that delinquency among marginalized young men is somehow an understandable, if not "normal," response to their situations. How are we to understand the experience of girls who share the same social and cultural milieu as delinquent boys? Despite seven decades of research on boys' gangs and crime, there has been no parallel trend in research on girls' involvement in gang activity. As Campbell (1990) correctly points out, the general tendency to minimize and distort the motivations and roles of girl gang members is the result of the gender bias on the part of male gang researchers, who describe the girls' experience from the boy gang member's viewpoint. The long-standing "gendered habits" of researchers have meant that girls' involvement with gangs has been neglected, sexualized, and oversimplified.[1] Girl members typically are portrayed as maladjusted tomboys or sexual chattel who, in either case, are no more than mere appendages to boy members of the gang. Collectively, they are perceived as an "auxiliary" or "satellite" of the boys' group, and their participation in delinquent activities (e.g., carrying weapons) is explained in relation to the boys (see Brown 1977; Flowers 1987; Miller 1975, 1980; Rice 1963).

This pattern was undoubtedly set by Thrasher (1927), who spent about one page out of 600 discussing the five or six female gangs he found.[2] A more recent example of the androcentrism of gang researchers comes from Jankowski's (1991) widely cited *Islands in the Streets*, which contains the following entries in his index under "Women":

• "and codes of conduct"
• individual violence over

- as "property"
- and urban gangs

One might be tempted to believe that the last entry might refer to girl gangs, but the "and" in the sentence is not a mistake. Girls are simply treated as the sexual chattel of male gang members or as an "incentive" for boys to join the gang (because "women look up to gang members") (Jankowski 1991, 53). Jankowski's work as well as other current discussions of gang delinquency actually represents a sad revisiting of the sexism that characterized the initial efforts to understand visible lower-class boy delinquency decades earlier.

Taylor's (1993) work *Girls, Gangs, Women and Drugs* goes a step further to provide a veneer of academic support for the media's definition of the girl gang member as a junior version of the liberated female crook of the 1970s. It is not clear exactly how many girls and women he interviewed for his book, but the introduction clearly sets the tone for his work: "We have found that females are just as capable as males of being ruthless in so far as their life opportunities are presented. This study indicates that females have moved beyond the status quo of gender repression" (Taylor 1993, 8). His work then goes on to stress the similarities between boys' and girls' involvement in gangs, despite the fact that when the girls and women he interviews speak, it becomes clear that such a view is oversimplified. Listen, for example, to Pat in answer to a question about "problems facing girls in gangs":

> If you got a all girls crew, um, they think you're "soft" and in the streets if you soft, it's all over. Fellas think girls is soft, like Rob, he think he got it better in his shit 'cause he's a fella, a man. It's wild, but fellas really hate seeing girls getting off. Now, some fellas respect the power of girls, but most just want us in the sack (Taylor 1993, 118).

Presently there are a small but important number of studies that move beyond stereotypical notions about these girls as simply the auxiliaries of boy gangs to more careful assessments of the lives of these girls (Campbell 1984, 1990; Fishman 1988; Harris 1988; Lauderback, Hansen, and Waldorf 1992; Moore 1991; Quicker 1983). Of particular significance are those elements of girl gangs that provide them with the skills to survive in their harsh communities while also allowing them to escape, at least for a while, from the dismal future that awaits them.

These ethnographies document the impact of poverty, unemployment, deterioration, and violence in the communities where these young women live. The girls share with the boys in their neighborhoods the powerlessness and hopelessness of the urban underclass. As Campbell (1990) notes in her ethnography of Hispanic girl gang members in the New York area, they exist in an environment that has little to offer young women of color. The possibility of a decent career, outside of "domestic servant," is practically nonexistent. Many come from distressed families held together by their mothers who are subsisting on welfare. Most have dropped out of school and have no marketable skills. Future aspirations are both gendered and unrealistic, with the girls often expressing the desire to be rock stars or professional models when they are older.

Their situation is further aggravated by the patriarchal power structure of their bleak communities. They find themselves in a highly gendered community where the men in their lives, although not traditional breadwinners, still act in ways that dramatically circumscribe the possibilities open to them. The Portrero Hill Posse, an African American girls group in Northern California, found themselves hanging together after having been abandoned by the fathers of their children and abused and controlled by other men (Lauderback, Hansen, and Waldorf 1992). Their involvement in selling crack and organized "boosting" (i.e., shoplifting) were among the few available resources for supporting themselves and their children.

Campbell (1990) describes much the same abandonment among young Hispanic women of New York who, constrained by being young mothers without husbands and raising children alone, spent their time "hanging out" and "doing nothing." In addition to the burdens of early motherhood, Moore (1991) also found significant problems with sexual victimization in her interviews with Chicana gang members in East Los Angeles. Faced with problems like these, it is clear that girls are drawn to gangs as much or more for the familialism and support they provide than the possible economic advantages associated with gang membership.

These ethnographies also clearly establish the multifaceted nature of girls' experiences in gangs. Importantly, there is no one type of gang girl. Some girl gang members did bear out the stereotypes. The Cholas, a Latina gang in the San Fernando Valley in California, rejected the traditional image of Latinas as "wife and mother," supporting instead a more "macho" homegirl image (Harris 1988). Moore (1991) found a similar pattern among some of the Chicana gang members in East Los Angeles, but also notes the price paid for rejecting the cultural norms of "being a woman." In documenting the sexual double standard of boy gang members as well as of barrio residents, Moore notes that girl gang members were labeled as "tramps" and symbolized as "no good," despite the girls' vigorous rejection of these labels; furthermore, some boy gang members, even those who had relationships with girl gang members, felt that "square girls were their future" (p. 75).

For the Vice Queens, an auxiliary to the Chicago Vice Lords of the early 1960s, toughness and independence were less an issue of rejecting cultural gender norms, and more a necessity to demonstrate "greater flexibility in roles" (Fishman 1988, 26–27). Growing up in rough neighborhoods provided this loosely knit group of about 30 teenage African American girls "with opportunities to learn such traditional male skills as fighting and taking care of themselves on the streets," particularly because it was expected that the girls learn to defend themselves against "abusive men" and "attacks on their integrity" (Fishman 1988, 15). Given the further deterioration of the African American community since the 1960s, these young women face an even bleaker future. In this context, Fishman speculates that "black female gangs today have become more entrenched, more violent, and more oriented [toward] 'male crime'" (Fishman 1988, 28). These changes, she adds, are unrelated to the women's movement, but are instead the "forced 'emancipation' which stems from the economic crisis within the Black community" (Fishman 1988, 28–29).

None of these accounts confirm the stereotype of the hyper-violent, amoral girls found in media accounts of girls in gangs. Certainly they confirm the fact that girls do commit a wider range of delinquent behavior than is stereotypically recognized, but these offenses appear to be part of a complex fabric of "hanging out," "partying," and the occasional fight in defending one's friends or territory. These ethnographies also underscore that although the "streets" may be dominated by young men, girls and young women do not necessarily avoid the "streets," as Connell (1987) suggests. The streets reflect the strained interplay between race, class, and gender.

For those with the conventional criminological perspective on gender, girls engaged in what are defined as "male" activities such as violent crime or gang delinquency are seen as seeking "equality" with their boy counterparts (see Daly and Chesney-Lind 1988). Is that what is going on? A complete answer to that question requires a more careful inquiry into the lives of these girls and the ways in which the gang facilitates survival in their world. Their lives are more complex than simple rebellion against traditional notions of femininity, and are heavily shaped by an array of economic, educational, familial, and social conditions and constraints. A focus on the meaning of the gang in girls' lives also means that comparisons with the experiences of the young men in their neighborhoods who are also being drawn to gangs will be possible. Our intent, then, is to move beyond the traditional, gender specific analyses of contemporary gangs to a more nuanced understanding of the ways in which gender, race, and class shape the gang phenomenon.

SOCIAL SETTING

Ethnicity

Hawaii is probably the most ethnically diverse state. The largest population groups are Japanese American (25 percent), European American (33 percent), Filipino American (13.9 percent), and Hawaiian/part-Hawaiian (17 percent); other non-Caucasian ethnic groups compose the rest of the population (Department of Business and Economic Development and Tourism 1993). Although Hawaii is ethnically diverse, it is not without racial or ethnic tensions. Class and ethnic divisions tend to reflect the economic and political power struggles of the state's past as a plantation society as well as its current economic dependence on mass tourism. In this mix, recent immigrants as well as the descendants of the island's original inhabitants are among the most dispossessed; consequently, youth actively involved in gangs are drawn predominantly from groups that have recently immigrated to the state (Samoans and Filipinos) or from the increasingly marginalized Native Hawaiian population.

Crime in Hawaii

Despite its image, Hawaii has many of the same crime problems as other states. In 1991, Hawaii ranked fortieth out of the fifty states in overall crime, but eighth in terms of property crime victimization. In the city and county of Honolulu, the nation's eleventh largest city (Federal Bureau of Investigation 1992,

79–106), where three quarters of the state's population lives and the state's capital of Honolulu is located, the pattern is much the same. Oahu's total crime rate is slightly more than half the national average for cities between 500,000 and 1 million (6,193 per 100,000 versus 9,535.1 per 100,000 nationally), but the state's property crime rate is considerably closer to the national average (Crime Prevention Division 1993). Previous research (Chesney-Lind and Lind 1986) has linked part of the property crime problem in the state to the presence of tourists.

Like other major cities, Honolulu has witnessed a rapid growth in police estimates of gang activity and gang membership. In 1988, the Honolulu police (HPD) estimated that there were 22 gangs with 450 members. In 1991, the number of gangs climbed to 45 with an estimated membership of 1,020. By 1993, the number of gangs reached 171 with 1,267 members (Office of Youth Services 1993).

METHODOLOGY

Hawaii policymakers, concerned about the trends in gang membership reported by the HPD, enacted legislation to develop a statewide response to youth gangs. Previous evaluations of this system included a quantitative assessment of the youth included in HPD's gang database, and it also compared arrest patterns among officially labeled gang members with those of nongang members. The results of that study, which are reported elsewhere (Chesney-Lind et al. 1992), suggest that stereotypes regarding gang members' involvement in serious criminal behavior are just that. Both boys and girls labeled by police as gang members are chronic, but not necessarily violent, offenders; moreover, the research raised serious questions about the assumed criminogenic character of gangs and underscored the need for a more qualitative understanding of gang membership among boys and girls.

Toward this end, in-depth interviews with 48 self-identified gang members were conducted from August 1992 through May 1993. The sample included interviews with 35 boys and 13 girls. Respondents were recruited through a snowball sampling technique (Watters and Biernacki 1989) from referrals provided by the interviewers' personal contacts as well as agency and school staff who work closely with high-risk youngsters. Four young people refused to be interviewed. Interviews were conducted in a wide variety of locations, and none were held in closed institutions. Interviewers were selected based on their knowledge about local culture and the streets and, when possible, matched according to gender.

The interview instrument was derived from similar research efforts in San Francisco (Waldorf 1993) and modified for use in Hawaii. The interview consisted of two parts in which the youth first responded to social survey questions regarding personal and familial characteristics, self-reported delinquency, and contact with the juvenile justice system. The second half of the interview was more qualitative in nature. Here, the informant responded to a series of open-ended questions regarding his or her gang's history, its organization, activities, membership roles, and his or her involvement with the group, and interaction with family, the community, and police.

GANGS, ETHNICITY, AND CULTURE IN HAWAII

The respondents are predominantly male (although we specifically sought out female gang members), and they are from "have-not" ethnic groups: the males are largely of Filipino (60 percent) or Samoan (23 percent) background. Slightly less than half of the boys were born in another country. The majority of the girls are Samoan (61 percent) or Filipino (25 percent) and born in the United States. The boys in the interview sample are slightly older than the girls; the mean age is 16.7 years for the boys interviewed, and 15.3 years for the girls. The average age of our sample is younger than the young adults found in HPD's gang database, partially because of our reliance on agency and school-based referrals. Most of the boys (94 percent) and all of the girls said they were attending school.

The majority of boys (60 percent) and girls (69 percent) live with both parents and are dependent on them for money—though about a third of the boys also work. About one fourth of the boys and girls report stealing to obtain money. Their family lives are not without problems—over half (55 percent) of the boys and three quarters of the girls report physical abuse. In addition, 62 percent of the girls state that they have been sexually abused or sexually assaulted.

Over 90 percent of the boys and three quarters of the girls were arrested, some many times. Indeed, more than a quarter of the boys and almost the same proportion (23 percent) of girls report being arrested 10 or more times. Boys committed a wider range of offenses than girls, with the most frequent being property offenses, vandalism, violent offenses, and weapons offenses. Girls were as likely to report status offense arrests as criminal offenses, but about a third of the girls were arrested for a violent crime. Both boys and girls say peer pressure was a major reason for their involvement in criminal activities, but boys were more likely than girls to mention needing money as a reason for their illegal activities.

All respondents described the visible presence of gangs in their neighborhoods, and in most cases, a family member could provide them with firsthand knowledge about gangs. Virtually all of the girls (90 percent) and boys (80 percent) had a family member, usually a sibling, who belonged to a gang. In terms of their own experiences with the gang, boys tended to be slightly older than the girls when they joined (respectively, 14 compared to 12), and despite popular conceptions, few respondents said that "joining" involved "initiation" or "jumping in." The boys' gangs were larger than the girls' groups, with 45 percent of the boys indicating that their group included 30 or more members. By contrast, almost half of the girls said their gangs had between 10 and 20 members, compared to only 23 percent of the boys.

Although the interviews were done with individual gang members, it is important to know that gangs in the Islands tend to be ethnically organized and generally exclusively male or female. Filipino youth and Samoan youth tend to share the stresses of immigration; these include language difficulties, parental-ization, and economic marginality. Beyond this, though, the cultures are very different. Samoan culture is heavily influenced by the Polynesian value system of collective living, communalism, and social control through family and village ties. In Samoa, although contact with the West has been present for a consid-erable period, there is still a clear and distinct Samoan culture to be found (un-like Hawaii). Samoan adults drawn from this traditional, communal society ex-perience cultural shock upon immigration when poverty forces isolation, frustration, and accommodation to a materialistic, individualistic society. As their children begin to feel caught between two very different systems of val-ues, and as the village system of social controls weakens, the pressures and problems in Samoan families multiply. Gender relations in traditional Samoan families are heavily regulated by Polynesian traditions of separation, obliga-tion, and male dominance, while girls and women have always found ways to circumvent the most onerous of these regulations (Linnekin 1990).

In contrast, Filipino immigrants come from a culture that has already been affected by centuries of colonialism. As a consequence, the Philippines is a myr-iad of discrete ethnic cultures that have been reshaped by Spanish and U.S. conquest and occupation. Of the many costs attending colonialism, one of the most insidious is that many Filipinos feel ambivalent about the value of their own culture. In addition, although pre-Hispanic women in the Philippines were dynamic and vital members of their ethnic groups, girls in modern Filipino fam-ilies are affected by the impact of colonial cultural and religious (largely Catholic) norms that stress the secondary status of women, a girl's responsi-bility to her family, and a concern for regulating female sexual experimenta-tion (Aquino 1994; Lebra 1991). Boys, on the other hand, are given consider-able freedom to roam, though they are expected to work hard, do well in school, and obey their parents. The downward mobility, overemployment, and cultural shock experienced by many adult Filipinos put special pressures on the cul-tural values of filial obligation and strain relationships with both sons and daughters.

Native Hawaiians have much in common with other Native American groups as well as with African Americans. Their culture was severely chal-lenged by the death and disease that attended contact with the West in the eighteenth century. Until very recently, Hawaiian was a dying language, and many Hawaiians were losing touch with anything that resembled Hawaiian cul-ture. Hawaiians, like urbanized Native Americans and low-income African Americans, have accommodated to poverty by normalizing early motherhood; high rates of high school dropout; and welfare dependency for girls and high rates of drug dependency, crime, and physical injury for Hawaiian boys.

LIVING IN CHAOTIC NEIGHBORHOODS: COMMON THEMES IN GANG MEMBERSHIP

A number of interrelated themes surfaced in the interviews with our respon-dents, which provide a framework for understanding youth involvement in gangs. The following discussion focuses on how everyday life in marginalized and chaotic neighborhoods sets the stage for group solidarity. At one level, the boredom, lack of resources, and high visibility of crime in their neglected communities create the conditions for turning to others who are similarly situated, and consequently, it is the group that realistically offers a social outlet. At another level, the stress on the family from living in marginalized areas combined with financial struggles creates heated tension and, in many cases, violence in the home. It is the group that provides our respondents with a safe refuge and a surrogate family. Although the theme of marginality cuts across gender and ethnicity, there were critical differences in how girls and boys, and Samoans, Filipinos, and Hawaiians express and respond to the problems of everyday life.

The "Hood"

One distinctive geographical factor about Hawaii is that many neighborhoods are class stratified rather than class/ethnic stratified. This is partly related to the history of the state's political economy (i.e., plantation, tourism) and the limited space of the island. These factors mean that a variety of low-income ethnic groups will live in proximity to each other.

Our respondents reside in lower-middle- and working-class neighborhoods. About a third (29 percent) of our respondents live in the central urban area of Oahu in the Kalihi district. This is a congested, densely populated area with a large Filipino population. It is filled with single family residences, housing projects, local small businesses, hospitals, and churches. Hawaiians and Samoans live along the fringes of the central district of Kalihi-Palama. This is an area that the police have targeted as being a high-crime neighborhood, particularly for drug sales, and this impression was confirmed through the observations and experiences of our respondents. Given law enforcement interest in this area, it is not surprising that several of our interviewees reported being tagged, harassed, and stopped by patrol units.

By contrast, similar ethnic groups are concentrated on the west end of the island, in what local residents refer to as the "plantation areas" and the "country." In some pockets of these rural neighborhoods, crime and drug transactions are visible as our respondents reported. Overall, however, neighborhoods in these rural areas are less crowded and relatively quiet; consequently, law enforcement surveillance operates differently in these areas than in the central district. Several of our respondents indicated that they were treated fairly by the police. In a few instances when youths were caught for a crime, the police sternly issued a warning and returned them home.

Despite differences in the density of and police attitudes toward these communities, these areas are similar to those described in recent gang ethnographies where the ongoing presence of crime combined with high rates of unemployment have resulted in a bleak and distressed environment (Rockhill et al. 1993). Not surprisingly, some of our respondents recognize that there has been little government investment in their neighborhoods, and all of them are quick to point out that there are few resources available for young people in their communities. They describe their lives in their neighborhoods as "boring." Simply put, being poor means being bored; there are few organized recreational activities, no jobs, no vocational training opportunities, no money to pay for entertainment, nowhere to go, and nothing happening for long stretches of time. Boys and girls alike echo this view: "there is nothing to do." How then do they cope on a daily level with having no money, no employment opportunities, and little to occupy their time?

Gang Provides a Social Outlet

Generally boys and girls have found the gang to be the most realistic solution to boredom. Our respondents uniformly state that their group provides a meaningful social outlet in an environment that has little else to offer. A sense of solidarity develops among those who face a similar plight, and as our respondents describe, their group provides a network of reliable friends who can be "counted on"; consequently, a large number of hours in school and outside of school are spent "hanging out" together and "wanting to have fun." How do they define "hanging out and having fun"? Much of their time together is spent in social activities, particularly sports. Both boys and girls indicate that they routinely engage in a variety of sports ranging from basketball to football to volleyball (mostly girls), and understandably, given the state's beaches, swimming, boogie boarding, and body surfing. Because program resources are either limited or nonexistent in their communities, our respondents are left on their own to organize their own activities. In many instances, they develop makeshift strategies to fill the time void. Because the local community center's hours are restricted, the girls from a Samoan group in the Kalihi area find themselves waiting for nightfall when they can climb the fence unseen, and swim in the center's pool.

Beyond sports, however, the social dimension of the group and the specific solutions to boredom operate differently in the lives of the girls as compared with the boys and, in many ways, is tied to traditional and cultural gender roles. For example, several of our female respondents, particularly our Samoan girls, indicate that they spend a great deal of their time together "harmonizing, going to dances and competitions and all that." Singing, dancing, and learning hula from family members are time honored activities within Pacific cultures, and the integration of these activities into gang life signifies an interface between traditional culture and the culture of the streets.

By contrast, the boys relieve the boredom and find camaraderie in the traditional sport of "cruising." Cruising in an automobile is a regular part of their life with the group, allowing them more mobility than our girl respondents, who are largely confined to the gym or park in their neighborhoods or who ride with boys or take the bus to other areas. For those girls who live in the more rural areas of the island, mobility is simply not an option. Not surprisingly, cruising for the boys is often accompanied by other expressions of masculinity, specifically "drinking," "fighting," and "petty thieving," including "ripping off tourists." All our male respondents state that they drink, usually beer, and the majority report regular use. The combination of boredom along with the limited avenues to express their manliness cuts across ethnic and community lines. Trip, an 18-year-old Samoan from Waipahu, describes his daily routine:

After school there is nothing to do. A lot of my friends like to lift weights, if there was someplace to lift weights. A lot of my friends don't know how to read, they try to read, but say they can't, and they don't have programs or places for them to go.... There are no activities, so now we hang around and drink beer. We hang around, roam the streets.... Yesterday we went to a pool hall and got into a fight over there.

A 14-year-old Filipino boy from the Kalihi area recounts a similar experience to Trip's:

Get up at 1:00 in the afternoon. Then take a shower, then at three o'clock, go with my friend to Pearlridge [shopping mall], look for girls, and then cruise in Tantalus, and we almost got into a fight. We was gonna drop off the girls and go back but they had too many guys so we turned around. We had 4 guys and they had 20.

Interestingly, although cruising is also connected for many of the boys with "looking for girls," girls responded that although they sometimes talk about boys in their gangs, they do not see the group as a vehicle for "looking" for boys.

This is not to say that girls are not involved in drinking or fighting like their boy counterparts; however, fighting and drinking are less frequent among the girls, with a few indicating that when they party, "they don't drink, smoke, or nothing," and "can't stand that stuff." Significantly fewer girls talked explicitly about getting into fights. Their fights usually have been because of "rumors" as Quente, whose group The Meanest Crew consists of a group of girls living in one of the city's largest and most densely populated housing projects in Oahu, explains:

Yes they say rumors they saw this person. The first day of school, they say my sister wanted to beat up this girl, but my sister never knew who this girl was.... Then my other sister, they was fighting, and then my sister her nose was bleeding, and my sister and my cousin started fighting, and I came and beat up this eighth-grade girl. She was big and fat. She was taller than me. Then after that we went to the office, and they say my sister and I gang up on that girl. Those Kuhio girls they say my sister wanted to fight but my sister didn't know them.... Those SOK started it.

We are told that members of The Meanest Crew and the SOK live in the same neighborhood, attend the same high school, and consider themselves rivals. SOK member Anna Marie, who is also from Kalihi and 15 years of age, reports that her group too gets in fights. Her first arrest for assault occurred three years ago when she was "mobbed" by another group, and she has since been arrested six to seven times for assault. All 16 of the members have been picked up for assault, fighting, stealing, and running away.

As our girls suggest, their involvement in fights has less to do with an attempt to gain an egalitarian position to their male counterparts, but instead, is directly related to the desperate boredom they experience. In this way, their situation is similar to their male counterparts. One 17-year-old Samoan girl explained her group's attempts to deal with boredom in the Kalihi district:

Before it got worse? [Then] after school everybody would meet at Brother Brian's Bar, drink, dance, talk story, then when the sun was going down that's when all the drug dealing started. And then [later] couple times we would go out and look for trouble. Some of us just felt hyped and would go out and beat up people. We went up to this park and had this one couple, and so for nothing we just went beat em up.

Gang Serves as Alternative Family

The impact of distressed communities is felt not only by young people but by their families as well. Our respondents come from several different types of family situations. In many cases their parents are "overemployed," holding two jobs in working class and service industry occupations. They are, for example, laundry workers, hotel maids, and construction workers. Given the high cost of living in Hawaii, this is a common practice among working-class families. Unfortunately, when both parents are struggling to stay afloat in this economy, supervision is absent in the home. A few youth indicated that they are essentially on their own because their single parent, who is consumed by his or her job, is rarely home to supervise. In some instances, parents have difficulty keeping a steady job and are either unemployed or underemployed for periods of time. As their children recognize and describe to us, supervision may be present, but it is filled with tension as parents try to cope with financial problems. In a small but important number of cases, the cultural and familial ties of parents required either the mother or the father to remain in their native land. This was true among a few of our Samoan and Filipino respondents.

In light of family financial pressures and limited time for parental involvement or supervision, it is not surprising that these young people feel a sense of isolation and consequently find support and solace among members of their group. As one Samoan girl plainly puts it:

[It's] good to just kick back and relax and have fun, but not get into trouble. We tell each other our problems. . . . I don't like to be a loner or feel isolated.

In sharing their problems at home with each other, the members of the group take on the role of a surrogate family. A common theme in the lives of our female and male respondents is that the gang serves as an alternative family. As Tina, a 15-year-old Samoan explains, "We all like sistas all taking care of each other." The symbolic kinship of the group is even reflected in the name of one female Samoan group called JEMA, which stands for Just Every Mother's Angel. Seventeen-year-old Daniella recounts the origins of her group's name.

We chose that because all the girls I hang out with, all their mothers passed away, and during elementary days, we all used to hang out and all our mothers were close yeah, so that's how we came up with that name.

The males express similar views to those of the "sistas." Kevin, a 17-year-old Hawaiian, likens the leader of his group to "like the father of the house." On meeting the leader, he reports that "[the] first time I saw him I felt like bowing. I didn't though. He said if I respected him, he would respect me." Or as Ricky, a 17-year-old Filipino states, "The gang is a closer family than my parents because they are there to help me everyday . . . unlike my parents."

The tension on the family is amplified by other factors. As noted earlier, among Samoan and Filipino families, the immigrant experience is frequently one of alienation because of differences in language and culture. The marginalization of the native Hawaiian people and their culture has a long history and has left them in an ambiguous cultural position. These ethnically diverse pressures on the family heighten the conflict at home and, in many instances, erupt into violence.

In this way, the group's surrogate family role takes on an even greater significance for the young people who report physical, emotional, and sexual abuse by a family member. As indicated earlier, 75 percent of the girls (6 out of 8 who were asked) and 57 percent of the boys (12 out of 21 who were asked) report "lickings" by one or both of their parents. In the midst of financial tension, physical abuse appears to be connected to the violation of cultural and gender role expectations. The girls, for example, indicate that their lickings were because of violations of a traditional sexual double standard: "not calling home," "coming home late," and "not coming home for the night." Staying out all night is interpreted differently for girls than for boys. When girls engage in these behaviors, this is "running away" and is often connected with "promiscuity." When boys don't come home for the night, this is normal adolescent behavior for working-class boys.

By comparison, all four of the Hawaiian boys and four of the nine Samoan boys reported that they were physically struck by one of their parents for delinquent behaviors such as "fighting," "stealing," and "smoking pakalolo [marijuana]." Kevin, a 17-year-old Hawaiian boy, described how his mother threw him down the stairs, cracking his ribs and bruising his spinal disc, when she found a bag of marijuana in his room. For two boys and one Samoan girl, their father's beatings were aggravated by alcohol and drug use, respectively. The experience of the four (out of eight) Filipino boys who stated that they received lickings differed from the South Pacific Islanders. According to the Filipino boys, the beatings were related to a wider range of behavior that their parents believed to be intolerable, such as a "bad attitude" and "poor grades." Dwane, a 17-year-old Filipino, recalled that his lickings stopped as he got older.

These young people's response to the abuse is usually one of reluctance and resistance to report the abuse, and must be viewed in a cultural context. Family loyalty is important among Filipino youth, where strong cultural pressures, language problems, and an understandable reticence to involve external agencies (and perhaps jeopardize immigration status) depress reporting of abuse. The Hawaiian and Samoan boys and girls who reported being physically abused also refused to call or permit official intervention (unless detected by school authorities). Despite child abuse education in the classrooms at all age levels, these young people viewed their loyalty to their parents as paramount. One 17-year-old Samoan male's loyalty to his father took precedence over his own victimization:

> Since my grandma passed away, I don't get along with my father. He comes home drunk and beat us up. He beats us up with those weight-lifting belts.

> The police never come, I don't tell nobody. I don't want nobody that's why,
> I don't want nobody butting in now. I run away when I can't stand it.

Family is the core of the Pacific Island culture. Traditionally social and economic activities took place within the context of the family. This familial arrangement, however, is severely ruptured in the Western economic context. In Samoa and other Pacific Islands, families live in open fales,[3] where behavior is clearly visible and, hence, children's behavior can be directly controlled. When a child is unruly, he or she can be sent to stay with relatives, given the extended sense of family there. Hawaii's *hanai* system provides a similar extended family arrangement for caring for troublesome children. Anna Maria, a 15-year-old Samoan girl, was taken out of her parents' home, spent two weeks in a shelter, and now lives with her auntie and uncle who also physically abuse her, but states that "it was far worse with my parents, that's why I stay with my auntie and uncle."

Although the "sistas" and "brothers" of the gang offer some level of support, it is understandably difficult for many to cope with everyday life. One 18-year-old Samoan girl who has been severely abused, physically and emotionally, by her parents, finds that her group provides "someone to talk to." In this particular case, the group has been especially important as she is fiercely loyal to her parents and rationalizes the beatings as a feature of the Samoan ways. "My parents aren't understanding. They are Samoan, and everything you do you get lickings"; moreover, she refuses to tell school and child protective services authorities because they will intervene. She must consequently contend with "wanting to kill myself because I'm tired of getting beat up." Many of them view their lives as "hopeless" and their future as being "jammed up." Their options seem limited as nearly half of them had contemplated suicide. Suicidal thoughts were more prevalent among the girls (71 percent or 5 of the 7 females asked) compared to the boys (33.3 percent or 6 of 18 males asked).

DIFFERENCES IN CRIME AND DELINQUENCY

Boy and girl gang members differ in the area of crime and delinquent behavior. Although girls commit more crime and engage in more fights than their stereotype would support, they are certainly less involved in this behavior than the boys. They are also far less involved in drug selling, robbery, and other types of criminal behavior.

As noted earlier, for boys, fighting—even looking for fights—is a major activity within the gang. If anything, the presence of girls around gang members depresses violence. As one 14-year-old Filipino put it, "If we not with the girls, we fighting. If we not fighting, we with the girls." Many of the boys' activities involved drinking, cruising, and "looking for trouble." Looking for trouble also meant being prepared for trouble—though guns are somewhat available, most of the boys we interviewed used bats or their hands to fight. Some of this is cultural—as one respondent explained:

> My friend has a gun, one of our boys had a gun, but one of our gang members said put it somewhere else, cause we're Samoans and Samoans fight with hands.

Another Samoan youth who lives in the country adds, "down here we no more guns, just fist fight." Some of this may also be strategic, because some respondents mentioned knowing where to get their hands on guns, but not carrying them regularly. The hiding of guns and carrying of baseball bats, for example, avoids arrest for possession of an illegal firearm because a bat can always be a piece of sporting equipment.

Another major difference between the girls and the boys was involvement in drug dealing. Although girls drink and use drugs in the gang, a number (though not all) of male gangs are involved in selling drugs. As a 17-year-old Filipino male who was in a leadership position with his gang noted, the gang is important because it provides "opportunities to make money and use drugs." The gang helps you "find drugs faster . . . [and] buy and sell drugs faster."

The boys' gangs did demonstrate a range of orientations to drug use and selling. Some only sold drugs ("Guys in my group don't do drugs, sell yea, but only weed"); other groups did not use drugs ("We don't sell no drugs, we cruise, we used to paint graffiti, but not any more"). For most of the boys, though, the gang was the site of drinking and doing drugs in a social way, "We do sports together, parties, we party every day, some guys do drugs and shit." One or two gang members belonged to groups that focused exclusively on drug selling. Logically, those most seriously involved in drug selling had moved to Waikiki and were selling to tourists. These gang members "sit on the wall and talk, look for vices,[4] if a deal comes up, go and make the deal. [We] don't get into that much trouble, most people in Waikiki know us." This variation in delinquent and criminal involvement of different gangs is consistent with other male gang studies (Fagan 1989).

As alluded to earlier, the violence associated with boys' gang life is largely an outgrowth of the violence in their neighborhoods, which explains why in many of the boys' interviews, protection was mentioned as a major reason to join the gang. As one young man put it, the gang gives "protection for when you go to school, some guys tough and that's your power . . . the gang's that power . . . you don't get picked on or beat up."

The violence that fuels membership in gangs, though, spills over into more general "trouble" as groups of young men begin to hang out, "Yeah, we have fights with other groups, sometimes when it is getting close to the weekend, there are fights. Sometimes one on one fights or the whole group against another group. . . . [we] just collide into each other and fight."

Experience with this kind of violence and drug use combined with the fact that almost all of these youth had relatives in gangs occasionally produces a reflective voice:

> Sometimes when my friends are in trouble, we go help my friends . . . that is how we get into fights and stuff. We play sports together, party, look for women, go to concerts, when we party sometimes my friends drink, but me I only drink a little . . . chill out . . . cruise . . . cause one of my uncles he used to drink and smoke a lot he died last year . . . when I think of him I think it is going to happen to me.

Only infrequently are nongang members the targets of violence; when they are, they are tourists assaulted for their money. As one 14-year-old Hawaiian youth puts it, "When we no more money, me and my friends walking around and get hungry, the first Jap[anese tourist] we see, we knock and take his money and go to McDonalds lidat [like that], eat and go home after." This behavior, though, was the exception. Most of the youths who engaged in gang behavior did drugs, sold drugs, and engaged in petty thefts—again chiefly as a group activity. As one 17-year-old Filipino puts it, "If one person go steal car, we all go steal car . . . they don't have to, but everybody go for watch." Another 17-year-old Samoan youth says, "I've been gang banging since I was fifth grade, I've been hitting [stealing?] cars and all kinds of shit."[5]

For girls, fighting and violence are part of life in the gang—but not something they necessarily seek out. Instead, protection from neighborhood and family violence is a major theme in girls' interviews. One girl simply states that she belongs to the gang to provide "some protection from her father." Through the group she has learned ways to defend herself physically and emotionally. "He used to beat me up, but now I hit back and he doesn't beat me much now." Another 14-year-old Samoan put it, "You gotta be part of the gang or else you're the one who's gonna get beat up." Though this young woman said that members of her gang had to "have total attitude and can fight." She went on to say, "We want to be a friendly gang. I don't know why people are afraid of us. We're not that violent." Fights do come up in the lives of these girls, "We only wen mob this girl 'cause she was getting wise, she was saying 'what, slut' so I wen crack her and all my friends wen jump in." Later this young women explained that the gang and its orientation to violence changed:

> At first [I] thought of the gang as a friendship thing, but as I grew into the gang, it just started to change. I started seeing it as, I guess, I don't know, I guess as trying to survive in the streets and everything, and that about it . . . protection, cause at the time I was scared, cause my sister and cousin used to beat me up and before I even joined the gang, you know how you would threaten your sister . . . my sister stole my mom's car and her money and my cousin use to steal her dad's money, and I knew all these things, and my sister would say, "We're going to beat you up if you tell dad."

In general, the girls talk about the trouble the gang gets into as a tonic for boredom. "Sometimes we like cause trouble yeah cause boring, so boring. So we like make trouble ah, for make scene, so we just call anybody, if they looking at us." Girls rarely carry weapons ("No, I don't carry weapons, but I can get it if I want to."). In fact, one girl said in answer to a question about knives, "I have knives, but only for food." This same 13-year-old girl saw some of the pointlessness of their violence:

> I think the girls and boys that don't join gangs are smart, but girls like me who are in gangs are stupid, they are just wasting their time cause dumb fighting over color, just for a stupid color.

Girls are also less involved in drug selling than boys. Arrests for running away from home and problems with status offenses are more commonly mentioned by girls, as are other problems on the streets. Also mentioned are problems with parents who insist on the double standard ("I couldn't handle, cause my parents always telling me do the things around the house, they never let me go out"), and the stereotypes of bad or wild girls: "I'm pretty sure a lot of people think we are prostitutes on the road, we just hang out with the mahus [transvestites] who crack us up."[6]

CONCLUSION

This article has stressed the need to explore gangs in their social context and to avoid totalizing notions of either boys' or girls' gangs. Previous research as well as our own interviews clearly suggest that such an approach is needed. One of the major conclusions one draws from listening to these young women and men is that the gang is a haven for coping with the many problems they encounter in their everyday life in marginalized communities. Paradoxically, the sense of solidarity achieved from sharing everyday life with similarly situated others has the unintended effect of drawing many gang youth—both boys and girls—into behaviors that ultimately create new problems for them.

On the broadest level, both the girls and boys are growing up in communities racked by poverty, racism, and rapid population growth. The gang is clearly a product of these forces. Shaped by the ethnicity, race, and gender of its participants, the gang takes on different shapes depending on its composition. Clearly, for both males and females, the gang provides a needed social outlet and a tonic for the boredom of low-income life. The gang provides friends and activities in communities where such recreational outlets are pitifully slim. Gender, though, shapes these activities. For girls, the list of prosocial activities is longer than for boys. For boys, getting together in groups quickly moves into cruising instead of hanging out, and that, in turn, leads to fights and confrontations with other groups of boys.

The violence that characterizes their family lives and their communities is another prod into the gang for most of these youth. Gangs provide protection for both girls and boys. Many youth are drawn from families that are abusive, and, particularly for girls, the gang provides the skills to fight back against the violence in their families. In a few cases, the violence the girls learn begins to express itself in relations with other girls. As Anne Campbell (1992) notes in reflecting on the meaning of this in her research: "If we are willing to allow young women to be exploited by poverty and crime—if we can offer them no way out of victimization—then we can hardly be surprised if they respond by nurturing a self-protective reputation for craziness" (p. 13). The violations of traditional notions of femininity then, particularly the "unacceptable" displays of toughness and independence, are hardly a reflection of their liberation from patriarchal controls. The costs of having been born female are not only clear in their lives, but are, in fact, attenuated by the economic dislocation of their communities.

The marginalization of working- and lower-working-class communities has specific meaning for young men as well. The displays of toughness and risk-taking described by the boys in our study are a source for respect and status in an environment that is structurally unable to affirm their masculinity. Their acts of intimidation and fighting are rooted in the need for protection as well as the need to validate their manliness. Police harassment of gangs, particularly in the cities, further strengthens their group solidarity and, at the same time, increases their alienation from conventional others (like store owners) in their neighborhoods.

Abuse and neglect shape experiences with their families as well, but here there are rather stark ethnic differences in the ways both the boys and girls experience abuse. First, girls are more likely to experience abuse, with problems of sexual victimization and sexual abuse appearing in their accounts of family life. For boys, the violence is further mediated by culture. Filipino boys report that they are more likely to be physically abused for failing to attend school, not getting good grades, and so on. Abuse also appears earlier in their lives. For Samoan and Hawaiian boys, the abuse appears later and is directly tied to delinquent and criminal behavior. Virtually no youth report such behavior to officials, and some go out of their way to hide the bruises and normalize the incidents. Samoan life is profoundly family centered; as a consequence, the youth rely on cultural strategies to deal with their problems—such as moving in with relatives. Filipino youth employ their own cultural tradition of *barkada*, which encourages the social grouping of young men and women, thereby facilitating the creation of a surrogate family system.

Gangs, though, do produce opportunities for involvement in criminal activity. Especially for boys from poor families, stealing and small time drug dealing make up for a lack of money. These activities are not nearly as common among the girl respondents. Instead, their problems with the law originate with more traditional forms of girl delinquency, such as running away from home. Their families still attempt to hold them to a double standard, which results in parental tensions and disputes that have no parallel among the boys.

Media constructions of gang behavior, then, which stress the violence done by gang members, need to be countered by far richer assessments of the role played by gangs in the lives of these young people. Gang participation and gang structure are clearly shaped by both gender and race. Products of distressed neighborhoods, the gangs emerge to meet many needs that established institutions—schools, families, communities—do not address. Many of the impulses that propel youth into gangs are prosocial and understandable—the need for safety, security, and a sense of purpose and belonging.

For boys, violence is certainly a theme in gang life, but it is as much a product of violent neighborhoods as it is a cause of the phenomena. Boys' experiences of violence and abuse within the family, although kept from official agencies by cultural norms stressing the centrality of the family, certainly provide an additional and powerful perspective on the violence of boys. For girls, violence (gang or otherwise) is not celebrated and normative; it is instead more directly a consequence of and a response to the abuse, both physical and sexual, that characterizes their lives at home.

Girls' participation in gangs, which has been the subject of intense media interest, certainly needs to be placed within the context of the lives of girls, particularly young women of color on the economic and political margins. Girl gang life is certainly not an expression of "liberation," but instead reflects the attempts of young women to cope with a bleak and harsh present as well as a dismal future. One 15-year-old Samoan girl captured this sense of despair when in response to our question about whether she was doing well in school, said, "No, I wish I was, I need a future. [My life] is jammed up."

Attempts to totalize these youth as amoral and violent must be seen as part of a larger attempt to blame them for their own problems in a culture where gang has become synonymous with race. As young women are demonized by the media, their genuine problems can be marginalized and then ignored. Indeed, they and their boy counterparts have become the problem. The challenge to those concerned about these youth is, then, twofold. First, responsible work on gangs must make the dynamics of this victim blaming clear. Second, research must continue to build an understanding of gangs that is sensitive to the contexts within which they arise. In an era that is increasingly concerned about the intersection of class, race, and gender, such work seems long overdue.

NOTES

1. For exceptions, see Brown (1977); Bowker and Klein (1983); Campbell (1984, 1990); Ostner (1986); Fishman (1988); Moore (1991); Harris (1988); Quicker (1983).

2. Thrasher did mention, in passing, two factors he felt accounted for the lower number of girl gangs: "First, the social patterns for the behavior of girls, powerfully backed by the great weight of tradition and custom, are contrary to the gang and its activities; and secondly, girls, even in urban disorganized areas, are much more closely supervised and guarded than boys and are usually well incorporated into the family groups or some other social structure" (Thrasher 1927, 228).

3. Open-air Samoan dwelling.

4. Members of the Honolulu Police Department's vice squad.

5. Gang-banging refers to being a part of a gang.

6. Hawaiian culture had an institutionalized role for transvestites. This cultural tradition has meant a greater acceptance of both cross-dressing and homosexuality in Hawaiian communities.

REFERENCES

Adler, Freda. 1975. *Sisters in crime*. New York: McGraw Hill.

Aquino, Belinda. 1994. Filipino women and political engagement. The Office for Women's Research, working paper series, volume 2 (1993-1994). Honolulu: University of Hawaii, Manoa.

Bowker, Lee, and Malcolm Klein. 1983. The etiology of female juvenile delinquency and gang membership: A test of psychological and social structural explanations. *Adolescence* 18:739–51.

Brown, W. 1977. Black female gangs in Philadelphia. *International Journal of Offender Therapy and Comparative Criminology* 21:221–28.

Campbell, Anne. 1984. *Girls in the gang*. Oxford: Basil Blackwell.

———. 1990. Female participation in gangs. In *Gangs in America*, edited by C. Ronald Huff. Newbury Park, CA: Sage.

———. 1992. Female gang members' social representations of aggression. Paper presented at the Annual Meetings, American Society of Criminology, New Orleans, LA.

Chesney-Lind, Meda. 1993. Girls, gangs and violence: Reinventing the liberated female crook. *Humanity and Society* 17:321–44.

Chesney-Lind, Meda, and Ian Lind. 1986. Visitors as victims: Crimes against tourists in two Hawaii counties. *Annals of Tourism Research* 13:167–91.

Chesney-Lind, Meda, Nancy Marker, Ivette Stearn, Allison Yap, Valerie Song, Howard Reyes, Yolanda Reyes, Jeffrey Stearn, and JoAnn Taira. 1992. Gangs and delinquency in Hawaii. Paper presented at the Annual Meetings, American Society of Criminology, New Orleans, LA.

Cloward, Richard, and Lloyd Ohlin. 1960. *Delinquency and opportunity: A theory of delinquent gangs.* New York: Free Press.

Cohen, Albert. 1955. *Delinquent boys: The culture of the gang.* Glencoe, IL: Free Press.

Connell, R. W. 1987. *Gender and power.* Stanford, CA: Stanford University Press.

Crime Prevention Division. 1993. *Crime in Hawaii.* Honolulu: Department of the Attorney General.

Curry, G. David, Robert J. Box, Richard A. Ball, and Darryl Stone. 1992. *National assessment of law enforcement anti-gang information resources: Draft 1992 final report.* West Virginia University: National Assessment Survey 1992.

Daly, Kathleen, and Meda Chesney-Lind. 1988. Feminism and criminology. *Justice Quarterly* 5:497–538.

Department of Business and Economic Development and Tourism. 1993. *Hawaii State Databook, 1992.* Honolulu: Author.

Fagan, Jeffrey. 1989. The social organization of drug use and drug dealing among urban gangs. *Criminology* 27:633–67.

Federal Bureau of Investigation. 1992. *Uniform crime reports 1991.* Washington, DC: U.S. Government Printing Office.

Fishman, Laura. 1988. The vice queens: An ethnographic study of Black female gang behavior. Presented at the Annual Meetings, American Society of Criminology, New Orleans, LA.

Flowers, R. B. 1987. *Women and criminality.* New York: Greenwood.

Hagedorn, John. 1988. *People and folks.* Chicago: Lake View.

———. 1992. Homeboys, dope fiends, legits and new jacks. Paper presented at the Annual Meetings, American Society of Criminology, New Orleans, LA.

Harris, Mary. 1988. *Cholas: Latino girls and gangs.* New York: AMS Press.

Jankowski, Martin Sanchez. 1991. *Islands in the street: Gangs and American urban society.* Berkeley: University of California Press.

Katz, Jack. 1988. *Seductions of crime.* New York: Basic Books.

Lauderback, David, Joy Hansen, and Daniel Waldorf. 1992. Sisters are doin' it for themselves: A Black female gang in San Francisco. *The Gang Journal* 1:57–72.

Lebra, Joyce. 1991. *Women's voices in Hawaii.* Niwot: University Press of Colorado.

Linnekin, Jocelyn. 1990. *Sacred queens and women of consequence*. Ann Arbor: University of Michigan Press.

Messerschmidt, James. 1986. *Capitalism, patriarchy, and crime*. Totowa, NJ: Rowman & Littlefield.

———. 1993. *Masculinities and crime*. Lanham, MD: Rowman & Littlefield.

Miller, Walter. 1958. Lower class culture as a generating milieu of gang delinquency. *Journal of Social Issues* 3:5–19.

———. 1975. Race, sex and gangs: The Molls. *Trans-Action* 11:32–35.

———. 1980. The Molls. In *Women, crime, and justice*, edited by S. K. Datesman and F. R. Scarpitti. New York: Oxford University Press.

Moore, Joan. 1978. *Home boys*. Philadelphia: Temple University Press.

———. 1991. *Going down to the barrio: Homeboys and homegirls in change*. Philadelphia: Temple University Press.

Muwakkil, Salim. 1993. Ganging together. *In These Times*, 5 April.

Office of Youth Services, State of Hawaii. 1993. *An interim report to the Legislature on the Gang Response System Act 300, 1992 SLH*. Honolulu: Author.

Ostner, Illona. 1986. Die Entdeckung der Madchen. Neue Perspecktiven fur die. *Kolner-Zeitschrift-fur Soziologie und Sozialpsychologie* 38:352–71.

Quicker, John. 1983. *Homegirls: Characterizing Chicana gangs*. Los Angeles: International University Press.

Reiner, Ira. 1992. *Gangs, crime and violence in Los Angeles. Findings and proposals from the District Attorney's Office*, executive summary. Los Angeles: District Attorney, County of Los Angeles.

Rice, R. 1963. A reporter at large: The Persian queens. *New Yorker*, 19 October.

Rockhill, Anna, Meda Chesney-Lind, Joe Allen, Nestor Batalon, Elise Garvin, Karen Joe, and Michele Spina. 1993. *Surveying Hawaii's youth: Neighborhoods, delinquency, and gangs*. Honolulu: Social Science Research Institute, University of Hawaii.

Ryan, William. 1972. *Blaming the victim*. New York: Vintage Books.

Skolnick, Jerome, Theodore Correl, Elizabeth Navarro, and Roger Rabb. 1989. *The social structure of street drug dealing*. Sacramento, CA: Office of the Attorney General, State of California.

Taylor, Carl. 1990. *Dangerous society*. East Lansing: Michigan State University Press.

———. 1993. *Girls, gangs, women and drugs*. East Lansing: Michigan State University Press.

Thrasher, Frederick. 1927. *The gang*. Chicago: University of Chicago Press.

Waldorf, Daniel. 1993. *Final report on crack sales, gangs and violence to the National Institute on Drug Abuse*. San Francisco: Institute for Scientific Analysis.

Watters, John K., and Patrick Biernacki. 1989. Targeted sampling: Options for the study of hidden populations. *Social Problems* 36:416–30.

CHAPTER 7

Women on the Edge of Crime

Crack Cocaine and the Changing Contexts of Street-Level Sex Work in New York City

LISA MAHER AND RICHARD CURTIS

INTRODUCTION

Nowhere is the gendered relation between women and the law more apparent in America at the moment than with respect to the current "war on drugs."[1] Perhaps the most startling and obvious example of this relationship is found in recent moves to "criminalize the pregnancies" of women who use illicit drugs. Such a strategy has been revealed as not only gendered, but racist and classist, being directed against a particular group of women who use a particular drug—i.e., poor minority women who smoke crack cocaine.[2]

The expanded interface between the criminal law and women's lives afforded by the "war on drugs" has been accompanied by increased administrative regulation which, in labeling these women "unfit mothers," has sought to remove their children, their welfare and Medicaid benefits and their housing—usually in that order. In New York City this situation, compounded by recent budget cuts has rendered women extremely vulnerable to exploitation and victimization by men—be it in the context of the "freakhouse" scene[6] or the street-level sex markets[7] on which this paper focuses.

In this paper, we elaborate the structural and "criminal" positioning of a group of women who smoke crack and engage in street-level sex work. We attempt to situate their consumption of crack, their "criminality" and their experiences of violence (both as perpetrators and victims) within the context of gender relations and occupational opportunities as they exist in the informal economy. . . .

Abridged from Lisa Maher and Richard Curtis, "Women on the Edge of Crime: Crack Cocaine and the Changing Contexts of Street-Level Sex Work in New York City," *Crime, Law, and Social Change*, Vol. 18, pp. 221–258, © 1992. Reprinted by permission of Kluwer Academic Publishers. *Ed. note:* Although text and footnotes were deleted, we preserved the footnote numbers that appeared in the original text.

The Prevalence of Women Crack Smokers

Although crack use is clearly declining,[13] the literature suggests that women may be more evenly distributed among populations of crack smokers than has historically been the case with respect to illicit drug use.[14] There is also some evidence to suggest that, at least among arrestee populations in New York City, similar proportions of men and women who come into contact with the criminal justice system test positive for cocaine.[15] In 1988, 43% of female drug commitments in New York State reported that the drug leading to their conviction was cocaine and only 31% reported crack. By 1989, however, 45% of women cited crack and only 34% cited cocaine as the drug leading to their conviction.[16] In 1988, the New York City Department of Corrections identified 2,280 inmates "addicted" to crack—56% of these inmates were women.[17] In a recent study of 886 intravenous drug users (IDUs) and their sex partners in Harlem, women used crack approximately 50% more frequently than men, leading the author to conclude that, in this sample, "women appear to prefer crack over any other drug."[18]

The Psycho-social Consequences of Women's Crack Use

Several studies have sought to document the psycho-social consequences of crack use.[19] While research on treatment populations indicates that compulsive crack use is structured by the contingencies of the urban setting, there is clearly a paucity of research on women's crack use. Earlier literature on women and narcotics use suggests that the psycho-social consequences of drug use may be gender-differentiated. Studies suggest that women drug users have more social, psychological and physical health difficulties than men. Women IDUs complain of more medical problems, and women in treatment have been documented to experience more medical problems than their male counterparts.[20]

Women IDUs are also thought to experience higher levels of stress, depression and anxiety and lower levels of self esteem.[21] These factors are compounded by the clinical and psychosocial consequences of AIDS and HIV infection among female populations, including high rates of gynecological and obstetrical disorders, the acceleration of HIV as a result of pregnancy, and the impact of HIV status on reproductive choice, child-bearing and child-rearing.[22] Research also indicates that women "addicts" tend to have fewer social supports and greater familial responsibilities than either nonaddict women or addicted males.[23] Perhaps most importantly, women IDUs are more likely to be subject to social stigmatization and alienation. Women appear to internalize negative social attitudes towards "female addicts" which are reinforced by the masculine norms and values of the addict subculture.[24] Moreover, the pervasiveness of the "commonsense" that drug use impedes maternal functioning serves to amplify the social stigmatization of women drug users.[25]

A number of recent studies have also suggested that "chronic crack use" is strongly correlated with high-risk behaviours implicated in the spread of HIV infection and sexually transmitted diseases.[26] Women sex workers are already a high risk group for HIV infection and women who are or have been partners of male IDUs constitute a significant population of women at risk for AIDS.[28]

Finally, our field observations to date suggest that not only are the psycho-social consequences of crack use particularly debilitating for women in the terms elaborated by previous research but, moreover, that crack use by poor minority women has served to stretch inter-generational relations and family resources to their limits—undermining traditional kin networks of care and domesticity among minority and particularly black women.[29]

The Nature, Extent and Impact of State Regulatory Responses

On a national level, both the number of drug arrests and the percentage of all arrestees charged with drug offenses have increased dramatically since 1980.[30] In New York City, the number of drug arrests increased from 18,521 in 1980 to 88,641 in 1988.[31] During 1989, there were 25,048 felony arrests for crack possession or sale in New York City, constituting the largest single offense category besides robbery. An additional 18,194 misdemeanour crack arrests were made in the same year.[32]

• • •

Between 1980 and 1986, an average of 22% of women incarcerated in New York were imprisoned for drug offenses.[36] In 1987, however, this proportion increased to 42%. By the end of 1989, 66% were incarcerated for drug offenses in New York State. Of these 1,059 women, 50% were Hispanic, 41% were black and 9% were white. Approximately 75% of these women reported having at least one child. The average minimum sentence was 24 months.[37] New York State has spent nearly three hundred million dollars over the past three years to build and operate new prison space for women.[38]

• • •

The singling out of "mothers" who are crack smokers for criminal and administrative sanctions has special implications for urban minority families. In New York State, where a positive toxicology screen on a newborn is considered presumptive evidence of neglect, child abuse and neglect petitions before the Family Court containing allegations of drug abuse quadrupled in the years 1986–1989.[40] At least 50% of identified toxicology positive infants are currently placed in foster care.[41] The overloading of foster care systems has given rise to the phenomenon of "boarder babies" in many hospitals and institutions.[42]

In response, a recent federal government report recommended that state and local agencies reduce "obstacles" to placing drug affected infants in adoptive homes, including the revision of existing laws on abandonment, expediting the termination of parental rights and inter-racial placements.[43] While the institutionalization of children in nonkin-based foster care is deplorable, state responses such as the creation of a category of kin-based foster care specifically for "crack babies" may serve to exacerbate intra-generational conflict, delay the reunification of mothers and their children, and perpetuate children's foster care status by promoting the commodification of relations between women crack smokers and their female kin. . . .

The Positioning of Women within the Informal Economy

. . . While the position of poor minority women within the informal economy mirrors their positioning within the labour and income transfer markets of the formal economy,[46] we suggest additionally that the relations and processes which serve to disadvantage these women within the formal economy are exacerbated within the illegal context of the drug/crack economy. In particular, occupational hierarchies within the informal economy draw on gender, ethnic and class divisions. . . . In the informal economy, women are confined to a secondary "secondary labour market"[47] that centres around the most saleable commodity they have—their bodies. . . . Specifically, our analysis addresses these areas:

Crack induced participation in the (sex segmented) informal economy. The widespread use of crack in many poor urban minority neighbourhoods has increased the number of women participating in street-level sex markets—often the only revenue generating strategy available to women within the informal economy.

Increased competition and hostility. Conditions of extreme competition and increased hostility between sex workers have exacerbated the atomization and social isolation of women crack smokers.

Changes in the price, structure and nature of sex work. Both crack-induced increases in the number of women sex workers and crack-accelerated shifts in the nature of the sex work (e.g., from vaginal intercourse to blow jobs, indoor to outdoor) have deflated the going rates for sexual exchanges.

Market conditions and the victimization of women. The price deflation of sexual services has in turn spawned a self-selection process of cheaper "rougher" dates which has made the stroll itself "rougher."

The emergence of "viccing" as a form of resistance. These cumulative processes have increased the level of violence within the market itself—the increasingly economically marginalized women "viccing" the dates ("vic him before he vic you"), the male smokers viccing women smokers and some women smokers viccing other women.

CRACK AND THE CURRENT STUDY

Despite the media predilection for attributing a range of preexistent social ills to crack cocaine, the curbside distribution and consumption of crack remains overwhelmingly concentrated in neighbourhoods which were *already* experiencing profound economic and social destabilization and disorganization prior to the advent of crack cocaine. These are neighbourhoods that, in the decades preceding the arrival of crack cocaine, suffered a massive exodus of human and economic capital. . . .

The research sites are located in precisely such neighbourhoods. The Southside, located in Williamsburg, has long been a site of highly structured organized drug distribution in Brooklyn. Ethnically, the Southside is dominated by Hispanics, although it is home to a sizeable enclave of Hasidic Jews. A well-established major trucking route, the site of prostitution strolls for more than a quarter of a century, runs through the area. In recent years, the Southside has witnessed a gradual decline of housing stock and there are large tracts comprised almost entirely of abandoned and boarded-up buildings. Crack distribution is modeled on the heroin markets which have been an entrenched feature of life on the Southside since the 1950s. Everyone who sells crack on the Southside is selling it for someone else. It is a highly structured and to some degree regimented marketplace of street-level distributors and consumers.

. . . By 1988, the phase of street-level distribution and consumption had peaked in the Southside. With a decline in the overall number of users and the failure of crack to attract new initiates, many previously flourishing drug markets began to experience a sizeable contraction. Since 1989, this shrinkage has led many hardcore distributors and users to concentrate themselves in pools which take on the appearance of a vortex: everyone is funnelled into small geographical areas where drug activity is heightened.

Bushwick, our second research site, is an example of such a vortex. Although no stranger to the drug trade, Bushwick had historically been a working class Italian neighbourhood which, over the years, generated a certain amount of mafia folklore. Since the late 1960s, however, the area has gradually come to be dominated by low income Latino populations (predominantly Puerto Ricans), and, more recently, Dominicans and Columbians have begun to move in. The housing stock in the general neighbourhood is primarily one- and two-family housing, although the drug market area itself consists of run-down apartment complexes and a lot of abandoned buildings set amongst a mix of light manufacturing and industry. The current vortex of active drug markets has evolved rapidly over the past two years and there are frequent confrontations over "turf" as drug dealing organizations compete to establish hegemony over respective markets.

VOICES FROM THE FIELD

It is within this context that we examine (i) the notion that women's emancipation escalates participation in crime and violence and (ii) the notion that women's crack use escalates participation in crime and violence.[53] . . .

1. Crack Induced Participation in the (Sex Segmented) Informal Economy

The widespread use of crack in poor urban minority neighbourhoods has increased the number of women participating in street-level sex markets.

. . .

All of the women who participated in the current study agree that "crack" increased the number of women working the strolls and had a significant impact on the kind of work they did, the renumeration they received and the interactions that occurred in and around street-level sex markets.

> Crack progressed more women out on the street. You see things you ain't never seen before—girls changin clothes on the street, shit that females would never do, they do now—you know that you would never see before—in this day and time you see now. (Bay)

> The people out here (in Bushwick) are worse than on the Southside—living worst—they're thirsty. Out here you see your people livin on the street—you see people ain't sleeping you know . . . they're like cavemen—if they could eat each other, they would—if it comes down to that. That's how this neighborhood is getting—very thirsty—that's what you call it. (Cookie)

This inter-relation between income generating strategies within the informal economy and crack has also served to structure patterns of consumption and use.

> [Is crack the main drug you use while you're working?] Yeah, because I can't go out sober on a date, because I don't like what I do and I do it for my (dope) habit. So I gotta be high on somethin before I get into that next car. [Do you think the crack does anything physically to you—does it like make sex any more/less enjoyable/bearable?] No, I don exactly enjoy what I do out there. I just, you know, caus it always has me like—I do my things quicker—I'm fast, I'm up. I just go in his car, do what I gotta do and I'm outta there already. No I don enjoy it. No way. (Vivian)

Some of the crack initiates reported subsequent initiation into heroin use in an attempt to moderate the effects of crack. As "Patricia"[58] told us, "Yeah because the crack gets so speedy and somebody tells you, I know how you can stop, you know, that speedy feeling—get a bag of dope."

Rather than assuming that women crack smokers "choose" sex work as the most desirable/convenient/lucrative way of financing their consumption of drugs, we began our fieldwork concerned to explore the range of opportunities for income generation available to women in the informal economy. Most of the women with histories of heroin use prior to initiation to crack reported having engaged in shoplifting or "boosting." As Rosie's account attests, this was not usually done in a random or indiscriminate way. Rosie's "boosting"—always in conjunction with males who "taught her everything"—can be seen as firmly embedded in a local context in which shoplifting was both possible and "tolerated" because of the function it performed in redistributing scarce resources.[59] . . . The fact that Rosie and her male cohorts knew *who* to approach shows how "crime"—as a form of redistribution—produces "complex chains of interaction resulting in local tolerance and shelter . . . for illegal activities."[60]

> [What kinds of things would you steal?] Les see, the coat—you know the feather one? [The down?] Yeah, is easy to sell. Let's see, some people buy,

you know, they would go to the store to buy a coat, right, so we would say you know, we could get it for you, you know, get it for you—give us less money [Which people—other junkies or . . .?] No no, no, regular people that, they was lookin in the store to buy so we would say you know, we could get that for you, just wait ousside and you pay us less money . . . What do you want—we can get it for you . . . they be waiting . . . [This was before the electronic tags came? Did that change it—has that changed?] Oh yeah, for they put that thing it's difficult to steal you know. [So back then you would steal stuff from the store—what other things, anything else? What about like robberies, robbing stores and robbing people?] No, only stealin', I'm not gon hurt nobody. (Rosie)

Similarly, Natalie had a male "ripping and running" partner. Together they'd go boosting, do the malls—Kings Plaza, Coney Island—all over. "I would steal it, he would sell it. We'd split the money evenly and get high together." Things are different today, however. Natalie has a heavy heroin and cocaine habit and smokes crack. She supports her consumption by working the stroll. As she puts it, "Once you're here, it's a rut, I don't think you can get out" (Natalie). Tina is a 23-year-old white woman from Long Island. She was introduced to heroin by her boyfriend and used to go "boosting" with a girlfriend out in the malls. Tina eventually moved to the Southside and ended up living with one of the Puerto Rican street sellers. With no car to go boosting, Tina became dependent on this guy to support her habit. After about a year, he was arrested and went to jail, and Tina began to work the stroll in order to finance her consumption. As she put it,

I'd rather go out and get mine and be with someone for fifteen minutes than hang out with one of those spics. You know what I'm saying? Suck their dicks, excuse the—you know—suck their dicks all night for the same amount. You know what I'm saying. I'm not down—you know. I'd rather do it the way I do it, than like do all the neighbourhood guys.

Neither Tina nor Natalie shoplift anymore. Down here, where the bodegas are at least three to a block, fast food, condoms and Bic lighters are the only legal commodities that do a roaring trade. There is nothing to boost and no malls to boost from in these neighbourhoods. Patricia recalled how once-upon-a-time she and another girl used to steal chains from people as they came out of a now defunct grocery store on a once busy avenue. They would take the chains to a local jeweller (who has since been murdered) who "fenced" them in exchange for cash. Her account indicates how the nature of the formal economy determines to a considerable degree the opportunities for revenue generation that are available in the informal economy.

There's a girl, now she's in jail, name Raka. We used to do things like that over here—snatched a police officer daughter chain right here on D. We didn't know she was a police officer daughter. [How is it that you and she got together?] She was robbin this guy with this other girl and the girl ran and she couldn't see nobody and I was just standing there watching them and she goes "yo, Patricia" and she was surprised that I responded, you know, and I blocked the guy and threw a bottle at him and hit him in the head and he ran and then, after that, like a couple of days, like everytime seem like we always be [dope]sick together. Somebody rich come out and she say, "I'm gonna push you into this guy, push you into him and snatch his chain, we'll run and I'll pass it." After like five or six times we started hangin out together. [Who you did this to?] These were people maybe comin out the grocery store, in front of P. When that store opened a lot of people used to stop there and we used to wait for them to come out. [Where you used to take the chains to?] Used to be the place where the guy got killed right across the street from you . . . no gunshots or nuttin, just stabbed and killed him.

Relations between the formal and informal economies clearly impact on, and are impacted on by, opportunities for income generation and reinvestment and redistribution provided by discrete and localized contexts for drug distribution and consumption. In examining differences in the rates, volumes and methods of income generation between marijuana and cocaine, Hamid concludes that the "feature of crack distribution which most differentiates it is the upward and outward flow of capital from the study population."[61] Unlike some earlier drug enterprises, cocaine revenues have been neither reinvested or redistributed at the local level.

We asked the women a series of questions designed to elicit their perceptions of the kinds of revenue-generating opportunities open to them within the local informal economy. It clearly emerged that gender relations are an important axis which serves to structure opportunities for income generation at the local level. The women's responses demonstrate the construction of gendered social meanings from both broad and localized patterns of interaction.

[What about, do girls do the sort of things that, you know, guys do out here—strip cars, steal cars or break into houses—do girls get involved in that?] It depend—on the neighbourhood, on the individual, how bad they're stressin and how bad you're sick. If I'm sick, I'm gon do anything to get my money, I don't care. I don't think I bop a little ol lady walking down the block . . . could be my moms, but I might think about takin one of the other bitches off. (Candy)

[Why don't girls strip cars, scrap metal—you think guys get upset if started doing that?] Yeah, they would probably try and get over if I came along . . . but it's too heavy and I don't have the tools . . . some girls can do that but with a guy, the one girl I know who strips cars by herself is a dyke— she's a mack truck mechanic . . . most of these girls don't know nuttin about cars. (Suzie Q)

[Do you think that it's harder for a guy to make money out here than a girl?] No, caus if they so bad, they go and stick somebody up. [What a woman couldn't do that?] I wouldn't. I may go in somebody pocket you know, like when I was out on the street but I wouldn't, not just cold blooded stick somebody up. [What other kinds of opportunities do women have to make money besides work on the stroll?] I don't know. The avenue is the only opportunity that comes to my mind. (Patricia)

• • •

Bay is a 26-year-old African-American woman who, at the time of writing, was seven months pregnant and had a bad case of syphilis. Bay is a sex worker and has sold drugs in the past. She claims she has never stolen from anyone but her family. She says that she would not sell drugs again because, as she put it, "I don like their (the managers') attitude, like if you come up short, they take it out on you. A lot of people will rip you off, be a dollar short for a vial—what can you do?" Bay currently alternates between sleeping on the streets and in a shelter for pregnant women. She has been cut off welfare and is finding it difficult to get sex work because of her pregnancy. We recently spent a day hanging out with Bay as she "hustled" for cash and crack. Watching her panhandle change whenever she could, con a junkie out of a stolen bedspread for $1 and re-sell it for $2, get free condoms from health workers and sell them to girls on the stroll, and, finally, try for over an hour to pick up a date, we were left with the indelible impression that, in the absence of sex work, it was difficult, if not impossible, for women to "get paid" in this neighbourhood.

> [Why do you think women stick to, like, boosting and turning tricks when they could do like rob people and shit, do all the things that men do?] That ain't their style, it's not their style—the guys would get pissed and the guys would start robbin the girls—they take it now, rob the girls, you know it, they take the shit, like the money they make from trickin and stuff, guys rip em off, they be bad out here. (Bay)

2. Increased Competition and Hostility

Candy is a 41-year-old European American woman who grew up on the Southside. . . . She currently shoots heroin and cocaine and smokes crack. Her health is deplorable. At 41, she is eight months pregnant as a result of having been raped by a client, her legs and breasts are abscessed, and she has a heart condition and a fluid retention problem—both exacerbated by a pregnancy for which she receives no prenatal care. She is also HIV positive. Somehow she manages to retain a great wit and a strong sense of empathy for others, which she struggles to keep covered up. Candy has been a sex worker, or as she puts it, a "ho" for about seventeen years "on and off" in both research sites. She is well placed to describe recent changes in the contexts of street-level sex work in these neighbourhoods. As she told us:

> Many moons ago I started off on D and P down by the Star Diner. There was three girls—Jo, Ellen and myself. O.K. By the train station, there was three of us out there . . . That was about fifteen years ago when it was real discreet . . . we had to do all the talkin, you know . . . it'll cost you a few dollars, you can give us a present if you want, you know, you can give us money for a meal you know. It was so much different and more fun back then too. [Did you have friends among the other girls them?] Those were friends—now these girls out here are just for the drug and theirself—no friendship, everyone's out to cut everyone's throat. [Back then were you all using drugs?] Of course, that's mainly what the whole deals about—drug using, you know what I'm sayin. We were friends and we'd help one an-

other out whether we were right or wrong . . . We'd stick together, it's like
I said, do a favour, call somebody up, go get a bag of dope . . . These people don't know how to be ho's. (Candy)

The absence of friendship is a recurrent theme in the women's conversations.
Most of the women characterize their relationships with other drug users as
"associates," even though these relations are more complex and perhaps less
instrumental than they initially appear.

A few women but friendships, no. Some of them say people come before
drugs. That's bullshit caus there's a lot of people I really care about—family and stuff—that I put the drugs before—you tryin to tell me I'm gonna
put some street junkie before them? (Tina)

• • •

Rosie is a 31-year-old Dominican woman who, at the time of writing, was seven
months pregnant with her fourth child. When Rosie came down to Bushwick
in about 1988, she had been using heroin and doing speedballs for about fifteen
years, but had not yet begun to smoke crack. Rosie walked onto a stroll dominated by crack smokers.

It was problem because you know, they want get a hit and you wanna get
a dope you know . . . they ones that crackhead, they even go for fi dollar,
three dollar. Yeah, we charge fifteen caus we need it. Like now I always
try to get twenny-five because like, I remember the crack, the coke, the
dope and I try to get more. But the one only smokin crack they don't care
to go for fi collar, because right there they got a bottle . . . [Do the dates
all wanna go with them caus they're cheap? And so what did you girls do
about this?] Yeah, we fight or watch them go out and when they come back
rip 'em off. Two of you together and we say I share with you whatever she
got. [But if you had like friends on the stroll down here?] Believe me, there's
no friend around here. [No friends—sorry—associates on the stroll, but
would they be like crack women or dope women?] Well most the people in
this days they be doing the dope and the crack, now I be all three, now I
do all three [You've been working on the stroll lately—how's it going?] Now
not too great caus I'm pregnant, it's hard to get a customer you know. [But
if it's just a blow job, it shouldn't make any difference?] That how I see but
I guess they don't see it that way. (Rosie)

Rosie's account is illuminating for a number of reasons. First, in these days
when "poly-drug use" has become a fashionable catch-all, her distinction between crack smokers and poly-drug users suggests the need for an analysis of
both the social and economic relations of poly-drug consumption, and, in particular, how poly-drug use relates to sex work and high risk behaviours. Secondly, Rosie's account verifies that not only are there "no friends out here" but
that relations between women on the stroll today are certainly "not like they
used to be." Increasingly, some of the interactions between the women are
characterized by mutual hostility and competition—to the point where, when
they are not "vicced" first by dates or male users, some will even "vic" each

other for increasingly hard-to-get cash and drugs. Finally, Rosie's experience of her pregnancy illustrates the relationship between sex work and constructions of femininity and sexuality. Although there is no good reason why Rosie could not continue to perform blow jobs, most dates clearly do not wish to engage pregnant sex workers.[64]

... Gender relations with intimates, where they survive the rigours of daily drug consumption by both partners, tend to be characterized by a reciprocal flow of violence between the street and the "home" (or other makeshift domestic setting).

> Last night I went up there [to the stroll]—you know I tricked ... took me about an hour and I made money and I have to tell him how much I made. I made forty-five dollars ... I said I made forty-five dollars here, I'm gon give you, you know caus he had got me straight yesterday. He doesn't have a dope habit—he doesn't never had one, he don't know what its like. He call me dope friend in front of everybody and lowlife bitch, bitch, suckin on white face dicks, you know, and this the same money that I share with him ... I mean ... after I gave him twenty-five dollars, I took twenty and you know that he smoked it all up right. I bought me a one on one (heroin and cocaine) and a crack, right. I had to give him half of my one on one so he wouldn't jump on me and beat me up—after I gave him twenty five dollars, then I had my crack, right ... and he want half my crack and caus I didn't give it to him, he jumped on me and beat me up and my sweater is all bloodied up from him beatin on me ... He knows I got no place to go. (Patricia)

On the street, the tenuous relations between genders—intimate or not—are undergirded by the same threat or reality of male violence and reinforced by the lack of any collective solidarity between the women. As Bay put it:

> The guys, they stress the females. The guys out here kick the girls' ass. That's where the girls got to watch okay? You got the girls competitioning each other, and you got the guys victimizing them, see? That's the line out here. [How come the girls don't get together and kick the boy's ass?] Because they're having their little rival, you know, all the girls are rivals. They're tryin to out-beat each other.

In particular, the women are conscious of the multitude of ways in which male crack users "disrespect" them.

> (Men are) bitches ... because since they got on crack, I learnt that they ain't no self respect for nobody. They treat you like shit—straight up, like shit. Disrespect—they lose all respect—treating them like a dog—word. (Bay)

• • •

3. Changes in the Price, Structure and Nature of Sex Work

Crack-induced increases in the number of women sex workers and crack-accelerated shifts in the nature of sex work (e.g., from vaginal intercourse to blow jobs, from indoor to outdoor) have both deflated the going rates for sexual exchanges and increased the levels of violence associated with the strolls. As Crystal put it, there is "less drugs and more violence" on the Southside. She explained that this has led to a situation where "a lot of girls is taking off dates and the dates is getting mad." . . . We got similar accounts from most of the women when we introduced a series of questions designed to elicit information about whether, how and why the strolls which they worked had changed in recent months. Asked about the Southside, women suggested a confluence of factors post-dating the TNT intervention. Most notable were the recurrent themes of crack's effect on the prices for sex work and increases in violence.

> [What has changed most about your work out here?] I'd be gettin more then that I'm gettin now, caus of this crack shit . . . or they wanted to get laid more than they do now caus of this AIDS thing okay . . . Now they don't want to pay no more than $10 and you don't want no more. (Candy)

• • •

Although they all smoked crack, the women pinpointed it as the prime culprit in limiting their ability to make money. "Crack" was repeatedly identified as having lowered the going rates for sex work and increased the numbers of "asshole dates" and male crack heads.

> The difference between here (Bushwick) and Manhattan is the guys are so cheap over here. All these bitches around here is crack heads so every trick you get now wanna give *crack fare*. [They don't wanna give you cash?] No, I'm saying "crack fare" because they know these bitches be doing—every bitch over here is a crack head so they just wanna give you that amount ($5) . . . These girls go out there just for crack fare. When it's over, when they want another crack, they go back—so why not let's just do this right from the beginning and we don't have to keep goin back an forth. (Kizzy)

• • •

> [I've heard it's much cheaper down here than it was on the Southside] I don't go out for less than twenty-five—over here, anywhere. I'll let twenty cars pass me, they can go. I don't know them. They don't know me, they can go. Two dollars. They go out for two dollars. I mean if I was sick—don't get me wrong—if I was dopesick and I needed a bag of dope, I'd go for ten dollars. I'm so sure I would. I'm sure any junkie would. (Mary)

> Oh man, they be go so low as a cap ($5 vial of crack)—dependin on how bad the person is stressin—they lose all the respect of yourselves—just totally bizarre if you ask me . . . The dates are rougher and nastier too—you're always gonna run into an asshole out there but there's more assholes now. With the girls, it's let's see who can beat each other, the majority of women try to challenge each other. It's pathetic . . . it's just fucked up, they just want that hit so bad—they're not pathetic, they're sick. (Bay)

> Normally you try to ask for fifteen for a blow job. These girls do it for five— less. That's, that's—you know—that's self degradation. You can't even

blame the men because of course if you can get a blow job for five instead of ten or fifteen, you're going to take it. It's like someone selling me a bag of dope for five dollars; of course I'm going to buy your dope instead of the dope for ten, you know. (Tina)

[Since you've been out here, it's gotten cheaper?] Yeah . . . we got a girl we call "Two Dollar Mindy." She go out . . . Mindy will stay with a date forty-five minutes and come back an she wanna get down on (share) a crack. [You mean she got less than five dollars?] . . . Two Dollar Mindy don't care about nobody, nuttin—long as she got two dollars. I've never seen a girl stay that long in a car an come back an she wants to get down. On a good date, she got four—she come back and she need a dollar." [What do you girls think about her doing that?] Oh they be talk, that's why they call her Two Dollar Mindy. Why would you pick up a girl for ten when you can get one for two? (Patricia)

While the drop in price was prompted in the eyes of some women by a drop in standards on the part of the "girls," it was clearly exacerbated by an increase in expectations, or "bang for the buck" on the part of the dates, which many women viewed as insulting and disrespectful. In fact, "viccing" by women was often precipitated when individual dates behaved in this way. . . . As Candy put it,

You don't have to be beautiful, can be the ugliest bitch on the street, bitch on the corner look like a million and you can look like a Bowery bum and he'll pick you up and she's standing there . . . They call themselves men and some of the girls out there really look like shit . . . I'm no raving beauty but there's a way to do everything—take care . . . I'm out there most of the time . . . and here comes a girl looking dynamite really stecked out, she can't pick up a date for jackshit and here comes this stank bitch looking terrible and dirty and she'll pick up a date faster than I will . . . A lot of Johns are afraid today because there's diseases goin around . . . but then again you'll get a guy who'll pick somethin like that up and leave me hangin there—I be there for hours and don't make a dime and here's this filthy bitch making money left and right.

In contrast to the emerging literature on women and crack cocaine which repeatedly asserts the primacy of sex-for-crack exchanges,[68] we found that women generally resist the lure of such exchanges. This is not surprising, given the fact that, within the current context of a deflated sex market, it is both time consuming and arguably more dangerous to support consumption through sex-for-crack transactions. . . .

You get a guy pull up to you and say, "Do you um um um, you goin out, I just wanna smoke, do you have a pipe?" Yeah, but "Do you smoke?" No I carry a fuckin pipe around for dicks like you and get busted. I've got a pipe of course I must smoke you stupid ass. And I tell the guy "Okay, hey honey if you wanna turn me on that's lovely but that's not gonna be my payment, you have to pay me cash up, I'm a ho." (Candy)

Moreover, as Kizzy—a 32-year-old African-American woman who worked as a "professional" prostitute in Chicago for many years before coming to New

York—told us, sex-for-crack exchanges, or "smokin dates" as the women refer to them, are both dangerous and "unprofessional."

> They fail to realize that crack affect everyone different—you know what I'm sayin. Whereas I might take a hit and sit here an' be cool, another person might take a hit and get to trippin, you know what I'm sayin, they might think anything—flip out. (Kizzy)

Sometimes some women do exchange sex for crack, but neither frequently, readily nor easily. Initially, most are extremely reluctant to elaborate just when and under what circumstances they would do it or have done it in the past. Over a long period of observation and several interviews, in which considerable relations of trust and support had been established. Candy gave us the following account.

> Okay. If I was stressin real bad and a guy tell me he's got two or three caps I might do it. I'm sorry, I'm no better than anyone else—shit, I don't put myself on a pedestal, if I was stressin bad enough I'd do it. But then after I do it—I think—you motherfucker man you give me two bottles and I gotta suck your dick . . . I get so mad at myself. . . .

Part of their resistance to sex-for-crack exchanges is couched in the inevitability of street-level gender relations whereby men constantly "get over women" and end up getting both "the head and the drugs."

> He smokin so lovely everytime he tell you okay you can take a pull, you take a pull an he wants you on the dick right away—let me enjoy the fuckin hit if you want me to smoke wit you. You take a hit and your're down there and ain't even let the shit out your mouth yet. You know what I'm sayin, he fuckin smokin lovely while you're just suckin rubber lovely. (Candy)

Despite recent crack-induced shifts in the price, structure and nature of street-level sex work, money still defines the nature of the interaction. Although prices are deflated and their work devalued, sex remains "work." For the most part, the women resist attempts by dates to mix "business and pleasure."

4. Market Conditions and the Victimization of Women

The price deflation of sexual services has in turn spawned a self-selection process of cheaper "rougher" dates which has made the strolls themselves "rougher" and more violent places to work. Despite the fact that they are often victims themselves, some of the women are reluctant to "blame" the dates. Rather, they attribute increases in victimization to crack-induced carelessness. As Kizzy told us:

> You can just about tell which guys be up to something. [But a lot of the girls obviously can't, because they be gettin all messed up out here now?] A lot of them be thirsty too and they be, they ain't got no time to judge you know.

Since we have been working in these neighbourhoods at least four women sex workers have been killed. One woman was hurled into a parking meter from a van being chased by the police; another was murdered and her decapitated body, minus her breasts, was found over by the railway tracks. Another woman, a "friend" of Patricia's, was beaten to death by a date.

> That's the one I'm a witness for in the case. She was workin. She was a crack head and he used to flip, used to go buy a bunch of crack right, give it to the girl and then, you know, do what you want but then he would flip out and then he'd beat em up. That was her date. (Patricia)

On a recent Sunday evening, one of the women, Juanita, was repeatedly stabbed and, again, her breasts were mutilated. At the time of writing, she remains in intensive care in a local hospital.

> I know Juanita from my old neighbourhood. I heard she got a hundred stitches. He cut her breasts off . . . He was hangin out in the lot. I can't understand. Why would you take somebody from the lot where everybody's there—you know, if he do something to you, all you gotta do is scream— and bring them to some secluded area? Two people . . . [But they were white guys we heard?] That why she went. To Hispanic and black people, if is white, it's okay—that's bull. (Patricia)

Another woman—Tessie—was found dead in an abandoned lot where many of the women sleep. She had two bullet holes in her head.

For many of these women, victimization on the streets merely extends a continuum of violence that began at home. These are women who, for the most part, experienced victimization and abuse as children. Candy was brutally raped by her father when she was eight years old. Her father attempted to rape her a second time, but Candy escaped and told her sister, who in turn told her grandfather. The grandfather "beat the shit" out of the father and kicked him out of the house. In 1990, she was raped by a date who drove her down to the waterfront and "beat the hell" out of her.

> I saw his face and I saw my father at the same time . . . We were right by the waterfront, okay, water again and I got raped. I've done everything, I lay, blowjobs, that and the other thing [crying] . . . still it's a different feeling, it's different to me . . . It just don't feel right . . . no matter what I am. (Candy)

• • •

Tina, who recently moved down to Bushwick, had been raped four times while working on the Southside. Suzie Q, a 32-year-old Jewish woman, is a former S&M Queen who lived in California for nine years. She has several porn videos to her credit and claims to have freebased at Hugh Hefner's Playboy mansion. However, these days are behind her and Suzie now works the stroll in Bushwick. She has been raped, and recently lost all her teeth as a result of a pistol whipping in East New York when two men tried to rob her and a friend for a dollar. Suzie is not alone. Most of the women report having been raped in the context of sex work and all of them report having been beaten in relation to either sex work or drugs.

[What happened yesterday? (She had a cut face and eye.)] Well, somebody tried to rip me off, two black guys, right there, they came from nowhere I didn't give up the money, they hit me, police came on time (they were passing by) but you know, hey I wasn't givin the money so I told them, you can kill me. They saw me gettin out of the (date's) car . . . They hit me . . . cut me, with a ring or something. I went to the Precinct, I was bleeding. (Rosie)

Although many of the women are currently homeless, which exacerbates their vulnerability to street predators, some are simultaneously victims of intimate abuse, as Patricia's story attests.

And, um, I can imagine myself like waitin til D go to sleep and killin him—caus—I promise myself once I get grown, nobody was gonna beat on me no more. Caus I can't take it. I don't want nobody beatin on me no more. I said, when I get grown nobody's gone ever hit me again . . . Now, it's startin to happen all over again . . . [sobbing] I'm scared, I'm gon kill him, I can't take it . . . I have no place to go, I got no place to go . . . Caus um, you know, he just takes an hit me for nuttin sometime. I mean it just bring back memories you know, and I be askin him "Why are you hitten me?" and then he'll say the same thing my mother say, "Just shut up"—and I cant fuckin take it . . . If there's a god, why, why is he makin me suffer like this? . . . I go in my pocket and give people my last, if I see people sick (dopesick). I share—I share with them. I sell my body and I give him. So, I can't take it . . . either I kill him or I kill me. . . .

5. The Emergence of "Viccing" as a Form of Resistance

The term "viccing" has become as much a part of the lexicon of crack use as more familiar phrases such as "beaming up," "talking to Scotty," "on a mission," "klingons," and "nickelonians." However, the use of robbery as a means of supporting drug consumption by women is not a new phenomenon, nor is it exclusive to crack use.[70] Some women have a long history of robbing dates within the context of income generation for drugs. Rosie told us of her "dope-fiend" days up in the Bronx:

Then I was like robbin more people. [How would you do that—how do you rob somebody?] Well, I was goin with guys, you know, maybe they want to go out and we used to set em up and I used to take em to a place and the guys would take the guy off . . . two guys or one . . . Well, I used to go on the street like, you know stand on the corner, guy come and say "Hey you go out?" (work as a prostitute), and I say yeah and take him to a place . . . to rob them . . . About 1986 . . . I startin gettin sick. [How much dope were you doing?] A bundle. [A day?] Yeah, caus all the money I was gettin . . . for dope. I wasn't even thinkin about clothes or food.

These women clearly distinguished between robbery, sex work and viccing.

There I started doing you know, started workin like a hooker, you know. I mean I was doing the job—I was gettin paid. [Where you were *really* working like a hooker, you weren't robbing or doing stuff?] No, no no—just doing the job and gettin paid you know. (Rosie)

While on face value, "viccing" dates appears to be nothing new, a further examination reveals that it is closely connected with crack-induced shifts in the context of street-level sex work. The fact that the act itself is little different to any other instrumental robbery belies the reality that the motivations undergirding it are more complex and, indeed, are intimately linked with women's collective sense of the devaluation of their bodies and their work. Viccing can be viewed as a way of contesting this devaluation and simultaneously as a means of adaptation to the changed conditions of street-level sex work post-crack.

> I robbed a guy up here not too long ago—5 o'clock Sunday morning . . . a real cheek gonna tell me $5 for a blowjob and that pisses me off—arguing wit them. I don't argue no more—jus get in the car sucker, he open his pants and do like this and I do like this, put my hand, money first. He give me the money I say "See ya, hate to be ya, next time motherfucker it cost you $5 to get me to come to the window" . . . Ain't give em shit for five bucks, you can't get nothing for five bucks . . . I rip off someone if he gonna be cute like that, but I don't rip anybody off . . . I haven't done that often, making a habit, but that guy got me so pissed off. Sunday morning I'm hungry, I'm stressin like a son of a bitch, I got my ride here stressed with me because he ain't done a blast and here come a sucker offer me five bucks an got pocket full of money . . . That's the guy that's *insulting* you and I don't like that . . . Like sorry, if I'm hungry or I'm stressin and I want a blast bad enough. I'll get in the car for $2 if I'm short, don mean you gon get your dick sucked . . . I was hungry, I wanted breakfast and I did it and my girl-friend, she's comin down the block . . . She said I know I saw you do the quick action . . . She said how much you get, I said $2, shit what, I said I'm hungry bitch. Two dollars she said, yeah I'm hungry too—so I bought some potato chips for 50 cents and two bags of 25 cent cookies . . . We both had breakfast for $2 . . . Two bucks he wanted to get laid . . . sonofabitch, imagine that shit and that sucker sit around for about two hours riding around cursin me out for that two dollars. (Candy)

There are, however, consequences attached to viccing dates—not the least of which are "cutting your own throat" and the ever present threat of retaliation.

> Like I lost a steady, he was a $30 blow job, used to come once a week and I was so ill this one day I took him in the bathroom and he paid me and I said "Not this day baby, I'm sorry" and I just took the money and ran down the stairs and he said "Where you goin?" and I said "I'm sorry I'm not in the mood today—later" . . . Now I lost that customer but at that point I didn't give a fuck, I was that sick . . . I just wanted to get mine, get straight and that all I cared about. Now I hurt because I miss that thirty bucks on that Wednesday morning you know. (Candy)

> I had to change my wig and everything. I do too much, do too much wrong—you know, I do too much stealin, rippin off motherfuckers—if dey identify me, I have to change up . . . My hairstyle, my style, have to look different . . . for my safety, do too much wrong. . . . (Felicia)

DISCUSSION

In many ways, recent changes in the structure, functioning and locales of drug markets can be seen as constitutive of changes in the prostitution markets that provide the context for street-level sex work. The city-wide "drying up" and consolidation of drug markets into "drug vortices" is mirrored by parallel shifts in the structure, functioning and locale of sex markets.[72] For example, the "drying up" of drug markets on the Southside has taken its toll on the once busy sex trade and any of the women who worked the stroll on the Southside have followed the drugs down to Bushwick.

The sex markets on which this research focuses have undergone considerable changes. The processes elaborated in this paper illustrate the interconnections or relations of mutual determination both amongst the constituent subeconomies of the informal economy and between the informal economy and the formal economy. They also illustrate how gender relations are conceived and structured within a specific social space. Heightened and exacerbated by the "war on drugs," negative social attitudes towards women are expressed in the victimization of women crack smokers by dates, male smokers, police and neighbourhood youth.[73] As Cookie's account indicates, male youth in particular appear to have internalized the sexist and racist social messages of the "war on drugs."

> [You were telling us that a lot of the young kids out here are beating up and harassing a lot of the crackheads?] Crackheads, dope addicts, and especially prostitutes—they don't like prostitutes . . . You know how much it hurts, you have to stay hit from a lil 11 or 12 year old kid—it happened to me that day . . . and all because they came up on the Avenue that night and I was the only one workin that corner. And they wanted to feel me—they wanted to feel my breasts, feel my ass, you know and then come on—"Let me get some of this, get some of that." I didn't know anything about them— I never seen em before in my life—all I knew was I wasn't about to let no little boy feeling my body you know. So I hit four of them . . . and I got into my dates car and I got away . . . Later on that evening, I'm on D and we're sittin on the ground you know—me and a friend of mine—we smokin and I was turnin him on and I got my back towards P—they came up on me, about six or seven of them . . . Somebody smacks me from the back and I turn around—there's a little kid on me you know—he just started pow pow pow you know, hitting on me and I'm on the ground—that block was full of more people than there's there now—about thirty people—dealers, crackheads, even the ones that just sit around there bullshitting, you know what I mean—everybody—you name it, was there. My people, *my so-called people*—nobody did nothin—everybody. Truly, walked away. In less than a minute, that garage door was empty. I was the only one there and it was the little kids beatin up on me. (Cookie)

What we have tried to illustrate is the need for both women's use of crack and their income generating strategies to be situated within the contexts of their lives. In our sample of street-level crack smokers, this has necessitated a consideration of the relationships between gender, crack, crime and violence as they are played out within the sex markets of the informal economy.

Recent increases in rates of participation by women in "criminal" activities such as robbery and assault may appear on face value to suggest a shift away from traditional female involvements.[74] However, our observations and interviews suggest that they may more accurately reflect an innovative "solution," albeit one that is deeply immersed, entrenched even, in the most traditional category of all—prostitution. . . . Within a context where blow jobs can be had for as little as two or three dollars, robbery, assault and petty larceny are going to be common events—committed against dates and other vics—but committed within a context provided by prostitution as the primary labor market or main hustle for women drug users. Viccing dates, conning guys, and retaliating when male crack users try to intimidate, harrass or rip them off may be forms of adaptation to the market.

Thus, these forms of illicit income generation, which appear to reflect extended criminality and excursions into the male domain, more accurately reflect these women's continued subjugation—not only their marginalization within prostitution, but the impact of recent changes in the sex markets themselves which have exacerbated women's vulnerability to violent victimization and necessitated adaptations in order to survive. Viccing has emerged as a response to these conditions. Rendered peripheral by the sex segmented labour markets of the informal economy and the crack accelerated commodification and devaluation of their bodies, these women make the most of the opportunities that come their way.

If we are correct in assuming that the women in this sample commit their robberies and assaults within the context of the deteriorating conditions of their "main hustle" (prostitution), it becomes important to illustrate their resistance to both localized and broader processes which circumscribe their options. . . . These women have merely sought to utilize the limited opportunities available to them . . . for "getting paid." By viewing and responding to their actions as lawbreaking, we neglect the conditions of their existence and criminalize what are, in effect, women's survival strategies.

CONCLUSION

The advent of crack cocaine can in no way be seen as "emancipatory" for women drug users.[77] Within the informal economy, women have neither been "masculinized" nor have opportunities for illicit income generation expanded or opened up where women are concerned. Within the context of curbside crack distribution and consumption studied here, women remain, for the most part, confined to marginal roles in the drug trade and traditional, even stereotypical, categories of female lawbreaking—prostitution, shoplifting, fraud and theft. . . .

The women we see and interact with neither strip cars nor fight turf battles. Men still very much control the informal economy in these neighbourhoods and the street drug scene in which social and occupational relations are increasingly embedded. Our observations suggest that men tend to monopolize opportunities both for income generation and violence within the informal economy. Moreover, our research lends support to broader theses which suggest that women's "violence" can only be understood within the social and economic context of male dominated structures and relations.

• • •

For women who smoke crack, it appears that any relationship between drug use and violence is overwhelmed by the relationship between masculinity and violence. Street-level sex work has long been recognized as a high risk occupation for violence. As Silbert and Pines have argued, "abuses on the job" constitute more than an occupational hazard and are a form of victimization of street prostitutes.[80] What we have attempted to illustrate are the ways in which the advent of crack cocaine, as an integral part of New York City's expanding informal economy, has accelerated the risks of violent victimization for women drug users. In particular, the "war on drugs" and the internalization of social messages which denigrate "crack heads" as the lowest form of drug lowlife are given expression in the victimization of women by (male) dates, (male) crack smokers, (male) neighbourhood youth and (male) police. In addition to reinforcing the persistent correlation between masculinity and violence in Western cultures, our research suggests that it is not the advent of crack per se, nor its "behavioural effects," that precipitates the violent victimization of these women and their "criminal" responses or resistances. Rather, the stigma which is indelibly attached to being a woman drug user and in particular, a "crack ho" or a "crack bitch," serves to sanction and reinforce at the local level the social legitimacy of violence against women.

Much feminist research has been concerned to demonstrate how women's apparent crime, deviance or other "unacceptable" behaviours, acts, omissions, shortcomings and deficits can be viewed in the context of physical, sexual and economic abuse. To utilize research to point this out is not, however, to take away from women's agency—to present women as mere "effects," rendered "victims" by overarching structures—but rather, to contextualize their agency within the terms of the sometimes conflicting and often complementary structures of patriarchy, racism and capitalism.

Our reading of these women's lives suggests that they are becoming neither more violent nor more "criminal." What they are becoming—within the contexts in which their daily lives and their drug use are situated—is both more vulnerable and more victimized.

NOTES

1. For a review and critical analysis of the "crack epidemic," see C. Reinarman, and H. Levine, "The Crack Attack: Politics and Media in America's Latest Drug Scare," in J. Best (ed), *Images of Issues: Typifying Contemporary Social Problems* (New York: Walter de Gruyter, 1989).

2. For a review, see L. Maher, "Criminalizing Pregnancy: The Downside of a Kinder

Gentler Nation," *Social Justice*, 1990 (17:3), 111–135 and D.E. Roberts, "Punishing Drug Addicts who have Babies: Women of Color, Equality and the Right of Privacy," *Harvard Law Review*, 1991 (194:7), 1419–1482.

⋮

6. ... A freakhouse is a house or apartment where men go to "freak"—both to "smoke lovely" [crack] and to engage in sexual exchanges with any number of women, for which the women receive either crack or money, or both. Freakhouses vary in form, composition and the kinds of exchanges that occur within. ... When women have lost their children, their incomes and their homes, freakhouses often present an alternative to squatting in derelict buildings, sleeping on the streets, in hallways and parks, or in the increasingly dangerous city shelter network. ...

7. We use the term "sex market" to suggest the relations of exchange that occur within the context of street-level prostitution and sex-for-drugs exchanges. These relations are structured by market and nonmarket forces operant at the local level, including social ecology, gender and ethnic composition, opportunities for income generation and the nature and strength of links between the formal and informal sectors.

⋮

13. Drug Abuse Warning Network (DAWN), 1990.

14. See, e.g., J.A. Inciardi, "Beyond Cocaine: Basuo, Crack and Other Coca Products," *Contemporary Drug Problems*, 1987 (14), 461–492; B. Frank et al., *Current Drug Use Trends in New York City: December 1987* (New York: New York State Department of Substance Abuse Services, 1987); P. Bourgois, "In Search of Horatio Alger," *Contemporary Drug Problems*, 1989 (16:4), 619–649; M. Clatts, "Sex for Crack: The Many Faces of Risk within the Street Economy of Harlem," paper presented at the Second Annual AIDS Demonstration Conference, Bethseda, MD.

15. Drug Use Forecasting, *Drugs and Crime in America* (Washington, D.C.: National Institute of Justice, 1990).

16. New York State Department of Correctional Services, *Female Drug Commitment Population 1987–1989* (Albany, New York: Department of Correctional Services, Division of Program Planning, Research and Evaluation, March 1990).

17. B. Frank and W. Hopkins, "Current Drug Use Trends in New York City: June 1989," in Community Epidemiology Work Group, *Epidemiological Trends in Drug Abuse: Proceedings* (Rockville, MD.: National Institute of Drug Abuse, June 1989).

18. Clatts, *op. cit.* Of the 388 women included in this study, 250 were IDUs and the remaining 138 were sex partners of IDUs.

19. See, e.g., A.M. Washton et al., "Crack: Early Report on a New Epidemic," *Postgraduate Medicine*, 1986 (50), 52–58; J. Strang et al., "Crack and Cocaine Use in South London Drug Addicts," *British Journal of Addiction*, 1990 (85), 193–196; Y.W. Cheung et al., "Experience of Crack Use: Findings from a Community-based Sample in Toronto," *Journal of Drug Issues*, 1991 (21:1), 121–140.

20. J. Mondanaro, *Treating Chemically Dependent Women* (Lexington, MA.: Lexington Books, 1988).

21. J.B. Cohen et al., "Women and IV Drugs: Parental and Heterosexual Transmission of Human Immunodeficiency Virus," *The Journal of Drug Issues*, 1989 (19:1), 39–56;

C. Robbins, "Sex Differences in Psychological Consequences of Alcohol and Drug Abuse," *Journal of Health and Social Behavior*, 1989 (30), 117–130.

22. R. Kapila et al., "Women with AIDS/ARC," in Abstracts, II International Conferences on AIDS, Washington, D.C., 1986; D.C. Wright et al., ""HTLV III/LAV Disease in Heterosexual Women," in Abstracts, II International Conference on AIDS, Paris, 1986; H. Minkoff et al., "Pneumocystis Carinii Pneumonia Associated with Acquired Immunodeficiency Syndrome in Pregnancy: A report of Three Maternal Deaths," *Obstetrics and Gynecology*, 1986 (67:2), 284–287; Centers for Disease Control, *AIDS Weekly Surveillance Report*, 3 August 1987, Atlanta, GA; A. Pivnick et al., "Reproductive Decisions among HIV-infected, drug-using Women: The Importance of Mother-child Coresidence," *Medical Anthropology Quarterly*, 1991 (5:2), 153–169.

23. V.J. Binion, *Women's Drug Research Project, Addicted Women: Family Dynamics, Self-perceptions and Support Systems* (Rockville, MD: Services Research Monograph Series, National Institute of Drug Abuse, 1979). See also M. Rosenbaum, *Women on Heroin* (New Brunswick, NJ: Rutgers University Press, 1981).

24. See, e.g., Binion, *op. cit.*, Rosenbaum, *op. cit.* See also J. Covington, "Gender Differences in Criminality among Heroin Addicts," *Journal of Research in Crime and Delinquency*, 1985 (22:4), 329–354.

25. See, e.g., E.S. Gomberg, "Historical and Political Perspective: Women and Drug Use," *Journal of Social Issues*, 1982, (38), 9–23.

26. See, e.g., M.T. and R.E. Fullilove, "Intersecting Epidemics: Black Teen Crack Use and Sexually Transmitted Diseases," *JAMA*, 1989 (44:5), 146–153; B. Sowder and G. Weissman, "NADR Project Revealing New Data on High-risk Behavior among Women," *NADR Network*, 1989 (1:2); D. Worth, "Minority Women and AIDS; Culture, Race and Gender," in D. Feldman (eds), *Culture and AIDS* (New York: Praeger, 1990); A. Kronlicizack, "Update on High-risk Behaviors among Female Sexual Partners of Injection Drug Users." *NADR Network*, (Special Issue), 1990; J.A. Inciardi, "Trading Sex for Crack among Juvenile Crack Users: A Research Note," *Contemporary Drug Problems*, Winter 1989; J.A. Inciardi et al., "Prostitution, IV Drug Use, and Sex-for-crack Exchanges among Serious Delinquents: Risks for HIV Infection," *Criminology*, 1991 (29:2), 221–235; Pivnick et al., *op. cit.*, M. Clatts, "Poverty, Drug Use and AIDS: Converging Lines in the Life Stories of Women in Harlem," in B. Bair and S. Cayleff (eds), *Wings of Gauze: Women of Color and the Experience of Health and Illness* (Wayne State University Press, 1993).

⋮

28. In New York City, where AIDS is currently the leading killer of women aged between 24 and 34 (New York City Department of Health, 1988), at least 120,000 current or former IDU males live with women in heterosexual relationships. See S. Staver, "Minority Women Grappling with Growing AIDS Problem," *American Medical News*, November 1987; Cohen *op. cit.*

29. See, e.g., C.B. Stack, *All Our Kin: Strategies for Survival in a Black Community* (New York: Harper Colophon Books, 1974).

30. S. Belenko et al., *Crack and the New York Courts: A Study of Judicial Responses and Attitudes* (New York: New York City Criminal Justice Agency, 1990).

31. S. Belenko, et al., "Criminal Justice Responses to Crack," *Journal of Research in Crime and Delinquency*, 1989 (28:1) 33–54.

32. Belenko et al., 1990 *op. cit.*

⋮

36. New York State Department of Correctional Services, *Female New Court Com-mitments 1976–1987* (Albany, New York: Department of Correctional Services, Di-vision of Program Planning, Research and Evaluation, 1988).

37. New York State Department of Correctional Services, *Female Drug Commitment Population 1987–1989* (Albany, New York: Department of Correctional Services, Division of Program Planning, Research and Evaluation, 1990).

38. *New York Correctional Association Reporter*, April 1991.

⋮

40. J.R. Fink, "Reported Effects of Crack Cocaine on Infants," *Youth Law News*, 1990 (11:1), 37–39.

41. Office of the Inspector General, *Crack Babies* (Washington, D.C.: OIG, June 1990).

42. A. Bussiere and C. Shauffer, "The Little Prisoners," *Youth Law News*, 1990 (11:1), 22–26.

43. Office of the Inspector General, *op. cit.*, at 15.

⋮

46. For example, a recent analysis of 1988 DUF data indicates that, while male ar-restees in New York had the highest rate of unemployment in 20 cities (57%), fe-male arrestees' rate was even higher, with almost 81% of women arrestees in New York City unemployed. Drug Use Forecasting. *op. cit.*

47. P.B. Dorienger and M. Piore, *Internal Labor Markets and Manpower Analysis* (Lexington, MA: D.C. Heath, 1971).

⋮

53. This thesis gained widespread publicity in 1975 with the publication of F. Adler's *Sisters in Crime: The Rise of the New Female Criminal* (New York: McGraw Hill, 1975). In this book, Adler posits the existence of a causal nexus between changes in the social roles of women attributed to the women's liberation movement and shifts in patterns and rates of women's lawbreaking. . . . The same year, R.J. Si-mon published *Women and Crime* (Lexington, MA: Lexington Books, 1975) ad-vancing what has become known as the "opportunity" thesis. . . . Numerous cri-tiques have been made of these theses. . . . The bulk of this research clearly indicates that neither the status of women lawbreakers nor patterns of female of-fending changed in the wake of women's "liberation." See, e.g., C. Smart, *Women, Crime and Criminology: A Feminist Critique* (London: Routledge and Kegan Paul, 1976); L. Crites (eds), *The Female Offender* (Lexington, MA: Lexington Books, 1976); C. Smart, "The New Female Criminal: Reality or Myth?" *British Journal of Criminology*, 1979 (19), 50–59; J.R. Chapman, *Economic Realities and the Female Offender* (Lexington, MA: Lexington Books, 1980); D. Steffensmeier et al., "Trends in Female Violence 1970–1977," *Sociological Focus*, 1979 (12:3), 217–237; D. Steffensmeier, "Sex Differences in Patterns of Adult Crime 1965–1977: A Review and Assessment," *Social Forces*, 1980 (58), 1080–1108; S.

Box and C. Hale, "Liberation and Female Criminality in England and Wales, *British Journal of Criminology* 1983 (23:1), 35–49; M. Chesney-Lind, "Women and Crime: the Female Offender," *Signs: Journal of Women in Culture and Society*, 1986 (12:1), 78–96.

⋮

58. Names and details of places have been changed in order to protect the anonymity of the women.

59. As Preble and Casey noted (*op. cit.*), heroin addicts in poor communities typically receive local level support by their income generating activities in exchange for providing a supply of cheap goods.

60. M.L. Sullivan, *Getting Over: Economy, Culture and Youth Crime in Three Urban Neighborhoods*, Ph.D. Dissertation, Columbia University (Ann Arbor: University Microfilms International, 1986) at 386.

61. A. Hamid, "Crack: New Directions in Drug Research," *International Journal of the Addictions*, 1991 (26:8), 829–830.

⋮

64. This was confirmed by many of the women in the current study, as well as by women in another Brooklyn site where research was undertaken by the authors on crack use in the context of freakhouses.

⋮

68. See, e.g., Fullilove and Fullilove *op. cit.*, Bourgois *op. cit.*, Clatts *op. cit.*, Inciardi *op. cit.*, and Inciardi et al. *op. cit.* . . .

⋮

70. See, e.g., P.J. Goldstein, *Prostitution and Drugs* (Lexington, MA: Lexington Books, 1979).

⋮

72. New York City has what can be described as a two-tiered system of street-level prostitution: an "exclusive" market concentrated in parts of midtown Manhattan and a hierarchy of second-tier street-level sex markets dispersed throughout the city. Most recently, however, the hierarchy of sex markets within this second tier appears to be breaking down in tandem with the breakdown of street-level drug markets in many neighbourhoods. Some of the second-tier sex markets have dried up, while others have been forced to absorb displaced women, resulting in an increasingly heterogeneous population of street-level sex workers. This process has arguably widened the gulf between the two tiers.

73. See, e.g., *New York Times*, 7/23/90; 9/25/90.

74. See, e.g., I. Sommers and D. Baskins, "The Situational Context of Violent Female Crime," paper presented at the Annual Meetings, American Society of Criminology, San Francisco, November 1991.

⋮

77. cf. Bourgois, *op. cit.* and Clatts, *op. cit.*

⋮

80. M.H. Silbert and A.M. Pines, "Occupational Hazards of Street Prostitutes," *Criminal Justice and Behavior*, 1984 (8:4), 395–399.

CHAPTER **8**

Women's Pathways to Felony Court
Feminist Theories of Lawbreaking and Problems of Representation

KATHLEEN DALY

INTRODUCTION

What brings women defendants to felony court? Why do these women get caught up in crime? How does their behavior become criminalized? Feminist scholars have made substantial strides in analyzing the place of women (or gender) in male-centered theories of lawbreaking, in bringing to light formerly "hidden" violence against women and children, in revealing the ways in which women victims of crime are treated by the justice system, and in challenging the conditions of incarcerated women pending trial or after conviction. A less developed area of feminist inquiry—perhaps the most *un*developed area—is the place of women and gender in *feminist* theories of lawbreaking or in *feminist* theories of justice and punishment for those accused and convicted of crime.

In this article, I want to contribute to a small, but growing, feminist literature on women lawbreakers and make this area more visible for feminist inquiry.[2] My discussion has four parts. In the first part, I sketch a composite of the leading feminist scenario of women's lawbreaking, and I identify the problems feminist scholars face in representing "criminalized women."[3] Part II describes the larger context of my research, the methods used to gather the information on the women, and the limitations of my data. In Part III, I present biographical material from a group of forty women, who were convicted of felonies in the years spanning 1981–1986 in the New Haven felony court. In

Abridged from Kathleen Daly, "Women's Pathways to Felony Court: Feminist Theories of Lawbreaking and Problems of Representation," *Southern California Review of Law and Women's Studies*, Vol. 2, pp. 11-52 (1992). Reprinted by permission of the Southern California Review of Law and Women's Studies. *Ed. note:* Although text and footnotes were deleted, we preserved the footnote numbers that appeared in the original text.

the last part of the article, I discuss how the women's biographies both conform and deviate from the leading feminist scenario. I conclude by summarizing the representational problems for feminist work on criminalized women.

I. FEMINIST REPRESENTATIONS OF WOMEN LAWBREAKERS

A. The Leading Feminist Scenario of Women's Lawbreaking

Little of a systematic nature is known of the biographies and backdrop of events that bring accused women to criminal court. Statistical studies of criminal courts give, at best, a thin account of women defendants' circumstances. At most, the studies may show the women's age, average level of education, paid employment situation, marital status and familial situation, and previous arrests or convictions. Qualitative research studies often focus on the reasoning underlying court officials' decisions.[4] When women's stories appear, they center on the immediate circumstances giving rise to lawbreaking.[5] One could, however, piece together interview studies of girls or women who have been arrested or incarcerated in the United States[6] or in England, Australia, Canada, and several European countries.[7] From this body of work, I constructed a feminist composite, the "leading scenario" of women's lawbreaking.[8]

Whether they were pushed out or ran away from abusive homes, or became part of a deviant milieu, young women begin to engage in petty hustles or prostitution. Life on the street leads to drug use and addiction, which in turn leads to more frequent lawbreaking to support a drug habit. Meanwhile, young women drop out of high school because of pregnancy, boredom or disinterest in school, or both. Their paid employment record is negligible because they lack interest to work in low-paid or unskilled jobs. Having a child may facilitate entry to adult women's networks and allow a woman to support herself in part by state aid. A woman may continue lawbreaking as a result of relationships with men who may also be involved in crime. Women are on a revolving criminal justice door, moving between incarceration and time on the streets. I term this the "street woman" scenario.[9]

The leading feminist scenario is better than previous ideas about women's lawbreaking for three reasons. First, the gendered and sexed contexts that bring adolescents to the street are brought into focus. For young women, this means running away from abusive or overly "strict" parents. Second, the gendered and sexed conditions of survival on the street are recognized. For women, this means that the primary source of their income—their bodies—is also a primary source of their victimization, whether they are victimized by male "clients" or intimates. Third, gender divisions of labor in adult responsibilities are brought into view. For women, this means that their children offer them a significant source of meaning and accomplishment; but women can also lose custody of their children if, in the view of the state, they are not good mothers.[11]

Despite considerable advances in the leading feminist scenario, questions continue to linger. For example, what lies in the "black box" between one's experiences of victimization as a child and of criminal activities as an adult? Is there something more than economic survival which propels or maintains women in a criminalized status? As I read and analyzed the women's biographies in my study, these questions became more pressing.

B. Problems of Representation

It has been easier for feminists to take on male-centered theories of women's lawbreaking than to find alternative theories with which to replace them. Initially, the issue is how to position oneself as a representor of women lawbreakers. Is the implied relationship defined in terms of "we and they"? *Or*, is it "we and us"? *Or*, is it something else? I will not review feminist inquiry on these matters. Instead, I will offer these observations on relations between "representor" and "represented." The "we" of academic feminist inquiry is not a criminalized group, and its class and racial/ethnic composition (among other indices of power) differs greatly from a criminalized group. A power and political relationship is simultaneously clarified and made more nebulous with these terms.[12] For some feminist scholars, there is no difference between "we" and "they." As one woman announced at a Mont Gabriel conference session, "I am an offender, and I am proud to say that." Another said, in a more private setting, "We connect because of our experiences with men who have been violent to us." The source of connection for the first woman is her deviant status in U.S. culture, regardless of whether she is lesbian, poor, or a woman of color. The connection for the latter woman is victimization and harm suffered at the hands of abusive or violent men, typically fathers, male kin, or male intimates. Although these personal experiences do not enter feminist criminological discourse routinely or explicitly, they define how feminists engage with the field of criminology.

While academic feminists' *own* exposure to victimization and criminalization is important, there is another crucial dimension to our enterprise: how we represent the lives and concerns of "others" and whether or not we see connections between these others and ourselves. There are at least five representational issues to consider. The first is terminology: what should we call women who have been arrested for crime? Are they "female criminals" or "female offenders"? Or are they "victims" who become "criminalized"? Or, is their lawbreaking simply "criminalized"? The second is emphasis: which dimension of women's lawbreaking should be emphasized? Some researchers focus on conditions that "criminalize survival," while others cast women as victims of structures and relationships. Still others center their attention on women's "resistance" to oppressive relationships, whether these are intimate, sexual, legal, or in the workplace.[16]

A third representational area is making claims of typicality or generalization. Pat Carlen suggests, for example, that there is "no typical criminal woman."[17] I take this to mean that it is not possible to describe *one* criminalization pattern that holds for all or even most women. But Carlen's comment raises the question of whether it is possible to make general claims or statements about sub-groups of women and variation in their experiences.

The fourth area is the source of representation: what "authority" will be the basis for describing a woman's biography or the circumstances that lead to her lawbreaking? Should it be *only* the woman's account? Can others, such as family members, intimates, counselors, psychologists, court officials, or court advocates be trusted to provide accurate information? If the sources of information differ, is the woman lawbreaker's account privileged over another's account?

A fifth set of representational problems in feminist inquiry is ethical: how much should one divulge about a woman's lawbreaking or her experiences while growing up, and how should that depiction be framed? For example, how much information about a woman's life should be revealed? If one wishes to understand the emotional or psychological dimensions of women's lives, can this be done in a way that does not reproduce the same "psy" script,[18] which casts deviance in individualistic and pathological terms?

These representational problems are central to describing and theorizing women's harms to others in the context of their lives. They pose knotty, vexing, and contentious questions for feminists. Along with my presentation of the New Haven women's biographies, I will describe reactions to my ideas by feminist colleagues. These reveal sources of discomfort in representing criminalized women.[19]

II. THE NEW HAVEN COURT STUDY

Study Method and Data

The women's biographies come from a larger study on problems of equality and justice in criminal courts.[20] I first gathered court information on all the women and a random sample of men whose criminal cases were disposed of by conviction in the New Haven felony court during 1981–1986 . . . From the wide sample, I selected forty women and forty men who were accused and convicted of the same or nearly the same statutory offenses. My aim in selecting this "deep sample" of eighty cases was to compare the sentences of a matched group of men and women, who were accused of similar statutory crimes and convicted (almost all by guilty plea) to similar statutory crimes, who were about the same age, who had previous felony convictions (or not), and who were the same race or ethnicity. The deep sample contains an assortment of seven felony offenses prosecuted in this court: homicide, aggravated assault, risk of injury,[23] arson, robbery, larceny, and drug offenses.

For the eighty deep sample cases, I obtained the presentence investigation reports (PSIs) and transcripts of the remarks made at sentencing. A PSI is a document written by a probation officer to guide the judge at sentencing. In Connecticut, it is a confidential state document, and it normally has a length of three to four single-spaced pages. The PSI contains sections describing the offense, the victim's and defendant's versions of the offense, the victim's desires in sentencing the defendant, the defendant's social history and prior record, the defendant's current work and family situation, mental health history, and drug or alcohol problems, and the probation officer's sentence recommendation. I used the PSI reports to construct a statistical profile of the defendants and an individual biography for each.

• • •

My analysis seeks to transform an abstraction called "the female defendant" into a woman with a biography and set of relations to others. By bringing some detail of a woman's life into view, I hope readers understand the conditions and circumstances that spawn violence and illegal forms of economic gain. Although such biographical context does not excuse, explain, or predict lawbreaking, it renders the women's circumstances palpable, and it gives an empathetic reading of their harms in the context of their lives, many of which are desperate and difficult.

· · ·

III. NEW HAVEN CRIMINALIZED WOMEN: STATISTICAL PROFILE AND BIOGRAPHIES

My portrait of the deep sample women has two parts. The first summarizes their biographies as a group, using a descriptive statistical approach. The second highlights individual pathways to the felony court, using a narrative form.

To develop the statistical portrait, I coded the PSIs with these questions: What were the women's social and economic circumstances growing up? Did they run away from home or finish high school? What was their paid employment record? Did they have children, and did they care for their children? What were their familial and economic circumstances at the time of the offense? Was there evidence of abuse in their household when growing up, or by current or past partners or spouses? Were they addicted to drugs and alcohol, and when did they begin using drugs? Had they been arrested or convicted before? Did they have psychological problems?

· · ·

A. Statistical Profile

The women's average age is twenty-five and ranges from seventeen to sixty years. Of the forty women, twenty-three are black, twelve are white, and five are Puerto Rican or Latin American. In tracing the women's present circumstances, I describe their situations at the time of the instant offense, meaning the offense for which they were convicted when I gathered information on the wide sample of cases in the summer of 1986.

1. Familial circumstances growing up   Half of the women were raised in single-parent families, and the other half, in two-parent families. While one-third were raised by both their biological mothers and fathers, another third were raised by their mothers alone. The remainder had a mix of familial circumstances, having been raised in families with their mothers and stepfathers, their mother's parents, other female kin, or a shift from mothers to state custody or other kin. Only two women could be described as growing up in middle-class households. A little less than half grew up in stable working-class families, while most lived in families whose economic circumstances were precarious. For two-thirds of the women, biological fathers were out of the picture—unknown to the women or not contributing to the support of their families. Physical abuse, toward the defendant or her mother and siblings, characterized the experience of one-third of the women while growing up.

• • •

2. Education, employment, and family   One-third of the women completed high school or the General Education Diploma (G.E.D.) equivalent, and only one woman had a four-year college degree. For those who did not complete high school, the main reason for dropping out was not related to pregnancy. Instead, the PSI narrative suggests a general lack of interest in school, failing grades, and high rates of absenteeism. For some women, a growing disinterest in school was related to a developing drug habit. With or without a high school diploma, three in ten women took additional skill training (e.g., daycare, secretarial work, hair styling). Two-thirds had either a sporadic or no paid employment record; and at the time of the offense, over eighty percent were not employed in a paying job.

About two-thirds of the women gave birth to one or more children, and the women's median age was nineteen to twenty years at the first birth. During the instant offense, thirty-five percent of women had child dependents (and in one case, an elderly parent) whom they cared for on a regular basis; and four in ten were supporting themselves or the children by state aid. . . . Whether in a current or previous relationship, three in ten women had been physically abused by their boyfriends or spouses.

• • •

3. Substance abuse, psychological problems, and prior record   Two-thirds of the women were addicted to alcohol, drugs, or both, and over half of them began their substance abuse at age twenty or younger. About one-third of them developed or continued their drug habit in association with a boyfriend or spouse. While most addicted women (seven in ten) had entered detoxification programs in the past, few had been successful in quitting drug use. Half the women were described as having psychological problems of some sort. These included a general aggressive personality, suicidal gestures, depression, and manic depression, as well as several other unspecified emotional or nervous problems. Fifteen percent had tried to kill themselves.

One-third of the women had never been arrested before, one-third had a moderate record of previous arrests or convictions (which I defined as arrests for one to five incidents), and one-third had more extensive records (six or more incidents). For those who had been previously arrested, the modal age at first contact with juvenile or adult authorities was seventeen to eighteen years. A minority (fifteen percent) were institutionalized in reform schools, mental hospitals, or state homes while in their teens.

Alcohol or drug abuse was typical for these women: It was especially high for women with a record of arrests and convictions. Sources for the probation officers' characterizations of the women's mental problems included the women's family members, school officials, and psychologists, as well as the women's behavior or memory. Thus, I cannot dismiss probation officers' accounts of the women's psychological problems or abnormal behavior (e.g., slashing wrists, hallucinating, jumping out of a window) as convenient ways of labeling the women's deviancy. Contrary to some observers,[39] there is something profoundly more complex than simply a medicalized or psychiatric "labeling" of women in professional discourse. In brief, the women themselves constructed and embraced these categories as a way of resisting and undermining parental (or at times, a male partner's) authority.

B. Biographies

In comparing the women's pathways to the court with the leading scenario, I found that "street women" characterized ten women, or one-fourth of my sample. A more frequent pathway is what I term "harmed-and harming women," with fifteen women falling into that group. I classified the remaining women as battered women (five), drug-connected women (six), and other (four).

· · ·

I begin by introducing the women I term "harmed-and-harming" and "battered." It is easier to show the differences and similarities of these women's pathways to felony court in comparison to the street women.

1. Harmed-and harming women The subgroup name, "harmed-and-harming women," inadequately conveys the physically and emotionally harmful experiences the women experienced while growing up, and the diverse and complex ways in which these experiences are reproduced in the women's harming behavior towards others. Although some women could be described as survivors, their friends or family members may note lingering emotional or psychological problems.

A common experience of harmed-and-harming women was physical or sexual abuse or neglect, and being (or labeled as being) "violent" or "acting out." Her mother, father, or both may have been addicted to alcohol, and her experiences growing up were chaotic and difficult. She may have had several different caretakers. Important loved ones died when she was young. She may have been identified by family members as a "problem child," "hard to manage," or "out of control." Typically, she was abused by an adult male, or neglected or abused by her mother. As she entered her teens, she became violent; alcohol consumption, drug addiction, or a psychological problem amplified an "acting out" or tough demeanor. Her criminal acts occurred when she was unable to control her rage, often when she was drunk or was unable to cope with an immediate situation. She may have a drug addiction or psychological problems. Emotional and psychological damage may have resulted from abusive and alcoholic parents, often in precarious economic circumstances. This, coupled with the women's inability to cope in particular situations, brought a significant portion of women before the felony court.

Fifteen women fell in this category; the following cases illustrate three pathway trajectories. Note that the words or phrases in quotation marks are, unless otherwise indicated, those of the probation officers writing the PSI.

a. Harmed-and-harming women—violence and alcohol

Dee Dee. Among the most desperate biographies was Dee Dee's, a twenty-four-year-old black woman, who stabbed a female acquaintance with a knife, causing serious injury (she pleaded guilty to second-degree assault). Dee Dee's experience while growing up was brutal and chaotic. She was removed from her parent's home and placed in state-supervised care at the age of seven. Her parents were alcoholics and never registered their children in school. Dee Dee and her three siblings were neglected, malnourished, and physically abused. They were first placed in the care of an aunt, but she died when Dee Dee was eleven. Dee Dee was placed in the care of a second aunt for several years, but because this aunt could not effectively control the children, they moved on to another aunt and their third caretaker. By their early teens, Dee Dee and one brother were diagnosed as "emotionally disturbed." She completed eight years of schooling and began to abuse alcohol in her teens. She gave birth to her first child at about the age of seventeen and to her second child when she was twenty-three; but because of a drinking problem, she was unable to care for either child. Just before the birth of her second child, Dee Dee served some time in jail for attempting to burn down a rooming house where her boyfriend lived. Soon after her release from jail, she was convicted of assaulting the same boyfriend. She and two male accomplices slashed the boyfriend with a mirror while he slept. Subsequently, she and the boyfriend were arrested for fighting with one another. Abused by her boyfriend, as well as neglected and abused by her parents, Dee Dee becomes violent when intoxicated. In this latest incident, she and the female victim had been drinking, and in Dee Dee's words, "my temper got over on me."

Latasha. White and nineteen years old, Latasha struck a police officer with a baseball bat as he was trying to arrest her for an assault she had committed earlier in the day against her ex-boyfriend's new girlfriend's mother. Latasha's father was a "severe alcoholic," and her mother said he "screwed up Latasha by using her to get back at me." Her parents separated when she was ten. Described by her mother as "incorrigible," Latasha started to abuse alcohol when she was thirteen. She was married for a short period of time in her teens, but she gave birth to a child by another man when she was eighteen. She was convicted of assault at seventeen. Her current offense occurred because she wanted her infant son back. Her boyfriend and his new girlfriend were living with the child at the girlfriend's mother's house. They believed Latasha was incapable of caring for her child.

· · ·

b. Harmed-and-harming women—violence and drugs

The major difference between the "violence and alcohol" group and "violence and drugs" group of harmed-and-harming women is the link between addiction to illegal drugs and crime. The story of Susan, for example, suggests themes of a harmed-and-harming woman while she was growing up, as well as her own violence toward others. Her addiction to drugs, however, gets her involved in property offenses rather than assaulting others.

Susan. A twenty-one-year-old Puerto Rican woman, Susan's most recent crime was a string of three robberies that she committed just after she was released from jail (she pleaded guilty to one count of first-degree robbery). She grew up in a family of six children. Her father was a "violent and abusive alcoholic," who beat his wife and children. A third-grade teacher described Susan as "aggressive and defiant." After completing six years of school, Susan was supposed to attend an alternative learning center, but the school refused her because of her history of assaultive behavior. She was first arrested at the age of twelve for breach of peace. As a member of a male gang, her role was having sexual relations with prospective gang members. Adjudicated a delinquent at age fifteen, she was placed in a juvenile facility, where she assaulted a staff member and two students. She ran away from this facility several times. She was then placed in a second facility, but she also ran away from there. During this time, a psychiatric evaluation described her as having "the ability to dehumanize her victims," having "no conscience," and being "violently asocial." She was placed in a third juvenile facility where she lived over a year. At this facility, she was described by staff members as "inordinately proud of her illegal activities" and acting "cocky, arrogant, tough, and manipulative." Susan said that she was asked to leave the facility because she triggered an interracial fight, which caused substantial damage to the facility. At the age of sixteen, she was convicted of shooting a teenage girl who resided at this facility. Susan was in jail for two years before being released at the age of eighteen. She was in and out of jail for the next several years because she violated her probation. She abuses both drugs and alcohol, and she seems to have committed her latest offenses to support a drug habit.

• • •

c. Harmed-and-harming women—psychological problems and inability to cope with current circumstances   Of the five women in this group, two were mentally disturbed, two were under the domination of men, and one could not handle the care of her infant. They either could not cope with an immediate situation, or they could not resist the will of a man they loved. None of them had a problem with drugs or alcohol, and with the exception of one woman, none of them had been arrested before. The three women who were convicted of risk of injury (an offense category that, if prosecuted in felony court, encompasses sexual or physical abuse of minors) are in this group of five, and all three had been physically or sexually abused while growing up.

• • •

2. Battered women   Although thirty percent of the women had been in relationships in which their boyfriends or husbands beat them, the five women I call "battered women" would not have appeared before the court had they not been in relationships with violent men.

Sharon. Sharon was sexually and physically assaulted as a child, and as an adult, her "crime" was fighting back against a violent intimate (she pleaded guilty to second-degree assault). Black and twenty-eight years old, Sharon grew up in New York City. She left home after she was raped at age fifteen. The PSI gives few details about the rape, but it appears that her father, an alcoholic, abused Sharon and other family members. Although Sharon's story is classic in terms of running away from an abusive family as an adolescent, she did not run to the streets; instead she was able to make something of herself. She had a child at age eighteen, and although she had completed only eight years of schooling, she trained as a nurse's aid and was steadily employed. Her difficulties began in her early twenties when she began to date Tim. He had a lengthy arrest record and was described as "disruptive, assaultive, and a seriously disturbed individual." They had a child together, but during their seven-year relationship, she "lived under constant harassment" from Tim. She recently tried to commit suicide. The circumstances which led to the current incident were that Tim came to her house drunk and threatened Sharon to let him into her apartment. Although she shot at him, he survived.

• • •

Carrie. Carrie, black and thirty-eight, was arrested for shooting a pistol at her boyfriend when he tried to hit her with his car (she pleaded guilty to reckless endangerment). Raised in the South, and one of twelve children, Carrie moved to New Haven when she was fifteen to live with an older sister. She finished ninth grade, but her arrest record suggests a life on the streets soon after. Her first conviction was for larceny at age seventeen. She was twice convicted for breach of peace at ages eighteen and nineteen, and she served about six weeks in jail. She married when she was twenty-one. At twenty-two she was convicted for prostitution; and at twenty-three, she was convicted for assault with a weapon and shoplifting. She was also convicted of shoplifting at ages twenty-three and twenty-five. She separated from her husband, and in her late twenties, she began to live with Chuck. Chuck had a record of gambling and drug convictions and had served time in jail. They lived together for ten years, and she was severely beaten by him during this period of time. On one occasion she was hospitalized for eleven days. She began abusing cocaine with Chuck; she also abused alcohol. In the last several years, she seemed to be turning her drug and alcohol abuse problems around. During the current incident, witnesses reported that Carrie was crying and yelling at Chuck to leave her alone.

Carrie's biography illustrates the problem of grouping women in one pathway group, either as a street woman, a harmed-and-harming woman, or a battered woman, because all three may characterize a woman's biography. My approach was to decide which feature was more important or overriding in bringing a woman before felony court. In her twenties, Carrie led the life of a street woman. But by the end of her twenties and over the next decade, she was in a relationship with a violent man who, like Carrie, abused cocaine.

3. Street women   The group I call "street women" had their share of physical and psychological damage while growing up or in their current relationships.

I distinguish a harmed-and-harming woman from a street woman in the following way: the latter eke out a living on the street, usually by a hustle. Many street women support their drug addiction by prostitution, theft, or selling drugs. Consequently, their arrest and conviction record is heavier, and they have spent time in jail. They did not get along with their parents, and many attempted to escape their parental situation as early as they could.

Kate. A thirty-five-year-old white woman, Kate fits the street woman profile in all respects. She and a black female accomplice held up a man on the street (first-degree robbery). Soon after Kate was born, her mother ended a twenty-year marriage to a man whom she described as "very bad" because he drank too much, gambled, and was a "womanizer." He beat her and her two sons. Although Kate's mother says her second spouse was a "good father," he too was an alcoholic. When Kate was growing up, her mother recalls that Kate had many problems in school; she ran away from home and associated with "negative influences." Kate describes herself as rebellious and unmanageable. She became distant from her family as an adolescent. She was placed in a residential program for problem children when she was twelve years old. When she was sixteen, Kate had a child, whom she gave up for adoption. During that same year, she was arrested for breach of peace. Since then, she has been convicted at least fifteen times for offenses such as prostitution, disorderly conduct, and drug offenses. She became part of the street life in her late teens. She drank heavily and was a heroin addict. She was in and out of prison starting from the age of twenty, spending three months to over a year incarcerated at a stretch. When she was twenty-four, she gave birth to a second child. Around that time she attempted to detoxify. She was able to care for her second child, and when she was thirty, she gave birth to a third child. The father of her third child beat her. He left the state and assumed custody of their child. The father of her second child takes care of that child; he would like to reconcile with Kate if she gave up drugs and left the street life. Kate's latest offense came about because she needed money to support her drug habit.

• • •

Penny. Penny, a twenty-four-year-old black woman, exemplifies the allure of selling drugs (sale of narcotics). Raised in a stable working-class family, her mother was the family's sole support. Although Penny did not complete high school, she obtained some vocational training. She began using drugs at sixteen and was a regular cocaine user by nineteen. Because she sniffs heroin instead of injecting it, she sees herself in control of her habit. For this reason, she has no interest in drug treatment. Described by the probation officer as "opting to lead a street life existence since mid-adolescence" and as being irresponsible because she sees "nothing wrong with her lifestyle or drug usage," Penny has sold drugs since the age of nineteen. She says that there is more money in dealing drugs than in working, and she views drug trafficking as a job in which she can get "the finer things of life." She claims that on a good day she can earn as much as $2,000. Penny was more confident of herself than most of the deep sample women. There was no indication that she suffered abuse as a child. She currently feels "in control" of her drug habit, and she is not in a relationship with a man who abuses her or is addicted to drugs.

. . .

With the exception of Penny, all the street women had a serious drug addiction. They supported their addiction through prostitution, drug sale, theft, and robbery. All but two were arrested for the first time in their late teens. For most, drug and alcohol use was part of the street scene. All of the women in the next group of "drug-connected women" were using or selling drugs in connection with boyfriends and family members. None of them is a street woman yet.

4. Drug-connected women The five drug-connected women used or sold drugs as a result of their relations with boyfriends or family members. Even the probation officers attributed the women's lawbreaking to the men in their lives. None of the women seems to be drug-addicted; their drug use is recent and experimental, and their arrest record is slim.

Winnie. Winnie, who is white and eighteen, grew up in a middle-class household; she stole silverware from her parents (first-degree larceny). She was a model student and had no problems at home until, at the age of sixteen, she started seeing Sam. Winnie continued to see Sam against her parents' wishes. Eventually, her parents evicted her from the house because they could not "tolerate her negative behavior." During her relationship with Sam, Winnie began to abuse alcohol and drugs. At seventeen, she married Sam, lived with his parents, and got pregnant. Sam and his parents wanted her to have the child, but her parents did not. She was hospitalized for depression for several months after she had an abortion. While married, she lived with her parents several times and stole from them to support Sam and herself. Her current arrest was a result of pawning her parents' silverware, estimated to be worth over $25,000 in value, for $200. Her parents said they never want to see her again.

. . .

5. Other Four women's biographies did not fit the profile of street, harmed-and-harming, battered, or drug-connected women. None of the women seems to have a problem with drugs or alcohol. The two women I have detailed information on did not grow up in damaging environments. None has been arrested before. Their offenses had economic motives unrelated to drug addiction or to a street life. Detailed biographical information is missing for two women, but the nature of their acts, the lack of prior records, and the lack of a drug or alcohol problem suggest their crimes arose from a simple desire for more money.

Prish. White and in her late forties, Prish recalls having a normal childhood and growing up in a working-class household. She was raised by her parents until they divorced when Prish was twelve. Her mother soon remarried. Prish is the only woman in the deep sample to have completed a four-year college degree. She married three times but never had children. Her most recent marriage to Michael took place when Prish was in her late thirties. Although he is a manic depressive, his condition is regulated by drugs, and their marriage is described as happy and stable. Soon after their marriage, Prish began working as a bookkeeper and office manager for a car dealership, the organizational victim in this offense. She worked there for eleven years. She made a good salary and seemed to have no gambling, drug, or other psychological problems. Prish has never been arrested before. Although she and her husband were building a house, they had no major debts. She embezzled over $125,000 from an employer during the last six years of her employment (first-degree larceny). While out on bond and awaiting trial, she secured another bookkeeping job with another car dealership in the area.

Maggie. Maggie, a black woman, was twenty-three years old when she and a male accomplice robbed an elderly man for whom Maggie had previously worked (first-degree robbery and kidnapping). Maggie and her brother (who has been incarcerated on a rape conviction) were raised by her mother's parents on a farm in the South while Maggie's mother lived in New Haven and provided economic support for her children. Maggie's mother returned to live with her children in the South when they were in their teens. Maggie is described as having "positive feelings toward her family." She finished high school, moved to New Haven after graduation, and completed a hair styling course. She worked in a manufacturing company for a year, and she was also a part-time companion sitter for an elderly woman. She gave birth to a child about six months before her current offense and supported the infant through state aid. The robbery victim knew Maggie because she had answered his advertisement to clean and care for an elderly man. It seems that she also had sexual relations with him for money. Maggie has never been arrested before, and she has no problem with drugs or alcohol. Her actions in this robbery, in which she wore a ski mask to hide her identity, wielded a butcher knife, ransacked the victim's house for valuables, and forced the victim into a car to get money with his bank card, suggest that something more than economic gain was involved. Although she says she was "desperate" and "didn't like being on [state aid]," she admits she "went there to scare the guy." I wondered if she also sought revenge because the victim had "pushed" her for sexual contact.

IV. SUMMARY AND DISCUSSION

A. Rethinking the Leading Scenario

My analysis of the New Haven women's biographies suggests that ten of them clearly fit the street woman model. Additionally, five other women may have street woman elements in their biographies. Allowing for the fact that the deep sample underrepresents women convicted of drug offenses, who are likely to be street women, I would estimate that no more than half of the women prosecuted in urban felony courts arrived by the street woman pathway.

• • •

Based on this group of female felons, I would not argue that the leading feminist "street woman" model is toppled. On the contrary, such a pathway is likely to be more common for women prosecuted in district or misdemeanor courts, where most criminal cases are disposed, than in felony courts. But I would argue for a more multidimensional portrait of why women get caught up in crime. In addition to the street woman pathway, there are other routes to felony court.

These routes include:

1. Abuse or neglect suffered as a child, or an "out of control" or violent nature, coupled with alcohol or drug abuse and psychological problems. The harmed-and-harming women tend to anger easily or become violent when drinking; they have difficulties caring for their children or being independent from dominating men.

2. Being (or having been) in a relationship with a violent man. Although a minority pathway to the court, this group of women has no other biographical element except being in a relationship with an abusive man.

3. Being around boyfriends, mates, or family members who use or sell drugs; or wanting more money for a more economically secure and conventional life.

I am struck by the content and consequences of the harmed-and-harming women's lives. This is where the street woman scenario can be misleading in overemphasizing the effects of criminalizing drugs or poverty. Having suffered abuse as children or adolescents, girls or young women not only run away from home to survive on the streets, they may also be emotionally crippled. Psychological problems, addiction to alcohol, and a violence-prone temperament coalesce to form a tough, violent, or abusive attitude toward others. At issue for the group of harmed-and-harming women is not just that their survival or poverty is criminalized[45] but that their anger or violence is criminalized.

Cathy Widom's research on the relationship between child abuse or neglect and adult arrest for crime shows that sixteen percent of girls who were officially adjudicated abused or neglected were arrested as adults, while the arrest rate for the control group (girls who were not adjudicated as neglected or abused) was lower, at nine percent.[46] Although one may question how the "abused/neglected" group is distinguished from the control group, or the use of adult arrest data as an indication of lawbreaking, Widom's research is the most rigorous to date in demonstrating that abused or neglected children are more likely to be involved with (or arrested for) crime as adults. Her study also suggests offense-based variability in arrest patterns for the abused/neglected and control groups of women. Specifically, she finds that as adults, abused/neglected females were not at "increased risk" to be arrested for violent offenses, although they were at increased risk to be arrested for property, drug, and public order offenses.[47]

Although the numbers are small, the New Haven women's biographies further explain Widom's findings for women arrested for violent offenses. Of the twenty-five women prosecuted for violent offenses (using Widom's definition of violence, which includes robbery), five were reacting to or fending off violent men. Thus, although Widom suggests that abused women turn their aggression inward more than men (e.g., resulting in psychiatric hospitalization), she fails to consider another important aspect of women's violence. Some women's aggression is spawned during adulthood in their relations with abusive and violent men, who precipitate the violence.

The offenses bringing a significant minority of women to the New Haven felony court were not in pursuit of economic gain. Instead, some women could not cope with their immediate circumstances, and some reacted violently when they believed others would harm them or when their honor was impugned.

· · ·

To the street woman scenario of hustling in the shadow of the law, we need to consider a number of the harmed-and-harming women (nine of fifteen) who did not commit crimes in the pursuit of economic gain. Instead, they were angry and harmed others. We also need to consider those women who may not have been abused or neglected as children, but who now suffer and respond to such violence at the hands of their mates. These women's experiences as victims and victimizers cannot be explained simply by economic conditions or struggles to survive economically. Rather, they reflect a process of reproducing physical and emotional harm.

B. Feminist Representations of Criminalized Women

As Mary Gilfus found in her interviews of incarcerated women, the boundaries between victim and offender are often blurred in describing the pathways of girls to the street and to the penal system.[50] The New Haven women's biographies are consistent with this theme not only because there is a connection between women's abuse by their families and running away to the streets, but also because women are victimized as adults by violent men. The concept of "blurred boundaries" is an important feminist contribution to the field of criminology. But, by joining victimization and criminalization, feminist scholars evade core questions about the conceptual status of "crime offender" and "crime victim."

For example, how should feminist scholars represent women who abuse, harm, or hurt others? Or women who steal from others? How should the idea of "responsibility" relate to these acts, or would feminist legal or criminological scholars propose a different definition of "responsibility"? These questions are difficult to contemplate because feminist work in crime and justice has focused almost exclusively on women's legal status and experiences as victims. Not surprisingly, initial feminist efforts to describe women lawbreakers discussed these women's acts in the context of their economic survival and their history of physical or sexual victimization. But where does victimization end and responsibility for acts that harm others begin? How do we characterize women when they do things that are wrong? A seamless web of victimization and criminalization tends to produce accounts which focus on victimization and leave little agency, responsibility, or meaning to women's lawbreaking.

Some feminist accounts of women's lawbreaking have created an unexplained "black box" between women's experiences growing up and their lawbreaking as adults. For example, a John Jay Forum[55] participant, who works with incarcerated women, said (paraphrasing): "We know that most women (in prison) were sexually or physically abused as children. Are there connections? I think there are."[56] As I listened to this woman, I wondered, what were the connections she assumed we should make? Was it a behavioral connection that women's harms to others were more explicable in light of the harms visited on them in the past? Or, was it a political connection of seeing incarcerated women, in general, as victims rather than victimizers?

Feminist scholars need to contemplate these and other possibilities in the victimization-criminalization "black box." At the same time, we should also consider how our analyses of women lawbreakers can be applied to men. Consider, for example, how "blurred boundaries" may be used to explain men's physical or sexual abuse of women or children. If we find that these men were physically or sexually abused while growing up, will we view them as both victimized and victimizing? In suggesting that feminist scholars should consider both men and women, not simply women, I am not proposing that we conceptualize men and women lawbreakers (or victims) in the same way. I am proposing that we abandon the implied gender-based overlay on victimization and criminalization (i.e., woman/victim; man/lawbreaker). Further, we must consider questions of redress or justice, not simply from the victim's viewpoint, but from both the victim's and lawbreaker's point of view.[59]

Recalling the five representational issues for feminists noted in Part I, there is terminology, emphasis, generalization, authoritative sources, and ethical matters. I conclude by discussing these five issues in light of research on women lawbreakers. With respect to *terminology*, "criminalized women" is today the preferred feminist term for accused, convicted, or sentenced women. This term is good for emphasizing the state's role in constructing crime, but it may be inadequate for describing noneconomic harms. Criminalized women also eludes questions of responsibility for harms. With respect to *emphasis*, scholars should pay more attention to the diverse pathways to lawbreaking and criminalization, and not focus solely on crime as work.

On the matter of *generalization*, it is crucial that feminist scholars plan research studies in such a way that we can be comfortable in making generalizations. Not all (or even most) research need be carried out with traditional social science concerns for generalization. Feminist approaches to gaining knowledge and producing data should be varied. At a minimum, some feminist scholars, especially those in law and the humanities, need to familiarize themselves with basic social science concepts, such as the meaning of "statistical significance" and the difference between making a generalization and making a "universalizing claim."[60]

With respect to *authoritative sources*, the time has come to suspend belief on "women's own stories" and resist privileging any one account of a biography. My proposal may seem heretical to feminist inquiry, but in reality it is not. My concern is that we do not succumb to an empiricist notion that women's "own stories" or accounts of themselves are closest to "the truth" or "the reality" of their lives. Such an approach can be useful as part of a collective experience of feminist consciousness raising, but as a method of gathering information about women's lives and behaviors, it alone is not satisfactory. Finally, the *ethical* question of how much to reveal about criminalized women's lives without lapsing into "voyeurism and vivisection"[62] cannot be assessed in the abstract. Rather, it must be considered carefully by every researcher when presenting material on these women.

Sandra Harding's concluding sentence in THE SCIENCE QUESTION IN FEMINISM[63] captures the magnitude of the task facing feminists in crime and justice: "I doubt that in our wildest dreams we ever imagined we would have to reinvent both science and theorizing itself in order to make sense of women's social experience."[64] For feminists working within and against the law and criminology, we are going to have to reinvent ideas about crime, punishment, and justice.

NOTES

⋮

2. I first presented the ideas discussed in this article at the International Feminist Conference on Women, Law, and Social Control, Mont Gabriel, Quebec (July 1991) [hereinafter Mont Gabriel Conference]. See PROCEEDINGS OF THE INTERNATIONAL CONFERENCE ON WOMEN, LAW, AND SOCIAL CONTROL, (Marie Andrée Bertrand, Kathleen Daly, & Dorie Klein eds., 1992). . . .

3. The concept "criminalized" is used by feminist and progressive analysts of crime to highlight the fact that women or men who are caught up in penal processes (i.e., arrested, convicted, or imprisoned) are not only lawbreakers, but have also been subjected to state officials' powers to arrest and punish. . . .

4. *E.g.*, as in my studies (by interview) of court officials, Kathleen Daly, *Rethinking Judicial Paternalism: Gender, Work-Family Relations, and Sentencing*, 3 GENDER & SOC'Y 9 (1989); Kathleen Daly, *Structure and Practice of Familial-Based Justice in a Criminal Court*, 21 LAW & SOC. REV. 267 (1987); and also in studies by Carol Smart, *Legal Subjects and Sexual Objects: Ideology, Law and Female Sexuality*, in WOMEN IN LAW: EXPLORATIONS IN LAW, FAMILY AND SEXUALITY 50 (Julia Brophy & Carol Smart eds., 1985); Coramae Richey Mann, *Race and Sentencing of Female Felons: A Field Study*, 7 INT'L. J. OF WOMEN'S STUD. 160 (1984).

5. *See, e.g.,* HILARY ALLEN, JUSTICE UNBALANCED: GENDER, PSYCHIATRY AND JUDICIAL DECISIONS (1987); MARY EATON, JUSTICE FOR WOMEN?: FAMILY; COURT AND SOCIAL CONTROL (1986); ANNE WORRALL, OFFENDING WOMEN: FEMALE LAWBREAKERS AND THE CRIMINAL JUSTICE SYSTEM (1990).

6. I draw from these studies: ANNE CAMPBELL, THE GIRLS IN THE GANG (2d ed. 1991); JANE ROBERTS CHAPMAN, ECONOMIC REALITIES AND THE FEMALE OFFENDER (1980); ELEANOR M. MILLER, STREET WOMAN (1986); MARSHA ROSENBAUM, WOMEN ON HEROIN (1981); Regina A. Arnold, *Processes of Victimization and Criminalization of Black Women*, 17 SOC. JUST. 153 (1990); Meda Chesney-Lind, *Girls' Crime and Women's Place: Toward a Feminist Model of Female Delinquency*, 35 CRIME &

DELINQ. 5 (1989); Meda Chesney-Lind & Noelie Rodriguez, *Women under Lock and Key: A View from the Inside*, 63 THE PRISON J. 47 (1983); Mary Gilfus, *From Victims to Survivors to Offenders: Women's Routes of Entry and Immersion into Street Crime*, 4 WOMEN & CRIM. JUST. (1992); Kim Romenesko & Eleanor M. Miller, *The Second Step in Double Jeopardy: Appropriating the Labor of Female Street Hustlers*, 35 CRIME & DELINQ. 109 (1989).

7. CRIMINAL WOMEN (Pat Carlen ed., 1985) [hereinafter Carlen, CRIMINAL WOMEN]; GENDER, CRIME AND JUSTICE (Pat Carlen & Anne Worrall eds., 1987); GROWING UP GOOD (Maureen Cain ed., 1989); TOO FEW TO COUNT (Ellen Adelberg & Claudia Currie eds., 1987); PAT CARLEN, WOMEN, CRIME AND POVERTY (1988) [hereinafter CARLEN, WOMEN, CRIME], Christine Alder, *"Unemployed Women Have Got It Heaps Worse": Exploring the Implications of Female Youth Unemployment*, 19 AUSTI., & N.Z. J. OF CRIMINOLOGY 210 (1986). Good reviews of the literature, with a focus on United States and British studies, are: FRANCES HEIDENSOHN, WOMEN AND CRIME (1985); ALLISON MORRIS, WOMEN, CRIME AND CRIMINAL JUSTICE (1987); Meda Chesney-Lind, *Women and Crime: The Female Offender*, 12 SIGNS: J. OF WOMEN IN CULTURE & SOC'Y 78 (1986).

8. Unlike other areas of feminist inquiry, the invisibility of women of color, especially black women, is not at issue in studies of crime and justice. The problem is how to address racial specificity without contributing to racist imagery. Like black men's share of men incarcerated, black women are half of the women incarcerated in the United States. Much of the theorizing on gender differences in crime or justice system practices, particularly for recent studies of urban populations, is about gender differences among populations of color. . . .

9. "Street woman" comes from the title of Miller's book, *supra* note 6.

⋮

11. I present these terms in such a way that the *gendered* push-pull patterns to the street, the conditions of surviving on the street, and the civil and penal powers of the state are highlighted. Each area affects men and women, but in gender-specific ways. Note, too, that my statements about men and women are keyed to gender relations *within* race and class groups.

12. *See* Talking about Women and Crime Forum, held at John Jay College of Criminal Justice, New York City, (Dec. 1991) [hereinafter John Jay Forum]. In two morning sessions, academics presented research on criminalized women, and in an afternoon session, practitioners and activists described their work. The latter group, which comprised some ex-prisoners, challenged the academics' implicit relational posture of "we" (academics) versus "they" (criminalized women). In the relationships among researchers, practitioners, activists, and criminalized women, identity politics as a basis of connection or cleavage is less at issue. More fundamental is how researchers plan studies and use research to promote change on behalf of criminalized people. For example, one participant at the John Jay Forum said that a good deal of research on criminalized women is "voyeurism and vivisection"; she called for "research to build a constituency" that seeks change.

⋮

16. MILLER, *supra* note 6, and Chesney-Lind, *supra* note 6, focus on the criminalizing of survival; CHAPMAN, *supra* note 6, and Gilfus, *supra* note 6, focus on the impact

of women's economic or physical victimization; and Arnold, *supra* note 6, analyzes women's lawbreaking as resistance.

17. Carlen, CRIMINAL WOMEN, *supra* note 7, Introduction.

18. The idea of "psy" professional discourse is developed by Carol Smart, drawing from Michel Foucault's ideas of how legal, medical, and psychiatric discourse serve to discipline and control members of subordinate groups. *See* CAROL SMART, FEMINISM AND THE POWER OF LAW (1989).

19. In this sentence and elsewhere, "representing" may also connote a defense attorney's relationship to a woman defendant. With the exception of legal feminists' research and writing on "women's self-defense work" (*see, e.g.*, Elizabeth M. Schneider, *Describing and Changing: Women's Self-Defense Work and the Problem of Expert Testimony on Battering*, 9 WOMEN'S RTS. L., REP. 195 (1986)), little else has been written on the relationship between feminist defense attorneys and criminalized women.

20. KATHLEEN DALY, GENDER, CRIME, AND PUNISHMENT. (1994).

⋮

23. The "risk of injury" statute broadly includes any harm to a minor, but normally, the prosecuted cases are physical and sexual abuse of children.

⋮

39. *See, e.g.*, EDWIN M. SCHUR, LABELING WOMEN DEVIANT: GENDER, STIGMA, AND SOCIAL CONTROL (1984).

⋮

45. *See* CARLEN, WOMEN, CRIME, *supra* note 7, and Chesney-Lind, *supra* note 6.

46. Cathy Spatz Widom, *Child Abuse, Neglect, and Violent Criminal Behavior*, 27 CRIMINOLOGY 251 (1989). Widom also finds differences between black and white women with a higher proportion of abused/neglected black women than abused/neglected white women (28% and 17%, respectively) having been arrested as adults in comparison to the control groups of black women and white women (19% and 11%, respectively). *Id.* at 263. Racial differences for the *oldest* of the four age groups are shown in Widom's Table 3. *Id.*

47. *Id.* at 264.

⋮

50. Gilfus, *supra* note 6.

⋮

55. *See supra* note 12 and accompanying text.

56. A John Jay Forum participant in the afternoon session, *supra* note 12.

⋮

59. *See* Kathleen Daly, *Criminal Justice Ideologies and Practices in Different Voices: Some Feminist Questions about Justice*, 17 INT. J. SOC. L. 1 (1989), elaborating and criticizing Carol Gilligan's "different voice" formulation (presented in IN A DIFFERENT VOICE (1982)) to aid feminists in reconstructing justice systems.

⋮

60. For example, in an otherwise wonderful essay on legal feminists' uses of narrative, Kathryn Abrams misuses concepts of generalization, universalizing, and statistical significance. See Abrams, "Hearing the Call of Stories," 79 *Cal. L. Rev* 971 (1991).

⋮

62. A John Jay Forum participant, *supra* note 12.
63. SANDRA HARDING, THE SCIENCE QUESTION IN FEMINISM (1986).
64. *Id.* at 251.

PART III

MASCULINITIES AND VIOLENCE

CHAPTER 9

Fraternities and Rape on Campus

Patricia Yancey Martin
Robert A. Hummer

Rapes are perpetrated on dates, at parties, in chance encounters, and in specially planned circumstances. That group structure and processes, rather than individual values or characteristics, are the impetus for many rape episodes was documented by Blanchard (1959) many years ago (also see Geis 1971), yet sociologists have failed to pursue this theme (for an exception, see Chancer 1987). A recent review of research (Muehlenhard and Linton 1987) on sexual violence, or rape, devotes only a few pages to the situational contexts of rape events, and these are conceptualized as potential risk factors for individuals rather than qualities of rape-prone social contexts.

Many rapes, far more than come to the public's attention, occur in fraternity houses on college and university campuses, yet little research has analyzed fraternities at American colleges and universities as rape-prone contexts (cf. Ehrhart and Sandler 1985). Most of the research on fraternities reports on samples of individual fraternity men. One group of studies compares the values, attitudes, perceptions, family socioeconomic status, psychological traits (aggressiveness, dependence), and so on, of fraternity and nonfraternity men (Bohrnstedt 1969; Fox, Hodge, and Ward 1987; Kanin 1967; Lemire 1979; Miller 1973). A second group attempts to identify the effects of fraternity membership over time on the values, attitudes, beliefs, or moral precepts of members (Hughes and Winston 1987; Marlowe and Auvenshine 1982; Miller 1973; Wilder, Hoyt, Doren, Hauck, and Zettle 1978; Wilder, Hoyt, Surbeck, Wilder, and Carney 1986). With minor exceptions, little research addresses the group and organizational context of fraternities or the social construction of fraternity life (for exceptions, see Letchworth 1969; Longino and Kart 1973; Smith 1964).

Reprinted from Patricia Yancey Martin and Robert A. Hummer, "Fraternities and Rape on Campus," *Gender and Society*, Vol. 3, No. 4, pp. 457–473, © 1989. Reprinted by Permission of Sage Publications, Inc.

Gary Tash, writing as an alumnus and trial attorney in his fraternity's magazine, claims that over 90 percent of all gang rapes on college campuses involve fraternity men (1988, p. 2). Tash provides no evidence to substantiate this claim, but students of violence against women have been concerned with fraternity men's frequently reported involvement in rape episodes (Adams and Abarbanel 1988). Ehrhart and Sandler (1985) identify over 50 cases of gang rapes on campus perpetrated by fraternity men, and their analysis points to many of the conditions that we discuss here. Their analysis is unique in focusing on conditions in fraternities that make gang rapes of women by fraternity men both feasible and probable. They identify excessive alcohol use, isolation from external monitoring, treatment of women as prey, use of pornography, approval of violence, and excessive concern with competition as precipitating conditions to gang rape (also see Merton 1985; Roark 1987).

The study reported here confirmed and complemented these findings by focusing on both conditions and processes. We examined dynamics associated with the social construction of fraternity life, with a focus on processes that foster the use of coercion, including rape, in fraternity men's relations with women. Our examination of men's social fraternities on college and university campuses as groups and organizations led us to conclude that fraternities are a physical and sociocultural context that encourages the sexual coercion of women. We make no claims that all fraternities are "bad" or that all fraternity men are rapists. Our observations indicated, however, that rape is especially probable in fraternities because of the kinds of organizations they are, the kinds of members they have, the practices their members engage in, and a virtual absence of university or community oversight. Analyses that lay blame for rapes by fraternity men on "peer pressure" are, we feel, overly simplistic (cf. Burkhart 1989; Walsh 1989). We suggest, rather, that fraternities create a sociocultural context in which the use of coercion in sexual relations with women is normative and in which the mechanisms to keep this pattern of behavior in check are minimal at best and absent at worst. We conclude that unless fraternities change in fundamental ways, little improvement can be expected.

METHODOLOGY

Our goal was to analyze the group and organizational practices and conditions that create in fraternities an abusive social context for women. We developed a conceptual framework from an initial case study of an alleged gang rape at Florida State University that involved four fraternity men and an 18-year-old coed. The group rape took place on the third floor of a fraternity house and ended with the "dumping" of the woman in the hallway of a neighboring fraternity house. According to newspaper accounts, the victim's blood-alcohol concentration, when she was discovered, was .349 percent, more than three times the legal limit for automobile driving and an almost lethal amount. One law enforcement officer reported that sexual intercourse occurred during the time the victim was unconscious: "She was in a life-threatening situation" (*Tallahassee Democrat*, 1988b). When the victim was found, she was comatose and had suffered multiple scratches and abrasions. Crude words and a fraternity symbol had been written on her thighs (*Tampa Tribune*, 1988). When law enforcement officials tried to investigate the case, fraternity members refused to cooperate. This led, eventually, to a five-year ban of the fraternity from campus by the university and by the fraternity's national organization.

In trying to understand how such an event could have occurred, and how a group of over 150 members (exact figures are unknown because the fraternity refused to provide a membership roster) could hold rank, deny knowledge of the event, and allegedly lie to a grand jury, we analyzed newspaper articles about the case and conducted open-ended interviews with a variety of respondents about the case and about fraternities, rapes, alcohol use, gender relations, and sexual activities on campus. Our data included over 100 newspaper articles on the initial gang rape case; open-ended interviews with Greek (social fraternity and sorority) and non-Greek (independent) students (N = 20); university administrators (N = 8, five men, three women); and alumni advisers to Greek organizations (N = 6). Open-ended interviews were held also with judges, public and private defense attorneys, victim advocates, and state prosecutors regarding the processing of sexual assault cases. Data were analyzed using the grounded theory method (Glaser 1978; Martin and Turner 1986). In the following analysis, concepts generated from the data analysis are integrated with the literature on men's social fraternities, sexual coercion, and related issues.

FRATERNITIES AND THE SOCIAL CONSTRUCTION OF MEN AND MASCULINITY

Our research indicated that fraternities are vitally concerned—more than with anything else—with masculinity (cf. Kanin 1967). They work hard to create a macho image and context and try to avoid any suggestion of "wimpishness," effeminacy, and homosexuality. Valued members display, or are willing to go along with, a narrow conception of masculinity that stresses competition, athleticism, dominance, winning, conflict, wealth, material possessions, willingness to drink alcohol, and sexual prowess vis-à-vis women.

Valued Qualities of Members

When fraternity members talked about the kind of pledges they prefer, a litany of stereotypical and narrowly masculine attributes and behaviors was recited and feminine or woman-associated qualities and behaviors were expressly denounced (cf. Merton 1985). Fraternities seek men who are "athletic," "big guys," good in intramural competition, "who can talk college sports." Males "who are willing to drink alcohol," "who drink socially," or "who can hold their liquor" are sought. Alcohol and activities associated with the recreational use of alcohol are cornerstones of fraternity social life. Nondrinkers are viewed with skepticism and rarely selected for membership.[1]

Fraternities try to avoid "geeks," nerds, and men said to give the fraternity a "wimpy" or "gay" reputation. Art, music, and humanities majors, majors in traditional women's fields (nursing, home economics, social work, education), men with long hair, and those whose appearance or dress violate current norms are rejected. Clean-cut, handsome men who dress well (are clean, neat, conforming, fashionable) are preferred. One soroity woman commented that "the top ranking fraternities have the best looking guys."

One fraternity man, a senior, said his fraternity recruited "some big guys, very athletic" over a two-year period to help overcome its image of wimpiness. His fraternity had won the interfraternity competition for highest grade-point average several years running but was looked down on as "wimpy, dancy, even gay." With their bigger, more athletic recruits, "our reputation improved; we're a much more recognized fraternity now." Thus a fraternity's reputation and status depends on members' possession of stereotypically masculine qualities. Good grades, campus leadership, and community service are "nice" but masculinity dominance—for example, in athletic events, physical size of members, athleticism of members—counts most.

Certain social skills are valued. Men are sought who "have good personalities," are friendly, and "have the ability to relate to girls" (cf. Longino and Kart 1973). One fraternity man, a junior, said: "We watch a guy [a potential pledge] talk to women . . . we want guys who can relate to girls." Assessing a pledge's ability to talk to women is, in part, a preoccupation with homosexuality and a conscious avoidance of men who seem to have effeminate manners or qualities. If a member is suspected of being gay, he is ostracized and informally drummed out of the fraternity. A fraternity with a reputation as wimpy or tolerant of gays is ridiculed and shunned by other fraternities. Militant heterosexuality is frequently used by men as a strategy to keep each other in line (Kimmel 1987).

Financial affluence or wealth, a male-associated value in American culture, is highly valued by fraternities. In accounting for why the fraternity involved in the gang rape that precipitated our research project had been recognized recently as "the best fraternity chapter in the United States," a university official said: "They were good-looking, a big fraternity, had lots of BMWs [expensive, German-made automobiles]." After the rape, newspaper stories described the fraternity members' affluence, noting the high number of members who owned expensive cars (*St. Petersburg Times*, 1988).

The Status and Norms of Pledgeship

A pledge (sometimes called an associate member) is a new recruit who occupies a trial membership status for a specific period of time. The pledge period (typically ranging from 10 to 15 weeks) gives fraternity brothers an opportunity to assess and socialize new recruits. Pledges evaluate the fraternity also and decide if they want to become brothers. The socialization experience is structured partly through assignment of a Big Brother to each pledge. Big Brothers are expected to teach pledges how to become a brother and to support them as they progress through the trial membership period. Some pledges are repelled by the pledging experience, which can entail physical abuse; harsh discipline; and demands to be subordinate, follow orders, and engage in demeaning routines and activities, similar to those used by the military to "make men out of boys" during boot camp.

Characteristics of the pledge experience are rationalized by fraternity members as necessary to help pledges unite into a group, rely on each other, and join together against outsiders. The process is highly masculinist in execution as well as conception. A willingness to submit to authority, follow orders, and do as one is told is viewed as a sign of loyalty, togetherness, and unity. Fraternity pledges who find the pledge process offensive often drop out. Some do this by openly quitting, which can subject them to ridicule by brothers and other pledges, or they may deliberately fail to make the grades necessary for initiation or transfer schools and decline to reaffiliate with the fraternity on the new campus. One fraternity pledge who quit the fraternity he had pledged described an experience during pledgeship as follows:

> This one guy was always picking on me. No matter what I did, I was wrong. One night after dinner, he and two other guys called me and two other pledges into the chapter room. He said, "Here, X, hold this 25 pound bag of ice at arms' length 'til I tell you to stop." I did it even though my arms and hands were killing me. When I asked if I could stop, he grabbed me around the throat and lifted me off the floor. I thought he would choke me to death. He cussed me and called me all kinds of names. He took one of my fingers and twisted it until it nearly broke. . . . I stayed in the fraternity for a few more days, but then I decided to quit. I hated it. Those guys are sick. They like seeing you suffer.

Fraternities' emphasis on toughness, withstanding pain and humiliation, obedience to superiors, and using physical force to obtain compliance contributes to an interpersonal style that de-emphasizes caring and sensitivity but fosters intragroup trust and loyalty. If the least macho or most critical pledges drop out, those who remain may be more receptive to, and influenced by, masculinist values and practices that encourage the use of force in sexual relations with women and the covering up of such behavior (cf. Kanin 1967).

Norms and Dynamics of Brotherhood

Brother is the status occupied by fraternity men to indicate their relations to each other and their membership in a particular fraternity organization or group. Brother is a male-specific status; only males can become brothers, although women can become "Little Sisters," a form of pseudomembership. "Becoming a brother" is a rite of passage that follows the consistent and often lengthy display by pledges of appropriately masculine qualities and behaviors. Brothers have a quasi-familial relationship with each other, are normatively said to share bonds of closeness and support, and are sharply set off from nonmembers. Brotherhood is a loosely defined term used to represent the bonds that develop among fraternity members and the obligations and expectations incumbent upon them (cf. Marlowe and Auvenshine [1982] on fraternities' failure to encourage "moral development" in freshman pledges).

Some of our respondents talked about brotherhood in almost reverential terms, viewing it as the most valuable benefit of fraternity membership. One senior, a business-school major who had been affiliated with a fairly high-status fraternity throughout four years on campus, said:

> Brotherhood spurs friendship for life, which I consider its best aspect, although I didn't see it that way when I joined. Brotherhood bonds and unites. It instills values of caring about one another, caring about community, caring about ourselves. The values and bonds [of brotherhood] continually develop over the four years [in college] while normal friendships come and go.

Despite this idealization, most aspects of fraternity practice and conception are more mundane. Brotherhood often plays itself out as an overriding concern with masculinity and, by extension, femininity. As a consequence, fraternities comprise collectivities of highly masculinized men with attitudinal qualities and behavioral norms that predispose them to sexual coercion of women (cf. Kanin 1967; Merton 1985; Rapaport and Burkhart 1984). The norms of masculinity are complemented by conceptions of women and femininity that are equally distorted and stereotyped and that may enhance the probability of women's exploitation (cf. Ehrhart and Sandler 1985; Sanday 1981, 1986).

Practices of Brotherhood

Practices associated with fraternity brotherhood that contribute to the sexual coercion of women include a preoccupation with loyalty, group protection and secrecy, use of alcohol as a weapon, involvement in violence and physical force, and an emphasis on competition and superiority.

Loyalty, group protection, and secrecy   Loyalty is a fraternity preoccupation. Members are reminded constantly to be loyal to the fraternity and to their brothers. Among other ways, loyalty is played out in the practices of group protection and secrecy. The fraternity must be shielded from criticism. Members are admonished to avoid getting the fraternity in trouble and to bring all problems "to the chapter" (local branch of a national social fraternity) rather than to outsiders. Fraternities try to protect themselves from close scrutiny and criticism by the Interfraternity Council (a quasi-governing body composed of representatives from all social fraternities on campus), their fraternity's national office, university officials, law enforcement, the media, and the public. Protection of the fraternity often takes precedence over what is procedurally, ethically, or legally correct. Numerous examples were related to us of fraternity brothers' lying to outsiders to "protect the fraternity."

Group protection was observed in the alleged gang rape case with which we began our study. Except for one brother, a rapist who turned state's evidence, the entire remaining fraternity membership was accused by university and criminal justice officials of lying to protect the fraternity. Members consistently failed to cooperate even though the alleged crimes were felonies, involved only four men (two of whom were not even members of the local chapter), and the victim of the crime nearly died. According to a grand jury's findings, fraternity officers repeatedly broke appointments with law enforcement officials, refused to provide police with a list of members, and refused to cooperate with police and prosecutors investigating the case (*Florida Flambeau*, 1988).

Secrecy is a priority value and practice in fraternities, partly because full-fledged membership is premised on it (for confirmation, see Ehrhart and Sandler 1985; Longino and Kart 1973; Roark 1987). Secrecy is also a boundary-maintaining mechanism, demarcating in-group from out-group, us from them. Secret rituals, handshakes, and mottoes are revealed to pledge brothers as they are initiated into full brotherhood. Since only brothers are supposed to know a fraternity's secrets, such knowledge affirms membership in the fraternity and separates a brother from others. Extending secrecy tactics from protection of private knowledge to protection of the fraternity from criticism is a predictable development. Our interviews indicated that individual members knew the difference between right and wrong, but fraternity norms that emphasize loyalty, group protection, and secrecy often overrode standards of ethical correctness.

Alcohol as weapon Alcohol use by fraternity men is normative. They use it on weekdays to relax after class and on weekends to "get drunk," "get crazy," and "get laid." The use of alcohol to obtain sex from women is pervasive—in other words, it is used as a weapon against sexual reluctance. According to several fraternity men whom we interviewed, alcohol is the major tool used to gain sexual mastery over women (cf. Adams and Abarbanel 1988; Ehrhart and Sandler 1985). One fraternity man, a 21-year-old senior, described alcohol use to gain sex as follows: "There are girls that you know will fuck, then some you have to put some effort into it. . . . You have to buy them drinks or find out if she's drunk enough. . . ."

A similar strategy is used collectively. A fraternity man said that at parties with Little Sisters: "We provide them with 'hunch punch' and things get wild. We get them drunk and most of the guys end up with one." "'Hunch punch,'" he said, "is a girls' drink made up of overproof alcohol and powdered Kool-Aid, no water or anything, just ice. It's very strong. Two cups will do a number on a female." He had plans in the next academic term to surreptitiously give hunch punch to women in a "prim and proper" sorority because "having sex with prim and proper sorority girls is definitely a goal." These women are a challenge because they "won't openly consume alcohol and won't get openly drunk as hell." Their sororities have "standards committees" that forbid heavy drinking and easy sex.

In the gang rape case, our sources said that many fraternity men on campus believed the victim had a drinking problem and was thus an "easy make." According to newspaper accounts, she had been drinking alcohol on the evening she was raped; the lead assailant is alleged to have given her a bottle of wine after she arrived at his fraternity house. Portions of the rape occurred in a shower, and the victim was reportedly so drunk that her assailants had difficulty holding her in a standing position (*Tallahassee Democrat*, 1988a). While raping her, her assailants repeatedly told her they were members of another fraternity under the apparent belief that she was too drunk to know the difference. Of course, if she was too drunk to know who they were, she was too drunk to consent to sex (cf. Allgeier 1986; Tash 1988).

One respondent told us that gang rapes are wrong and can get one expelled, but he seemed to see nothing wrong in sexual coercion one-on-one. He seemed unaware that the use of alcohol to obtain sex from a woman is grounds for a claim that a rape occurred (cf. Tash 1988). Few women on campus (who also may not know these grounds) report date rapes, however; so the odds of detection and punishment are slim for fraternity men who use alcohol for "seduction" purposes (cf. Byington and Keeter 1988; Merton 1985).

Violence and physical force Fraternity men have a history of violence (Ehrhart and Sandler 1985; Roark 1987). Their record of hazing, fighting, property destruction, and rape has caused them problems with insurance companies (Bradford 1986; Pressley 1987). Two university officials told us that fraternities "are the third riskiest property to insure behind toxic waste dumps and amusement parks." Fraternities are increasingly defendants in legal actions brought by pledges subjected to hazing (Meyer 1986; Pressley 1987) and by women who were raped by one or more members. In a recent alleged gang rape incident at another Florida university, prosecutors failed to file charges but the victim filed a civil suit against the fraternity nevertheless (*Tallahassee Democrat*, 1989).

Competition and superiority Interfraternity rivalry fosters in-group identification and out-group hostility. Fraternities stress pride of membership and superiority over other fraternities as major goals. Interfraternity rivalries take many forms, including competition for desirable pledges, size of pledge class, size of membership, size and appearance of fraternity house, superiority in intramural sports, highest grade-point averages, giving the best parties, gaining the best or most campus leadership roles, and, of great importance, attracting and displaying "good looking women." Rivalry is particularly intense over members, intramural sports, and women (cf. Messner 1989).

FRATERNITIES' COMMODIFICATION OF WOMEN

In claiming that women are treated by fraternities as commodities, we mean that fraternities knowingly, and intentionally, *use* women for their benefit. Fraternities use women as bait for new members, as servers of brothers' needs, and as sexual prey.

Women as bait Fashionably attractive women help a fraternity attract new members. As one fraternity man, a junior, said, "They are good bait." Beautiful, sociable women are believed to impress the right kind of pledges and give the impression that the fraternity can deliver this type of woman to its members. Photographs of shapely, attractive coeds are printed in fraternity brochures and videotapes that are distributed and shown to potential pledges. The women pictured are often dressed in bikinis, at the beach, and are pictured hugging the brothers of the fraternity. One university official says such recruitment materials give the message: "Hey, they're here for you, you can have whatever you want," and, "we have the best looking women. Join us and you can have them too." Another commented: "Something's wrong when males join an all-male organization as the best place to meet women. It's so illogical."

Fraternities compete in promising access to beautiful women. One fraternity man, a senior, commented that "the attraction of girls [i.e., a fraternity's success in attracting women] is a big status symbol for fraternities." One university official commented that the use of women as a recruiting tool is so well entrenched that fraternities that might be willing to forgo it say they cannot afford to unless other fraternities do so as well. One fraternity man said, "Look, if we don't have Little Sisters, the fraternities that do will get all the good pledges." Another said, "We won't have as good a rush [the period during which new members are assessed and selected] if we don't have these women around."

In displaying good-looking, attractive, skimpily dressed, nubile women to potential members, fraternities implicitly, and sometimes explicitly, promise sexual access to women. One fraternity man commented that "part of what being in a fraternity is all about is the sex" and explained how his fraternity uses Little Sisters to recruit new members:

> We'll tell the sweetheart [the fraternity's term for Little Sister], "You're gorgeous; you can get him." We'll tell her to fake a scam and she'll go hang all over him during a rush party, kiss him, and he thinks he's done wonderful and wants to join. The girls think it's great too. It's flattering for them.

Women as servers   The use of women as servers is exemplified in the Little Sister program. Little Sisters are undergraduate women who are rushed and selected in a manner parallel to the recruitment of fraternity men. They are affiliated with the fraternity in a formal but unofficial way and are able, indeed required, to wear the fraternity's Greek letters. Little Sisters are not full-fledged fraternity members, however; and fraternity national offices and most universities do not register or regulate them. Each fraternity has an officer called Little Sister Chairman who oversees their organization and activities. The Little Sisters elect officers among themselves, pay monthly dues to the fraternity, and have well-defined roles. Their dues are used to pay for the fraternity's social events, and Little Sisters are expected to attend and hostess fraternity parties and hang around the house to make it a "nice place to be." One fraternity man, a senior described Little Sisters this way: "They are very social girls, willing to join in, be affiliated with the group, devoted to the fraternity." Another member, a sophomore, said: "Their sole purpose is social— attend parties, attract new members, and 'take care' of the guys."

Our observations and interviews suggested that women selected by fraternities as Little Sisters are physically attractive, possess good social skills, and are willing to devote time and energy to the fraternity and its members. One undergraduate woman gave the following job description for Little Sisters to a campus newspaper.

> It's not just making appearances at all the parties but entails many more responsibilities. You're going to be expected to go to all the intramural games to cheer the brothers on, support and encourage the pledges, and just be around to bring some extra life to the house. [As a Little Sister] you

have to agree to take on a new responsibility other than studying to maintain your grades and managing to keep your checkbook from bouncing. You have to make time to be a part of the fraternity and support the brothers in all they do. (*The Tomahawk*, 1988)

The title of Little Sister reflects women's subordinate status; fraternity men in a parallel role are called Big Brothers. Big Brothers assist a sorority primarily with the physical work of sorority rushes, which, compared to fraternity rushes, are more formal, structured, and intensive. Sorority rushes take place in the daytime and fraternity rushes at night so fraternity men are free to help. According to one fraternity member, Little Sister status is a benefit to women because it gives them a social outlet and "the protection of the brothers." The gender-stereotypic conceptions and obligations of these Little Sister and Big Brother statuses indicate that fraternities and sororities promote a gender hierarchy on campus that fosters subordination and dependence in women, thus encouraging sexual exploitation and the belief that it is acceptable.

Women as sexual prey   Little Sisters are a sexual utility. Many Little Sisters do not belong to sororities and lack peer support for refraining from unwanted sexual relations. One fraternity man (whose fraternity has 65 members and 85 Little Sisters) told us they had recruited "wholesale" in the prior year to "get lots of new women." The structural access to women that the Little Sister program provides and the absence of normative supports for refusing fraternity members' sexual advances may make women in this program particularly susceptible to coerced sexual encounters with fraternity men.

Access to women for sexual gratification is a presumed benefit of fraternity membership, promised in recruitment materials and strategies and through brothers' conversations with new recruits. One fraternity man said: "We always tell the guys that you get sex all the time, there's always new girls. . . . After I became a Greek, I found out I could be with females at will." A university official told us that, based on his observations, "no one [i.e., fraternity men] on this campus wants to have 'relationships.' They just want to have fun [i.e., sex]." Fraternity men plan and execute strategies aimed at obtaining sexual gratification, and this occurs at both individual and collective levels.

Individual strategies include getting a woman drunk and spending a great deal of money on her. As for collective strategies, most of our undergraduate interviewees agreed that fraternity parties often culminate in sex and that this outcome is planned. One fraternity man said fraternity parties often involve sex and nudity and can "turn into orgies." Orgies may be planned in advance, such as the Bowery Ball party held by one fraternity. A former fraternity member said of this party:

> The entire idea behind this is sex. Both men and women come to the party wearing little or nothing. There are pornographic pinups on the walls and usually porno movies playing on the TV. The music carries sexual overtones. . . . They just get schnockered [drunk] and, in most cases, they also get laid.

When asked about the women who come to such a party, he said: "Some Little Sisters just won't go. . . . The girls who do are looking for a good time, girls who don't know what it is, things like that."

Other respondents denied that fraternity parties are orgies but said that sex is always talked about among the brothers and they all know "who each other is doing it with." One member said that most of the time, guys have sex with their girlfriends "but with socials, girlfriends aren't allowed to come and it's their [members'] big chance [to have sex with other women]." The use of alcohol to help them get women into bed is a routine strategy at fraternity parties.

CONCLUSIONS

In general, our research indicated that the organization and membership of fraternities contribute heavily to coercive and often violent sex. Fraternity houses are occupied by same-sex (all men) and same-age (late teens, early twenties) peers whose maturity and judgment are often less than ideal. Yet fraternity houses are private dwellings that are mostly off-limits to, and away from scrutiny of, university and community representatives, with the result that fraternity house events seldom come to the attention of outsiders. Practices associated with the social construction of fraternity brotherhood emphasize a macho conception of men and masculinity, a narrow, stereotyped conception of women and femininity, and the treatment of women as commodities. Other practices contributing to coercive sexual relations and the cover-up of rapes include excessive alcohol use, competitiveness, and normative support for deviance and secrecy (cf. Bogal-Allbritten and Allbritten 1985; Kanin 1967).

Some fraternity practices exacerbate others. Brotherhood norms require "sticking together" regardless of right or wrong; thus rape episodes are unlikely to be stopped or reported to outsiders, even when witnesses disapprove. The ability to use alcohol without scrutiny by authorities and alcohol's frequent association with violence, including sexual coercion, facilitates rape in fraternity houses. Fraternity norms that emphasize the value of maleness and masculinity over femaleness and femininity and that elevate the status of men and lower the status of women in members' eyes undermine perceptions and treatment of women as persons who deserve consideration and care (cf. Ehrhart and Sandler 1985; Merton 1985).

Androgynous men and men with a broad range of interests and attributes are lost to fraternities through their recruitment practices. Masculinity of a narrow and stereotypical type helps create attitudes, norms, and practices that predispose fraternity men to coerce women sexually, both individually and collectively (Allgeier 1986; Hood 1989; Sanday 1981, 1986). Male athletes on campus may be similarly disposed for the same reasons (Kirshenbaum 1989; Telander and Sullivan 1989).

Research into the social contexts in which rape crimes occur and the social constructions associated with these contexts illumine rape dynamics on campus. Blanchard (1959) found that group rapes almost always have a leader who pushes others into the crime. He also found that the leader's latent homosexuality, desire to show off to his peers, or fear of failing to prove himself a man are frequently an impetus. Fraternity norms and practices contribute to the approval and use of sexual coercion as an accepted tactic in relations with women. Alcohol-induced compliance is normative, whereas, presumably, use of a knife, gun, or threat of bodily harm would not be because the woman who "drinks too much" is viewed as "causing her own rape" (cf. Ehrhart and Sandler 1985).

Our research led us to conclude that fraternity norms and practices influence members to view the sexual coercion of women, which is a felony crime, as sport, a contest, or a game (cf. Sato 1988). This sport is played not between men and women but between men and men. Women are the pawns or prey in the interfraternity rivalry game; they prove that a fraternity is successful or prestigious. The use of women in this way encourages fraternity men to see women as objects and sexual coercion as sport. Today's societal norms support young women's right to engage in sex at their discretion, and coercion is unnecessary in a mutually desired encounter. However, nubile young women say they prefer to be "in a relationship" to have sex while young men say they prefer to "get laid" without a commitment (Muehlenhard and Linton 1987). These differences may reflect, in part, American puritanism and men's fears of sexual intimacy or perhaps intimacy of any kind. In a fraternity context, getting sex without giving emotionally demonstrates "cool" masculinity. More important, it poses no threat to the bonding and loyalty of the fraternity brotherhood (cf. Farr 1988). Drinking large quantities of alcohol before having sex suggests that "scoring" rather than intrinsic sexual pleasure is a primary concern of fraternity men.

Unless fraternities' composition, goals, structures, and practices change in fundamental ways, women on campus will continue to be sexual prey for fraternity men. As all-male enclaves dedicated to opposing faculty and administration and to cementing in-group ties, fraternity members eschew any hint of homosexuality. Their version of masculinity transforms women, and men with womanly characteristics, into the out-group. "Womanly men" are ostracized; feminine women are used to demonstrate members' masculinity. Encouraging renewed emphasis on their founding values (Longino and Kart 1973), service orientation and activities (Lemire 1979), or members' moral development (Marlowe and Auvenshine 1982) will have little effect on fraternities' treatment of women. A case for or against fraternities cannot be made by studying individual members. The fraternity qua group and organization is at issue. Located on campus along with many vulnerable women, embedded in a sexist society, and caught up in masculinist goals, practices, and values, fraternities' violation of women—including forcible rape—should come as no surprise.

NOTE

1.   Recent bans by some universities on open-keg parties at fraternity houses have resulted in heavy drinking before coming to a party and an increase in drunkenness among those who attend. This may aggravate, rather than improve, the treatment of women by fraternity men at parties.

REFERENCES

Adams, Aileen and Gail Abarbanel. 1988. *Sexual Assault on Campus: What Colleges Can Do*. Santa Monica, CA: Rape Treatment Center.

Allgeier, Elizabeth. 1986. "Coercive Versus Consensual Sexual Interactions." G. Stanley Hall Lecture to American Psychological Association Annual Meeting, Washington, DC, August.

Blanchard, W. H. 1959. "The Group Process in Gang Rape." *Journal of Social Psychology* 49:259–66.

Bogal-Allbritten, Rosemarie B. and William L. Allbritten. 1985. "The Hidden Victims: Courtship Violence Among College Students." *Journal of College Student Personnel* 43:201–4.

Bohrnstedt, George W. 1969. "Conservatism, Authoritarianism and Religiosity of Fraternity Pledges." *Journal of College Student Personnel* 27:36–43.

Bradford, Michael. 1986. "Tight Market Dries Up Nightlife at University." *Business Insurance* (March 2): 2, 6.

Burkhart, Barry. 1989. Comments in Seminar on Acquaintance/Date Rape Prevention: A National Video Teleconference, February 2.

Burkhart, Barry R. and Annette L. Stanton. 1985. "Sexual Aggression in Acquaintance Relationships." Pp. 43–65 in *Violence in Intimate Relationships*, edited by G. Russell. Englewood Cliffs, NJ: Spectrum.

Byington, Diane B. and Karen W. Keeter. 1988. "Assessing Needs of Sexual Assault Victims on a University Campus." Pp. 23–31 in *Student Services: Responding to Issues and Challenges*. Chapel Hill: University of North Carolina Press.

Chancer, Lynn S. 1987. "New Bedford, Massachusetts, March 6, 1983–March 22, 1984: The 'Before and After' of a Group Rape. *Gender & Society* 1:239–60.

Ehrhart, Julie K. and Bernice R. Sandler. 1985. *Campus Gang Rape: Party Games?* Washington, DC: Association of American Colleges.

Farr, K. A. 1988. "Dominance Bonding Through the Good Old Boys Sociability Network." *Sex Roles* 18:259–77.

Florida Flambeau. 1988. "Pike Members Indicted in Rape." (May 19):1, 5.

Fox, Elaine, Charles Hodge, and Walter Ward. 1987. "A Comparison of Attitudes Held by Black and White Fraternity Members." *Journal of Negro Education* 56:521–34.

Geis, Gilbert. 1971. "Group Sexual Assaults." *Medical Aspects of Human Sexuality* 5:101–13.

Glaser, Barney G. 1978. *Theoretical Sensitivity: Advances in the Methodology of Grounded Theory*. Mill Valley, CA: Sociology Press.

Hood, Jane. 1989. "Why Our Society Is Rape-Prone." *New York Times*, May 16.

Hughes, Michael J. and Roger B. Winston, Jr. 1987. "Effects of Fraternity Membership on Interpersonal Values." *Journal of College Student Personnel* 45:405–11.

Kanin, Eugene J. 1967. "Reference Groups and Sex Conduct Norm Violations." *The Sociological Quarterly* 8:495–504.

Kimmel, Michael, ed. 1987. *Changing Men: New Directions in Research on Men and Masculinity*. Newbury Park, CA: Sage.

Kirshenbaum, Jerry. 1989. "Special Report, An American Disgrace: A Violent and Unprecedented Lawlessness Has Arisen Among College Athletes in all Parts of the Country." *Sports Illustrated* (February 27): 16–19.

Lemire, David. 1979. "One Investigation of the Stereotypes Associated with Fraternities and Sororities." *Journal of College Student Personnel* 37:54–57.

Letchworth, G. E. 1969. "Fraternities Now and in the Future." *Journal of College Student Personnel* 10:118–22.

Longino, Charles F., Jr., and Cary S. Kart. 1973. "The College Fraternity: An Assessment of Theory and Research." *Journal of College Student Personnel* 31:118–25.

Marlowe, Anne F. and Dwight C. Auvenshine. 1982. "Greek Membership: Its Impact on the Moral Development of College Freshmen." *Journal of College Student Personnel* 40:53–57.

Martin, Patricia Yancey and Barry A. Turner. 1986. "Grounded Theory and Organizational Research." *Journal of Applied Behavioral Science* 22:141–57.

Merton, Andrew. 1985. "On Competition and Class: Return to Brotherhood." *Ms.* (September) 60–65, 121–22.

Messner, Michael. 1989. "Masculinities and Athletic Careers." *Gender & Society* 3:71–88.

Meyer, T. J. 1986. "Fight Against Hazing Rituals Rages on Campuses." *Chronicle of Higher Education* (March 12):34–36.

Miller, Leonard D. 1973. "Distinctive Characteristics of Fraternity Members." *Journal of College Student Personnel* 31:126–28.

Muehlenhard, Charlene L. and Melaney A. Linton. 1987. "Date Rape and Sexual Aggression in Dating Situations: Incidence and Risk Factors." *Journal of Counseling Psychology* 34:186–96.

Pressley, Sue Anne. 1987. "Fraternity Hell Night Still Endures." *Washington Post* (August 11):B1.

Rapaport, Karen and Barry R. Burkhart. 1984. "Personality and Attitudinal Characteristics of Sexually Coercive College Males." *Journal of Abnormal Psychology* 93:216–21.

Roark, Mary L. 1987. "Preventing Violence on College Campuses." *Journal of Counseling and Development* 65:367–70.

Sanday, Peggy Reeves. 1981. "The Socio-Cultural Context of Rape: A Cross-Cultural Study." *Journal of Social Issues* 37:5–27.

———. 1986. "Rape and the Silencing of the Feminine." Pp. 84–101 in *Rape*, edited by S. Tomaselli and R. Porter. Oxford: Basil Blackwell.

St. Petersburg Times. 1988. "A Greek Tragedy." (May 29):1F, 6F.

Sato, Ikuya. 1988. "Play Theory of Delinquency: Toward a General Theory of 'Action.'" *Symbolic Interaction* 11:191–212.

Smith, T. 1964. "Emergence and Maintenance of Fraternal Solidarity." *Pacific Sociological Review* 7:29–37.

Tallahassee Democrat. 1988a. "FSU Fraternity Brothers Charged" (April 27):1A, 12A.

———. 1988b. "FSU Interviewing Students About Alleged Rape" (April 24):1D.

———. 1989. "Woman Sues Stetson in Alleged Rape" (March 19):3B.

Tampa Tribune. 1988. "Fraternity Brothers Charged in Sexual Assault of FSU Coed." (April 27):6B.

Tash, Gary B. 1988. "Date Rape." *The Emerald of Sigma Pi Fraternity* 75(4):1–2.

Telander, Rick and Robert Sullivan. 1989. "Special Report, You Reap What You Sow." *Sports Illustrated* (February 27):20–34.

The Tomahawk. 1988. "A Look Back at Rush, A Mixture of Hard Work and Fun" (April/May):3D.

Walsh, Claire. 1989. Comments in Seminar on Acquaintance/Date Rape Prevention: A National Video Teleconference, February 2.

Wilder, David H., Arlyne E. Hoyt, Dennis M. Doren, William E. Hauck, and Robert D. Zettle. 1978. "The Impact of Fraternity and Sorority Membership on Values and Attitudes." *Journal of College Student Personnel* 36:445–49.

Wilder, David H., Arlyne E. Hoyt, Beth Shuster Surbeck, Janet C. Wilder, and Patricia Imperatrice Carney. 1986. "Greek Affiliation and Attitude Change in College Students." *Journal of College Student Personnel* 44:510–19.

CHAPTER 10

Is "Doing Nothing" Just Boys' Play?

Integrating Feminist and Cultural Studies Perspectives on Working-Class Young Men's Masculinity[1]

Joyce E. Canaan

In 1976, Paul Corrigan wrote a paper entitled "Doing Nothing," in which he explored how some working-class young men spent their informal time together on the streets on Saturday nights. As he described it, "doing nothing" meant talking, developing "weird ideas" such as smashing milk bottles and, for some, fighting. These activities structured both time and social relations; the former was filled and the latter were solidified by "doing nothing" collectively.

As my title suggests, this chapter questions some of these assumptions in Corrigan's work, and in the youth subculture perspective that has developed in cultural studies more generally. I do so by exploring how some white working-class young men among whom I conducted ethnographic research use the activity of fighting in the construction of masculine subjectivity and subculture. I will argue that although the youth subcultures perspective rightly explores how working-class young men's fighting rests on and expresses their subordinate class position, it does not consider how fighting also elaborates their dominant position in terms of gender relations.

To do this, I want to extend recent feminist analyses of male violence. These analyses stress both the formal and informal means by which male violence against women is perpetrated. They suggest that male socialization presumes and encourages violence; violence against women is therefore seen as part of a more pervasive and determining system of male values through which patriarchal social relations are organized.

These analyses explore how male violence against women is part of a social value system which extols male strength, control and competition and re-

Reprinted from Joyce E. Canaan, "Is 'Doing Nothing' Just Boys' Play? Integrating Feminist and Cultural Studies Perspectives on Working-class Young Men's Masculinity," in *Off-Centre: Feminism and Cultural Studies*, edited by Jackie Stacey, Sarah Franklin, and Celia Lury, pp. 109–125, (1991). Reprinted by permission of the author.

inforces these values in social institutions and through the media. But they do not explore in depth how class and race also shape male violence. While these analyses emphasize the centrality of socialization to male identity, their focus on the effects of this socialization on women prevents them from considering the contradictory ways in which men themselves experience this socialization. Nor do these analyses examine the relationship between male violence against women, other men and themselves[2] (Bart, 1989; Hanmer and Saunders, 1984; Russell, 1984; Walby, 1990).

This chapter explores how the young men among whom I conducted research conjoin gender and sexuality in their constructions of masculinity, and shows the links between male violence against women and violence against men.[3] The next section, which provides the background for the central ethnographic section, describes the research method and setting and provides a brief review of the relevant literature. The ethnographic section explores how the young men with whom I talked construct and interpret drinking and fighting in contradictory ways. I conclude by showing how bringing together feminist and cultural studies perspectives enables a more nuanced understanding of masculinity to be developed than that which either perspective alone provides.

BACKGROUND INFORMATION

Data for this chapter were collected at two youth clubs which I visited four times each. I told youth club leaders that I wanted to talk to white young men between 16 and 24, so they selected groups willing to talk to me. I told these young men that I wanted us to talk about their spare time activities. The initial interview was structured; I asked them what they did from morning until night during the week and on weekends. Since most of them began talking about fighting as their most esteemed leisure activity, I directed my questions to this activity so that they could discuss it in detail. Interviews were taped. I then listened to these interviews and wrote down questions which they raised. I used these questions as the basis for my next interview with subjects.[4]

Most data for this chapter were collected from young men in two communities in Wolverhampton.[5] One community, Wilton Manor, has a youth unemployment rate of 11.9 per cent; the other, Carr Lake, has a youth unemployment rate of 21.8 per cent.[6] My qualitative findings substantiate these statistics; most of the young men to whom I spoke at Wilton Manor were semi-skilled or unskilled labourers who performed jobs such as mechanic, painter and decorator and dustman. Most at Carr Lake were unskilled and unemployed. The employed young men at Wilton Manor, in their mid to late teens, claimed to fight frequently, while the mostly unemployed young men from Carr Lake, in their early twenties, claimed to fight less than before.

Some comments by the older young men suggest some reasons for these differences. They state that they are beginning to find fighting frightening as weapons replace fists and as they face legal repercussions if caught because they are over 16. Those who are unemployed claim that they have less money and drink and go out less than previously. They therefore have fewer opportunities to fight. Finally, these older young men have already developed a notion of masculinity and therefore have less need to test it. For these reasons at least, the mostly unemployed young men with whom I spoke from Carr Lake fight less than their more often employed and somewhat younger counterparts from Wilton Manor. While these findings are not definitive, they suggest that fighting is not a key activity of many unemployed young men; only their wealthier counterparts can afford to drink enough to achieve the mental state necessary for fighting.

This research is informed by three bodies of literature: cultural studies analyses of youth, feminist analyses of male violence and recent studies of men and masculinity. The youth subcultures perspective of cultural studies rests on earlier sociological research on working-class young people. While these studies are ostensibly about both genders, they actually focus on young men. Although Chicago sociologists in the 1920s and 1930s explicitly explored how poor youths (as well as poor people of other ages) meaningfully responded to social disorganization in their neighbourhoods, these studies' focus on male "gangs" indicates that for them "youth" meant young men (Canaan, 1990). Similarly, Miller's study of the so-called delinquent values of working-class young people (1978) characteristically was male-oriented. He stressed that these young people have certain "focal concerns" which include: getting into trouble by breaking the law, demonstrating "toughness" by being strong and brave when physically threatened, and "search[ing] for excitement" during weekly "nights on the town" when they drink, listen to music, have sexual adventures and where young men fight over young women. This short burst of excitement is followed by a longer period of boredom when they are "hanging out" and doing "nothing" (Miller, 1978, p. 145). Clearly, this list of focal concerns and activities indicates that the "young people" being studied are male. There is no attempt to explore how young women make sense of and are affected by these male-oriented focal concerns or whether they have focal concerns of their own.

Much of the work on youth subcultures within cultural studies similarly ignores gender in developing an explicitly class-based analysis of working-class male youths' focal concerns. For example, Cohen notes that working-class young people who lack the monetary resources to participate in leisure consumption as fully as their middle-class counterparts "manufacture excitement" of their own, based on their focal concerns, to affirm their class position (Cohen, 1978, p. 269). He claims that the components of these concerns rest on those which Miller delineated (e.g., "trouble," "toughness" and "excitement" (1978, p. 270)), which again indicates that he focuses on working-class young men alone. Most of the later cultural studies projects maintain this exclusive focus.[7] Some explore how (male) youths most marginalized from middle-class institutions elaborate class-based identities in and through leisure consumption (Hall and Jefferson, 1976; Hebdige 1979). Others, such as Corrigan (1976) and Willis (1977), examine these (male) youths' activities in middle-class institutions, thereby suggesting how marginalization in these institutions provides the basis for these young men's leisure consumption. Willis also notes that his subjects view fighting as a key means of articulating their focal concerns of masculinity, "dramatic display, [and] the solidarity of the group" (Willis, 1977, p. 34). It enables them to distinguish themselves from their more conformist working-class counterparts and to resist dominant middle-class cultural values more generally.

While these mostly white male researchers claim to be elaborating an understanding of working-class "youths" in general, later researchers show that this understanding rests on data collected from, and the elaboration of analyses applicable to, white working-class male youths (Amos and Parmar, 1981; Clarke, 1982; McRobbie, 1980; McRobbie and Garber, 1974; Mac an Ghail, 1988). These later researchers explore how other subordinate young people (e.g., working-class young women and black youths) are affected by the activities of their more powerful white male counterparts.

This chapter focuses on male fighting because the young men to whom I spoke, just as those spoken to by other researchers, view fighting as "the moment when you are fully tested in the alternative culture" (Willis, 1977; p. 35). As I shall show, at this moment they elaborate and affirm some key components of what masculinity means to them.

While this analysis, like those of the new men's studies (e.g., Brod, 1987; Kimmel, 1987), examines men and masculinity from the perspective of the men who are experiencing it, it differs from men's studies in that it considers the consequences of male experience for women. Indeed, as Griffin and I argue elsewhere (Canaan and Griffin, 1990), it is difficult, if not impossible, for a dominant group such as men to explore how their power affects subordinate groups and to develop strategies through which they voluntarily give up their power. Feminists, it can be argued, must therefore continue to study men and masculinity, and must continue to make men feel uncomfortable, because feminist work offers insights into how male power works and affects us. It might also help us develop more effective strategies that challenge male power.

ETHNOGRAPHIC EVIDENCE

The mostly white working-class young men with whom I spoke did not suddenly start fighting during adolescence. As Andrew, from Wilton Manor notes, he learnt about fighting by seeing others do it when he was a boy:

> **A:** When there has been fights, there's been little six- or seven-year-olds there, like. Not that them doing [it], they just come for the excitement of it. But I think that also puts it [fighting] into their heads cos them going when them six or seven. They ay gonna get hit, but I think that puts the idea what you gotta do when you'm older.

Andrew suggests that boys obtain a glorified picture of fighting by standing on the outskirts and seeing only its "excitement" while experiencing none of its pains or terrors. Realizing its importance for their elders, they learn early about the centrality of fighting to masculinity.

According to Andrew, fighting becomes increasingly important as little boys start growing up:

A: Once you get to school, I mean, little five-year-old, he don't give a shit about who's hard or not . . . But once you start growing up, you get people who start coming up and fighting you and you have to defend yourself. And it just starts from there, it's sommat you can't avoid.

Andrew's comments suggest that the need to fight is not something which males acquire "naturally"; they do so in and through the social contexts in which they act.[8]

Perhaps not surprisingly, given its prominence in primary school, fighting is also central to the construction of the male peer group system during secondary school. As Andrew and his friend Keith, also from Wilton Manor, maintain:

K: It's like, when you'm at school, you've always got a cock of the school. Or a few people who are harder than the rest. They have to fight to see who's the hardest in school . . .

A: The strongest, who can lamp everybody.

K: You only get about 15 guys in the whole school that are the hardest.

A: . . . [T]hey'll hang around together in a gang. Then you have the next hardest lot go round in a gang and then you get the bottoms. The ones who just ay there! . . .

Those who are hardest, or strongest, and most capable of "lamping" or beating up their opponent form the top peer group.[9] Group members fight each other to determine who is the "cock," or the most powerful male. This term refers to both a male animal known for its aggressiveness and to the male genitals. The male genitals are also explicitly acknowledged in the term for the least masculine young man, "wanker." This suggests that hardness is embodied and symbolized through the male genitals, which are considered most formidable when hard.

During secondary school young women are also thought to affirm this male criterion. Andrew notes that they find hard young men most desirable:

A: You find the girls go out with the harder ones. They set a reputation when they go out with the girls, no matter how they look. Like you'll find a girl will go out with them . . . [T]he girls go with them to look good being seen with them. They think it's good to be seen with a hard person.

The relationship between hardness and sexual attractiveness to young women suggests that these young men are developing forms of masculinity that are constituted and affirmed in and through their relations with young women. Andrew's comments suggest that he views these relationships with some ambivalence. On the one hand, he acknowledges that young women have a certain power because they prefer the hardest males. On the other hand, he denigrates them precisely because they exercise power in this way. His comment that young women choose such males because they "think it's good to be seen with a hard person" suggests that they exercise power merely to raise their own status. Yet his discussion of drinking and fighting, and, indeed, that of the other young men with whom I spoke, suggests that they too use hardness to build up their status. This suggests that young men denigrate young women for using the criterion in the same way as they do themselves. Evidently young men maintain that hardness is something which only young men should recognize in each other.

As Andrew and his friend Jonathan note, hardness is also exhibited spatially. These young men note that their "territory," like them, is assessed according to its hardness:

> **JC:** So about territory, when did you first start thinking about this as your territory? . . .
>
> **J:** But you don't sort of say one day, "This is Wilton Manor territory," like but as you grow up, you see other people who belong to the estate like fighting 'cos of the territory. Then you think, "We should do that."
>
> **A:** Not just that, you don't want other kids coming over here, starting to cause trouble and thinking they can get away with things, and before you know it, the area's got a name. "Oh, you can go up there and do what you want." . . . It's got a reputation, like.

Just as boys come to value fighting by seeing their elders doing it, so they come to esteem their territory by watching their elders fight to defend it. The fact that a territory is defined by its degree of hardness suggests that it functions symbolically as the materialization of their collective bodily strength.

The working-class young men with whom I spoke view the *notion* of hardness as central to the *activity* of fighting. This can be seen in the following conversation between myself and several young men from Wilton Manor, Andrew, Keith and David:

> **JC:** What makes someone really hard?
>
> **K:** Fighting. If he's got the ability to fight and he can beat other guys, he's hard.
>
> **A:** You fight someone, like, say if he [K] had a fight with him [D], right, and he lamped him, right, and say me, we had a bit of argument or sommat. I'd be scared of him [K] and then people just don't want to fight.
>
> **K:** See, if I really smashed his face in . . .
>
> **A:** bashed him to a pulp . . .
>
> **K:** then they'd have seen it, they'd have thought, "Oh, don't mess with him, 'cos he can fight."
>
> **A:** Even though you might be able to beat him.
>
> **D:** It's intimidation . . .
>
> **A:** It's an attitude.

K: It's being better than the rest. Knowing that they know that you are the best.

These comments suggest that the fight is the ultimate demarcator of hardness. It is the means by which the "best" is selected from the "rest." But fighting need not occur frequently. Indeed, those who fight on any occasion are less esteemed than those who only fight occasionally. As Andrew notes, when young men see, or hear about, other young men's hardness, they are unlikely to start a fight when tensions arise between them. A hard young man may merely "intimidate" rather than fight another. By displaying an "attitude" that he is harder than they, he implicitly imposes his power on them, which is usually enough for them to acquiesce to his point of view. Thus, this is considered superior to fighting.

Categories of Masculinity and the Concept of Hardness

The concept of hardness contains at least two components, *acting* and *being* hard, as Jonathan and Andrew observe:[10]

J: I mean, how hard you act and how hard you am are two different things. Like there's some people who act really hard but they just ay at all. Put down in one punch. Whereas other people keep themselves to themselves and you go up to them, you have a fight with them, and they tek your punch, no trouble, and when they throw a punch at you, you know about it.

A: You can be hard and act hard, and you cannot act hard and be hard, or you can act hard and not be hard. I think the best of them is to be hard and not act hard.

These remarks suggest several things. They suggest that being and acting hard rank social contexts as well as people. How hard one *is* refers to what happens in a fight, where a young man's supposedly "true nature" is revealed. How hard one *acts* refers to one's actions in other contexts. Because one's nature as revealed in the fighting situation is thought to shed light on one's activity in other contexts, the fighting context is separated from and ranked above all other contexts. The fight is the "last move in and final validation of" the components of hardness that are displayed in other contexts (Willis, 1977, p. 35).

The components of acting and being hard explicitly rank three forms of masculinity: those who do not act but are hard; those who act and are hard; and those who act hard but are not. These young men's comments and those of two young men from Carr Lake, Steve and Neil, show that the preferred form is being but not acting hard:

JC: Don't people think you're a wanker if you don't fight?

S: Nay.

N: A mate'll respect you if you walk away from drunkenness.

S: If anyone comes up to you and says, "Do you want a fight?", you say, "Fuck off." If they doe, you just beat them up. You give them a chance to walk away. Say, "I don't want to fight, alright? I doe want no trouble, just gu away like." You'm still standing your ground, you'm standing there saying, "Gu away."

The fact that being but not acting hard is the preferred form of masculinity substantiates the point made in the last section that fighting does not occur frequently. One who is "standing the ground," even when drunk, is most respected. He only fights when there is no way not to do so. The expression "standing his ground" suggests that while such a young man does not fight, he also does not walk away. By preventing a fight he shows that he can "manfully" control himself without flying off the handle when the first spark of tension arises. He thereby displays his masculinity in another way. While the other initially proposes a fight, the protagonist's decision to reject this proposal enables him to redefine the situation. If the other accepts this redefinition, the protagonist effectively demonstrates that he is the more powerful of the two. In so doing, he shows that he is not only powerful when fighting, but that he, more than others, determines when he will and will not fight.

As this suggests, there is a simultaneous valorization of fighting and of not fighting as signs of hardness. This same mentality is evident in the nuclear deterrent strategy which constructs the fantasy of omnipotence as the last defensive strategy in a war which, it is hoped, will never reach the point where this omnipotence is demonstrated.

One who "stands his ground" is, as this trope suggests, able to occupy space because he successfully makes his might known to others. Because he can keep the other at a distance and thereby defines the situation, he is able to operate on and control this other. He has a particular kind of male power; his presence and literal staying power imply the threat of violence.

This exercise of force and skill requires what Seidler defines as "self-control." One must be able to hide his inner fears and vulnerabilities from himself and others. In speaking of his own experience, Seidler observes that he was

> brought up to denounce whatever fear I was feeling . . . I learnt not to show my fear to others as I learnt to hide it from myself. But also I discovered that in hiding my fear I hid my vulnerability . . . We fear that if we allow our softer feelings to surface we shall never be able to regain control of ourselves. (1985, pp. 150, 159).

Seidler's usage of the term "soft" indicates that the "hardness" of thought central to masculinity requires that vulnerabilities and feelings be stifled.[11]

One who is but does not act hard exercises force, skill and self-control in several ways. In the fighting situation, he may physically fight, which, if successful, means that he uses his strength so skillfully that he can beat his opponent. While fighting, he also controls the pain that he feels from the blows he receives. If he decides not to fight, he aims to control how the situation proceeds mentally, thereby demonstrating that his force and skill extend beyond physical to mental action. He may also exercise mental control in other situations by displaying an attitude of hardness and the implied threat of violence that makes others submit to him. He thereby shows that he is harder than others outside as well as inside the fighting situation.

The second kind of masculinity is evident in the young man who acts and is hard. Just as with the first kind, he exercises force and skill as well as control in a fight, although he is more likely to fight than not to fight in a tense situation than the first kind. Unlike the first kind, he exercises these abilities in other contexts. This suggests that he does not temper his force and skill by control outside the fighting situation. That is, he is viewed as being somewhat out of control in nonfighting contexts. On the other hand, because such a young man *does* exhibit hardness in a fight, he is viewed as being hard. Because he does display this key male attribute in the most important context in which it can be displayed, his form of masculinity is esteemed. Although less esteemed than one who does not act hard, he is preferred over the third type.

The third type of young man acts but is not hard. He displays his hardness in all contexts *except* the fight. In the crucial fighting context he is defeated and, consequently, his "true nature" (which in this case is shown to be false because he misrepresents himself) is revealed. As Keith notes, "If you keep yourself to yourself, nothing will happen, but if you start going 'round acting hard or something, when you ay, people are going to come down on you."

One who acts hard everywhere but in the fighting context is not only *not* considered hard, he is considered a sham. This suggests that hardness is not acceptable as a pose; it must be grounded in male identity. Otherwise the way a young man acts outside the fighting context is not substantiated in it. Probably because such a young man misuses the notion of hardness, he finds himself rejected by peers who "come down on" him. This indicates that the peer group provides evaluative criteria of masculinity which it then publicly imposes on those who do not comply with its dictates. This imposition, in turn, both consolidates and reaffirms these criteria.

But these three kinds of masculinity are not the only ones that these young men elaborate. Elsewhere some of them discuss a more ambiguous, fourth kind of masculinity, that of the "wanker," which they construct in relation to a fifth, a non-"wanker" kind. Neither of these two kinds of male fight: they neither act nor are hard. They are evaluated differently from the other kinds and from each other, as Andrew and Keith note:

A: You got some kids like Tom, he woe fight, but it doe make him a wanker or nothing like that.

K: No, cos we know he doe want to fight . . . You know he wouldn't fight, but you know he's your mate. That's because that's his way, he woe fight.

A: Someone ay got to be hard to be your mate. If someone's a complete wanker, we doe want him. If you doe fight, it doe mean you'm soft . . . He's got more sense than some people.

Andrew suggests that the difference between these two kinds of masculinities is the difference between young men who are "hard" and those who are "soft." He notes that softness is associated with one who is a "wanker." Such a young man *never* demonstrates hardness, in or outside of the fighting context. Since hardness is central to masculinity, a wanker seems to be the least preferred form of masculinity.[12]

It is significant that the term wanker quite literally means one who engages in masturbatory sex. This indicates that those who have sex without a woman and without penetration (the importance of which the requisite hardness of "cocks" suggests) are not "real men." This also suggests that only those who have sex with women are "real men." The young men with whom I spoke link hardness with heterosexuality in other ways. Steve claims that he is more likely to have a fight when he is out with a young woman than at other times because it is a means by which he can "show off in front of a wench." Andrew and Jonathan elaborate this point:

A: [B]oys want to fight in a way to look good to girls. It's a manly thing, ay it?

J: It's macho . . .

A: Yeah. 'Cos you can cause some trouble then. That's even more reason, ay it? The girl's there, someone's causing trouble, you ain't just gonna laugh it off. They [girls] think, "What's he doing? He's a bit of a wanker, ay he?" Whereas if you stand up and have a go . . . you try and impress them, don't you?

J: Thing is, you've got more of a chance of getting into a fight when there's a girl there, 'cos there's a lot of fights happen caused over girls, like. Like you'm going out with someone, someone tries to get off with her, that's it.

A: That's why territory fights can start, 'cos you've been out with a girl from that area. You start going down and people from that area won't like it, 'cos she's going out with someone from another area. Before you know it, they'll have a go at you and then the whole area's having a fight, ay they?

These young men suggest that fighting is "manly" and thereby enables them to demonstrate their hardness to young women. But they claim that they are motivated to fight in this situation not just because they want to show off, but because they fear that their female partner might consider them "a bit of a wanker" if they do not fight. This suggests that they feel somewhat uncertain around and need to demonstrate their masculinity to young women.

However, the fact that these young men maintain that other young men may try "to get off with her" indicates that they consider young women to be pawns in a competitive game that is played by and for males only. But young women are not mere tokens in this game; they are considered the cause of such competition between young men, which can become very violent, as Andrew and Jonathan note:

A: Girls can cause trouble between mates easily. They can split two best mates apart.

J: Easily.

A: To hating each other. To want to kill each other.

Young women are blamed for the consequences of actions between the victors. And Andrew's comment that young men get so angry at each other when young women ostensibly cause fights raises the question of how young men feel about and act towards the supposed female perpetrator of divisiveness between men. If they can hate and "want to kill" the other whom they view as an equal, how might they feel about and act towards a subordinate antagonist?

Some idea of the ways young women experience their role as tokens in a male game can be seen by considering how Hilary, a 16-year-old white working-class young woman at a college outside Wolverhampton, interprets her relationships with young men:

> **H:** Like, what you got to do when you're out with somebody, right, they always try it on with you . . . A bloke will go off with a slag, right, but when it's time to get married, they'll look for the quiet, well, not quiet, but decent girl . . . So when a bloke tries it on you, you kick him in the donkeys and tell him to get lost . . . When I was going out with this bloke, right, he tried it on with me and I thumped him and everything. And after he said to me, "Well, at least I know you'm decent now," you know what I mean. So sometimes it's a test.

Hilary's comments indicate that young men's aim to demonstrate hardness in their heterosexual relationships has serious ramifications on their relationships with young women. They make these relationships into competitive "test[s]" similar to those in which they compete against male peers. If young women fail the "test," they will be labelled "slags" and thus considered sex objects to be used instrumentally by males. If they pass the "test," at this point in their lives their male partners are likely to drop them for a "slag," or "sexually easy" young woman. Young men thereby make heterosexual relationships a context in which they struggle against young women in a contest that the latter cannot win. Clearly, young men view young women as even more subordinate than the softest young men because they do not compete against the former.

This subordination of young women to young men is further suggested by the fact that going out with young women from another territory is thought to cause territorial fights. Such an action is considered a violation of *territory*. Young men give no thought to whether such a violation also includes a violation of young women, which Hilary's comments suggest. This indicates that young men view young women as part of their territory, of their collective materialization of bodily strength.

The construction of masculinity around hardness thus has direct consequences for young women. Young women cannot choose their partners; the young men in their territory seek to control this themselves. Even more ominously, once they enter into relationships with young men, they may be seen as objects through which their partner's masculinity is displayed to other young men.

It is not just heterosexuality that is central to these young men's preferred forms of masculinity, but a heterosexuality that is literally and figuratively substantiated in and through the male genitals. As I have suggested, during secondary school Andrew and his mates viewed the hardest or most powerful young men as "cocks" and now view the softest young men as "wankers." This indicates that the male genitals play a central role in these young men's constructions of masculinity. They constitute masculinity through two opposing sexual orientations of the male genitals: penetrative sex with a young woman and nonpenetrative, masturbatory sex (where such "hardness" is unnecessary and "softness" prevails).[13] The former is preferred and the latter is denigrated. This indicates even more starkly how the preferred form of masculinity of the young men with whom I spoke does not just denigrate young women but constructs the latter only as subordinate objects of sexual desire.

While the fifth kind of masculinity, like that of the wanker, involves not fighting, it has more positive connotations. If it is a young man's "way" not to fight, and if, simultaneously, he is not "soft," then he is considered to have force and skill and to exercise mental control because he *chooses* not to fight. Andrew makes this point when talking about his friend Jonathan:

> **A:** [H]e [Jonathan] doe go to any of the fights. That don't make him a wanker. I think that makes [him] pretty good . . . I think he's standing out from the rest and I think that's better . . . That shows he's got it up here [points to his head]. He knows what he's on about.

Andrew approves of Jonathan's conduct because it indicates that Jonathan exercises mental self-control—he "has it up here." This indicates that there us a mental equivalent to bodily hardness. Like bodily hardness, mental hardness assumes that one has a kind of self-control. Like one who is but does not act hard, such a young man thinks before he acts; he relies on mental capacities to avoid a fight. Unlike the former, however, such a young man never fights. He therefore is in a different category to the former and, indeed, to most other young men. For he chooses not to construct his masculinity with the criteria that they use. Partly because the masculinity which he develops relies upon a notion of self-control, and partly because this masculinity calls upon the strategy of mental self-control used by the most esteemed young men, this form of masculinity is acceptable to and even admired by other young men. Thus Jonathan is respected because he thinks before he acts.

While this form of masculinity, which stresses mental capacities, is admired, it is not the preferred form. My male subjects view their bodies as the main source of their power and esteem. This is not surprising, since those of them who work do skilled or unskilled manual labour; they at least partly affirm their male identities in and through this labour and the wage packet it provides. This differs from middle-class young men, who view their minds as their source of power and control at work, and strive to sharpen their mental control in leisure (Canaan, 1990).

All five types of masculinity which these working-class young men develop rest on the bipolar opposition of hardness and softness. Cocks are hard, wankers are soft, and all other kinds of young men exhibit hardness, its mental analogue, or softness to a greater or lesser degree.

This ethnographic analysis of these forms of masculinity adds to the feminist understanding of male violence in several ways. It demonstrates that the category of hardness provides the idiom with which masculinity is articulated. It further suggests that this masculinity is located in and symbolized by the hard state and heterosexual orientation of their genitals. Relationships with young women thereby presume and are affirmed by penetrative sex. Because this constitutes young women as mere signifiers of male power, young women hold a subordinate position in the male world. Because this world is the more encompassing one, and because young men strive to control young women in their spatial territory as well as in relationships, this suggests that in both public and private contexts young women's movements are limited and monitored by young men. Finally, if these young men construct forms of masculinity that so centrally focus on demonstrating the potential of physical might over male subordinates, might they not also extend this demonstration into their relationships with young women, the gender they consider subordinate to their own?

It is significant that young men construct several distinct forms of masculinity even within a relatively homogeneous population of mostly white, heterosexual working-class young men. This has implications for both feminism and cultural studies. For feminism, it suggests that the social construction of male violence must be understood as mediated by complex and contradictory notions of masculinity, class identity and subculture. For cultural studies, it suggests that analyses of working-class male fighting cannot simply be considered as the expression of their class position.

CONCLUSION

This chapter has aimed to show how some working-class young men's construction of masculinity is highly contradictory and multifaceted. The fact that masculinity can take several forms, even among a small fragment of white working-class heterosexual male youths, suggests that masculinity is not a unified entity. It can mean different things to different young men in different contexts. Not all of these forms rest on and affirm violence, which suggests that violence against women is not something that is central to all forms of masculinity. Working-class male violence is not something that singularly expresses working-class identity or masculine identity; it is a particular conjunction of these two, and other, factors. In addition, this analysis suggests that male violence is constructed as much through gender as class; it is central to masculinity in general and takes particular forms among distinct groups of working-class young men, which reveals much about their class and gender as well as their sexual orientation and age.

By integrating cultural studies analyses of males fighting other males, which stress class relations, and feminist analyses of male violence against females, which stress gender relations, I have sought to contribute to a more complex, textured and multivocal perspective on masculinity. Both class and gender must be seen in a more encompassing framework, one which considers how people organize these, and other components, into their identities.

NOTES

1. This chapter uses data collected from four months of participant–observer research at a college outside Wolverhampton. I also spent one month at youth clubs in two other communities outside Wolverhampton.

2. Michael Kaufman (1987) calls this "the triad of men's violence."

3. I do not mean to suggest that fighting is exclusively male; during my research among upper middle-class American teenagers (Canaan, 1990) I heard about fights between young women, which other studies explore in more detail (e.g. Campbell, 1984). Nor do I mean to suggest that violence is limited to working-class males. My data on American upper middle-class young men in the longer version of this chapter suggest that they develop forms of verbal violence that are much more insidious than those of working-class British young men.

4. The research which I conducted can only loosely be termed ethnographic. Unlike the more traditional anthropological ethnography on American suburban upper middle-class teenagers (Canaan, 1990) which I wrote, this research was neither long-term nor very extensive. Yet just as an anthropological ethnography, it was qualitative and aimed to tease out the terms and strategies with which working-class young men constructed some aspects of their identities.

5. From the earliest days of the Industrial Revolution until recently, Wolverhampton has been a central site for the manufacturing and distribution sectors of the British economy. However, these sectors are currently diminishing in importance as the service sector of the economy expands. The manufacturing that remains is moving away from old industrial cities such as Wolverhampton. That which is left relies on a smaller workforce. The level of unemployment in Wolverhampton has been relatively higher than elsewhere in the country and this is especially true for young people. In the early 1980s one-third of all young people were unemployed (Willis et al., 1988).

6. Names of communities and of the young people to whom I talked are pseudonyms.

7. Exceptions include: Griffin (1985), McRobbie (1981), McRobbie and Garber (1976) and McRobbie and Nava (1984).

8. Other data for this study and my prior study of white middle-class suburban American young people (Canaan, 1990) suggest that young people have contradictory ideas about the "natural" and "cultural" components of their conduct. Sometimes they emphasize one component, at other times the other, and sometimes they acknowledge both. Further research is needed to clarify in what circumstances they emphasize these factors.

9. The criterion of hardness does not simply constitute the most powerful group of young men in school. Other male groups are also ranked by hardness. The next hardest group occupies the middle rung. Those at the bottom rung who "just ay there" probably seem invisible because they do not fight and therefore do not demonstrate hardness.

10. When I gave this chapter as a paper at the University of Exeter, Jeff Meiners noted that his students use a third criterion, "looking hard," that is, dressing in a way which conveys hardness.

11. If these "soft" qualities are not contained, males may feel very threatened. Interestingly, Holloway's (1984) male subjects use the term "soft" as a verb to describe

how they feel when attracted to a woman. This suggests that such attraction is fundamentally threatening to masculinity because it requires that one reveal the qualities that one previously attempted to conceal:

Wendy: But I think that there's a question about . . . how much you show yourself to be vulnerable.

Martin: But you do, just by showing that you're soft on somebody. It seems to me that when you've revealed that need, you put yourself in an incredibly insecure state. You've before managed by not showing anyone what you're like. By showing them only what is publicly acceptable. And as soon as you've shown that there is this terrible hole in you—that you want somebody else—then you're in an absolute state of insecurity. (Holloway, 1984, p. 246).

Martin's description of the display of vulnerabilities as that which makes him feel so incomplete that he has a "terrible hole" inside, suggests how fundamental the containment of vulnerabilities is to the construction of masculinity.

12. Chris Griffin at the University of Birmingham pointed out that this was a distinct type of masculinity.

13. The upper middle-class American teenagers I worked with use a slang term, "weaponhead." They gloss this as a male who is controlled by his genitals rather than his brain, which suggests that the male genitals can function as a kind of lethal weapon. The implications of this term for male violence against women are dangerously suggestive (Canaan, 1990).

REFERENCES

Amos, V., and Parmar, P. (1981), "Resistances and responses: the experiences of black girls in Britain," in A. McRobbie and I. McCabe (eds.) *Feminism for girls: An Adventure* (London: Routledge & Kegan Paul), pp. 129–48.

Bart, P. (1989), "Rape as a paradigm of sexism in society—victimization and its discontents," in R. D. Klein and D. L. Steinberg (eds). *Radical Voices* (Oxford: Pergamon), pp. 55–69.

Brod, H. (ed.) (1987), *The Making of Masculinities: The New Men's Studies* (Winchester, Mass.: Allen & Unwin).

Campbell, A. (1984), *The Girls in the Gang* (Oxford: Basil Blackwell).

Canaan, J. E. (1990), "Individualizing Americans: the making of American suburban middle class teenagers," PhD thesis, Department of Anthropology, University of Chicago.

Canaan, J. E., and Griffin, C. (1990), "Men's studies: part of the problem or part of the solution?", in J. Hearn and D. Morgan (eds) *Men, Masculinity and Social Theory* (London: Unwin Hyman).

Clarke, G. (1982), "Defending ski-jumpers: a critique of theories of youth subcultures', stencilled paper no. 72, Centre for Contemporary and Cultural Studies, University of Birmingham.

Cohen, S. (1978), "Breaking out, smashing up and the social context of aspiration," in

B. Krisberg and J. Austin (eds), *The Children of Ishmael* (Palo Alto, Calif.: Mayfield), pp. 257–79.

Corrigan, P. (1976), "Doing nothing," in S. Hall and T. Jefferson (eds), *Resistance Through Rituals: Youth Subcultures in Postwar Britain* (London: Hutchinson), pp. 103–5.

Griffin, C. (1985), *Typical Girls? Young Women from School to the Job Market* (London: Routledge).

Hall, S., and Jefferson, T. (eds) (1976), *Resistance Through Rituals: Youth Subcultures in Postwar Britain* (London: Hutchinson).

Hanmer, J., and Saunders, S. (1984), *Well-Founded Fear* (London: Hutchinson).

Hebdige, D. (1979), *Subculture: The Meaning of Style* (London: Methuen).

Holloway, W. (1984), "Gender difference and the production of subjectivity," in J. Henriques et al. (eds) *Changing the Subject* (London: Methuen), pp. 227–63.

Kaufman, M. (1987), "The construction of masculinity and the triad of male violence," in M. Kaufman (ed.), *Beyond Patriarchy* (Toronto: Oxford University Press), pp. 1–29.

Kimmel, M. (ed.) (1987), *Changing Men: New Directions in Research on Men and Masculinity* (New York: Sage).

Mac an Ghail, M. (1988), *Young, Gifted and Black* (Milton Keynes: Open University Press).

McRobbie, A. (1980), "Settling accounts with sub-cultures: a feminist critique," *Screen Education*, vol. 34, pp. 37–49.

McRobbie, A. (1981), "Just like a *Jackie* story," in McRobbie and McCabe, op. cit., pp. 113–28.

McRobbie, A., and Garber, J. (1976), "Girls and subcultures: an exploration," in S. Hall and T. Jefferson (eds) *Resistance Through Rituals: Youth Subcultures in Postwar Britain* (London: Hutchinson), pp. 209–22.

McRobbie, A., and Nava, M. (eds) (1984), *Gender and Generation* (London: Macmillan).

Miller, W. (1978), "Lower class culture as generating milieu of gang delinquency," in B. Krisberg and J. Austin (eds), *The Children of Ishmael* (Palo Alto, Calif.: Mayfield), pp. 139–55.

Russell, D. E. H. (1984), *Rape in Marriage* (New York: Macmillan).

Seidler, V. (1985), "Fear and intimacy," in A. Metcalfe and M. Humphries (eds), *The Sexuality of Men* (London: Pluto Press), pp. 150–80.

Willis, P. E. (1977), *Learning to Labour: How Working Class Kids Get Working Class Jobs* (Aldershot: Saxon House).

Willis, P., et al. (1988), *The Youth Review: Social Conditions of Young People in Wolverhampton* (Aldershot: Avebury).

CHAPTER 11

Masculinity, Honour, and Confrontational Homicide

KENNETH POLK

INTRODUCTION

While it is well established that males account for most homicide offenders (Wolfgang 1958; Wallace 1986; Silverman and Kennedy 1987; Falk 1990; Johnson and Robinson 1992), perhaps less well known is that slightly over half of all homicides are likely to be male-on-male events, that is, involving men both as offenders and victims. In a national study in Canada, homicides with both male victims and male offenders accounted for 53 per cent of all homicides (Silverman and Kennedy 1987), while an investigation in New South Wales (Australia) reports a virtually identical 54 per cent (Wallace 1986).

What factors account for these distinctively masculine homicides? Unfortunately, the literature is scanty regarding such killings, despite their relative frequency. Ever since the pioneering study of Wolfgang (1958), analysis of the victim–offender relationship has been a central feature of most homicide investigations. None of the major investigations, however, has carried out an analysis of these relationships for the specific group of male-on-male homicides.

Some rough clues can be found in the larger studies, however, since these are likely to report relationship data by gender of victims. Since close to 90 per cent of all offenders are male, it can be presumed that the bulk of cases where males are victims will also be cases where males are offenders, and then male victims can be compared with female victims. Such analysis will show that females are likely to be victimised by other family members (notably husbands, but sometimes parents), whereas in contrast males are much more likely to be

Reprinted from Kenneth Polk, "Masculinity, Honour, and Confrontational Homicide," in *Just Doing Business?*, edited by Tim Newburn and Elizabeth A. Stanko, Routledge, pp. 166–188, © 1994. Reprinted by permission of Routledge and the author.

victimised by either "friends" or "strangers" (Wolfgang 1958: 207; Wallace 1986: 73).

This observation that homicides among males are more likely to fall outside of the family network in fact doesn't carry us very far in developing an understanding of what is going on in these killings. For example, in Philadelphia (Wolfgang 1958: 207), almost two-thirds (64 per cent) of male homicide victims were killed by either friends, acquaintances, or strangers (in contrast to 21 per cent of female victims). While that information has traditionally featured strongly in discussions of homicide, it actually does not provide information about why friends kill, or why strangers kill, let alone why such killings should involve men more often than women. If a male kills a friend, he does not do so because the person is a friend, but because something has happened between them. Other factors are present which push an offender to do what would otherwise be unthinkable (taking the life of someone close). Similarly, people are not killed because they are strangers, rather because something occurs which transforms the scene to the point where the taking of life of a person otherwise remote to the offender becomes a possibility.

Initially relationship data appear to be a bit richer when the focus shifts to the "motive" (Wolfgang 1958; Falk 1990) or the "circumstances" (Maxfield 1984) of the homicide. A potentially useful bit of information is found in Wolfgang's observation that a large proportion (41 per cent) of male homicide victims were killed as a result of a "trivial" altercation. In his text Wolfgang speaks of the "significance of a jostle, a slightly derogatory remark, or the appearance of a weapon in the hands of an adversary" going on to comment that:

> A male is usually expected to defend the name and honor of his mother, the virtue of womanhood . . . his age, or his masculinity. Quick resort to physical combat as a measure of daring, courage, or defense of status appears to be a cultural expectation, especially for lower socio-economic class males of both races. (Wolfgang 1958: 188–89)

When Wolfgang provides actual case examples of male-on-male homicide, these fit this formulation, including cases where a victim refused to pay a $2 bet in a card game, where a victim would not share his wine with his flophouse roommate, or when a victim in the course of an argument referred to the offender as a "Dago."

Unfortunately, the matter becomes a bit confused when the data are treated quantitatively, since almost as many female offenders (28 per cent) as male offenders (38 per cent) in Wolfgang's study committed homicide because they were provoked by a "trivial altercation" (Wolfgang 1958). Further, it is necessary to go beyond these terms, and perhaps follow the words of his text more closely, since it is obvious that in a strict sense people don't kill because of a trivial provocation. That is, there has to be something behind the apparently inconsequential event which generates the heated response which results in lethal violence.

One possibly helpful avenue of thought has been opened by Katz (1988) in a discussion of how humiliation and rage push individuals to the point where homicide becomes possible. Luckenbill (1977) has presented a view of homicide as proceeding through a set of stages, from an initial provocation to the ultimate killing. He urges that any view of homicide must be a dynamic one: "homicide does not appear as a one-sided event with an unwitting victim assuming a passive, non-contributory role. Rather, murder is the outcome of a dynamic interchange between an offender, victim, and, in many cases, bystanders" (Luckenbill 1977: 185).

While perhaps providing a starting point in thinking through the processes involved in lethal encounters, neither Katz nor Luckenbill examines the critical masculine character of homicide. For ideas regarding masculinity and violence, a much richer source of information is to be found in the ideas of Daly and Wilson (1988). While much of their argument is concerned with the question of why it is that homicides in situations of sexual intimacy are more likely to involve males than females, they also recognise the role that masculine competition and honour play in male-on-male killings.

Drawing heavily upon the ideas of Daly and Wilson, the present research has been able to identify patterns within the general category of male-on-male homicides (Polk and Ranson 1991). A significant proportion of male-on-male killings occur during the course of other crime, as where the threat implicit in armed robbery becomes real, at the cost of the life of either the victim or offender in the robbery. A smaller proportion involve situations where males well at the boundaries of conventional life employ planned and intentional violence as a technique of conflict resolution.

The largest grouping of male-on-male killings, however, are a result of confrontations which begin as a contest over honour or reputation (Polk and Ranson 1991; following the usage first suggested by Daly and Wilson 1988). It is the purpose of the present discussion to discuss the structure of this form of homicide, and to identify the particular elements that make up this distinctive masculine scenario of violence.

THE DATA

The data for the present investigation, which is part of an on-going investigation of homicide (Polk and Ranson 1991), are drawn from the files of the Office of the Coroner of Victoria, Australia. These files contain a number of reports which are collected for the purpose of carrying out the coronial inquest, and include an initial police report of the incident, an autopsy report regarding the cause of death, a toxicology report if such is relevant, a police prosecutor's brief, and the report of the inquest itself. The most helpful of these documents is the prosecutor's brief, which typically contains lengthy witness statements as well as transcripts of interviews with defendants where these have been taken.

There were a total of 380 homicides reported in the years 1985–89. For each homicide a lengthy case history was prepared drawing upon the material in the coronial files. These case studies were then subjected to a qualitative analysis of the themes which characterised the relationship between the victim and the offender. These themes where then analysed, and yielded a number of distinctive scenarios of violence. Among these were the confrontational homicides, of which there were 84 cases (this scenario accounting for 22.1 per cent of all homicides).

CONTESTS OF HONOUR AND LETHAL VIOLENCE

Confrontational homicide has its source in the willingness of males, first, to lay down challenges to the honour of other males, and second, the masculine readiness to engage in physical violence in response to such challenges, as is made clear in our first case study:

> Gabe W. [age 32, soldier] boarded a train at Flinders Street Station after an evening of drinking with his friends (his blood alcohol level was subsequently established to be 0.224). When Gabe attempted to take a seat where Mike M. was sitting with his feet spread across two seats, Mike ordered him in a clearly insulting manner to move on and find a seat elsewhere. Challenged, Gabe refused to move on, and attempted to force his way onto the seat. Mike leaped up and struck Gabe, and the two fought. Although Gabe received a number of blows, and was kneed in the face, he finally managed to pin Mike down.
>
> Witnesses relate that at this point Gabe said: "If you don't stop now, I'll break your neck." Then, believing that Mike would stop, Gabe released him. Mike instead produced a knife, stabbing Gabe three times in the chest. One of the blows penetrated the heart. Gabe collapsed and died in the aisle. (Case No. 4714–86)

This represents almost the ideal type of confrontational homicide. The incidents moved rapidly from initial exchange to the fatal wounding. It is not possible to know the nonverbal cues that preceded the violence. Once words were exchanged, the males quickly responded to the public challenge to their masculine reputation. There was no planning or premeditation regarding the death, since the parties could not have known even minutes before that a lethal encounter was about to ensue. Words led quickly to a fight, the fight in turn escalated to the point where a deadly weapon was employed.

MASCULINITY, HONOUR AND WHEN WHAT APPEARS TRIVIAL BECOMES A LIFE-THREATENING MATTER

One further issue in this narrative is that the precipitating events appear exceptionally trivial when contrasted with the disastrous outcomes (Gabe's death and Mike's subsequent sentence to prison). These apparently minor triggering events are a common feature of the confrontational killings:

> Late one Saturday night, Anthony N. (age 19, unemployed) was walking back towards their home after attending a local "Octoberfest." They had enjoyed a pleasant evening of drinking (Anthony's blood alcohol level was later established at 0.08). In a small park, they met up with another group, including Don B. (age 18, unemployed) and Peter T. Before setting out, this second group had armed themselves with broken billiard cues and knives.
>
> One of the young women in Anthony's group was part of the triggering of the confrontation when she asked if she could ride Peter's

bike. He replied: "You can have a ride if I can ride you." Insults and challenges began to flow back and forth between the groups. At one point, Anthony is recorded as having said to Don: "You're a bit young to be going to Octoberfest, aren't you?" Don responded with: "Don't call me a kid."

The exchanges escalated into pushing and shoving. Anthony said: "If you want to have a go, I'll have a go back." Don then threw a punch at Anthony, and the fight was on. At first it was a general group scuffle, and at one point Anthony broke a beer stein (obtained at Octoberfest) over the head of a member of Don's group.

The main group conflict began to simmer down, but Anthony and Don sought each other out and continued their personal dispute. At first Don was armed with the broken pool cue, but Anthony was able to take it off of him. Peter then handed Don a knife. Witnesses agree that at this point, Anthony kept repeating to Don: "I'll kill you, I'll kill you." Don was able to come in close to Anthony, however, and slashed out with his knife, stabbing Anthony in the left thigh, right hand, and finally the left side of his chest. By now all eyes of the groups were on the two. They saw Anthony stagger, and he began to bleed profusely. The two groups broke off the fight, each going their separate ways.

One of Anthony's friends asked if he was feeling all right, to which he replied; "I think I have been stabbed." The friends helped him to a nearby house and called an ambulance, but Anthony died before medical help arrived. (Case No. 3661–85).

As before, the initial set of precipitating events appear inconsequential to the outside observer. Daly and Wilson (1988) have warned, however, that care must be used in understanding the nature of these apparently trivial events:

> The typical "trivial altercation" homicide in America is an affair of honor with strong resemblances to the affairs of honor that have been described in other cultures. . . . The precipitating insult may appear petty, but it is usually a deliberate provocation (or is perceived to be), and hence constitutes a public challenge that cannot be shrugged off. It often takes the form of disparagement of the challenged party's "manhood": his nerve, strength or savvy, or the virtue of his wife, girlfriend or female relatives. (Daly and Wilson 1988: 69)

Such perceptions are actually consistent with Wolfgang's observations. After noting the apparently "trivial" character in some of the disputes leading to homicide, Wolfgang (1958) went on to comment that it is the observers in the criminal justice system (rather than the social analysts) who, drawing upon middle- and upper-class values which have shaped legal norms, describe the disputes which lead to homicide as trivial in origin. For the working- or lower-class players in the homicide drama, the challenge to manhood is matter of consequence.

THE SETTING OF CONFRONTATIONAL VIOLENCE

Another characteristic of these events is that they occur in definitively public and leisure scenes. One of the most common of these leisure scenes of course is the pub:

> Dennis [age 23, unemployed] and a group of three friends had been celebrating the birthday of one of the group when they stopped in the Doutta Galla Pub at 9.30 in the evening. Fred [age 31] was there drinking alone. The initial provocation for a fight was the challenging eye contact between Fred and one of Dennis's friends. The friend said: "I don't like this arsehole Turk [Fred was born in Turkey] . . . he looks sleazy." Fred then approached the friend and said: "What are you staring at?" To which the friend replied: "What are you on about?" Fred then claimed: "You're staring at me," to which the friend replied, "Get out of here." One of the other members of the group attempted to intervene at this point, and Fred told him: "Fucking keep your head out of it." In reply, the one who had attempted to intervene said: "Well, fuckin' cop this," and punched Fred in the head.
>
> An all out bar room brawl developed. Fred produced a knife, and slashed his attacker across the stomach, and followed this by stabbing his opponent in the staring contest in the leg. Dennis and his friends, and other patrons in the bar armed themselves with billiard cues and surrounded Fred, who then sought shelter behind the bar. When Dennis reached over to pull him from behind the bar, Fred stabbed him in the chest. One of Dennis's friends, known in the pub as "Dogsbody," pummelled Fred several times over the head with a cue. Fred twisted around and was able to stab his attacker twice in the body. Patrons then started shouting: "Let's kill him, he's stabbed Dogsbody, let's kill him!"
>
> Fred attempted then to seek shelter in the pub office behind the bar, where the barman was counting the night's takings. Fred locked the door, and pleaded: "Don't let them get me, they're going to kill me." Several men kicked at the door until they were able to break it down. Fred then grabbed the barman, and held a knife to his throat, threatening to kill the barmen if the group approached any closer. Someone yelled "The Turkish cunt has got him," and the group started throwing bottles at Fred to make him release the barman. When the barman was able to break free, Fred was showered with an avalanche of bottles. The police entered at this point, and the fight subsided. Dennis was found, dead, on the floor (his blood alcohol was 0.309). (Case No. 3631–87)

There is much in this that suggests a classic confrontation. The scene is a pub. There is a large social audience of other males who are witness to, and even participants in, the violence as it erupts. The initial provocations are what others might define as petty, including the mutual jousting with eye contact known as "eyeing off." Alcohol features in this event, not only in the sense that it has been consumed by the participants, but more importantly because it helps define the nature of the leisure scene where males relax among other males, some known and others unknown. In such scenes, the social audience plays a critical role in providing social supports for violence as an appropriate way of dealing with the challenge. It is not uncommon, as happened in this narrative, for members of the audience to do more than provide a backdrop for the violence, since they in fact may come to play an active role in the unfolding combat.

HONOUR AND THE PROTECTION OF WOMEN

There are numerous specific sources for the honour contest that flares to violence. One common theme is that men are quick to respond to insults directed at their female companions:

> One weekend night, Tommy F. [age 29, unemployed] and his friend Charlie began their round of drinking first at the Crab Cooker restaurant, then gravitated to the Bowling Green Hotel where they remained, drinking for several hours. Another group came in much later in the evening, including Mike D. [age 26, assembly worker], Pete, and Rog, who was a boy friend of Jennie [a waitress at the pub].
>
> At closing time, as Tommy and Charlie were leaving, they passed Rog and Jennie in the hallway. In passing, Tommy made a comment to Jennie which Rog took to be an insult. An argument developed between Rog and Tommy that led to a fight between them on the sidewalk outside. Tommy was punched to the ground, and the fight broke up with Tommy and Charlie withdrawing to their car which was parked nearby.
>
> Shortly afterwards, Rog, Jennie, Mike and Pete came out of the hotel to head for home. Tommy and Charlie had waited for them, and the two once again approached and proceeded to confront and challenge Rog. When the other males joined in, Tommy pulled a knife and backed away to his car.
>
> Mike and Pete gave chase to the car. Mike picked up a piece of timber, and began to hit the car repeatedly. Tommy suddenly leaped out of the car, and stabbed Mike with his knife. Badly hurt, Mike fell to the ground. Tommy kicked him several times in the head, then jumped back into the car and drove off. The knife, had penetrated Mike's heart, he died before the ambulance arrived (his blood alcohol level was 0.05). (Case No. 3264–86)

As in the previous account, the violence here emerges in a pub environment. Here the initial insult was directed at a woman, and the males felt compelled as a matter of honour to respond. One further interesting feature of this story is how quickly the social audience can move to centre stage in the evolving conflict. In this narrative, the ultimate victim of the homicide was peripheral to the initial flow of insults that initiated the violence, but became swept up in the events and the violence spilled outward to involve the wider group.

COLLECTIVE VIOLENCE

In many of these accounts, the violence is clearly collective in character. One form that this can assume is found in the following case:

Colin [age 17] was a member of a loosely organised group known as "Bogans," while Charles [age 19] was identified as a "Headbanger." Both were
attending a disco in a local tennis centre, when a group of the Bogan males
became involved in an argument with a group of girls who were hanging
out with the Headbangers. After a brief exchange of taunts and insults, one
of the girls punched Colin, who retaliated with a punch in return. Charles
came over and attempted to pull the girl away. Colin called Charles a cow-
ard and a wimp, and began to throw punches at Charles. At this point, a
general fight began between the two groups, involving 10–12 people.
Charles then pulled out a knife, and stabbed Colin several times in the chest
and abdomen. Colin died shortly after (his blood alcohol level was found to
be 0.079). (Case No 1931–87)

In this account, the disco provides an open, public setting in which groups of
males circulate, thereby opening up the possibility of conflict. Both groups involved in this account are distinctively working class, but set off from each
other rather clearly in terms of clothing and hair styles. One of the factors in
this narrative is the active role played by the female Headbanger, since it was
her punching of the Bogan male that initiated the physical violence.

Given the group nature of the conflict found in these last accounts, a natural question which follows concerns the extent to which these findings indicate the presence of gang behaviour in Victoria. The media, certainly, have
popularised the idea of gangs and gang violence in Melbourne. Melbourne newspapers have focused attention on the behaviour of groups such as the "3147
gang" (so-called because of the postal code of the neighbourhood), and one forensic specialist was quoted as being concerned that Victoria was "heading towards becoming a state of warring gangs" (*Melbourne Herald-Sun*, 7.8. 1991:
2).

Assessing the issue of the degree to which there is a "gang problem" in
Victoria requires some clarity and agreement regarding the use of the term
"gang." There is nothing new, obviously, about collective forms of trouble in
Australia. Newspapers in Melbourne and Sydney complained of the "larrikin"
problem over a century ago, and somewhat before that there was the "Kelly
gang," so central now to Australian mythology of colonial life.

In the United States gangs and gang violence tend to be given a highly
specific meaning. One concise definition offered in the US was:

> A youth gang is a self-formed association of peers, bound together by mu-
> tual interests, with identifiable leadership, well-developed lines of author-
> ity, and other organisational features, who act in concert to achieve a spe-
> cific purpose or purposes which generally include the conduct of illegal
> activity and control over a particular territory, facility, or type of enter-
> prise. (Miller 1980: 121)

While there is not complete agreement among writers, it would seem that in
the American scene the term "gang" is likely to refer to a group that has a relatively high degree of organisation, with an explicit leadership structure, a defined territory which is part of the gang identity, and clear colours or other in-
signia which set them apart. Using these rough guide-lines, it would appear
that such formalised gangs are rarely encountered in Australian communities.

While for a short time after the appearance of the movie *Colors* there was a bit of faddish copying of American gang characteristics (including the wearing of colours), in the Melbourne environment there is little that resembles American street gangs. There are no groups who are formally organised, who maintain a clear sense of territory (including control of that territory), who consistently through time maintain a distinctive set of colours and clothing, and who rely on formal leadership.

At the same time, there are groupings of young people, especially originating in lower and underclass environments, whose collective behaviour is seen by the wider community as "troublesome." The groupings tend to be loosely organised, including their leadership structure. While they may emerge from a particular neighbourhood, their activities are spread over a reasonably wide geographical area. These informal groups may spend some time in their neighourhoods, but it is also highly likely that they will be mobile, often flowing through the major spokes of the public transportation system (buses, trams and trains) into such readily available public spaces as train stations, shopping malls, pubs, parks or reserves, and, of course, the streets, laneways and sidewalks that make up the "street" scene.

What seems characteristic of collective violence in Australia is that much of the conflict between groups seems to result from what can be seen as the "social friction" that occurs as groups flow past each other in public space, often outside the neighbourhood of either group. Walmsley (1986) has observed a similar form of group movement, friction, and confrontations over honour in the UK:

> One troublespot in Newcastle was a small area of about four streets containing twelve pubs. Groups of young people moved from pub to pub during the evening and this led, towards closing time, to friction between groups suddenly arriving at a pub. . . . Such situations produce violent incidents whether inside or outside the pub. Again violence sometimes occurs when large numbers of people leave rival establishments (e.g., dance halls) at about the same time. Ramsay describes three violent late-night incidents at burger stalls. In each case "individual worth and identity were at stake, in front of other bystanders, in an impersonal setting." Provocative remarks were made, or something was seen by one party as provocative and the incidents escalated into violence. (Walmsley 1986: 17–18)

Such accounts are virtually identical with those described in the present case studies. It should be noted that the friction which occurs in the social space is probably highly concentrated in terms of the times when violence is likely to result. These open and public places are often occupied in the daylight and early evening hours by groups of other conventional citizens, whose separate claims to the space are likely to exert a dampening effect on violence. One is more likely to fight in front of an audience of masculine "mates," and is inclined in other directions if the audience includes aunties, younger sisters, grandfathers, or strangers occupying disparate age and gender roles.

Where group identities exist in Victoria, such as "Bogans," "Headbangers," "Wogs," or "Skips," at least in the period being studied, these are loosely defined and derive more from general and widely spread lifestyles, rather than membership in territorial based gangs. As indicated in the accounts above, group identities can nourish collective violence in Victoria, as seen in the disco encounter between the Bogans and Headbangers. The nature of that collective violence, however, seems tied more to issues having to do with the uses of public spaces, rather than in protection of home territory.

VIOLENCE WHERE THE ACTION IS BROKEN

While in the homicide narratives up to this point the violence has proceeded rapidly and spontaneously from the initial insult or challenge to lethal violence, there is in some accounts a break in the interaction when one of the partici-pants leaves to obtain a weapon:

> Mick F. [age 36, unemployed] started his drinking at the house of a friend late in the afternoon, and then the two of them moved off to their local, the Victoria Hotel. They continued drinking "shout for shout" for some time (Mick's blood alcohol was later found to be 0.147).
>
> In the middle of the evening, the group was approached by Jimmy S. (age 53), another of the pub regulars. Jimmy, also feeling the effects of al-cohol (some hours later, his blood alcohol was still found to be 0.197), up-braided Mick for some insulting comments he had made towards his "mis-sus" (observers commented that a trivial exchange had occurred between the two earlier in the day, or at least in their view the comments were triv-ial). There were mutual insults and challenges, and finally Mick hauled back and struck Jimmy, a short fight ensued, with Jimmy being rather badly beaten. Hurt as well as drunk, Jimmy needed help from bystanders to make his way out of the pub.
>
> Mick and his group settled back to their drinking, when they were in-terrupted by Jimmy's de facto wife, who proceeded to abuse Mick for his beating of Jimmy. Then, Jimmy himself re-entered the bar. Without a word he walked up to Mick, pulled out a knife, and stabbed him once in the chest. As before, Jimmy was set upon, this time by the friends of Mick. Jimmy was assisted out of the pub by his de facto spouse. Help was summoned for Mick, but the knife had penetrated his heart and he died before he could reach hospital. (Case No. 3778–85)

This is similar in many respects to the previous accounts of such violence. The action was played out in a pub. Insults directed at a woman companion pro-voked one of the males to initiate physical violence. In this particular narra-tive, the older male was publicly humiliated by the beating administered in front of both peers and his de facto wife. He then broke away from the scene to fetch a knife, and re-engaged the fight bringing it to a swift and deadly con-clusion.

Another case of such a breaking of the action is of interest both because of the nature of the provoking incident, and because it provides an illustration of what Wolfgang (1958) termed "victim premeditated" homicide:

> Gregor B. [age 24, machine operator] and his friend Ned set out one evening for a pub crawl. After many drinks, and while they were at their third ho-

tel, Gregor went to the toilet. When coming out of the toilet, Gregor became involved in an argument with a woman who, like him, had too much to drink (Gregor's blood alcohol level was found later to be 0.120). The nephew of the woman, Albert S. [age 18], intervened, shoving Gregor away. The two pushed at each other, arguing heatedly. The pub bouncer came over, and ordered Gregor to leave the pub.

When Ned came out, he found Gregor waiting in his car. Gregor was furious, explaining that he had been bashed up and "called a wog" (Gregor was a recent migrant from Yugoslavia). Gregor then asked to be driven home so he could fetch his shot gun and bring it back in order to force his attackers to apologise. They went to Gregor's house to pick up the weapon. Gregor's wife pleaded with him to either stay home, or leave the gun behind, but he replied that this was ". . . something he simply had to do."

Gregor and Ned returned to the pub just on closing time. As Albert and his group came out, Gregor threatened them with the shot gun, insisting that they all line up along the wall. They all stood quietly until Gregor turned to say a word to Ned, who was still in his car. At that moment Albert rushed Gregor, knocking him down and taking control of the gun.

Three of Albert's friends began to beat and kick Gregor. Albert ordered Ned out of the car, and when Ned refused, smashed one of the car windows. Ned sped off. Albert then added his bit to the beating of Gregor, hitting him with the butt of the shot gun. He then pointed the gun at Gregor, and fired a shot which hit him in the neck, killing him instantly.

When apprehended a few minutes later, Albert said: "He was going to shoot me . . . I acted in self-defence. I know I acted rashly. Is the bloke all right, the bloke I shot? . . . I wanted to shoot the tires out . . . When I first got the gun, I tried to shoot it in the air but it wouldn't go off . . . I thought he wouldn't be hit . . ." Circumstances suggest that Albert may not have intended to shoot when he did. Forensic tests revealed that the gun had a sensitive trigger. Further, Albert very nearly shot his own friends as well, one of them, in fact, receiving a burn mark on his jeans because he was close to the line of fire when Gregor was shot. (Case No. 2069–86)

As in the previous account, one of the actors has broken off the action to search out a weapon, in this case a gun, to carry back to the scene, except here the male became a victim of his own weapon. We see as well in this account the role that ethnic slurs can play in the events which stir up males to the point where they take up violence.

ETHNICITY AND MASCULINE CONFLICT

Given the markedly multicultural environment of contemporary Australian cities, it is inevitable that, as in the previous case study, ethnic identities provide the spark for masculine confrontation:

V. [age 27, unemployed] was originally from Vietnam, but had lived in Melbourne for some time. He was planning to move to Queensland in a few days to accept a job offer. A group of his friends (all Vietnamese) decided to throw a party in his honour.

The group went along Racecourse Road to the local shops and pub to obtain the supplies for the party. While part of the group went into the Palace Hotel to buy beer, V. and a friend went across the road to buy some pizza. As they crossed the road, a battered green sedan pulled up with what the Vietnamese could only describe as "western" males inside. These men alighted from their car, and started verbally to abuse the two Vietnamese, followed this with threats to use a chopping knife that one of the group produced. V. remained alone briefly while his friend went to summon help from their friends in the pub.

At the same time as the group of Vietnamese arrived on the scene, a further group of "western" males poured out of the pub. A general mêlée developed, in which the Vietnamese group apparently threw beer bottles at their attackers in an attempt to defend themselves. Surrounded now by the original group augmented by those that had come from the pub, the outnumbered Vietnamese broke ranks and began to run to the safety of their flats further among Racecourse Road.

The green car followed in pursuit, grabbing and beating whatever stragglers they could reach. One of these was V., who was viciously beaten, including a severe blow to his head. Found shortly later unconscious in the street, V. was taken to Royal Melbourne Hospital where he died three days later of brain damage from the head injuries. (Case No. 666–85)

This again shows how the frictional contact of persons moving through public space may result in masculine violence. In this account the violence occurs in the city streets, and the provoking incidents originate in ethnic conflict, here conflict between "Old Australians" and the newly emerging Vietnamese community. In some instances, such clashes occur between ethnic groups:

As was his usual custom, Edgar L. [age 19] left his suburban home to go into the China Town section of the city in order to take Kung Fu lessons. He met his friend Keith L. in Little Bourke Street, where they played some of the machines in the "Tunza Fun" amusement parlour for a few minutes, then went off to their Kung Fu lessions. Their class finished at 2.30 p.m., and the two first had coffee with friends, then returned to the Tunza Fun at about 3.30, and started playing the Kung Fu Master machine which was their particular favourite. Suddenly, 6 Vietnamese youths approached and started to strike both Edgar and his friend. Edgar then turned and challenged the group, saying (according to one witness): "Come on, I'll do ya." One of the Vietnamese group came in close, produced a knife, and stabbed Edgar once in the chest. The Vietnamese group then quickly slipped away. Edgar staggered outside, and collapsed on the sidewalk, where he died a few minutes later (the knife had penetrated his heart).

The police investigation was able to pull together only scanty details of this homicide. They were unable to identify or locate any of the six Vietnamese young people involved. One of Edgar's friends recalled seeing the Vietnamese group sitting outside a Little Bourke Street restaurant earlier in the afternoon, and commented that this group had previously caused trouble for Chinese young people in the street. Further, there was some provocation on Edgar's part, since earlier he and his friends had been yelling out anti-Vietnamese insults in Chinese as they had been walking down the street on their way back from their lessons. (Case No. 1047–85)

Here the frictional movement of the two groups occurred in one of Melbourne's most popular laneways, the narrow street that contains some of the better-known restaurants in the city. In this incident, tensions between an older and more firmly established ethnic group (Chinese) and the more recent arrivals (Vietnamese) provided the background for the lethal violence.

A DEVIANT CASE: A CONFRONTATION INVOLVING WOMEN

While this analysis has proceeded with the presumption that confrontational homicides are definitively male behaviour, there is among these cases one in which the central actors were female:

Carol [age 31, single mother] was walking to the local supermarket near the council flats where she lived, when she became involved in an argument with Donna (age 21) and Tricia. The two women apparently felt that Carol had insulted them, and was responsible for graffiti alluding to their lesbian relationship. As the argument heated up, Donna suddenly punched Carol, grabbed her by the hair, and threw her on the ground. Since Carol had her six month old baby with her, she thought that a defensive response was called for, and she managed to break off the conflict and run with her child back to her own flat.

Carol then armed herself with a small wooden baton, and had two male friends drive her so that she could ". . . go down there to get them two bitches." The men stood by the car while Carol went to the front door of Donna and Tricia's flat, calling out: "Now, come on out and fight me." Tricia came to the door, and alleged that Carol hit her across the face with the baton. Tricia then woke Donna who had been napping. Donna grabbed a knife and went outside. When she saw the weapon, Carol said: "Hey, you don't have to use the knife." Carol then backed off, and started running for the car. Donna followed, shouting "I'm going to fuckin' kill you." Donna lunged forward, and stabbed Carol in the chest. Carol's right pulmonary artery was cut, and she bled to death at the scene. It was later established that Donna had a long history of violence, and had previously stabbed Tricia during one of their domestic disputes. (Case No. 4202–88)

There is much in common with other of the confrontations which have fatal outcomes. Insults are exchanged, a fight breaks out, the action breaks off and one of the parties leaves to fetch a weapon, and then returns to a scene where the final violence takes place. There was, as well, one further case where two women who had been close friends became embroiled in an argument over a male who had written to both of them while the two were in prison. Again, the argument flared up quickly and spontaneously from an initial set of insults to the final killing (Case No. 2174–87).

While these cases share much in common with the other confrontations we have observed, these two differ in that they involve women as the major participants. While women can draw upon the confrontational scenario in a scene of conflict, this is exceptionally rare, since well over 90 per cent of these events involve males. Despite these deviant cases, it can be concluded that confrontational violence is overwhelmingly and distinctively masculine in its makeup.

THE ISSUE OF CLASS, GENDER AND ECONOMIC MARGINALITY

It is the present contention that it is important to see confrontations as "contests of honour" in which the maintenance of "face" or reputation is a central matter. Further, these are seen as quintessential masculine matters. In looking for explanations, theorists such as Katz (1988), whose ideas are not grounded in gender, are not likely to be of much help. If we take Katz as providing a general view of homicide (as he proposes), then the great number of cases where the homicide falls well outside of events involving a spontaneous interplay of humiliation and rage (central to his description of "typical homicide") raise fundamental questions about the adequacy of his view. His theory cannot encompass the many carefully premeditated homicides on the part of jealous husbands, the planned homicides of depressed males who kill their wives as part of their own suicide plan, the rationality of some homicides where males employ violence to resolve a long-term conflict with another male, or even the strange and complex motivations involved in neonaticide where in most cases the young women simply deny the birth. Even where the particular interaction between rage and humiliation might have some relevance, since something like this happens in some of the confrontational homicides, Katz's inadequate and flawed treatment of the gender elements of homicide requires us to look elsewhere for ideas regarding the nature of confrontational homicide.

Luckenbill's (1977) suggestion that homicide be examined as a "situated transaction" fares only slightly better. Some of the confrontational homicides appear to correspond to the step-by-step movement from initial provocation to the ultimate killing laid down by Luckenbill. There are, unfortunately, two kinds of problems in this formulation. One is an empirical matter. Despite having a wealth of useful data in the records available to the present investigation, it is often not clear what the "opening moves" of a homicide might have been. Quickly evolving scenes, such as those in the opening case studies (such as the fight on the train between Gabe and Mike), permit an observer to construct an account of the social dynamics as these moved through the various phases described by Luckenbill. Other homicides are more extended in time, and it is no longer possible to trace back to the opening move. Further, Luckenbill argues that his model applies to all homicides, when clearly such events as neonaticide or where depressed husbands intent on their own suicide kill their wives, fall outside his formulation.

Much more important, however, is the second matter. Luckenbill's argument is posed in gender neutral terms. While many of the confrontational homicides can be described as moving through the stages he specifies, Luckenbill offers no clues as to why it is highly likely that such confrontations are masculine. Neither Katz nor Luckenbill are likely to be of much theoretical relevance because neither addresses the question of why it is that males are likely to become involved in this pattern of violence.

Much more close to the mark are the ideas of Daly and Wilson (1988) who have argued that it is particularly males who become involved in violence around the issue of reputation:

> A seemingly minor affront is not merely a "stimulus" to action, isolated in time and space. It must be understood within a larger social context of reputations, face, relative social status, and enduring relationships. Men are known by their fellows as "the sort who can be pushed around" or "the sort that won't take any shit," as people whose word means action and people who are full of hot air, as guys whose girlfriends you can chat up with impunity or guys you don't want to mess with. In most social milieux, a man's reputation depends in part upon the maintenance of a credible threat of violence. (Daly and Wilson 1988: 128)

The theoretical account provided by Daly and Wilson is one of the few that recognises the diverse forms of masculine violence that make up contemporary homicide patterns. It is their argument that the general thread of masculinity that runs through homicide reflects forms of male aggressiveness that can be accounted for by evolutionary processes. While their formulation is helpful in moving us towards an understanding of the masculine character of violence, in its present form it needs some expansion to encompass the class elements of this form of homicide.

A possible line of argument which might help here has been advanced recently by the anthropologist Gilmore (1990). In reviewing data on masculinity across a number of cultures, Gilmore concluded that there were three essential features to masculinity: "To be a man in most of the societies we have looked at, one must impregnate women, protect dependents from danger, and provision kith and kin" (1990: 223). In many societies, these "male imperatives" involve risks, and masculinity can be both dangerous and competitive:

> In fulfilling their obligations, men stand to lose—a hovering threat that separates them from women and boys. They stand to lose their reputations or their lives; yet their prescribed tasks must be done if the group is to survive and prosper. (Gilmore 1990: 223)

At this level, the argument is consistent with that of Daly and Wilson. Can these ideas be expanded to include the underclass character of this violence as well? A possible line of reasoning is established in Gilmore's argument about the impact of differential social organisation on masculinity:

> The data show a strong connection between the social organization of production and the intensity of the male image. That is, manhood ideologies are adaptations to social environments, not simply autonomous mental projections or psychic fantasies writ large. The harsher the environment and the scarcer the resources, the more manhood is stressed as inspiration and goal. (Gilmore 1990: 224)

If Gilmore is correct, it would seem reasonable to argue by extension that the contemporary male who possesses economic advantages is able to provide the base for the procreative, provisioning and protective functions through his economic resources, and these same resources provide the underpinning for his competition with other males for a mate. In other words, physical prowess and aggression no longer become necessary for the economically advantaged male to assure his competence in reproduction, provision or protection.

For males at the bottom of the economic heap, however, the lack of access to economic resources has the consequence of rendering these issues, and therefore their sense of masculinity, as problematic. For such males, the expression and defence of their masculinity may come through violence. Messerschmidt, for one, has argued along these lines:

> Some marginalized males adapt to their economic and racial powerlessness by engaging in, and hoping to succeed at, competition for personal power with rivals of their own class, race and gender. For these marginalized males, the personal power struggle with other marginalized males becomes a mechanism for exhibiting and confirming masculinity. . . . The marginalized male expresses himself through a "collective toughness, a masculine performance "observed and cheered by his "buddies." Members of the macho street culture have and maintain a strong sense of honor. As he must constantly prove his masculinity, an individual's reputation is always at stake. (Messerschmidt 1986: 70)

There are deeply rooted aspects of culture which place men in a competition with other men in terms of their reputation or honour. Assuming that Gilmore (1990) is correct in his assertion that the bases of masculine rivalry derive from competition regarding mating, provisioning and protecting, males who are well integrated into roles of economic success are able to ground their masculinity through methods other than physical confrontations and violence. For economically marginal males, however, physical toughness and violence become a major vehicle for the assertion of their masculinity and a way of defending themselves against what they see as challenges from other males.

It is the defence of honour that makes what might be considered a "trivial" provocation for some to be the grounds for a confrontation which builds to homicide. Wolfgang was one of the early observers of the phenomenon of the apparent triviality of events which provoke some homicides:

> Despite diligent efforts to discern the exact and precise factors involved in an altercation or domestic quarrel, police officers are often unable to acquire information other than the fact that a trivial argument developed, or an insult was suffered by one or both of the parties. (Wolfgang 1958: 188)

It seems clear, however, that what is trivial to a firmly respectable observer may be quite central to the marginal actor's sense of masculinity. Daly and Wilson (1988) have argued along similar lines, that for some men it is important that they maintain their sense of honour, that they do not allow themselves to be "pushed around," that they maintain a "credible threat of violence" (Daly and Wilson 1988: 128).

SUMMING UP

Confrontational homicide involves behaviour which is essentially a contest of honour between males. In the initial stages of the encounter, what the participants in a confrontational killing intend is first to argue, then to fight. The argument which produces that fight is spontaneous, as are the events which follow. These conflicts typically occur in leisure scenes, especially scenes where males predominate. The venue is a public setting, taking place in and around pubs, in streets or laneways, in public parks or reserves, parties or barbecues, and in public transport settings such as bus stops, train stations, or even on the train or buses themselves. In most of such scenes, an active role is played by the social audience, particularly male peers. The social nature of these situations is reinforced by the role of alcohol, the use of which has been found to be a feature of a great majority of these homicides.

The lethal violence is not premeditated, at least at the starting point of the conflict. Some confrontation scenes move rapidly to the point where deadly violence is employed, as where the parties begin with a fist fight, then raise the stakes by pulling knives. Others are more complex, however, and may involve one of the parties leaving the immediate scene to return a short time later with a weapon. In some instances the conflict may become elaborated into a feud which simmers for weeks or months before the lethal violence results.

Through it all resound the joint themes of masculinity and lower social class position. Extreme violence in defence of honour is definitively masculine. But, not all males feel compelled to defend their reputation or status with such violence. Why it is that some males pursue violence to secure their reputation or status, while others avoid such challenges, is a major theoretical question which must guide further research.

REFERENCES

Daly, M. and Wilson, M. (1988) *Homicide*, New York: Aldine de Gruyter.

Falk, G. (1990) *Murder: An Analysis of Its Forms, Conditions, and Causes*, London: McFarland & Company.

Gilmore, T. C. (1990) *Manhood in the Making*, New Haven: Yale University Press.

Johnson, C. M. and Robinson, M. T. (1992) *Homicide Report*, Washington, DC: Government of the District of Columbia, Office of Criminal Justice Plans and Analysis, 717 Fourteenth St. NW, Washington, DC 20005.

Katz, J. (1988) *The Seductions of Crime: Moral and Sensual Attractions of Doing Evil*, New York: Basic Books.

Luckenbill, D. F. (1977) "Criminal homicide as a situated transaction," *Social Problems* 26: 176–86.

Maxfield, M. (1984) *Fear of Crime in England and Wales*, London: HMSO.

Messerschmidt, J. W. (1986) *Capitalism, Patriarchy and Crime: Towards a Socialist Feminist Criminology*, Totowa, N.J.: Rowan & Littlefield.

Miller, W. B. (1980) "Gangs, groups and serious youth crime," in Shichor, D. and Kelly, D. H. (eds) *Issues in Juvenile Delinquency*, Lexington, MA: Lexington Books.

Polk, K. and Ranson, D. (1991) "Patterns of homicide in Victoria," in Chappell, D., Grabosky P. and Strang, H. (eds) *Australian Violence: Contemporary Perspectives*, Canberra: Australian Institute of Criminology.

Silverman, R. A. and Kennedy, L. W. (1987) "Relational distance and homicide: the role of the stranger," *Journal of Criminal Law and Criminology* 78: 272–308.

Wallace, A. (1986) *Homicide: The Social Reality*, Sydney: New South Wales Bureau of Crime Statistics and Research.

Walmsley, R. (1986) *Personal Violence*, Home Office Research Study No. 89 London: Her Majesty's Stationery Office.

Wolfgang, M. E. (1958) *Patterns in Criminal Homicide*, New York: Wiley.

PART IV

CROSSROADS AND INTERSECTIONS OF CLASS-RACE-GENDER, POLITICS, AND JUSTICE

CHAPTER 12

Policing Woman Battering

KATHLEEN J. FERRARO

The definition of woman battering as a social problem in the 1970s initiated debate about how to control and prevent violence between intimates. Feminists have argued that the control of intimate violence depends on fundamental restructuring of gender relations and the empowerment of women. Mental health professionals have promoted therapeutic intervention for offenders and victims of domestic violence. Most experts agreed that battered women need more legal protection (Hart et al., 1984; Schechter, 1981; Stanko, 1985; Taub, 1983; Walker, 1985; U.S. Commission on Civil Rights, 1978). The police are the "front line" of the official response to battering. Past research shows that police did not arrest men who battered their wives, even when victims were in serious danger and directly asked officers to arrest (Berk and Loseke, 1981; Black, 1980; Brown, 1984; Davis, 1983; Parnas, 1967). Activists in the battered women's movement saw failure to arrest as tacit support for battering, contributing to the inability of women to escape violent relationships and in the escalation of abuse to domestic homicides (Police Foundation, 1976).

Since 1976, civil suits, legislation, and policy initiatives have challenged police inaction (Ferraro, 1989). In 1984, the U.S. Attorney General's Task Force on Family Violence recommended that "family violence should be recognized and responded to as a criminal activity" and law enforcement agencies should "establish arrest as the preferred response in cases of family violence" (Hart et al., 1984:10, 17). Advocates for battered women insist that police should arrest men who use violence against their wives and lovers (Ferraro, 1989). This "get tough" stance is supported by legislative changes that expand police power to arrest.

Reprinted from Kathleen J. Ferraro, "Policing Woman Battering," *Social Problems*, Vol. 36, No. 1, pp. 61–74, © 1989. Reprinted by permission of the Society for the Study of Social Problems.

By 1986, six states passed laws *requiring* arrests when probable cause exists and the offender is on the scene. Probable cause is established by the presence of witnesses, visible injuries, or property damage that indicate a crime has been committed. Forty-seven large city police departments had adopted a policy of mandatory or presumptive arrests for family fights by 1986 (Crime Control Institute, 1986). In 28 other states and the District of Columbia, police *may* arrest for a misdemeanor spousal assault on the basis of probable cause (Lerman and Livingston, 1983). Officers cannot arrest for misdemeanor assaults between unmarried people unless the assault is observed by the officer, an arrest warrant has been issued, or a citizen signs a complaint. The changes in the statutes are a response to the fact that most assaults against wives occur in private settings and fall in the misdemeanor category. Without expanded arrest powers, police cannot arrest batterers unless the assault is felonious or witnessed by an officer. Eighteen states require officers to provide information on legal options and services, and in eleven states police must transport victims to hospitals or shelters. Twenty-nine states also provide for temporary restraining orders, in which courts order abusers to stay away from their victims (Buzawa and Buzawa, 1985).

The push to arrest batterers enhances police power to arrest, but mandatory arrest policies limit the discretion of police officers to dismiss woman battering as a "civil matter." Policies that require arrest also limit discretion of complainants in that they ignore the wishes of the victim. Many battered women experience ambivalence about pressing criminal charges or fear retribution if they do so (Ferraro, 1988). Yet academic research purports to demonstrate the superior effect of arrest. Sherman and Berk (1984) found that violence was less frequently repeated when arrests were made than when battering incidents were mediated or resolved through physically separating the couple. Their findings have gained widespread recognition in police culture.

While laws and policies regarding woman battering have changed, the police response to battering relies heavily on extra-legal factors in police decision making (Bell, 1985; Berk and Loseke, 1981; Black, 1980; Davis, 1983; Smith and Klein, 1984; Waaland and Keeley, 1985). Observational studies of police work have consistently supported Black's (1971) early finding that the closer the relationship between victim and assailant, the less likely police are to arrest. Thus, even when departmental policies instruct police to arrest, officers continue to rely on victim and offender characteristics in deciding whether a law has been broken.

The response of police in the field to formal rules and policy about battering is embedded in a social context. As Manning (1971:162) notes, a police officer "moves in a dense web of social action and social meanings, burdened by a problematic, complex array of ever-changing laws." To better understand how these extra-legal considerations reduce protection of battered women, we must look at how police work is done. The purpose of this paper is to examine the web of actions, meanings, and changing laws through which police construct their response to battering. I begin with a description of the emergence of new laws and policies about policing domestic disputes in Phoenix, Arizona. I then outline four dimensions of police response to battering and conclude by summarizing the difficulties of implementing the presumptive arrest policy for domestic violence.

ARIZONA'S DOMESTIC VIOLENCE LAW AND POLICY

Most misdemeanors in Arizona result in a citation and release of the offender. In 1980, the state legislature passed a domestic violence bill that: (1) prohibits officers from citing and releasing domestic violence offenders; (2) expands police power to arrest on the basis of probable cause and requires officers to provide information to victims about procedures and available services; and (3) provides for orders of protection that can be obtained through any court, without filing for divorce. The orders provide grounds for arrest if a batterer goes near his victim. Two local judges drafted the bill. They were responding to two county coalitions on domestic violence that were putting pressure on police and courts to do more to protect battered women. In addition, police and lower court judges had complained that their hands were tied by constraints on arrests and by unwilling victims. The authors of the bill were fully aware of the practical limitations of controlling intimate violence through court orders.

The new law went into effect in July 1980. It had very little impact on law enforcement in Arizona. The police departments did not change their arrest policies. Officers had available one more tool for dealing with domestic violence, but did not view the law as an indication that arrests should increase. By 1983, the Maricopa County Task Force Against Domestic Violence, composed primarily of shelter and mental health workers, convinced a state representative that more legislation was required to force police to arrest batterers. A committee formed to draft a bill mandating arrest for domestic violence. The Phoenix Chief of Police, Ruben Ortega, discouraged the group from pressing for the law, promising that he would adopt a mandatory arrest policy and would encourage other chiefs to do so. Police administrators said that the superior court judge heading the family court had made several complaints to Chief Ortega about failure to arrest violent husbands. At the same time, Chief Ortega was appointed to the U.S. Attorney General's Task Force on Family Violence. After traveling around the country listening to testimony about the need to crack down on wife abuse, he returned to Arizona to help implement the recommendations of the Attorney General's Task Force. In May 1984, the Phoenix police department adopted a presumptive arrest policy. It stated that:

> Officers *should* arrest domestic violence violators even if the victim does not desire prosecution. When probable cause exists, an arrest should be made even if a misdemeanor offense did not occur in the officer's presence (Ortega, 1984:1, emphasis added).

The policy was publicized in the local papers and on television. All police officers received training on the new policy from their sergeants and from members of the domestic violence coalition.

The Phoenix presumptive arrest policy represented only one minor change in an extensive city and county criminal justice system. Other cities in the county did not immediately alter their policies regarding domestic violence, although some since have done so. The city and county prosecutors did not increase prosecutions, and judges did not sentence batterers to jail. The Phoenix police were not supported in their policy shift by correlative changes in other parts of the system.

The police department figures indicate that the rate of arrest at the scene for family fights more than doubled in the second month after the policy was implemented. In 1983, the average monthly arrest rate was 33 percent. In June 1984, it was 67 percent, at which time a clarifying statement emphasized that probable cause was still a requirement for arrest. Officers told us that "ridiculous" arrests were annoying the judges who, in turn, complained to the chief. The chief reminded the officers that the policy did not override the constitutional requirement of reasonable grounds for arrest. This clarification created some confusion among officers. Some told us things were back to normal; others said they were only supposed to arrest in cases where there was serious injury and witnesses. This apparent hedging by the administration undermined the policy's initial forcefulness about the importance of arrest. In July 1984, the official arrest rate dropped to 52 percent, and by August it was 42 percent.

METHODS

The Phoenix presumptive arrest policy offered an opportunity to observe the street level response to an administrative crackdown on battering. I asked Chief Ortega for permission to study the Phoenix police, and after some prodding from my college dean, he agreed to grant me entree. I interviewed Chief Ortega, four assistant chiefs, and the detective in charge of family fights to gather administrative perceptions of the policy before beginning ridealongs. Our team of six field observers entered the field in May 1984, three weeks after the presumptive arrest policy was adopted. Two male professors, one female professor, and three female graduate students conducted the observations. The observers rode with officers on ten-hour weekend evening shifts for 44 nights. Phoenix is divided into five districts with separate stations in each. The districts are divided into beats. Officers do not cross district boundaries but may enter unassigned beats within their districts. Three districts were observed. The two districts with the highest concentration of low income and transient individuals were selected because they represented the highest proportion of domestic violence calls. One district primarily composed of middle income whites was also observed. Officers were told that we were studying domestic violence and were instructed to respond to as many family fight calls as possible. On many evenings we were assigned to "roving cars," which had no beat boundaries and that could respond to family fight calls anywhere in the district.

During the ten-hour shifts, we accompanied officers on every aspect of their duties. During periods in which there was no activity, we questioned officers about the new presumptive arrest policy, their experiences with family fights, and their opinions about the appropriate response. Observers carried yellow pads for recording information and verbatim quotes. Information about police work in general was outlined, but officers' statements about and actions at family fights were recorded in as much detail as possible on the day following observations. At family fight calls we observed the police intervention and spoke with victims whenever possible. When arrests were made, we sometimes went to the station to observe the booking process. In one case, an observer was called to court as a witness to an assault.

In most cases, observers did not attempt to influence police behavior, even when they disagreed with decisions. Observers did not suggest arrest or nonarrest at the scene. When officers signalled completion of the call by saying goodby to the victim and walking toward their car, I sometimes suggested—consistent with the new statute—that they provide victims with information about services and orders of protection. In several cases I also suggested officers request the services of the on-call mental health team, but only after they began to leave the scene.

We observed the police respond to 69 reports of family fights. Of these, 34 involved married or formerly married couples, 15 involved cohabitees or former lovers, 13 involved neighbors or other relatives, and 7 were false reports. Although 20 of the cases do not involve woman battering, they were dispatched and referred to as family fights by the officers.

POLICE RESPONSE UNDER THE NEW POLICY

The intent of mandatory and presumptive arrest policies is to treat domestic violence "as a crime." Thus, officers are supposed to arrest batterers regardless of other characteristics of the situation. That was not what we observed. Out of 69 family fight calls, 49 involved spouses, cohabitants, estranged lovers, or current lovers and fit the definition of battering. Officers made no arrests in 40 of these cases (82%); arrests were made in only 9 (18%) of the battering incidents, in spite of the presumptive arrest policy. In 25 (51%) cases, police used conciliation, which means talking to the people and emphasizing the importance of the relationship over the dispute. Very few cases involved a therapeutic style of social control, and none could be classified as compensatory, in which the officer would attempt to gain redress for the violence inflicted on the victim.

These results are similar to those reported by Black (1980:156) in cases involving married and common law couples: 70 percent conciliatory, 26 percent penal, 2 percent therapeutic, and 2 percent preventative. Black (1980:158) found that for those cases where penal action was taken, 26 percent were arrests. This is quite striking in that Black's observations were conducted prior to the emergence of the battered women's movement and statutory and policy changes in policing battering. The consistency over time attests to the complexity of the police response to battering and the difficulty of altering it.

Department policy is only one factor influencing police decision making at family fights. As Berk and Loseke (1981:342) note, police responses are "rife with situationally determined contingencies." In their research, using police reports, presence of both disputants on the scene, women's willingness to sign complaints, victims' allegations of violence, and male alcohol consumption were all positively correlated with the decision to arrest (Berk and Loseke, 1981:341–42). Our observations suggest that these factors continue to play a major role in decision making even when arrest is the preferred policy.

Officers evaluate each call to decide whether it is really a "family fight." A set of behaviors in one context might lead one officer to arrest, while similar behaviors in another context might lead another officer to take no action. Most of the time officers rejected arrest as an option after weighing certain considerations. However, when they did arrest, they often invoked some of the same considerations. The following categories summarize the considerations impinging on the decision making process at family fights: legal, ideological, practical, and political.

Legal

By legal considerations I mean to emphasize how police think about and use their understandings of the laws and statutes they are officially charged with enforcing. The most obvious instances of these laws being "applied" might be the 9 arrests we observed.

There were two arrests the police classified as misdemeanor spousal assaults that seemed consistent with the intent of the new policy. In the first case, the couple was married the day before the assault. A neighbor called the police after she saw the husband assault his wife. All three people were sitting quietly at the apartment when we arrived. The couple was Hispanic and lived in a low-income neighborhood. The woman had a deep cut on her forehead and said she wanted to press charges. Police called paramedics to treat the cut, took photographs for evidence of injury, and took the man to jail. With all legal and policy criteria met and a compliant offender, officers did not hesitate to make an arrest.

A second case where the wife was the only victim involved an argument in the presence of a female friend who called the police when the husband threatened his wife with a knife. When police arrived, all three people denied any conflict. Police searched the husband and found a knife. The presence of a weapon satisfied the legal criterion of assault even though the victim and witness said no assault or threat occurred. The officer perceived danger and arrested the man.

In two cases, men were violent in the presence of officers and both were arrested. In the first case, a 65-year-old man was drunk and wrestling with his son. Two male police officers grabbed the man, cuffed him, and loaded him into a back-up police car. In the second case, a man spit on his girlfriend and punched a male neighbor in the mouth. When the officer arrived, the man greeted him at the front door with a raised ball bat. The officer drew his gun, and the man slammed the door in his face. Police subsequently chased and captured the offender, threw him to the floor, tightly cuffed his hands and feet and carried him to the car.

This case was the only instance where police asked the victim to make a "citizen's arrest." The charges against him were simple assault against a male bystander and spitting at his girlfriend. The officer perceived him as a dangerous character and one who showed a lack of respect for the law. The officer told the observer the assault charge might not hold because the bystander was trespassing; the spitting charge was obviously weak. He therefore instructed the girlfriend to place her foot on the "hog-tied" man's back and say, "I place you under citizen's arrest."

Most of the time, however, the police did not arrest anyone when called to the site of reported domestic violence. One legal ground for this decision is that, at the time of the research, the domestic violence statute did not extend to cohabitants, although the law now has been changed to include them. Of the 15 cases observed involving cohabitants, lovers or exlovers, three resulted in arrests. Arrests involving violence in nonmarried couples did not fall within the purview of the new policy. Presumptive arrest relied on enhanced power to arrest in misdemeanor domestic violence cases. When couples were not married, officers did not consider arrest, even if there were legal grounds for it. For example, it is always possible to arrest if a citizen signs a complaint, but that option was used only once in 69 cases. In that case, the offender was violent to a male neighbor, threatened a police officer, and attempted to escape. In this and the other two cases where an unmarried person was arrested, the high level of danger was more significant to officers than the fact that the new policy did not formally apply. In most cases observed, however, officers did not consider arresting unmarried cohabitees.

In one case, for example, a live-in boyfriend broke down the front door when his girlfriend refused to let him in. He was very drunk, and she did not want to see him, as they were both recovering alcoholics. He tore up their apartment, breaking and destroying her personal belongings. He also hit her in the face, and she had a small cut where her glasses bridged her nose. Three officers arrived at the scene, and the two patrolmen asked their sergeant what to "make" the call. He told them no crime had been committed, except against the landlady for destruction of the apartment door.

Several crimes could have been constructed from these facts, including assault, criminal damage, endangerment, and threatening or intimidating. The officers might have encouraged the woman to sign a citizen's complaint. Either a stranger or a husband committing identical acts would have been defined differently, but the sergeant focused on the cohabitant status of the relationship and decided that no crime had been committed.

Another legal consideration was seen when officers searched for probable cause for arrest. The detective in charge of family fights told us that the presence of visible injuries, property damage, weapons, or witnesses establishes probable cause. The statute permitting misdemeanor arrests based on probable cause authorizes officers to determine whether the situation permits a reasonable conclusion that a crime has been committed. But this determination is, of course, discretionary. For most officers, severe visible injuries or the use of weapons constituted probable cause, but minor injury, property damage, and the presence of child witnesses did not. Officers' interpretations of probable cause undermined the policy because they used a level of evidence high enough for felony arrests. Administrative directives that emphasized the importance of probable cause led many officers to conclude that they had wide discretion in this area.

After receiving the directive about probable cause, one officer said that "things are back to normal." He made no arrests in the three family fights we responded to in one night of observations. In one case, for example, a woman fled her home after her husband beat and choked her. She had taken one child with her, but the other remained at her mother's home where her husband had gone and subsequently assaulted her brother. The husband was drunk and violent, and the woman was afraid he would either hurt the baby or take it away where she could not find them. She had bruises on her neck from the choking, and her mother had witnessed the assault on the brother. They lived in a housing project, and she had to walk three blocks to use a phone to call the police. It was 2:00 A.M. when we arrived on the scene. The officer told her there was nothing he could do. He said the baby was not in danger and that everything was okay. He told her to call if anything else happened. The victim was frightened and believed her husband was "crazy" and capable of serious violence. The officer did not agree and offered her no information or advice except to "call back."

This incident could have met the standards of probable cause. The victim was anxious to press charges, had visible signs of injury, and there were witnesses to the assault on her brother. The man was a few blocks away at his mother-in-law's home, but the officer made no attempt to contact him. He did not suggest that the victim sign a complaint. Legally, his decision not to arrest could be justified by the absence of probable cause as no serious injury or weapons were present. His interpretation of the new policy required these elements for an arrest. But the officer's actions in this case are not what would be expected based on the "get tough" rhetoric or the presumptive arrest policy.

The domestic violence statute specifies the destruction of property, or criminal damage, as a crime. In several cases, women were not physically attacked, but their property was destroyed. These cases included tire slashing, smashed windshields, a waterbed punctured with an ice pick, doors kicked in, and the two cases described above. In all but one case, officers told victims that nothing could be done. The officers said that Arizona is a community property state. Therefore, everything belongs to both people, and one cannot be charged for destroying one's own property. Yet the legislature and courts have recognized that community property means half, not total, ownership. When jointly held property is destroyed, the half not owned is destroyed as well as the half that is. The one case of arrest for criminal damage indicates that it was a legitimate charge if officers wanted to use it.

Legal criteria are not the most salient in police decision making. Presumptive arrest implies that legal standards are the most important consideration for family fights, but in the cases we observed the legal interpretation of events was strongly influenced by other considerations.

Ideological

Ideological considerations are those background beliefs and ideas about battered women and family fights that police officers use to evaluate specific incidents. They include general ideas police have about the people they encounter, specific ideas about family fights, and images of danger. These ideas emerge through police practice, although officers may be predisposed to interpret other people as adversaries. As Manning (1971:156) emphasizes, the occupational culture of police sets the standards for a "good policeman" and prompts the assumptions police officers use in shaping their work.

Police tend to dichotomize the community into normal and deviant citizens (Ferraro, 1989). Normal citizens abide by society's rules through maintaining employment, sobriety, a family, and a modestly clean home. They are heterosexual, white, and speak English. Deviants serve as the "other" for police officers; they are publicly intoxicated or high, homeless, involved in crime, live in run-down houses, have atypical family structures, and/or speak foreign languages. Habitual problems are endemic to their lifestyle.

According to this view, a normal citizen who violates a law responds to police intervention with shame and anxiety. A "normal" wife beater is perceived as situationally deviant, his behavior the product of particular strain or a response to a threatened divorce. Such a man, officers believe, may be deterred by arrest because both violence and arrest are extraordinary and undesirable events for such people. On the other hand, arrest and violence are viewed as routine events for deviant men. Officers on patrol often referred to Mexicans, Indians, gay men, and people in the housing projects as "low lifes," "scum," or "these kind of people." Officers believed arrests were a waste of time and meaningless for these people because violence is a way of life for them. Empirically, middle income, professional men do engage in repetitive wife beating (Weller, 1988). However, representative surveys find higher rates of wife beating among low-income and unemployed men (Gelles and Straus, 1988; Straus et al., 1980). Police ideology about the types of situations in which violence occurs may be grounded in experience.

In one case, a Hispanic woman who spoke little English approached us at 3:00 A.M. for help as we responded to another call. She complained, through a 14-year-old neighbor, that her husband was drunk, violent, and threatening to take her children away. We found the man intoxicated, sitting among a pile of beer cans. Three small boys sat nearby. The officers (one man and one woman) resolved the problem by walking the woman and children to an apartment a few doors away. They told the woman to call the police if there was any more trouble although she had no telephone or money. The residents were not friends of the woman and were not happy to have her. We left the woman sitting on the porch and walked past the husband who waved good-by to us. The low level of protection provided by this arrangement and the imposition on neighbors did not concern the officers. The male officer expressed frustration at dealing with Spanish speakers and people in the projects.

Police also held stereotypes about battered women. One repeatedly expressed idea was that battered women were likely to drop any charges that might be filed. They often asked for arrest at night when they were angry and then refused to testify or lied about the abuse when later contacted by detectives or prosecutors. The presumptive arrest policy is supposed to take the burden of prosecution off the victim. Still, it is difficult to prosecute an assault when the victim denies it occurred. One officer argued that the policy would lead to more homicides because once women knew arrests would be made they would stop calling the police for help. He said,

> A lot of these people, especially in this district, just want you to do something to stop it for the night. They want us to get somebody to leave. They could do that for themselves, but they want us to do it. If they can't call us, because we'll arrest, then they don't have anybody to help them, and instead of somebody leaving for the night, somebody's going to get killed.

Several officers thought there were fewer reports of family fights because the word had gone out about arrests. However, department figures indicated an increase in calls. Police statistics showed an average of 83 reports a month in 1983. In the first month of the policy, 327 family violence reports were received. The number steadily dropped over the first five months of the policy, but in September there were still 157 calls.

The police believe battered women choose to remain in abusive situations. Most officers believed adult women could leave violent situations if they wanted to. If they stayed with a violent man, it was not the responsibility of police to try to control the violence. An officer expressed this belief in a case involving a young, black woman staying in a run-down motel in a low-income section of town. Her boyfriend hit her, took all her clothes, and left in their car. They had recently moved to town, and she had nowhere to go and no money or clothes. Officers arranged for her to spend the night with others in the motel. On leaving, one officer commented, "This is your typical family fight. They don't really want to do anything." He did not empathize with the woman's lack of alternatives, but rather typified her as willfully choosing an abusive situation.

Officers expressed a range of attitudes toward battered women. At the sympathetic end of the continuum, a female officer, herself a formerly battered woman, strongly supported the new policy. She said,

> What is a woman really supposed to do if she has no job skills and a couple of kids, and he's been tellin' her he'll kill her if she leaves? What is she gonna' do? A lot of people can't understand why she stays, but I can really empathize with that. Sure there are a few dingbats that are just so stupid they don't know enough to leave. But I think most women who get beat up really don't have anyplace else to go and they're afraid.

This woman was the only officer who expressed sympathy with the battered woman's situation. Three other female officers mentioned appreciation for the new policy, but the other female officers (15) were either neutral or antagonistic toward the policy. Several female officers openly expressed disdain for family fight calls, citing the danger involved and unwillingness of victims to follow through. One female officer said she believed women who dropped charges should be held in contempt of court.

Male officers also expressed a range of attitudes about woman battering and the policy, but the negative evaluations were more extreme. At the critical end of the continuum, one male officer expressed the belief that a man's home is his castle where he should be allowed to do what he wants. He believed most wife beating was provoked by the woman. He had recently punched a hole in his own living room wall during an argument with his wife. From his perspective, arresting men for destroying their own property was an outrageous infringement on liberty. For officers who view arrests as a waste of time or an illegitimate infringement on private life, presumptive arrest is an illogical policy.

Officers also held implicit images of dangerous situations. For two nights we drove down alleys and kept watch for a man wearing women's clothing who was suspected of rape. Officers believed he was dangerous. Reports of "drive-by" shootings by gangs and gang conflicts were also perceived as dangerous and worth investigating. Certain bars and neighborhoods were described as extremely dangerous, and one bar was singled out for intervention "before somebody gets killed."

Battered women, on the other hand, were usually not perceived as being in dangerous situations. Women cried and shook with fear as they told officers their husbands or lovers were going to hurt them. But repeatedly officers responded with a "call if anything happens," rather than giving them the immediate protection they sought. Everything appeared to officers to be "under control" because they could see no visible signs of danger. To women who were battered and were experienced with their assailants' patterns of violence, the danger was real and frightening, and easy to see. The divergent perceptions of danger held by battered women and police resulted in a minimal effort to intervene in cases which appeared to officers as stable.

Practical

The statute and policy did not specify the degree of inconvenience and probing required of officers at family fights. So if both husband and wife denied the existence of a fight, or if both accused the other of violence, it was left to the officer's discretion whether intervention of any kind was appropriate.

The policy did not specifically state that offenders had to be on the scene for arrests to be made. Neither did it encourage officers to search for men who had fled. In order for us to observe an arrest, the offender had to have been on or near the scene. In 28 cases (40%) the man was not on the scene at the time of police arrival. Either he had left, or the woman had called from a location other than that of the dispute. In these cases, the officers were supposed to write detective's reports that would allow a detective to follow up the next day. It was not always apparent whether reports were written because several police units were on the scene. Officers with whom we were not riding did not commonly share information about the calls. In cases where our assigned officer was the primary respondent to the call, it was possible to determine whether detective's reports were written. In most cases, they were not.

Although failure to file a report is not a technical violation of the presumptive arrest policy, it does undermine the intent to "get tough." In practice, if the batterer is not on the scene, no punitive action will be taken, even if the woman has left her home to seek safety while her abuser remains at home. In one case a woman called police from her friend's home after her drunken husband smashed her car windshield with a ball and chain and threatened to kill her and her children. She asked the officers to go to her home and arrest him. The officers said they could not do that without a warrant or unless she accompanied them because her home was in another district. The officer told me the woman would not accompany them, but I heard her tell him that she would. They left her at her friend's home, telling her to call if he came around. Whether the policy only applied to cases where the offender was on the scene was irrelevant for the officers. In their view, there was no danger of the violence continuing that night and so the policy was not invoked. The officer said it was a typical family fight and that, although the woman was angry that night, she would cool down the next day and forget about charges. As Davis (1983:275) notes, the police at family fights are concerned with achieving a situational "semblance of order" rather than finding a solution to the larger relational problem.

Arizona domestic violence statute 13-3601 D includes the requirement for officers to inform victims of the procedures and resources available for the protection of victims, namely orders of protection, emergency telephone numbers of the police, and telephone numbers of emergency services in the area. Officers were supplied with domestic violence cards that listed magistrates, shelters, and hotlines along with their phone numbers. In only 2 of the 69 cases we observed did officers provide this information to victims without being prompted by the observers. Officers did not see providing the victim with information as relevant to restoring order in the situation and so they seldom did it (see Davis, 1983).

Police also had access to a special mental health team on weekend nights. The Family Stress Team was made up of mental health professionals who were on call to respond to mental health problems. Officers stated that the team did good work and was a good resource, but they called them only four times in the 69 cases we observed. When arrests were made, they did not see a need for mental health assistance. As long as the immediate problem was resolved, and order was restored, officers did not consider relevant those options for more long term solutions, such as calling the stress team or providing the victim with community service information.

In four cases (6%) the problem was defined as "resolved prior to arrival." In these cases either no one answered the door, or someone appeared at the door and told police everything was under control. Officers did not insist on entering the home when the resident requested them to leave. In these situations, there was no complainant, no apparent violence, and thus no problem for the police to handle. In domestic violence situations this response is disturbing, as it is unknown whether the victim is being forced to keep quiet or ask the police to leave.

Officers also spoke about cases they called "mutual combat," where there was aggressive interaction rather than explicit violence. A man physically assaulting a woman who was screaming and yelling at him could be construed by officers as mutual combat, particularly in cases where the woman was intoxicated. Officers said they would not arrest in these cases because it was not possible to determine who was at fault. Directives from the Assistant Chief of the Patrol Division discouraged arrest when both parties were violent at a misdemeanor level. In such cases, it was difficult to get testimony from either party, as they could not talk without incriminating themselves.

Arresting both spouses could also create practical problems of placing children. The police could use local social services to foster children temporarily.

This is difficult and time consuming and may be as frightening to children as their father's violence. While some officers explicitly stated that the presence of children would not inhibit them from making an arrest, others recounted instances in which arrests had not been made because they would have had to foster children out.

Although the presumptive arrest policy was intended to remove the decision to arrest from the victim, establishing probable cause is more difficult if a woman refuses to testify to her abuse. Some battered women do not press charges because they love their husbands. But there may be other reasons why arrest would not be in a woman's best interests. In follow-up interviews conducted during a second stage of this research, one victim said she did not want her husband arrested because he had recently obtained a job after six months of unemployment. He might lose his job if he missed a day of work or if his employer learned he had been arrested. Other women worried about immigration authorities and did not want to get too close to the law. Why a woman does not want to press charges may not be clear to the responding officer. But if she unequivocally states that she does not want to press charges, officers may recognize her competence and knowledge of what is best for her. Although the intent of presumptive arrest policies is to shift the responsibility for arrest from the woman to the police, some officers continued to consider the practical consequences of arrest for the victim and her children.

Finally, time is a practical consideration. Since it takes at least an hour to process an arrest, officers are less likely to arrest when they are about to finish their shifts. Moreover, officers view time as a resource to be saved for "important" cases. An arrest makes officers unavailable for other activities during the booking procedure. During this time, officers are off the street, unable to respond to other calls. One officer lamented that once she had been unable to respond to an armed robbery call because she was transporting a woman to a shelter. She implied that the armed robbery was more important and exciting. This was cited by other officers in explaining why they would not transport victims to a safe place. Although time is never sufficient to account for arrest/nonarrest decisions, it combines and probably interacts with legal, ideological and other practical considerations in shaping an officer's response to a given incident.

Internal and External Politics

In the police department, there is a tension between administrative policy makers and street level actors. Administrators are attuned to professional and community level politics, while patrol officers are attuned to the politics of the street. The presumptive arrest policy was interpreted by officers through their perceptions of administrative motives.

Traditionally, domestic violence is a low status offense. The presumptive arrest policy tried to elevate its importance. But without clear-cut rewards or incentives, officers doubted the political significance of the policy. Some officers believed the policy was just for show, and some said it came from pressure from judges. But most did not know why they were suddenly urged to alter their responses in these cases. Family fights remain low status, undesirable calls for most officers.

One final consideration is the political organization of the housing projects. The projects have committees that officers perceive as "really powerful" and having "a direct line to the chief's office." Officers believe that project residents despise them and that the committees are eager to complain about police misconduct. Graffiti in these neighborhoods suggest that the contempt is not entirely imaginary. Two officers explained that they had been transferred from the projects because of fabricated complaints brought to the chief by the project committee. The belief that the committees had influence with the chief and that people are more than willing to complain about police misconduct was not conducive to a presumptive arrest policy. Officers were hesitant to arrest without sufficient evidence or victim cooperation when they feared retribution from the committees.

Legal, ideological, practical, and political considerations do not exhaust the factors that influenced police decision making at family fights. Sometimes legal considerations voiced in one context were contradicted by actions in another. The process of police responses to domestic violence situations is not entirely rational or accessible to observers. Still, seeing how police took these factors into account in their work helps us to understand how the new law and policy were in fact enacted.

DISCUSSION

The officers in this study did not implement the presumptive arrest policy in a uniform way. The observational data show that discretion persists in spite of well publicized policy changes and training on domestic violence. In part, lack of adherence to the policy can be traced to the confusion produced by policy clarifications after the fact, which was evidence that the chief was "backing off." Publicly, Chief Ortega maintains a "get tough" stance on arresting batterers. Training on the policy did not resolve questions about its political meaning within the department. Officers were free to guess how much importance they should attach to a policy that drastically altered their traditional approach to domestic violence. No explicit incentives were offered for compliance, and no penalties were attached to evasion of the new policy. These were situational problems that may be remedied by a more vigorous, explicit administrative plan to increase arrests. The level of tension and conflict between administrators and patrol officers varies by locale. A department with strong leadership and morale may have more success at implementing a presumptive arrest policy.

On the other hand, these data indicate that each case is evaluated in terms of its relationship to a web of considerations, including legal, ideological, practical, and political issues. Officers can be encouraged to interpret situations in a given manner, but the interpretive process remains tied to these influences. For example, officers may be told to arrest regardless of the victim's wishes, yet still evaluate her recalcitrance in light of the perceived power of the housing project committees or the time taken away from other work. Policy directives did alter police behavior in this study, as evidenced by the two arrests for misdemeanor wife assaults. They did not, however, eliminate the impact of the web of considerations on police decision making.

Information on the factors that discouraged arrests is useful in designing programs to enhance arrests. The legal and political considerations described reflect officers' concerns with what will happen if arrests are made. If they perceive that high standards of evidence are required for prosecution and observe low rates of prosecution, they are likely to see most arrests as a waste of time. Mandatory and presumptive arrest policies implemented in the absence of change in other parts of the legal system will probably have little lasting impact on how police respond to domestic violence. If the official rhetoric about "treating domestic violence as a crime" embodied in the task force recommendations is genuine, changes must occur at the prosecutorial, judicial, and correctional levels in tandem with changes in law enforcement practices.

Concerns about the power of housing project committees suggest that police officers recognize the impact of citizen complaints on their work lives. The recent surge in law suits against police departments may have some impact on street level decision making (Woods, 1986). At the local level, the relationship between police officials and battered women's advocacy groups could have a positive impact on police response. If officers view policies as rhetoric to quiet the "women's libbers," they are not likely to be concerned about the consequences of their street level decisions. However, if they believe that failure to provide adequate protection will result in complaints that include their name and badge number and may lead to disciplinary action, they may be more thorough in their response to victim's complaints. Education and organizing by battered women's advocates can likely influence police perceptions of the power of battered women.

REFERENCES

Bell, Daniel J. (1985) "A multiyear study of Ohio urban, suburban, and rural police dispositions of domestic disputes." *Victimology* 10:301–10.

Berk, Sarah F. and Donileen R. Loseke (1981) " 'Handling' family violence: situational determinants of police arrest in domestic disturbances." *Law and Society Review* 15:317–46.

Black, Donald (1971) "The social organization of arrest." *Stanford Law Review* 23:1087–1111.

———(1980) *The Manners and Customs of the Police.* New York: Academic Press.

Brown, Stephen (1984) "Police responses to wife beating: neglect of a crime of violence." *Journal of Criminal Justice* 12:277–88.

Buzawa, Eva and Carl C. Buzawa (1985) "Legislative trends in the criminal justice response to domestic violence." Pp. 124–47 in Alan J. Lincoln and Murray A. Straus (eds.), *Crime and the Family.* Springfield, IL: Charles C. Thomas.

Crime Control Institute (1986) "Police domestic violence policy change." *Response* 9:16.

Davis, Philip W. (1983) "Restoring the semblance of order: police strategies in the domestic disturbance." *Symbolic Interaction* 6:216–74.

Ferraro, Kathleen J. (1988) "Prosecution of felony assaults against women." Paper given at the annual meeting of the American Society of Criminology, Chicago, IL.

———(1989) "The legal response to battering in the United States." Pp. 155–84 in Jalna Hanmer, Jill Radford, and Elizabeth Stanko (eds.), *Women, Policing, and Male Violence.* London: Tavistock.

Gelles, Richard J. and Murray A. Straus (1988) *Intimate Violence.* New York: Simon and Schuster.

Hart, William L., John Ashcroft, Ann Burgess, Newman Flanagan, Ursula Meese, Catherine Milton, Clyde Narramore, Ruben Ortega, and Frances Seward (1984) Attorney General's Task Force on Family Violence. Washington, DC: U.S. Department of Justice.

Lerman, Lisa G. and Franci Livingston (1983) "State legislation on domestic violence." *Response* 6:1–28.

Manning, Peter K. (1971) "The police: mandate, strategies, and appearances." Pp. 149–93 in Jack Douglas (ed.), *Crime and Justice in American Society.* Indianapolis, IN: Bobbs-Merrill.

Ortega, Ruben B. (1984) Operations Digest No. 84–85:1–2.

Parnas, Raymond (1967) "The police response to the domestic disturbance." *Wisconsin Law Review* 2:914–60.

Police Foundation (1976) *Domestic Violence and the Police: Studies in Detroit and Kansas City.* Washington, DC: The Police Foundation.

Schechter, Susan (1981) *Women and Male Violence: The Visions and Struggles of the Battered Women's Movement.* Boston, MA: South End.

Sherman, Lawrence W. and Richard A. Berk (1984) "The specific deterrent effects of arrest for domestic assault." *American Sociological Review* 49:261–72.

Smith, Douglas A. and Jody R. Klein (1984) "Police control of interpersonal disputes." *Social Problems* 31:466–81.

Stanko, Elizabeth A. (1985) *Intimate Intrusions: Women's Experience of Male Violence.* London: Routledge & Kegan Paul.

Straus, Murray, Suzanne K. Steinmetz, and Richard J. Gelles (1980) *Behind Closed Doors.* Garden City, NY: Anchor.

Taub, Nadine (1983) "Adult domestic violence: the law's response." *Victimology* 8:152–171.

U.S. Commission on Civil Rights (1978) *Battered Women: Issues of Public Policy.* Washington, DC: U.S. Government Printing Office.

Waaland, Pam and Stuart Keeley (1985) "Police decision making in wife abuse: the impact of legal and extralegal factors." *Law and Human Behavior* 9:355–66.

Walker, Lenore E. (1985) "Psychological impact of the criminalization of domestic violence on victims. *Victimology* 10:281–300.

Weller, Sheila (1988) "Middle-class murder." *Ms.* May:56–61.

Woods, Laurie (1986) *Resource List: Battered Women: Litigation.* New York: National Center on Women and Family Law.

CHAPTER 13

What Is to Be Gained by Looking White People in the Eye?
Culture, Race, and Gender in Cases of Sexual Violence

SHERENE RAZACK

> Was it just that old race thing that had thrown her off when her
> eyes met Grace's? Her neighbour Wilma's father said he'd never
> in his adult life looked a white person in the eye. He'd grown up
> in the days when such an act very often ended in a black per-
> son's charred body swinging from a tree. For many years,
> Blanche worried that it was fear which sometimes made her re-
> luctant to meet white people's eyes, particularly on days when
> she had the lonelies or the unspecified blues. She'd come to un-
> derstand that her desire was to avoid pain, a pain so old, so
> deep, its memory was carried not in her mind, but in her bones.
> Some days she simply didn't want to look into the eyes of people
> raised to hate, disdain, or fear anyone who looked like her.
> (Neely 1992, 111)

CONVERSATIONS ABOUT CULTURE

"I had a Vietnamese doctor who wouldn't look me in the eye when we discussed
the risks of amniocentesis," a woman says to me angrily at a Christmas party
and wonders whether or not the doctor ought to be compelled to put aside his

Abridged from Sherene Razack "What is to be Gained by Looking White People in the Eye? Culture, Race, and Gender in Cases of Sexual Violence," *Signs: Journal of Women in Culture and Society*, Vol. 19, No. 4, pp. 894–923, © 1994. Reprinted by permission of the University of Chicago
Press. *Ed. note:* Although text and footnotes were deleted, we preserved the footnote numbers
that appeared in the original text.

cultural peculiarities in the interests of his white, Western patients. Eye contact, a perennial favorite as a marker of the perils associated with cross-cultural encounters, is a popular topic these days. A Crown attorney's book on the cultural attributes of his Aboriginal clients garners praise, particularly for his description of how Aboriginal men's failure to look judges in the eye is a mark of respect rather than an admission of guilt (Ross 1992).[1] In academe, professors are reportedly "going for the judicial jugular," subjecting judicial decisions on Aboriginal issues to scrutiny and itemizing the "difficulties courts face as they are called to sit in judgment of another culture and, in the case of land claims, another time" (MacQueen 1992, A4). The controversy over culture, and specifically over the cultural bias of the judiciary, has also emerged in the context of sexual violence against Aboriginal women and women of color, although Aboriginal women more often have been at the center of the debate.[2] In his opening submission to the court in a sexual assault case involving a sixty-three-year-old Roman Catholic bishop and young Aboriginal girls under his charge at a residential school thirty years ago, a Crown prosecutor proposed to build his case of nonconsent on a bedrock of culture.[3] Referring to the role of the expert witness he intended to call to testify, an anthropologist specializing in Aboriginal culture, the Crown argued: "The purpose of [Dr. Van Dyke's] evidence is to put into context what these witnesses mean when they say, 'I did it because he told me to do it.' That is an indication of a reflection of their cultural background, the way they perceive this individual" (*R. v. O'Connor* 1992, 16). Yet, culture used in service of proving the nonconsent of young Aboriginal girls who have been sexually assaulted is highly unusual. Far more typical is culture used as a defense of the accused when the accused is of Aboriginal or non-Anglo-Saxon origin.

The cultural contexts of victims of violence and their attackers have also interested black and Aboriginal feminist researchers and women's advocacy groups, but in this context there is likely to be more of an awareness of the dilemmas and contradictions that surface whenever cultural considerations are taken into account. For instance, feminist service providers to immigrant women have stressed the need to understand how culture shapes refugee and immigrant women's experiences of and responses to violence (Rafiq 1991). Activists also note, however, that in a racist society any discussion of culture and violence in immigrant communities can be interpreted by white society as "another sign of backwardness" (Thobani 1993, 12). That is, violence in immigrant communities is viewed as a cultural attribute rather than a product of male domination. In the face of racism, it has sometimes not made sense for feminists working in the context of violence against women in immigrant and Aboriginal communities to talk about culture at all. When women from nondominant groups talk about culture (among whom I count myself), we are often assumed by others to be articulating a false dichotomy between culture and gender; in articulating our difference, we inadvertently also confirm our relegation to the margins. Culture talk is clearly a double-edged sword. It packages difference as inferiority and obscures gender-based domination within communities, yet cultural considerations are important for contextualizing oppressed groups' claims for justice, for improving their access to services, and for requiring dominant groups to examine the invisible cultural advantages they enjoy.

This article is an attempt to examine the uses to which culture is put in the courts when the issue is violence against racialized women.[4] It is equally an attempt to explore the risks of talking culture for women of color and Aboriginal women. We need to ask, Can we move the discussion about culture from cultural modes of making eye contact to what is to be gained and lost by looking white people in the eye? Both within their communities and outside of them, the risks racialized women encounter when they talk about culture in the context of sexual violence are manifested on several levels. First, many cultural communities understand culture and community in ways that reflect and leave unchallenged male privilege. Indeed, the notion of culture that has perhaps the widest currency among both dominant and subordinate groups is one whereby culture is taken to mean values, beliefs, knowledge, and customs that exist in a timeless and unchangeable vacuum outside of patriarchy, racism, imperialism, and colonialism. Viewed this way, culture maintains "a superautonomy that reduces all facets of social experience to issues of culture" (Calmore 1992, 2185). Second, racialized women who bring sexual violence to the attention of white society risk exacerbating the racism directed at both men and women in their communities; we risk, in other words, deracializing our gender and being viewed as traitors, women without community. These risks are particularly acute when, as so often happens, it is the dominant group who controls the interpretation of what it means to take culture into account.

When the terrain is sexual violence, racism and sexism intersect in particularly nasty ways to produce profound marginalization. In using the pronoun *we*, I do not want to claim, however, that as a woman of color I experience this to the same degree or incur the same risks as do Aboriginal women in Canada in talking culture. For each group, the risks are different and, more important, their need to talk about culture in spite of these risks emerges out of different histories and present-day realities. Aboriginal women often confront sexual violence in a context in which several generations have been victims of sexual violence. There is, too, a legacy of harsh socioeconomic realities. The continued denial of sovereignty and the Canadian government's consistent refusal to honor treaties and resolve land claims are profound injustices. Further, the categories *Aboriginal women* and *women of color* clearly are not homogeneous. What I would suggest we share is the fact that both women of color and Aboriginal women are obliged to talk about culture and violence within the context of white supremacy, a context in which racism and sexism and their intersections are denied. Both groups of women, therefore, in talking about their cultural specificities, run the risk, in different ways, of being granted some cultural differences but only at the expense of acknowledging their experience of sexual and racial violence. Culture becomes the framework used by white society to preempt both racism and sexism in a process that I refer to as culturalization. The risks of talking culture require us to exercise great caution whenever cultural considerations enter legal discourse or discussions about access to services. In working through the risks and in identifying how cultural considerations often work in the service of dominant groups, I hope to explore how

Aboriginal women and women of color might talk about the specificities of their cultural experiences without risking a denial of the realities of violence, racism, and sexism in their lives.

THE CULTURALIZATION OF RACISM

Contemporary discussion about culture and violence takes place within the context of modern racism, a racism distinguished from its nineteenth-century counterpart by the vigor with which it is consistently denied. In its modern form, overt racism, which rests on the notion of biologically based inferiority, coexists with a more covert practice of domination encoded in the assumption of cultural or acquired inferiority. The culturalization of racism, whereby black inferiority is attributed to "cultural deficiency, social inadequacy, and technological underdevelopment," thrives in a social climate that is officially pluralist (Essed 1991, 14; Calmore 1992, 2131). We speak more of cultural and ethnic differences and less of race and class exploitation and oppression. The concept of culturalized racism is important, it seems to me, for three reasons. First, it highlights a major feature of how modern racism works: its covert operations. Second, it explains why denial is so central to how racism works. To quote Philomena Essed, "There are two levels at which racism as ideology operates: at the level of daily actions and their interpretations and at another level in the refusal to take responsibility for it" (Essed 1991, 44). If we live in a tolerant and pluralistic society in which the fiction of equality within ethnic diversity is maintained, then we need not accept responsibility for racism. We can conveniently forget our racist past and feel secure in the knowledge that at least the residential schools are closed. Like the Dutch society Essed writes about, whose newspapers put the word *racism* in quotation marks, Canadians are outraged when racism, particularly indirect racism, is named, as it is not supposed to exist. What is denied is that "whites regularly idealise and favour themselves as a group" (Essed 1991, 43). Thus, there can sometimes be a more or less general rejection of overt racism and at the same time "an increasing reluctance to see race as a fundamental determinant of white privilege and black poverty" (Essed 1991, 30). Third, a "declaration of faith in a plural, diverse society," comments Homi Bhabha, serves as an effective defense "against the real, subversive demands that the articulation of cultural difference—the empowering of minorities—makes upon democratic pluralism" (Bhabha 1992, 235). Cultural differences are used to explain oppression; if these differences could somehow be taken into account, oppression would disappear. According to this logic, as Arthur Brittan and Mary Maynard noted in *Sexism, Racism, and Oppression*, power is subsumed under culture, and oppression is reduced to a symbolic construction in which there are no real live oppressors who benefit materially and no real oppressed people to liberate (Brittan and Maynard 1984, 19). In effect, minorities are invited to keep their culture but enjoy no greater access to power and resources.

In the context of law, because democratic pluralism means, to borrow Bhabha's aphorism, that "multiculturalism must be seen to be done, as noisily and publicly as possible," white judges are being urged to be culturally sensitive (Bhabha 1992, 232). Judges begin to practice what Dwight Greene has described for the American context as a kind of "pluralistic ignorance": "Mostly affluent white males talking among themselves about what are the reasonable choices for poor people of color to be making in situations virtually none of the judges have ever been in" (cited in Calmore 1992, 2136). In Canada, white judges have been discussing Aboriginal culture and its relevance to the sentencing of Aboriginal males convicted of sexual assault, among other offenses. At least three judicial education programs have been undertaken to "sensitize" judges to issues of cultural diversity among immigrant as well as Aboriginal communities (projects conceived of as entirely separate from gender sensitivity training, thereby rendering racialized women invisible). Sensitivity in this context means learning how to read culturally specific behavior in the courtroom setting. When it is the behavior of generic women (read white) that must be translated, sensitivity includes such things as understanding that a victim of a sexual assault may giggle on the witness stand not to express her agreement with the sexual assault but rather to convey her discomfort (Tyler 1992). For women of color and Aboriginal women who are sexually assaulted, cultural sensitivity, as I shall show below, can be about both victims and offenders unable to make eye contact. In the context of the latter, sensitivity is often about the culturalization of rape: how cultural and historical specificities explain and excuse the violence men direct at women. Culture, working in tandem with judicial tendencies to minimize the harm of rape, then becomes a mitigating factor in the sentencing of Aboriginal and minority men convicted of sexual assault.

THE CULTURALIZATION OF SEXISM

Culture as a Defense: Aboriginal Offenders

In cases of sexual assault when victims and their attackers are of the same race, it is often assumed that it is gender and not race that is the meaningful factor at work influencing how rape is "scripted" in court (Marcus 1992, 392). Yet, as Kristin Bumiller has pointed out, rape trials are most often about fallen angels who must prove their innocence in contributing to their fall from grace. The emphasis in a rape trial on the victim's purity "reinforces the presumption that punishing violent men is justified to the extent that women are worthy of trust and protection" (Bumiller 1991, 97). Racialized women, however, are considered inherently less innocent and worthy than white women, and the classic rape in legal discourse is the rape of a white woman. The rape script is thus inevitably raced whether it involves intraracial or interracial rape. The criminal justice system, Jennifer Wriggins argues, takes less seriously the rape of black women either by black men or white men (Wriggins 1983, 121). Examples from the Canadian context of Aboriginal offenders, while they show that male judges continue to minimize the harm of sexual assault, also confirm that race never absents itself from the rape script. Rather, racial and cultural differences and the implication that colonization has had a devastating impact on Aboriginal men all contribute to making invisible the harm that is done to Aboriginal women who are sexually assaulted. Additionally, viewing Aboriginal men as dysfunctional (and not, e.g., oppressed) indirectly serves to confirm the superiority of white men.

In Margo Nightingale's study of Aboriginal women in sixty-seven cases of sexual assault, Canada's history of colonization pervades the legal environment just as extensively as do historical and social attitudes toward women, and it becomes impossible to untangle which factor is contributing most to lenient sentencing of Aboriginal males accused of sexual assault (Nightingale 1991). For instance, Nightingale notes that the stereotype of the drunken Indian still operates to ensure that alcohol abuse is viewed as more significant for Aboriginal than for white offenders. What is interesting, however, is the gendered response to this stereotype. For an Aboriginal man accused of rape, alcohol abuse can be seen as a mitigating factor, sometimes a root cause of the violence against women. For an Aboriginal woman who is raped, however, intoxication becomes a form of victim blaming. A woman who has passed out, Nightingale notes, is often considered to have suffered less of a violation, and the number of victims who are passed out is greatly exaggerated.[6] Similarly, the ostracism that might be suffered by a woman who complains of rape in an isolated northern community is not noticed while the suffering a male offender might experience in a jail far from home where no one speaks his language has occasionally been taken into account.

Just what are the statements that flag race and gender coming together under the banner of culture to diminish the reality of sexual assault and its impact on Aboriginal women? Nightingale identified perhaps the most notorious Canadian case to date to illustrate the combination of gender and cultural bias in sexual assault sentencing. In *R. v. Curley, Nagmalik, and Issigaitok*, a sentence of seven days was meted out to three Inuit men found guilty of having intercourse with a female under the age of fourteen. Relying on his experience in the Eastern Arctic, Judge Bourassa considered the culture of the accused men and was especially lenient on the basis that, according to his information, in Inuit culture, a young woman is deemed ready for intercourse upon menstruation. An assumed cultural difference was also used to bolster the defense's argument that the accused men were ignorant of Canadian law on sexual assault. On appeal, cultural considerations continued to shape the rape script by eclipsing the realities of the violence done to the young girl. Although the sentence was increased to reflect the view that ignorance of the law was no excuse, there was no effort made to determine if the victim had in fact suffered great harm (Nightingale 1991, 92–94).[7]

Similar cultural considerations have arisen in cases where the defense has argued for a community-based treatment program as an alternative to prison. In *R. v. Naqitarvik*, the same Judge Bourassa accepted the community-based solution on the basis that the community's unique cultural methods of dealing with sexual assault (in this instance a healing circle) had a significant role to play in healing the offender. On appeal, the issues once again revolved around culture as the court elected to impose a stiffer sentence on the basis that the community-based program was no more than a counseling program and that, further, "the witnesses in this case do not describe a culture markedly different than that in the rest of Canada. Rather, the incident itself arose as the victim and her sister played music on a modern player for which there was an electric cord," an indication in the court's eyes that Inuit culture was sufficiently modern that it could not be characterized as different from the mainstream (Nightingale 1991, 92–93).

Judges, and the lawyers who argue the cases before them, can work with a notion of cultural difference as inferiority but recognize, at the same time, the damaging impact of colonization (at least in sexual assault cases if not in land claims where such recognition would have a bearing on the restitution of land); that is, they sometimes display a willingness to consider the history of colonization and its present-day effects as mitigating factors in the sentencing of Aboriginal males.[8] One reads in decisions, for instance, some empathy for sexual offenders who come from "the worst Indian reserve in the province" (*R. v. T.* 1989, 8). In *R. v. Whitecap and Whitecap*, the very difficult social and economic conditions on the Red Earth Indian reserve are noted (*R. v. Whitecap [R. T.] and Whitecap [D. M.]* 1989); in *R. v. Okkuatsiak*, the offender is described as a victim of the economic conditions in Nain (*R. v. Okkuatsiak* 1987, 234). Judges also note in their decisions the vicious cycle of sexual abuse that began with residential schools (*R. v. J. [E.]* 1991). What is absent here is any acknowledgment of the impact of this history of colonization and its present-day legacy on Aboriginal women as the victims of sexual assault. This is how gender and race conflate to produce an absence of the realities of Aboriginal women.

At the time of Nightingale's study, few Aboriginal women had written of the cultural bias of the judiciary in cases of sexual assault involving Aboriginal men, perhaps wary, as Nightingale speculates, that such a critique would only serve to further criminalize Aboriginal men and leave Aboriginal women open to the charge of race treason, very much as Anita Hill was during her testimony regarding Clarence Thomas. Since then, Teressa Nahanee, a member of the Squamish Indian Nation, has strongly protested the gender bias of Northern judges. Reviewing both reported and unreported decisions in the sentencing of Inuit males accused of sexual assault during the period 1984–89, Nahanee concluded, as did Nightingale, that lenient sentencing of Inuit males cannot be defended on the basis of cultural sensitivity: "This [lenient sentencing] is simply a process whereby white patriarchs bond with brown patriarchs in justice administration. The northern judiciary keep Inuit male sex offenders in the North by accepting cultural defenses put forward by Inuit males accused in rape cases. Inuit women claim the 'culture' defined in this sentencing process does not represent 'Inuit modern culture,' or traditional practices. It is culture defined by flown-in, southern, white anthropologists who take a text-book approach to culture" (Nahanee 1992, 5). Indeed, Pauktuutit, the Inuit Women's Association of Canada, as Nahanee reports, has launched a constitutional challenge of sentencing decisions on the basis that lenient sentencing of Inuit males in sexual assault cases interferes with the right to security of the person and the right of equal protection and benefit of the law of Inuit women (Nahanee 1992, 3). Along the same lines as Nightingale (and the evidence uncovered in my own research), Nahanee elaborates on how race is confused with culture and comes to be used as a mitigating factor in the sentencing of Inuit male offenders. Instead of using the "reasonable man" standard, she writes, the Northern court "has invented a fictional Inuit man": "He can be many things. He can be a high-ranking public official, raised 'traditionally,' a family man, with no criminal record for whom the crime is unpremeditated. Or, he is not well educated, under the influence of alcohol, unemployed, with no previous record. No matter what elements of the fiction are used, he is Inuit [*sic*] and he will not be sentenced to more than two years less a day" (Nahanee 1992, 34).

Both Nightingale and Nahanee have rightly focused on cases in which cultural sensitivity rested on a highly gendered, unsophisticated view of culture and, I would add, on a gendered view of the impact of colonization. My own research into cases of sexual assault has confirmed their conclusions.[9] Recently, however, some judges have been more careful of the gendered consequences of viewing rape through the lens of race and/or culture as well as history. For example, in *R. v. M. (G. O.)*, the court noted: "The seriousness of the offence does not vary in accordance with the colour of the skin of the victim, her cultural background or the place of her residence" (*R. v. M. [G. O.]* 1990, 81); in *R. v. Ritchie*, it is noted that sexual assault "is not acceptable in society whether it be within the Indian society or the general society" (*R. v. Ritchie* 1988, 1). There is an emerging awareness of the dangers of relying on culture as a mitigating circumstance. In *R. v. J. (H.)*, this use of culture is specifically refuted: "There have been instances when Canadian judges were persuaded to bend the rules too far in favour of offenders from Native communities or disadvantaged backgrounds. When that happens a form of injustice results; specific victims and members of the public generally are given cause to believe that the justice system has failed to protect them. . . . H. J. cannot properly be portrayed as a naive young man who should only be pitied and not condemned. He is not a 'child of the forest' " (*R. v. J. [H.]* 1990, 3). If Aboriginal offenders are no longer "children of the forest," the dangers for Aboriginal women of deficient and clumsy attempts on the part of legal players in the justice system to interpret culture and history remain nonetheless. It continues to be primarily white male judges and lawyers with little or no knowledge of history or anthropology who interpret Aboriginal culture and its relevance to the court. Wrapped in a cloak of sensitivity to cultural differences and recognition of the consequences of colonization, the anthropologizing of sexual assault continues to have gendered overtones and to maintain white supremacy as securely as in days of more overt racism and sexism.

Eye Contact and the Cultural Differences Approach

In 1989, a Crown attorney with extensive experience prosecuting Native offenders in the North wrote an article on how cultural bias affects the sentencing of Native accused men. Two years later, the article became a book. In *Dancing with a Ghost*, Rupert Ross begins from the standpoint of cultural sensitivity, urging lawyers and judges to critically examine their own cultural assumptions and advising them to do their best to discover Aboriginal realities and truths (Ross 1992, 2). Ross explains with an example: "I have learned, to my chagrin, that in some northern reserve communities looking another straight in the eye is taken as a deliberate sign of disrespect for their rule is that you look inferiors straight in the eye" (Ross 1992, 2). He then goes on to elaborate how such cultural differences have an impact on sentencing. Significantly, Ross is responding to his perception that sentencing of Native offenders has been too harsh and at variance with the wishes of Aboriginal communities themselves. His identification of cultural differences, then, is intended to avoid this outcome. Largely anecdotal, Ross's commentary serves to highlight where cultural interpretation through white male eyes can take us in the area of sexual assault.

Ross intends to make an argument for community-based justice and for lenient or nonexistent jail terms, an outcome he considers justifiable if it can be shown that Aboriginal communities both desire it and can offer protection to the community. The first part of this argument, that Aboriginal communities desire this outcome, relies on anecdotes of the victims themselves. A teenage rape victim refuses to testify, Ross reports, because she believes that her assailant has paid enough of a penalty while waiting for the case to come to trial (Ross 1992, 2). . . . Ross feels certain that Aboriginal communities do not want violent, abusive men punished but instead healed and forgiven. Describing the sentencing of a young man who had beaten his wife in an alcoholic rage, Ross compares his own position that such an offense required a jail term as a deterrent to that of the men and women of the community. Aware perhaps that he might well be criticized for a gender-blind account of community, Ross notes that, while the community leaders asking that the young man remain in the community were all male, the courtroom was jammed with women. As he speculates, "Each of those ladies knew that when his jail term was over he would come back. If he came back feeling reviled by the women of the village, his problems with women would only grow worse. If, in contrast, they demonstrated their forgiveness, their support and their waiting welcome, the opposite result might occur. In their view, while jail sentences might on occasion be necessary for the protection of all, the person who has to pay that price should not be cut off from community affection and support. To do so would only put the community further at risk" (Ross 1992, 6). Finally, to support his speculation that Aboriginal women endorse community sanctions as an alternative to jail, Ross cites the 1989 report by the Ontario Native Women's Association (which he mistakenly dates 1990) that recommends the establishment of healing houses for women, children, and abusers (Ontario Native Women's Association 1989).

While it would be wrong to overdramatize the impact of Ross's cultural interpretations or to fail to note that he himself warned that his comments were restricted to isolated Aboriginal communities of his experience in Northern Ontario, his comments have been taken up by the chief judge of the Yukon territories, Heino Lilles, and reflect the approaches taken in some recent sexual assault cases in the North. Judge Lilles's own theorizing about cultural bias is noteworthy not only because of his position in the justice system and his involvement in various judicial education programs but because, like Ross's, his statements are accompanied by an acknowledgment that Aboriginal communities are highly disadvantaged communities. These interpretations are not, in other words, overtly racist; rather, they are presented as culturally sensitive, even antiracist initiatives (Lilles 1990, 1992).[10]

Like Rupert Ross, Chief Justice Heino Lilles has spent some of his professional life within the context of Northern justice and hence has had ample opportunity to see how harshly the criminal justice system has dealt with Native offenders, a situation he attributes to two principal factors: "The social and economic poverty in which many Natives live, and a subtle, unintentional but persistent discrimination by the decision makers in the criminal justice system" (Lilles 1990, 330). If players in the judicial system can do little about poverty, they can certainly address discrimination, and it is to this end that Judge Lilles writes about culture and cultural bias. Decision makers in the justice system in the North, including police, lawyers, and judges, come from a cultural, social, and economic background different from that of the majority of persons in the communities where they serve, notes Judge Lilles. Such individuals are unintentionally biased; that it is to say, they may possess "an inclination, bent, or predisposition to make decisions a certain way, based on the sum total of the individual's own cultural and social experiences" (Lilles 1990, 343). Put this way, the problems of Northern justice originate in poverty as well as in a "misinterpretation" of cultural differences (Lilles 1990, 330). Admitting that it is difficult to generalize about Aboriginal values (but apparently not so difficult to do so about white culture), Judge Lilles nevertheless proceeds to rely on a chart comparing the value systems of Aboriginal peoples and non-Aboriginal peoples and to suggest how these differing values enter into judicial proceedings.[11] The question of eye contact surfaces once again, and Lilles, relying on Ross, notes that the justice system often unnecessarily criminalizes and labels young Aboriginal people because of the assumption (based on their alleged tendency not to make eye contact) that they are unreliable, remorseless, and uncooperative (Lilles 1990, 341).

It is important to note that under the umbrella of cross-cultural sensitivity Judge Lilles includes a number of practices that do not originate in culture but rather in the material practices of Northern justice. Thus, Crown prosecutors prosecute more readily because they are unwilling to overrule the police; police charge more readily; the level of policing is 200–300 percent greater than in other jurisdictions; few support services exist as alternatives to jail. All these factors contribute to a scenario that is explained away by poverty and misunderstandings of cross-cultural encounters. Significantly, the word *racism* does not throughout Lilles's article. If cultural differences and poverty are the source of the problems of Northern justice, then Aboriginal and community-based justice in which, presumably, cross-cultural concerns disappear, is at least one important strategy toward greater justice.[12] It is precisely this option that is now being considered in the disposition of some sexual assault cases and in two recent cases in which Judge Lilles presided, although, significantly, it is a white judge who is in the position of deciding what a community-based disposition should be.

HEALING OFFENDERS

Culture as a defense and the pursuit of a "culturally relevant disposition" in the case of *R. v. P. (J. A.)* revolved around the Aboriginal concept of healing, an approach to justice described in the *Report of the Aboriginal Justice Inquiry of Manitoba* as follows:

The underlying philosophy in Aboriginal societies in dealing with crime was the resolution of disputes, the healing of wounds and the restoration of social harmony. It might mean an expression of regret for the injury done by the offender or by members of the offender's clan. It might mean the presentation of gifts or payment of some kind. It might even mean the forfeiture of the offender's life. But the matter was considered finished once the offence was recognized and dealt with by both the offender and the offended. Atonement and the restoration of harmony were the goals—not punishment. [*Report of the Aboriginal Justice Inquiry* 1991, 27]

P. pleaded guilty to sexually assaulting his two daughters and a foster child over the course of several years. The assaults began when each of the girls reached the age of thirteen years. The defense urged the court to adopt a community-based disposition in lieu of a period of incarceration (normally a two-year minimum and a maximum of life imprisonment for sexual intercourse with a minor). Notwithstanding the serious breach of trust involved, Judge Lilles agreed to the community-based disposition on the basis of three factors, each of which bears examination for how culture, community, and colonization can be used to compete with and ultimately prevail over gender-based harm. First, the chief (on behalf of the five clan elders) supported P.'s bid for a community-based disposition. As described by Judge Lilles in his decision and later in an article, the chief spoke in some detail about the community's efforts to recover from the devastating effects of colonization and in particular the Alaskan highway, which passed through the community in 1942. Alcohol, sexual abuse at residential schools and in homes, and the breakdown of the traditional community structure resulted, in the chief's words, in a "time of great cultural downfall" (*R. v. P. [J. A.]* 1991, 305). The community's response was to break the cycle of abuse through a healing circle in which both victims and offenders would come forward for treatment and rehabilitation. Also testifying on P.'s behalf were a number of witnesses, including one of his daughters and his wife who supported the call for a community solution already in place in the community in the form of a weekly collective counseling session. A third factor in P.'s favor was the fact that he had been a leader in bringing Native culture back to the community and possessed, in the eyes of the judge, "the potential to be a future leader in the Teslin community" (*R. v. P. [J. A.]* 1991, 315). Aware that his decision was likely to attract censure, Judge Lilles accepted the community alternative, as does Rupert Ross, on the basis that a community disposition can be "hard time" and even more difficult for the offender than a term of imprisonment. As he elaborates, "In this case I heard evidence about the humiliation which accompanies disclosure of an offence like this in a community the size of Teslin. 'First one must deal with the shock and then the dismay on your neighbour's faces. One must live with the daily humiliation, and at the same time seek forgiveness not just from the victims, but from the community as a whole.' For in a Native culture, a real harm has been done to everyone. A community disposition continues that humiliation, at least until full forgiveness has been achieved" (*R. v. P. [J. A.]* 1991, 317). Culture and community remain in this decision unexamined and ungendered while the subtext of colonialism (never named as racism and thus a legacy of the past and not part of the present) informs white judicial cultural sensitivities.

It is mainly within remote, Northern communities that culturally relevant sentencing has occurred. In the Northwest Territories, there is, as Judge Lilles is concerned to note, "an exceptionally harsh system of justice" with an imprisonment rate of 790 per 100,000 population as compared to 112.7 for the rest of Canada and 426 per 100,000 for the United States (Lilles 1992, 330). Arguably, such an environment demands that alternatives to incarceration be explored. At the very least they demand that we examine the root causes of the problems apparent in the judicial system. In this context, it seems sensible to explore, as Judge Lilles has advised, the potential of probation reviews as a means of monitoring whether or not community-based dispositions are working. What is worrying is the offender-centered features of this approach, the almost entirely male cast of spokespersons for the community, the denial of racism as a key factor affecting the treatment of all Aboriginal peoples, and sexism in Aboriginal women's lives. Of concern, too, is the failure to question whether what may be appropriate for a small Aboriginal community of 300 may be transposed to altogether different contexts.

Lilles's decision in *R. v. P. (J. A.)* has not to my knowledge drawn public criticism but another decision of Judge Lilles, also involving sexual assault and healing, has. The connections between *R. v. P (J. A.)* (1991) and *R. v. Hoyt* (1991) are instructive in that cultural considerations in the former appear in the latter despite significant differences in context. Between 1965 and 1971, John Hoyt, a white probation officer in Whitehorse (the capital of the Northwest Territories, population 60,000) who also served as a volunteer assisting Native youth, molested three minors of Aboriginal origin whom he supervised on a camping trip and whom he counseled and befriended. In view of Hoyt's early guilty plea, over forty letters of reference, the devastating impact on Hoyt's family, and a remorseful offender who would like to assist his victims in their "healing," Judge Lilles imposed a fine of $2,000 per victim. While he did not ultimately accept the defense's suggestions that Mr. Hoyt contribute to the community by "researching alternatives in sentencing for sexual abuse cases, assist the authorities in developing badly needed programming for sexual offenders, assist the Native community, while allowing him to facilitate the healing process for himself and his victims," Judge Lilles did concede that such suggestions were "very attractive" (*R. v. Hoyt* 1991, 17). The Court of Appeal in January 1992 dismissed an appeal by the Crown that the sentence was too light (*R. v. Hoyt* 1992).

The Lilles decision in *Hoyt* did draw criticism from the Yukon Association for the Prevention of Community and Family Violence. As the authors of the response argued, Judge Lilles gave no weight to the one victim who testified about the harm done to him and presumed on the weakest of evidence that there was no risk of recidivism, notwithstanding the testimony by Mr. Hoyt's psychologist that the accused's understanding of the consequences of his behavior for his victims was limited. Finally, on the judge's attraction to the defense's proposal of community work, the authors state their association's response bluntly: "To be crass, one wonders if the criminal offence of arson qualifies one for the position of fire marshall" (Forde, Pasquali, and Peterson 1991, 7).

Judge Lilles's decisions may simply be illustrative of a more generalized tendency to dispense offender-centered rather than victim-centered justice in cases of sexual assault, but what is interesting about the *P. (J. A.)* and *Hoyt* decisions is the extent to which they reflect the judge's acceptance of community-based dispositions and of healing in particular, concepts that are intended to reflect his sensitivity to the social and economic conditions of Aboriginal communities in the North, to their history of colonialism, and to specific cultural differences. That Judge Lilles is himself a white man and that Hoyt, a white probation officer, is one of those players in the justice system whom Judge Lilles earlier identified in his article as likely to possess cultural biases, seems not to have altered the strategy or encouraged a cautious interpretation of cultural considerations. The victims, in this case Aboriginal boys, also were not considered in the eager acceptance of community-based justice.

Judges dispensing justice in Canada's North are confronted with the vulnerability of Aboriginal children in the North. There are many cases involving pedophiles who are also authority figures, a heritage of colonialism that surfaces in the rape of a sister by a brother who was himself raped as a child by a white authority figure, high suicide rates among young people, and extensive alcohol abuse. Judges must thread their way through culture and history in order to determine who is offender and who is victim. In this context there are only victims, but they are certainly not all equally placed. While a few decisions do not constitute a trend, *Hoyt* and *P. (J. A.)* and others nevertheless suggest that judging in this context demands more careful attention to the meaning of community, history, and culture. . . .

BETWEEN A ROCK AND A HARD PLACE: ABORIGINAL WOMEN'S RESPONSES TO SEXUAL VIOLENCE

Community has not been a safe place for women, and Aboriginal women have not failed to note this. The Ontario Native Women's Association's study on violence confirmed what many earlier studies had noted: the level of violence directed against women and children in Aboriginal communities and families was much higher than for non-Aboriginal populations. . . . Indeed, male violence was one reason why the Native Women's Association of Canada (NWAC) went to court in 1991 for the right to sit at the table during the constitutional talks on Aboriginal self-government. Arguing that their exclusion from the table posed a grave threat to Aboriginal women, NWAC explained to the court the basis for its fears: "Why are we so worried as women? . . . We have a disproportionately high rate of child sexual abuse and incest. We have wife battering, gang rapes, drug and alcohol abuse and every kind of pervasion imaginable has been imported into our lives. The development of programs, services, and policies for handling domestic violence has been placed in the hands of men. Has it resulted in a reduction of this kind of violence? Is a woman or a child safe in their own home in an Aboriginal community? The statistics show this is not the case" (*Native Women's Association of Canada*, applicants' memorandum 1992, 14). . . .

Confronting male domination within Aboriginal communities has required an understanding of how white domination of Aboriginal communities has contributed to the causes and extent of male violence. As the Ontario Native

Women's Association stressed in its report on violence, Aboriginal people do not have self-government and are regulated in much of their everyday affairs through the federal government. This continuing colonization and the devastating impact of past domination are the contexts in which Aboriginal family violence must be examined (Ontario Native Women's Association 1989, 23). Unlike judicial consideration of colonization, however, Aboriginal women stress the contemporary dimensions of colonization and its impact on both men and women. Aware of racism but equally concerned about the violence inflicted on women and children, respondents to the Ontario Native Women's Association's study on Aboriginal family violence were emphatic that they did not condone violence and wanted it stopped: 82 percent of respondents wanted their abusers charged even though they also expressed a fear of the wider implications of involving Canadian police in Aboriginal family disputes. The association's report emphasizes healing of all members of the family but solidly maintains, "Of course, the needs and safety of the abused woman and children are more urgent at first" (Ontario Native Women's Association 1989, 50). Its recommendations reflect this priority, referring first of all to the need to provide services and healing lodges for women and children who are victims of violence and second to treatment programs for batterers.

In other reports by Aboriginal women on family violence, it is clear that the twin realities of racism and violence inform the analysis of strategies. In Alberta, the author of a report on abused Aboriginal women notes that for "too many Aboriginal women the inability of Aboriginal communities to protect her and her children from abuse means the only option is to relocate outside the community" (Courtrille 1991, 23). Victimized in their own communities and victimized outside of it, even in shelters, such Aboriginal women do indeed find themselves between a rock and a hard place: either violence or the double victimization and harsh reality of being without community and family . . . (see also Northwest Territories Status of Women Council 1990b). . . . In *Voices of Aboriginal Women: Aboriginal Women Speak Out about Violence* . . . Aboriginal women make clear why they prefer an approach to violence that is community-centered and focused on healing: "Most of the Aboriginal victims of family violence are women and children and the offenders are men. The Aboriginal victims must deal with the offender or be subject to exile outside the community, from their home, far from close relatives. It is important to realise that the victims and members of the family are victimized again by the system because they must leave their home and community. Aboriginal women feel that it is the offender that is most in need of help to break the cycle of violence, but is the most ignored. But the women do not want to give up their right to safety. So the logical approach is to intervene and take the offender away from home" (Canadian Council on Social Development and Native Women's Association of Canada 1991, 25–26). The dilemma that Aboriginal women face in being forced to choose between their personal safety and community was expressly acknowledged in the *Report of the Aboriginal Justice Inquiry of Manitoba*. . . . Justices Hamilton and Sinclair . . . conclude with a discussion of healing and Aboriginal women:

> As the victims of childhood sexual abuse and adult domestic violence, they
> have borne the brunt of the breakdown of social controls within Aborig-

inal societies. There was substantial support for an entirely new system, to break the cycle of abuse and to restore Aboriginal methods of healing designed to return balance to the community, rather than punish the offender. . . . We recommend that women be involved in the implementation of our recommendations, and that they be represented on the various administrative bodies that will become necessary. While the role of Aboriginal women in Aboriginal society is not well understood in non-Aboriginal circles, we have been told, and accept, that a resumption of their traditional roles is the key to putting an end to Aboriginal female mistreatment. The immediate need is for Aboriginal women to begin to heal from the decades of denigration they have experienced. But the ultimate objective is to encourage and assist Aboriginal women to regain and occupy their rightful place as equal partners in Aboriginal society. [*Report of the Aboriginal Justice Inquiry of Manitoba* 1991, 507]

Responses such as this speak of healing and community but also speak of the safety of women and of equality; they are different in a significant way from the forgiving approach noted by Ross and Lilles because they attempt to come to terms with women's realities at the intersection of racism and sexism.

White judges and lawyers seeking neat culturally sensitive, ungendered solutions to justice have not often stopped to question their authority to interpret Aboriginal culture, history, and contemporary reality. Self-reflexivity has been entirely absent from discussions of culture and the courts. Talal Asad's point that "'cultural translation' is inevitably enmeshed in conditions of power—professional, national, international" would suggest that Canadian courts must begin with the *contemporary* fact of white supremacy in and out of the courtroom and not simply get by with a passing reference to its history and hazy references to contemporary cultural biases and social conditions (Asad 1986, 163). There are, however, perils in calling for an interrogation of notions of culture in a legal context. Clearly, women and children who are victims of violence do not stand in relation to culture as do their assailants. We will need to ask, as Leila Abu-Lughod did about the Bedouin communities she studied, how cultural responses work to sustain the power differences within groups, such as the difference in status between men and women (Abu-Lughod 1991, 162). This does not then become a dichotomy between culture and gender but an interrogation into how culture is gendered and gender is culturalized. A second, equally compelling issue is that a discussion about culture may well displace an inquiry into domination. . . . It is not difference that is feared, Cherrie Moraga notes, but similarity. The oppressor fears "he will discover in himself the same aches, the same longings as those of the people he has shitted on . . . he fears he will have to change his life once he has seen himself in the bodies of the people he has called different" (Moraga 1992, 26). The eagerness with which theories of cultural difference are taken up in the justice system while racism and sexism remain unnamed is a reminder that culture is treacherous ground to travel.

• • •

RISKS FOR IMMIGRANT WOMEN

When immigrant women plead for cultural considerations to be taken into account, they can very quickly find themselves backed into a multicultural corner. As Homi Bhabha commented (in reference to the exoneration of Clarence Thomas from the charge of sexual harassment of Anita Hill), "Suddenly, lip service is paid to the representation of the marginalized. A traditional rhetoric of cultural authenticity is produced on behalf of the 'common culture' from the very mouths of minorities. A centralizing, homogeneous mode of social authority is derived from an ever-ready reference to cultural 'otherness'" (Bhabha 1992, 235). The culturalization of racism, whereby minorities are seen as culturally inferior, makes any foray into cultural difference risky. Attempts by women of color to draw the connections between racism, sexism, and violence have sometimes floundered in the wake of these powerful currents of racism. How will the story of rape from within one's own cultural group be heard by the dominant group when, as Yasmin Jiwani concluded from her study of South Asians in the media, South Asian women, "whether muslim, hindu or sikh," are portrayed "as victims trapped in the patriarchal mould of the east" (Jiwani 1992, 14)? . . . As Jiwani recounts, responses from white women to articles on Muslim women and the veil included the sentiment that, in comparison to Eastern women, Western women should consider their own men "as gems of enlightenment and kindness" (Jiwani 1992, 14).

· · ·

Although women of color, like Aboriginal women, have consistently named patriarchal violence within the context of racism and the histories of colonialism and imperialism, the second part of the message is unlikely to be heard as strongly as the first. Women of color have often found it necessary, for instance, to distance themselves from the culturalization of violence while arguing at the same time for culturally sensitive services for women who have been victims of silence. Thus the Coalition of Immigrant and Visible Minority Women of British Columbia states in its report to the British Columbia Task Force on Family Violence that "no culture condones violence" (Jaffer 1992, 204). A study done by African women in Toronto observes that culture is a "cocoon in which people, especially men, hide and use to oppress others" (Musisi and Muktar 1992, 22). . . .

Immigrant women have described their problems around violence as one of equality of access and the services to assist survivors of violence as suitable only to the needs of Anglo-Saxon and/or French-Canadian women (Rafiq 1991, 12). From this point of departure, cross-cultural service delivery becomes the goal for service providers of the dominant groups. Yet rarely is it noted that majority group members usually know very little about the impact of racism on the lives of the racialized women they serve. For instance, a handbook for service providers working with immigrant women includes a chapter on culture that begins with the notion that "it is just a gap in awareness that we need to fill in order to improve the quality of our service" (Coutinho 1991, 49). . . . The practical steps she suggests to improve cross-cultural service delivery emphasizes learning about behavioral differences such as eye contact and a variety of "cultural cues" that identify a person's cultural identity. Culture is once again taken to encompass a specific set of readily identifiable values, practices, and responses that characterize all the members of a particular group. More important, those who use broad generalizations about various cultures (nonrationality, stress on spiritual grace rather than material comfort, etc.) reveal an enormous potential to stereotype and rank cultures according to racist assumptions. The popularity of cross-cultural awareness sessions, in which service providers of the dominant group learn about cultural cues from charts that categorize the values of various cultures indicate that, while little has shifted in terms of who provides service and how those services are provided, immigrant women's demands for equality of access can be absorbed handily by a smattering of stereotypes acquired by white service providers and legal professionals in the name of cross-cultural sensitivity.

CULTURE AS AN OPPOSITIONAL WEAPON

The risks of talking culture are immense. What is too easily denied and suppressed in this discussion is power. . . . Dominant groups too readily adopt the cultural differences approach, relieved not to have to confront the realities of racism and sexism. The challenge is therefore how to reduce massive inequalities in communication so that racialized women can speak as well as be heard as they intended, without risking further marginalization.

Cross-cultural sensitivity training will be of little use unless it is pursued in the context of the greater empowerment of the subordinate group. The project of working across cultures must, for a start, include an acknowledgment of contemporary relations of domination and how they are lived. For example, the cross-cultural training endorsed by the Aboriginal Justice Inquiry of Manitoba includes not only matters relating to Aboriginal culture but also issues of discrimination and profiles of the enormous socioeconomic injustice that is contemporary Aboriginal reality. More important, cross-cultural training is pursued alongside of self-determination and the creation of a separate Aboriginal justice system. For our part, immigrant women such as myself, who are not faced with the issues of land claims and sovereignty, must watch out instead for the ethnicization of our concerns. Legal professionals and service providers must come from our own communities. While it may be worthwhile to communicate cultural differences to members of the dominant group, we also ought never to forget how rooted such differences are in our histories of racial oppression. . . .

Cultural considerations might be effectively deployed if they remain grounded in the realities of domination. In the courtroom, the cultural background of racialized women can be used to explain the structural constraints of our lives. . . . To fully contextualize the lives of women and children who are sexually assaulted, feminists working in law take a risk that information is likely to be used against women and children as much as for them. In talking about culture and domination, therefore, while we will have to stand on firm ground and stay away from broad unsubstantiated generalizations about cultural values and practices, we will also have to be careful in how we choose to describe specific practices of domination against racialized women. There can be no casual, unreflective use of culture in the courts.

NOTES

1. Crown attorneys refer to lawyers representing the state in federal jurisdiction.

2. The Aboriginal people of Canada include Indian, Metis, and Inuit people. *Indian* typically refers to Aboriginal people entitled to be registered as Indians (Status Indians) according to the Indian Act of Canada, although there are many people of Indian ancestry not entitled to register under the Act for a variety of reasons; *Metis* refers to Aboriginal people of mixed blood, and *Inuit* refers to Aboriginal people known formerly as Eskimos. The word *Native* is also used to refer to Indian, Metis, and Inuit people.

3. In Canada, many Aboriginal children were forcibly removed from their homes and taken away to residential schools run by the Catholic church. Allegations of rampant sexual and physical abuse are increasingly common, and many cases have been proven.

4. I have used the term *racialized women* to refer to women whose ethnicity, as indicated by skin color, accent, religion, and other visible markers, denotes that they are of non-Anglo-Saxon, non-French origin. In the eyes of the two dominant groups, such women are raced.

⋮

6. There are obviously parallels here to how intoxicated non-Aboriginal victims of sexual assault are treated, but I would argue that the pervasiveness of the stereotype of the drunken Indian ensures that, for the judiciary and for society, Aboriginal women's intoxication offsets the harm of sexual assault.

7. Note that consent is not an issue in the case of rape of a girl under fourteen years of age.

8. It has been suggested that Judge Bourassa's original attraction to a community disposition in *R. v. Naqitarvik* stemmed in fact from his special concern for the survival of a small and fragile Arctic Inuit community (Bell 1991, 37).

9. Twenty-nine cases prior to 1989 and ten cases from 1989 to 1992 confirm Nightingale's conclusions on sexual assault cases in predominantly Northern jurisdictions.

10. Note that the word *disadvantaged* implies that the problem is one of bad luck. There is thus no agent of domination, whereas to say *oppressed* implies that oppressors exist.

11. A chart of Native and white value systems is popular not only among judges in their training sessions but is also used by some sexual assault centers in their recent bid to understand cultural differences. One handout used by the Hamilton Sexual Assault Centre correctly attributes the original description of Native values to Justice Thomas Berger 1977, 1:93–99. The Berger report was highly influential and remains a frequently cited description of Native culture.

12. Ideas for Aboriginal justice systems and community-based initiatives have been advanced for some time in Canada, particularly by Aboriginal communities them-

selves. Most recently, the Law Reform Commission has cautiously endorsed the idea. While the commission is careful to explore potential difficulties, gender-based concerns are not among these (Law Reform Commission of Canada 1991, 16–23). A public inquiry into the administration of justice for Aboriginal people in Manitoba concluded more strongly that a separate Aboriginal justice system was required but stressed also that Aboriginal self-government and the settlement of land claims were necessary steps before justice could be served. The concerns of Aboriginal women are addressed in this report (*Report of the Aboriginal Justice Inquiry of Manitoba* 1991, 639–74).

REFERENCES

Abu-Lughod, Leila. 1991. "Writing against Culture." In *Recapturing Anthropology,* ed. Richard Fox, 137–62. Santa Fe, N.Mex.: School of American Research Press.

Asad, Talal. 1986. "The Concept of Cultural Translation in British Social Anthropology." In *Writing Culture: The Poetics and Politics of Ethnography,* ed. James Clifford and George E. Marcus, 141–64. Berkeley and Los Angeles: University of California Press.

Bell, Jim. 1991. "The Violating of Kitty Nowdluk." *Arctic Circle,* July/August, 32–38.

Berger, Thomas. 1977. *Northern Frontier, Northern Homeland: The Report of the Mackenzie Valley Pipeline Inquiry.* Ottawa: Supply and Services Canada.

Bhabha, Homi. 1992. "A Good Judge of Character: Men, Metaphors, and the Common Culture." In *Race-ing Justice, En-gendering Power: Essays on Anita Hill, Clarence Thomas, and the Construction of Social Reality,* ed. Toni Morrison, 232–50. New York: Pantheon.

Brittan, Arthur, and Mary Maynard. 1984. *Sexism, Racism, and Oppression.* Oxford: Blackwell.

Bumiller, Kristin. 1991. "Fallen Angels: The Representation of Violence against Women in Legal Culture." In *At the Boundaries of Law,* ed. M. A. Fineman and N. S. Thomadsen, 95–112. New York: Routledge.

Calmore, John O. 1992. "Critical Race Theory, Archie Shepp, and Fire Music: Securing an Authentic Intellectual Life in a Multicultural World." *Southern California Law Review* 65(5):2129–2230.

Canadian Council on Social Development and Native Women's Association of Canada, 1991. *Voice of Aboriginal Women: Aboriginal Women Speak Out about Violence.* Ottawa: Canadian Council on Social Development.

Courtrille, Lorraine. 1991. *Abused Aboriginal Women in Alberta: The Story of Two Types of Victimization.* Edmonton: Misener-Margetts Women's Resource Centre.

Coutinho, Tereza. 1991. "Culture." In Rafiq 1991, 49–64.

Essed, Philomena. 1991. *Understanding Everyday Racism: An Interdisciplinary Theory.* Newbury Park, Calif.: Sage.

Forde, Jan, Paula Pasquali, and Alexis Peterson. 1991. "A Victim-centred Approach." *Yukon News,* July 12, 7–9.

Henderson, James Youngblood "Sakej." 1992. "The Marshall Inquiry: A View of the Legal Consciousness." In *Elusive Justice,* ed. Joy Manette, 35–62. Halifax: Fernwood.

Jaffer, Mobina. 1992. Is Anyone Listening? *Report of the British Columbia Task Force on Family Violence.* Vancouver.

Jiwani, Yasmin. 1992. "To Be and Not to Be: South Asians as Victims and Oppressors in the *Vancouver Sun.*" *Sanvad* 5(45):13–15.

Law Reform Commission of Canada. 1991. *Report No. 34 on Aboriginal Peoples and Criminal Justice.* Ottawa: Law Reform Commission of Canada.

Lilles, Heino. 1990. "Some Problems in the Administration of Justice in Remote and Isolated Communities." *Queen's Law Journal* 15:327–44.

———. 1992. "A Plea for More Human Values in Our Justice System." *Queen's Law Journal* 17:328–49.

MacQueen, Ken. 1992. "Academia Goes for the Judicial Jugular." *Toronto Star*, December 18, A4.

Marcus, Sharon. 1992. "Fighting Bodies, Fighting Words: A Theory and Politics of Rape Prevention." In *Feminists Theorize the Political*, ed. Judith Butler and Joan W. Scott, 385–403. New York: Routledge.

Moraga, Cherrie. 1992. "La Guera." In *Race, Class, and Gender: An Anthology*, ed. Margaret L. Andersen and Patricia Hill Collins, 20–27. Belmont, Calif.: Wadsworth.

Musisi, Nakanyike, and Fakiha Muktar. 1992. *Exploratory Research: Wife Assault in Metropolitan Toronto's African Immigrant and Refugee Community.* Toronto: Canadian African Newcomer Aid Centre of Toronto.

Nahanee, Teressa. 1992. "Sex and Race in Inuit Rape Cases: Judicial Discretion and the Charter." Unpublished typescript in possession of the author.

Native Women's Association of Canada and Her Majesty the Queen, reasons for judgment. 1992. Fed. C.A., June 11, Mahoney, J. A.

Native Women's Association of Canada, Gail Stacey-Moore and Sharon McIvor and Her Majesty the Queen, The Right Honourable Brian Mulroney and the Right Honourable Joe Clark in RE the Referendum Act, applicants' memorandum of fact and law in the Fed. Ct. (Trial Division), September 18, 1992, file No. T 2283–92.

Neely, Barbara. 1992. *Blanche on the Lam.* New York: Penguin.

Nightingale, Margo. 1991. "Judicial Attitudes and Differential Treatment: Native Women in Sexual Assault Cases." *Ottawa Law Review* 23(1):71–98.

Northwest Territories Status of Women Council. 1990a. Open Letter to Madame Justice Conrad. June 18.

Northwest Territories Status of Women Council. 1990b. *We Must Take Care of Each Other: Women Talk about Abuse.*

Ontario Native Women's Association. 1989. *Report on Aboriginal Family Violence.* Thunder Bay, Ont.

Rafiq, Fauzia, ed. 1991. *Toward Equal Access: A Handbook for Service Providers Working with Survivors of Wife Assault.* Ottawa: Immigrant and Visible Minority Women against Abuse.

Report of the Aboriginal Justice Inquiry of Manitoba. Vol. 1. *The Justice System and Aboriginal People.* 1991. Winnipeg: Queen's Printer.

Ross, Rupert. 1992. *Dancing with a Ghost: Exploring Indian Reality.* Markham, Ont.: Octopus.

Thobani, Sunera. 1993. "There Is a War on Women." A Desh Pradesh workshop. *Rungh: A South Asian Quarterly of Culture, Comment and Criticism* 1(1&2):12.

Tyler, Tracey. 1992. "Are Judges Guilty of Gender Bias? The Jury's Out." *Toronto Star*, December 2, A1, A17.

Wriggins, Jennifer. 1983. "Rape, Racism, and the Law." *Harvard Women's Law Journal* 6:103–41.

CASES CITED AND RELATED CASES

R. v. Betancur. Dist. Ct. (Ont.). 1985. December 20, reasons for sentence, Weiller, J., file no. I.SA 362.

R. v. Drozdkik. County Ct. (B.C.). 1988. March 31, reasons for sentence, Boyd, J., file no. CC870536.

R. v. E. G. C.A. (Ont.). 1987. *Ontario Appeal Cases* 20:379.

R. v. Hoyt. C.A. (Yukon). 1992. January 17, oral reasons for judgment, Taqqert, Lambert, and Hollinrake.

R. v. Hoyt, Terr. Ct. (Yukon). 1991. July 18, reasons for sentence, Lilles, C.J.T.C.

R. v. J. (E.). S.C. (Yukon). 1991. March 15, judgment delivered orally, Madison, J., file no. 90-06337.

R. v. J. (H.). Pr.C. (B.C.). 1990. January 17, reasons for sentence, Barrett, J., file no. 1095FC.

R. v. Kowch. S.C. (Yukon). 1989. March 20, file no. 87-4661.

R. v. L. (K.). P.C.(Man.). 1989. September 18, reasons for sentence, Meyers, J.

R. v. M. (G.O.). S.C.(NWT). 1990. *Canadian Criminal Cases* 54 (3d): 81.

R. v. Moses. 1992. Terr. Ct. (Yukon). *Canadian Criminal Cases* 71 (3d): 347–85.

R. v. O'Connor. S.C.(B.C.). 1992. December 2, 1992, excerpts of proceedings at trial.

R. v. O'Connor and Aboriginal Women's Council, Canadian Association of Sexual Assault Centres, Disabled Women's Network Canada, the Women's Legal Education and Action Fund, and the Canadian Mental Health Association. C.A. (B.C.). 1993. June 30, written reasons for judgment of application for intervenor status, Taylor, J.A., Wood, J.A., Hoolinrake, J.A., Rowles, J.A., and Prowse, J.A., concurring.

R. v. Okkuatsiak. 1987. Nfld. & P.E.I.R. 65:233.

R. v. P. (J.A.). 1991. 6 C.R. (4th) 126. R. v. P. (J.A.). *Northwest Territories Reports* [1991].

R. v. Ritchie. County Ct. (B.C.). 1988. March 2, reasons for sentence. Houghton, C.C.J., file no. CC39/87.

R. v. Roach. S.C. (Yukon). 1987. December 8, file no. 523.87.

R. v. S. (D.D.). Prov. Ct. (Ont.). 1988. November 2, reasons for sentence, Langdon, J.

R. v. T. (J. J.). C.A. (Sask.). 1989. April 26, judgment delivered orally, Tallis, J.A., Vancise, and Gerwing, J.A., concurring.

R. v. Vaneden. Terr. Ct. (Yukon). 1988. February 1, reasons for sentence, Ilnicki, J.

R. v. Whitecap (R.T.) and Whitecap (D.M.). C.A. (Sask.). 1989. January 5, judgment delivered orally, Gerwing, J.A., Tallis, J.A., concurring. Wakeling, J.A., in dissent.

CHAPTER 14

Feminism, Punishment, and the Potential of Empowerment

LAUREEN SNIDER

> The main criterion for determining the success or failure of re-
> forms should be the impact of the changes made on the lives of
> the women involved.[1]

> In accepting law's terms in order to challenge law, feminism al-
> ways concedes too much.[2]

> We can't dwell on the blame. We have to move on. The longer
> we spend blaming, the more time it will take.[3]

INTRODUCTION

The purpose of this paper is to argue that the focus in feminist thought on
women's injuries at the expense of women's uniqueness and progress is one-
sided and harmful. In policy terms, it leads to an emphasis on punishment and
victimization rather than empowerment and transformation. . . .

The emphasis on injuries and punishment has its origins in anger. As
women have gradually rediscovered their history, redefined their entitlements,
and realized the extent, viciousness and pervasiveness of misogyny in Western institutions and cultural practices over private and public spheres, they

Abridged from Laureen Snider, "Feminism, Punishment, and the Potential of Empowerment,"
Canadian Journal of Law and Society, Vol. 9, No. 1, pp. 75–104, © 1994. Reprinted by permission
of the Canadian Journal of Law and Society. *Ed. note:* Although text and footnotes were deleted,
we preserved the footnote numbers that appeared in the original text.

have become justifiably angry. Rage is a usual companion of social move-ments—the anger of black people in United States, for example, will be fuelling riots for some time to come. Indeed, reformers typically get more angry as movements succeed, because the rage comes to be seen as increasingly legiti-mate and the dangers of expressing it openly lessen. On political and ideolog-ical levels, calls for vengeance and punishment are appealing to those seeking change because they attract the attention of mass media and of political elites. However, this paper will argue that strategies built on rage which employ crim-inal law and the criminal justice system tend to backfire. By focusing feminist energies on villains and victims, political and theoretical attention is directed away from tactics with greater potential to empower and ameliorate.

This paper should not, however, be read as advocating a dichotomous, black-and-white renunciation of all arguments based on injury or punishment, or a blanket rejection of criminal law under all circumstances. Such a "mas-culinist" discourse,[4] an arrogant insistence on the virtues of a particular posi-tion to the exclusion of all competing ones, embodies the very characteristics of social theory we should be questioning. The aim here is to suggest that fem-inism may have over-emphasized the negative, and it might be time to shift the balance. . . .

PUNISHMENT AND CRIMINAL JUSTICE SYSTEMS

Theory and Criminal Justice

• • •

History illustrates that law has generally acted to reinforce dominant gender, race and class patterns. In conjunction with other institutions of the state, it has aligned itself structurally with both capitalism and patriarchy, and played a key role in maintaining hegemony, defined as "the process(es) of generating the 'spontaneous consent' of the governed to the rule of a particular social group (class) through the development and promotion of ideologies that act as a so-cial cement."[14] The documented struggles of working class people, people of colour and women throughout the 18th and 19th centuries illustrate the close connection between legal rule, in its administrative, civil, and criminal guises, and dominant classes, races and genders.[15] Thus the potential for using law to facilitate liberative struggle is real, but success is likely to be hard to come by—the struggle may fail or, worse, prove counterproductive over time.

• • •

Feminist scholars have themselves pointed out the patriarchal nature of law in general, the ways its form, language, and substance reflect and reinforce male or elite or racist views, and have alluded to its tendency to boomerang against women.[21] Yet building strategies upon it is still the norm.[22] Criminal-ization is politically appealing because it simplifies conflicts by stressing moral indignation over reason, offering "a concrete terrain of struggle, a reachable result."[23] But what if the result is not ameliorating for women; if strengthening criminal law plays into the hands of those who would disempower women?

Criminal justice lacks transformative potential because it does not operate in the same way as other mainstream institutions; it fills different ideological and structural roles. Criminal justice refers to a set of institutions whose primary role is to further social control, a task made easier if its "clients" are delegitimized, rendered voiceless and powerless, ideologically and structurally isolated from the working class. The work of transforming lawbreakers from political rebels to despised criminals took place during the early stages of industrial capitalism, before the dominance of monopoly capitalism, and has stood remarkably firm since that time.[24] In criminal justice, the official mandate of police, courts, and criminal justice officials is to control and coerce (and thereby "protect," which is the official legitimation for the first two).[25]

Institutions outside the social control/punishment nexus accomplish tasks which benefit a large multiclass client group—they educate, heal, serve deities, provide public transportation or child-care. At a more basic level they also control and coerce, but that is not their primary role. They have legitimate functions, potentially useful to all classes, genders and ethnic groups, and can be called to account if they control or coerce at the expense of these central duties. Schools, for example, can be forced to change their procedures if they are punishing children rather than teaching them to read; general hospitals will be publicly criticized if they merely control patients as opposed to treating illness.

· · ·

Although passing criminal laws is a public process, full of sound and fury, enforcing them in the institutions of criminal justice remains a complex and largely invisible one.

Empirical Evidence

Let us look first at initiatives employing criminal law to further feminist goals. In this area, the effect on the women the legislation aimed at empowering—the battered or assaulted woman—must be the prime, if not the only criterion for evaluating the success or failure of law reform.[36] When doing this, one notices first the cases where "reform" has actually worsened the plight of the victimized. Women found themselves facing contempt charges for refusing to testify against batterers,[37] for example, or arrested for pointing a gun to stop a beating.[38] In other instances, women were forced to contend with heightened state interference in their lives, facing social workers eager to investigate everything from finances to sex lives.[39]

Moving to case studies, initiatives where the use of criminal law has been pronounced successful are much more equivocal on closer analysis. Jane Ursel[40] outlines the struggle in Manitoba to force courts and police to take wife battering seriously, beginning with a 1983 directive from the Attorney General instructing police to charge all wife abusers. While the argument is complex, she maintains that changes in criminal law have significantly improved the position of female victims. Let us look at the evidence presented. First, the number of charges against abusers has gone up, a slow but steady increase since the 3673 charges laid in 1983—itself up from 2458 in 1982.[41] Attrition rates have been reduced, particularly at the courtroom level, and criticisms by judges and lawyers of the Attorney General's 1983 directive to charge abusers has largely evaporated. "More appropriate" sentences[42] have been obtained for abusers. Crown appeals have also increased[43] so presumably some "inappropriate" sentences are still being imposed. The percentage of offenders receiving a court-imposed sanction has increased from 48 to 64%; the percentage of those receiving fines alone as sanctions is down; probation and mandatory counselling dispositions are up; and jail sentences have increased from 2 to 7% of cases. Most of the offenders processed have working- or lower-class origins, are under 40 (70%), and have prior records (70%). They have low-level jobs if employed at all, and little education. (Data on racial origin were not presented, but it would be a safe bet that many of those charged are native or Metis in origin.)

The argument for interpreting this material as evidence of the success of employing criminal law is weak, particularly on the one criterion that counts—bettering the life of the victim. As indicated above, there is no reason to conclude that arresting and charging more suspects is helpful to the women involved, or even that it represents the option she would have preferred. As always, the men arrested are not a representative sample of abusers—they are the abusers with the fewest resources and the least ability to resist. It is abundantly clear from self-report studies and other sources,[44] that poor men and natives are not the only, or even the most serious offenders against women. Mobilizing class bias (and probably racism as well) in the name of justice, *and of feminism*, is not a clever strategy.

Second, the fact that most of those arrested have prior records is presented as evidence of their "dangerousness."[45] But an equally plausible interpretation is that those with records are the easiest subjects for police to arrest, process and convict, as they are already stigmatised and labelled. Is there any reason to believe that putting more poor young males through the public trauma of criminal justice processing, and subjecting more of them to jail or "mandatory counselling" and compulsory therapeutic programmes, which have the highest records of failure,[46] accomplishes any purpose except to provide more jobs for middle- (and some working-) class officials in criminal justice? The one documented effect of imprisonment is to make those subject to it more resentful, more dangerous, more economically marginal, and more misogynous. Those arrested are disproportionately men already subjected to the injuries of class, racism and often childhood abuse as well. Moreover, there is no literature showing that punitive sanctions, particularly applied to marginalized offenders for expressive rather than instrumental offences[47] have any transformative or deterrent effect.[48]

On the other hand, once separated from criminal justice and its mission of punishment, Ursel presents evidence that shows certain feminist initiatives have made a real difference to the lives of Manitoba women. The number of community-based women's assault services increased from five to 23 in the period under study. Ten of these are shelters, several are nonresidential programmes, and all are apparently controlled by women. In addition, programmes to train police recruits have been set up (laudable from ideological and practical perspectives, however slim their chances of transforming paranoid and patriarchal police subcultures), as well as treatment groups for batterers, and a Women's Advocacy Program. Funding for battered women has tripled, from $300,000 in 1983–1984 to $1.7 million in 1987. (However it is unclear how much money will go towards increased punishment of offenders, and how much for amelioration and empowerment of female victims.) Ursel points out that feminists employed in provincial and federal bureaucracies outside criminal justice played a crucial role throughout, supporting the principle of community-based programmes run by local women even at the expense of their own department and their own jobs.[49]

Thus we see evidence of real progress produced by feminists and their allies through struggle and engagement with mainstream institutions and government departments. But little success was achieved when changes were channelled through criminal justice—a finding consonant with similar studies elsewhere.[50]

The effect of initiatives directing police to arrest males accused of assaulting their partners has been extensively studied in the United States. An early study, much publicized in the media, reported that arrest decreased the chance of future assaults.[51] Subsequent studies—six replications were commissioned by the National Institute of Justice of Dade County (Miami), Atlanta, Charlotte, Milwaukee, Colorado Springs and Omaha—have not supported an arrest effect. For example, Dunford et al.,[52] in Omaha, found no difference in recidivism between assailants who were counselled, separated (the assaulter was sent away from the home for a 12 to 24-hour period), or arrested. Still, such initiatives have often been interpreted as evidence of the success of feminist initiatives. Dobash and Dobash,[53] summarizing studies in the United States and the United Kingdom, see American feminism as instrumental in altering police practices and changing prosecution offices. The result, it is argued, has "advanced the agenda of social change" and produced "greater democratization of agencies of the State."[54]

Spurred by equal protection suits, the practice of mandatory arrest and mandatory police response to complaints of battering have become almost commonplace in the United States and (less dramatically) in Canada. The San Francisco Family Violence Project, launched in 1980, "succeeded in heightening public awareness and altering persistent patterns [of denial and non-response by police] within criminal justice."[55] Similarly, the Duluth Domestic Abuse Intervention Project, "another successful programme,"[56] instituted a pro-arrest policy that produced, from 1982 to 1984, a 47% reduction in repeat calls and a 77% rate of guilty pleas (1992:181). Phrased differently, this meant that the percentage of women in the local shelter involved in court cases increased from 17% in 1980 to 43% in 1983. And in London, Ontario, the number of arrests increased from one in every 16 calls in 1979 to three of every four in 1983,[57] and victims were deemed more satisfied as well.[58] The Dobashes conclude that "significant progress" in establishing "meaningful consequences" for abusers[59] has occurred. The Santa Barbara Family Violence Project, on the other hand, has been pronounced a failure because it did not produce more prosecutions and arrests.[60]

This North American record is contrasted with the situation in Britain where police and courts have, by and large, resisted initiatives to force them to arrest and prosecute suspected abusers on a routine basis. Efforts to protect women through civil injunctions have also been largely ineffective, as judged by the women themselves, although dramatic increases in the number of injunctions granted have occurred. Injunctions jumped from 6400 in 1980 to 15,539 in 1987.[61]

However, to interpret the increased use of criminal justice as evidence of the success of feminist initiatives to empower women (and particularly women victims of physical and sexual assault) is to make an unwarranted leap of faith and logic. Surely an increase in the number of injunctions and/or arrests shows only that social control is a growing and prosperous industry. To be fair, the Dobashes recognize the downside of criminal justice despite their optimistic conclusions. As they point out, one of the first documented effects of mandatory arrest legislation was the increase in the number of women arrested, usually for using violence to defend themselves against their attackers.[62] They also note that criminal justice systems discriminate against men of colour. Moreover, the traditional prejudices court officials harbour against nontraditional women (usually those who offend against patriarchy by living without males to control them), results in increased discrimination and harassment against them. And feminist dependence on criminal justice has legitimized the expansionary agenda of the criminal justice system.[63]

Moreover, the most urgent need is to transform the community to which abusers return, and institute structural change at this level. The chances of doing this are surely diminished when all our efforts are directed toward initiatives that end up scapegoating marginal minority males. This is not to suggest that those arrested are predominantly innocent—there is no evidence of this—nor to argue that their offences be trivialized or ignored. The violence must be halted. And the Dobashes and others may be correct in pointing to changes in criminal law as important *symbolic* victories. But the key question remains: to what degree have such victories for feminism as a movement (still largely middle-class and white) been achieved at the expense of working- and lower-class women, women of colour and native peoples? . . .

Certain conclusions are inescapable: policies mandating arrest and punishment do not provide solutions to the real problems of women—they do not ameliorate the day-to-day realities of battering, rape, and assault, and they may increase stress by adding a public level of suffering, at the hands of the criminal justice system, its practices and officials, to that endured in the private sphere. Reform initiatives seeking to promote liberal, humane or feminist values through criminal justice systems have failed, while initiatives promoting increased criminalization (as long as the discretionary powers of officials are not challenged) have largely succeeded, in North America at any rate. Many of the latter—victims' rights movements in the United States provide good examples—are consonant with dominant ideological forces in that they seek to intensify control over potentially dissident groups in an era of high unemployment and fiscal crisis. Whatever their origins, they are accordingly embraced with some enthusiasm by state authorities, the media and relevant corporate elites, translated into law, and end up intensifying state control. Under the pretence of responding to pressure from such groups, including calls by feminists for longer sentences for rapists and sexual assaulters, many American states are passing statutes that weaken the standards of evidence required for conviction and allow preventive detention, arrest without warrant and seizure of property. At the same time funding for counselling, therapy, or women's shelters has been systematically eliminated.[65] None of this means the state is implacably patriarchal. As illustrated by Ursel's work,[66] among others, there are interstices where feminists, inside and outside state structures, have made a difference. However, institutional sites and types of law vary. They occupy different structural niches with different potentials for resistance and transformation. Macrolevel and organizational level realities combine to make the institutions that comprise the criminal justice system the least likely candidates for transformative struggles. It is essential, therefore, to shift the balance of struggle away from criminal law and into arenas with greater ameliorative and empowering potential. The symbolic gains achievable through public forays to change criminal law must be balanced against the losses and costs of this strategy. We must be particularly attentive to their consequences for the most vulnerable women, whose fates cannot be easily disentangled from the lives of their partners and lovers. . . .

THE PERILS AND PLEASURES OF RIGHTS STRUGGLES

Rights struggles are also problematic as foci for social action. While usually outside the jurisdiction of criminal law and the discourse of punishment, they do privilege law rather than social restructuring, and they do assume law reform is a legitimate way of redressing social problems. . . .

Rights, be they legal or constitutional, and the rights discourses and litigation they may or may not require, must be contextualized, broken down, situated. . . . Feminists should engage law, in the following ways: first, to remove any remaining impediments, laws which stand in the way of full legal equality or which "disadvantage women as a sex class";[70] second, to prevent the passage of laws which will create new barriers (this includes struggles to prevent new and disabling interpretations of previously existing laws); and third, to establish concrete rights, cutting across both class and gender, which will consolidate present gains and empower future generations of women. Thus, rights struggles may need to become less central, but they will still be necessary under certain conditions. . . . The aim should be to secure concrete rights—to day care, minimum income, or the like—rather than abstract rights such as equality.

The Potential of Struggles Using Noncriminal Law

Some aspects of civil and administrative (but not criminal)[71] law may provide opportunities dissenting groups can use to secure structural as well as ideological change. Played out against a minimally liberal state and media, conflicts may be transformed into sites of ideological struggle, highlighting the injustices facing women (or workers, native peoples, lesbians, and similar groups). Through such struggles dominant ideologies (and ultimately hegemony) can be challenged, for the credibility of dominant beliefs rests on people's isolation and shame, and on the tendency to individualize or blame oneself when discrepancies between dominant ideology and daily reality are confronted. The ideological, legal and political changes created through rights struggles may lead to long-term change and tangible progress. In addition, limited structural change can be precipitated. This is the best case scenario; the pitfalls, as many have pointed out, are numerous.[72]

. . .

The most damning argument against rights struggles is the simplest one: that laws creating equal rights for women have not been effective. They have "failed to produce substantive changes in the everyday lives of women or in the relations of power between women and men."[78] Equal pay legislation in Canada, for example, has apparently achieved minuscule gains, and only for the most privileged female workers. Could we have achieved more universal and expeditious results by struggling to increase the percentage of the female workforce in unions,[79] or upping the minimum wage,[80] rather than chasing the chimera of legal equality? Fineman[81] and Weitzman[82] have both pointed out that equal rights (to family income, assets, and children) in divorce law can disadvantage women and children because legal presumptions on the equality of spouses ignore the realities of structural discrimination against women, as both mothers and wage labourers. And, although the ideological "fit" is quite different, we have already seen the dangers of attempting to make women's conditions in criminal justice systems "equal" to those of men.[83]

. . .

Engaging Law to Remove Barriers

The second condition which may necessitate engagement with law is the removal of legal impediments. As Smart has pointed out,[85] first-wave feminists became involved with law reform because of the need to abolish laws which accorded special privileges to men. Laws that reinforce patriarchy and serve as barriers to feminist goals of empowerment and amelioration are far from obsolete despite the fact that earlier generations of feminists succeeded in removing the most egregious legal barriers in Anglo-European countries. Laws denying women the right to own property or retain it after divorce, laws making children the property of the father, laws barring women from education and shutting them out of professions, are now gone. Ironically, however, many of the laws that impede women's struggles today are boomerangs, the product of earlier attempts to secure abstract rights that are now, through universalism and technology, being used against women.

. . .

Limits on the Powers of Law

Foreseeing the dangers of impending legislation is an important task. However, we must not forget that this attention to law is rendered necessary by the fact that women are still relatively powerless. *Laws have the potential to be interpreted in ways which hurt women because women lack the power to resist such interpretations.* Laws, however complex and ambiguous, do not generally wreak havoc upon dominant groups. They are practically never interpreted in ways which threaten the rights of males or upper-class people, because both dominant ideology and social practice direct judges away from this reconstruction of reality. . . . Legal action is sometimes important not because law in itself will increase the power of women, for history shows repeatedly that law has limited independence from structural forces, and limited potential to act as an independent instrument of social change. But legal battles may be a means to an end; the end being to increase the power of women on ideological, political, or economic levels. They must never replace strategies designed to empower, nor be confused with them. Law reform, then, is best envisaged as a defensive tactic, to be used when it cannot be avoided. Like surgery or growing old, it is only advisable when the alternative course of action is worse.

The secondary role law plays in battles for meaningful change highlight another point that should guide political action: concrete rights—to guaranteed employment, universal Medicare, day care or reproductive rights—are tactically preferable to abstract ones. . . . Struggles for concrete universalistic rights should develop constituencies that cut across gender as well as class and ethnic lines. Because the ultimate success of feminism depends on collective struggle with alliances of like-minded people, avoiding the divisive potential of battles for special exclusionary rights, as opposed to universal ones, is crucial. . . .

Limiting rights struggles to concrete issues where large, cross-class and cross-gender coalitions are a reasonable possibility, in areas with the potential to empower and politicize such as health care and employment, then, maximizes the chances of long-term success. Should the reform be passed into law, it may be tactically important to press for new bureaucratic arrangements within state structures to implement the changes. Maximum leverage will be achieved if the new bureaucracy is controlled by feminists or "friends." This is a controversial recommendation because state bodies are subject to cooptation and inertia, but consolidating a reform in this way provides a set of allies inside state structures who then have vested interests in retaining and expanding the benefit secured. Arguments generated from the inside—mounting defences against competing organizational priorities or protecting one's share of a shrinking budget pie—are more likely to be successful. Ongoing pressure from the outside is still essential, however, to give allies on the inside the leverage they need. They have to be able to tell their political masters that the recommended policy change is really very conservative when one considers what those angry women demonstrating in the streets are demanding! External pressure, then, makes a necessary progressive policy appear to conservative state officials as the better of two unpalatable courses of action. External groups are also necessary to ensure that key beneficiaries of the reform remain those outside state structures, not officials or politicians.

There is also much to be done without invoking law. On the ideological level, educating the public and convincing people of the validity of feminist causes, through legal, extra-legal, and non-legal struggles, employing a variety of means and embracing a number of institutional levels, is crucial to secure long-term change. . . . Public struggle is a key way to change dominant ideologies about women, and thus an important device for achieving the generational changes that are essential if real progress is to occur.

This process can be best illustrated by looking at the struggles of another group, workers, and their campaigns for the right to refuse dangerous work. Although this struggle was more superficial than the one feminists confront— because the psychological processes confronting feminist aims are rooted deeply in human psyches—opposition from the forces of capital and state were initially virulent, extensive, and very powerful. Only very slowly, through a series of highly public struggles, demonstrations, speeches, publications and confrontations with the police and army, did workers successfully challenge the fervently held belief that facing hazardous conditions was part of the job contract, a condition of employment accepted whenever they "freely" took a job. In one set of state-sponsored hearings, for example, managers with Canadian Pacific Railways argued that running along the tops of railway cars (in a train going 50 miles an hour) was not dangerous as long as the workers were careful—and it was their habit of abusing liquor that made so many of them fall off.[91] A series of very ineffective laws were passed at first, by political states that were, in some instances, directly controlled by the forces of capital.

Gradually, however, dominant ideology changed—and the limits of "reasonable" business behaviour and "reasonable" risk shifted. Gradually, conditions that had been accepted as part of the employment bargain in 1890 became marks of the irresponsible employer by 1940. Law did not cause this transition—in many instances, the power to pass laws outlawing dangerous conditions did not exist until long after the conditions had declined and become characteristic of the "bad apples" on the fringe of respectability. Indeed criminal law was almost totally absent, criminal prosecutions of employers virtually unknown. The struggle to refuse dangerous work was also facilitated by the fact that many hazardous conditions were rendered unnecessary by technological improvements, thus removing the crucial link between unsafe conditions and profit maximization, making reforms financially expedient and considerably lessening resistance from capital. Nevertheless, the development of safer technologies was itself spurred by employee resistance to dangerous conditions. Whatever the reasons, prevailing definitions of acceptable levels of risk for first-world employees did change dramatically over the last 100 years. The result is that people work shorter hours, in cleaner, lighter, better ventilated conditions, with more break time and more protection against arbitrary dismissal. They also live longer. It is this process of ideological and structural change that feminism, ideally, buys into by entering the public arena.

Alternatives—Theory and Praxis

The attempt to construct a specifically feminist jurisprudence, an elaborate structure of formal law based on women's values and reflecting women's realities, represents one alternative.[92] Although I would argue that this initiative is deeply flawed—it rests on the premise that law, particularly but not exclusively criminal law, can effect structural change and deliver empowering remedies, it encourages a passive discourse of victimisation, and it colludes with "law's overinflated view of itself"[93]—some of its elements are useful.

• • •

Pressure from feminism in recent decades has forced law to take account of certain female acts of care (such as the decision to bear a child), but such acts have been misinterpreted in a dominance/subordination discourse. The struggle for reproductive choice, where women seeking to control the timing and amount of nurturance they will provide are seen as selfish and antifamily, illustrates this dilemma.

In the struggle to control law and shape dominant ideology, patriarchy has used women's concern for others, particularly their families, to split and weaken feminism. It has successfully pitted women who see themselves primarily as mothers and spouses against those whose identities rest on their roles outside the family. Feminist movements themselves have sometimes unwittingly given the forces of reaction ammunition, by de-emphasizing the key roles women play in socializing and nurturing, preferring "hard" discourses based on rights and privileging criminal law. This is not surprising, given that women's special responsibilities and roles have been used against them so often, and with such devastating effect, but it is shortsighted.

Conservative groups have argued that women can only fulfill their responsibilities for caring and nurturance if they eschew power in the public sphere. Given structural conditions that deny parents employed outside the home any right to child care, supported by dominant ideologies that limit the working father's household responsibilities to "helping the wife" if he chooses to do so, this false dichotomy of choices contains, like most ideological constructions, a kernel of truth. In the struggle to construct counter-hegemonic positions, feminist theorists must begin by pointing out the sexist assumptions and cultural contingencies that underlie such reasoning. Women's roles as mothers and nurturers, as agents of socialization upholding humane people-centred values in a capitalist world where selfish individualism is the norm, can and must be reconciled with women's right to empowerment, to full citizenship in public and private arenas.

• • •

Empowerment, then, on the ideological, economic, and political levels, is the key to transforming women's lives—and to ultimately preventing gender-related injuries. In the short term, better access to services, changes in the unjust distribution of time, money, and work that now benefits men at the expense of women, in both public and private spheres, are all important goals.[101] Such strategies require a certain engagement with law, particularly civil and administrative. And criminal law has a place here as well. The struggles to secure legal reforms that redefined rape as sexual assault and rediscovered wife battering as a moral evil have ideological and symbolic significance—if only because of the unfortunate centrality criminalization and control discourses enjoy in public arenas. Obviously, short-term intervention strategies that allow the state to intervene and stop men from beating and raping women are essential and, whether due to a failure of imagination or not, the only ones we now have rely on criminal law. All the same, minimizing the damage done by criminal law is equally essential.

Indeed, many fruitful ideas have come out of feminist recognition of the damage criminal law and control campaigns have inflicted on poor, black and native men and women, and their communities. Building on Quaker and abolitionist traditions, "feminist peacemakers" have been pushing governments to provide preventative community-based education for male and female children. They have also fought to secure funding for victim/survivor services and offender restoration, to minimize if not eliminate the social conditions that foster rape-prone societies. These are nonpunitive actions that directly and indirectly alleviate human suffering;[102] they promote healing rather than punishment. Other initiatives we could build upon are also "out there," being debated in academic and media circles. For example, many people of colour insist that progressive academic theorists have forgotten the key role families have played in their struggles, as collective sources of strength and resistance against racism.[103] In a related vein, Sugar and Fox[104] point out the key roles family and concepts of connectedness and healing have played in aboriginal cultures. All of these provide building blocks and starting points for feminist strategies.

CONCLUSION

Feminism is at risk of emphasizing the negative, adopting punishment and injury-obsessed agendas at the expense of positive, empowering and ameliorating ones. There is a temptation to rely too much on law and legal reform, whether through changes in criminal law, rights struggles, or the development of grand legal theory. Negative agendas partake of victimization and punishment discourses which take power away from women. The argument in this paper favours specificity: we must recognize that different types of law and different institutional sites have different transformative potential. The potential will vary by nation-state and historical period as well. Although it is impossible (and undesirable) to lay out in advance all the strategies that feminists may find useful (since they must be tailored to local ideological and material conditions), analyses of the evidence will at least make some of the blind alleys more obvious. Such general guidelines, informed by theoretical and empirical analysis, remain both possible and essential guides to effective social action.

NOTES

1. E. Comack, "Legal Recognition of the 'Battered Wife Syndrome': A Victory for Women?" (Paper presented at the American Society of Criminology Meetings, San Francisco, November 1991), citing J. Ursel, "Considering the Impact of the Battered Women's Movement on the State: The Example of Manitoba" in E. Comack & S. Brickey, eds., *The Social Basis of Law: Critical Readings in the Sociology of Law*, 2d ed. (Toronto: Garamond, 1991) 261.

2. C. Smart, *Feminism and the Power of Law* (London: Routledge, 1989) at 5.

3. P. Monture-Okanee, "The Violence We Women Do: A First Nations View" in C. Backhouse, ed., *Challenging Times: The Women's Movement in Canada and the United States* (Montreal: McGill-Queen's Press, 1992) 76.

4. C. Gilligan, *In a Different Voice* (Boston: Harvard University Press, 1982).

⋮

14. H. J. Maroney, "Using Gramsci for Women: Feminism and the Quebec State, 1960–80" (1988) 17:3 *Feminist Perspectives on the Canadian State* 26.

15. B. Palmer, *Working Class Experience: Rethinking the History of Canadian Labour, 1800–1991* (Toronto: McClelland & Stewart, 1992); E. P. Thompson, *The Making of the English Working Class* (New York: Vintage Books, 1966).

⋮

21. C. MacKinnon, *Sexual Harassment of Working Women: A Case of Sex Discrimination* (New Haven: Yale University Press, 1979); C. MacKinnon "Feminism, Marxism, Method and the State: An Agenda for Theory" (1982) 7:3 Signs 515; C. MacKinnon "Feminism, Marxism and the State: Toward Feminist Jurisprudence" (1983) 8:2 Signs 635; A. Howe, "The Problem of Privatized Injuries: Feminist Strategies for Litigation" (1990) 10 Society 119; Gilligan, *supra* note 4.

22. C. Brants & E. Kok, "Penal Sanctions as a Feminist Strategy: A Contradiction in Terms?" (1986) 14 *International Journal of Sociology of Law* 269.

23. T. Pitch, "From Oppressed to Victims: Collective Actors and the Symbolic Use of the Criminal Justice System" (1990). 10 Studies in Law, Politics and Society 103.

24. R. S. Ratner, "Rethinking the Sociology of Crime & Justice" in R. S. Ratner & J. L. McMullan, eds., *State Control: Criminal Justice Policy in Canada* (Vancouver: University of British Columbia Press, 1987).

25. Under the guise of protecting the public, criminal law and its institutions function to stigmatize and de-legitimate despised individuals, causes or groups.

⋮

36. This discussion focuses on male assault of female partners. We have too few studies on lesbian or gay battering to know whether similar patterns prevail in these "family" units or not.

37. "Battering Victims Sentenced" *Toronto Star* (10 August 1986) A8.

38. *Winnipeg Free Press* (18 March 1992).

39. L. Snider, "The Potential of the Criminal Justice System to Promote Feminist Concerns" (1990) 10 Studies in Law, Politics and Society 143. See also S. Caringella-

MacDonald, "Marxist and Feminist Interpretations on the Aftermath of Rape Reforms" (1987) 12 Contemporary Crises 4; D. Klein, "Violence Against Women: Some Considerations Regarding its Causes and its Elimination" (1981) 27:1 Crime and Delinquency 64; R. Elias, "Which Victim Movement: The Politics of Victim Policy" in W. Skogan et al., eds., *Victims and Criminal Justice* (Berkeley: Sage Publications, 1989); P. Morgan, "From Battered Wife to Program Client: The State's Shaping of Social Problems" (1981) 9 Kapitalistate 17; Geller, *supra* note 35; J. Roberts, *Sexual Assault Legislation in Canada: An Evaluation Report*, vols. 1–9 (Canada: Department of Justice, Minister of Supply and Services, 1991).

40. Ursel, *supra* note 1.

41. This would seem to indicate that feminist pressure was having an effect on government attitudes before policy was changed.

42. Ursel, *supra* note 1 at 272.

43. *Ibid.* at 275.

44. Canada, Solicitor General, *Bulletin on Reported and Unreported Crimes, Canadian Urban Victimization Survey #1-4* (1984).

45. Ursel, *supra* note 1 at 279.

46. S. Walker, *Sense and Nonsense About Crime* (Monterey, CA: Brooks/Cole, 1985).

47. Expressive offences refer to those committed for primarily emotional motives, as ends in themselves, to demonstrate sexual prowess or win status in a peer group, for example. Rape, especially group rape, much juvenile delinquency and recreational drug use are examples of crimes that are frequently expressive in nature. Corporate crime, professional theft, fraud and bank robbery, on the other hand, are typically instrumental offences committed as a means to an end, the end frequently being monetary gain. As more "rational" offences, they are more amenable to preventive strategies that alter the cost and payoff structure of the offence. Like all ideal-type dichotomies, the distinction between expressive and instrumental offences, while useful for classificatory purposes, is never absolute. Most offences (and offenders) exhibit some features of both types.

48. Walker, *supra* note 46.

49. Ursel, *supra* note 1 at 274.

50. Roberts, *supra* note 39; D. Spohn & J. Horney, *Rape Law Reform: A Grassroots Revolution and Its Impact* (New York: Plenum Press, 1992).

51. L. W. Sherman & R. A. Berk, "The Specific Deterrent Effects of Arrest for Domestic Violence" (1984) 49:2 American Sociological Review 261.

52. F. Dunford, D. Huizinga & D. Elliott, "The Role of Arrest in Domestic Assault: The Omaha Police Experiment" (1990) 28:2 Criminology 183.

53. R. Dobash & R. E. Dobash, *Women, Violence and Social Change* (London: Routledge, 1992).

54. *Ibid.* at 203.

55. *Ibid.* at 180.

56. *Ibid.*

57. *Ibid.*

58. P. Jaffe, D. A. Wolfe, A. Telford & G. Austin, "The Impact of Police Charges in Incidents of Wife Abuse" (1986) 1:1 Journal of Family Violence 37.

59. Dobash & Dobash, *supra* note 53 at 183.

60. *Ibid.* at 183–84.

61. *Ibid.* at 192–93.

62. *Ibid.* at 199.

63. *Ibid.* at 206–09.

⋮

65. Elias, *supra* note 39.

66. Ursel, *supra* note 1.

⋮

70. K. Lahey, "Civil Remedies for Women: Catching the Critical Edge" (1988) 17:3 Feminist Perspectives on the Canadian State 92.

71. As we have seen, changes in criminal law tend to enlarge the domain of punishment while offering no concrete benefits to women at risk. At best they might have the potential for symbolic advance but not structural change. The distinction is a crucial one because it means the everyday lives of women are unlikely to be made better by, for example, new criminal laws proscribing heavier punishment for rapists, but they may be transformed by statutes delivering higher wages, day care or paid maternity leave.

72. J. Handler, "Social Movements and the Legal System: A Theory of Law Reform and Social Change" (New York: Academic Press, 1978); J. Handler, "Dependent People, the State and the Modern/Postmodern Search for the Dialogic Community" (1988) 35 UCLA Law Review 998; Cohen, *supra* note 9.

⋮

78. Findlay, *supra* note 18 at 31.

79. R. Warskett, "Valuing Women's Work: Dealing with the Limits of State Reform" (1988) 17:3 Feminist Perspectives on the Canadian State 67.

80. L. Mitchell, "What Happens on the Way to the Bank: Some Questions About Pay Equity" (1988) 17:3 Feminist Perspectives on the Canadian State 64.

81. M. Fineman, "Dominant Discourse, Professional Language and Legal Change in Child Custody Decisionmaking" (1988) 10:4 Harvard Law Review 727.

82. L. Weitzman, *The Divorce Revolution* (New York: Free Press, 1985).

83. Geller, *supra* note 35; K. Daly & M. Chesney-Lind, "Feminism and Criminology" (1988) 5:4 Justice Quarterly 497; N. H. Rafter, "Chastizing the Unchaste: Social Control Functions of a Women's Reformatory, 1894–1931" in S. Cohen & A. Scull, eds., *Social Control and the State* (Oxford: Martin Robertson, 1983); N. Rafter, *Partial Justice* (Boston: Northeastern University Press, 1985).

⋮

85. Smart, *supra* note 2.

⋮

91. M. Bliss, *A Living Profit: Studies in the Social History of Canadian Business, 1883–1911* (Toronto: McClelland & Stewart, 1974).

92. MacKinnon, "Feminism, Marxism, Method and the State: An Agenda for Theory", *supra* note 21; MacKinnon, "Feminism, Marxism, Method and the State: An Agenda for Theory", *supra* note 21; Howe, *supra* note 21; Pitch, *supra* note 23.

93. Smart, *supra* note 2 at 22.

⋮

101. T. S. Dahl, "Taking Women As a Starting Point: Building Women's Law" (1986) 14 International Journal of Sociology of Law 239.

102. F. Knopp, "Community Solutions to Sexual Violence" in H. Pepinsky & R. Quinney, eds., *Criminology as Peacemaking* (Bloomington, IL.: Indiana University Press, 1991) 181.

103. H. Carby "White Woman Listen! Black Feminism and the Boundaries of Sisterhood" in *The Empire Strikes Back: Race and Racism in 70s Britain* (London: Hutchinson, 1982); F. Anthias & N. Yuval-Davis, "Contextualizing Feminism—Gender, Ethnic and Class Divisions" (1983) 15:62 Feminist Review 59.

104. F. Sugar & L. Fox, "'Nistum Peyako Seht'Wawin Iskwewak': Breaking Chains" (1989) 3:2 C.J.W.L. 465 at 482.

CHAPTER 15

"The Black Community," Its Lawbreakers, and a Politics of Identification

REGINA AUSTIN

I. DISTINCTION VERSUS IDENTIFICATION: REACTIONS TO THE IMPACT OF LAWBREAKING ON "THE BLACK COMMUNITY"

There exists out there, somewhere, "the black community." It once was a place where people both lived and worked. Now it is more of an idea, or an ideal, than a reality. . . . "The black community" of which I write is partly the manifestation of a nostalgic longing for a time when blacks were clearly distinguishable from whites and concern about the welfare of the poor was more natural than our hairdos. Perhaps my vision of the "'quintessential' black community" is a historical, transcendent, and picturesque. I will even concede that "the community's" infrastructure is weak, its cultural heritage is lost on too many of its young, and its contemporary politics is in disarray. I nonetheless think of it as "Home" and refer to it whenever I want to convey the illusion that my arguments have the backing of millions.

"The black community" of which I write is in a constant state of flux because it is buffeted by challenges from without and from within. (The same is true for "the dominant society," but that is another story.) There are tensions at the border with the dominant society, at the frontier between liberation and oppression. There is also internal dissension over indigenous threats to security and solidarity. "Difference" is as much a source of contention within "the community" as it is the factor marking the boundary between "the community" and everyone else. . . .

Abridged from Regina Austin, " 'The Black Community,' Its Lawbreakers, and a Politics of Identification," *Southern California Law Review*, Vol. 65, pp. 1769–1817, © 1992. Reprinted by permission of the author. *Ed. note:* Although text and footnotes were deleted, we preserved the footnote numbers that appeared in the original text.

Nothing illustrates the multiple threats to the ideal of "the black community" better than black criminal behavior and the debates it engenders. There is no shortage of controversy about the causes, consequences, and cures of black criminality. To the extent there is consensus, black appraisals of questionable behavior are often in accord with those prevailing in the dominant society, but sometimes they are not. In any event, there is typically no unanimity within "the community" on these issues.

For example, some blacks contend that in general the criminal justice system is working too well (putting too many folks in prison),[3] while others maintain that it is not working well enough (leaving too many dangerous folks out on the streets). Black public officials and others have taken positions on both sides of the drug legalization issue.[4] Black neighbors are split in cities where young black men have been stopped and searched by the police on a wholesale basis because of gang activity or drug trafficking in the area.[5] Those with opposing views are arguing about the fairness of evicting an entire family from public housing on account of the drug-related activities of a single household member, the propriety of boycotting Asian store owners who have used what some consider to be excessive force in dealing with suspected shoplifters and would-be robbers, and the wisdom of prosecuting poor black women for fetal neglect because they consumed drugs during their pregnancies.

Whether "the black community" defends those who break the law or seeks to bring the full force of white justice down upon them depends on considerations not necessarily shared by the rest of the society. "The black community" evaluates behavior in terms of its impact on the overall progress of the race. Black criminals are pitied, praised, protected, emulated, or embraced if their behavior has a positive impact on the social, political, and economic well-being of black communal life. Otherwise, they are criticized, ostracized, scorned, abandoned, and betrayed. The various assessments of the social standing of black criminals within "the community" fall into roughly two predominant political approaches.

At times, "the black community" or an element thereof repudiates those who break the law and proclaims the distinctiveness and the worthiness of those who do not. This "politics of distinction" accounts in part for the contemporary emphasis on black exceptionalism. Role models and black "firsts" abound. Stress is placed on the difference that exists between the "better" elements of "the community" and the stereotypical "lowlifes" who richly merit the bad reputations the dominant society accords them.[9] According to the politics of distinction, little enough attention is being paid to the law-abiding people who are the lawbreakers' victims. Drive-by shootings and random street crime have replaced lynchings as a source of intimidation, and the "culture of terror" practiced by armed crack dealers and warring adolescents has turned them into the urban equivalents of the Ku Klux Klan.[10] Cutting the lawbreakers loose, so to speak, by dismissing them as aberrations and excluding them from the orbit of our concern to concentrate on the innocent is a wise use of political resources.

Moreover, lawless behavior by some blacks stigmatizes all and impedes collective progress. For example, based on the behavior of a few, street crime is wrongly thought to be the near exclusive the domain of black males; as a result, black men of all sorts encounter an almost hysterical suspicion as they negotiate public spaces in urban environments[11] and attempt to engage in simple commercial exchanges.[11] Condemnation and expulsion from "the community" are just what the lawbreakers who provoke these reactions deserve.

In certain circumstances the politics of distinction, with its reliance on traditional values of hard work, respectable living, and conformity to law, is a perfectly progressive maneuver for "the community" to make. Deviance confirms stereotypes and plays into the hands of an enemy eager to justify discrimination. The quest for distinction can save lives and preserve communal harmony.

On the downside, however, the politics of distinction intensifies divisions within "the community." It furthers the interests of a middle class uncertain of its material security and social status in white society. The persons who fare best under this approach are those who are the most exceptional (i.e., those most like successful white people). At the same time, concentrating on black exceptionalism does little to improve the material conditions of those who conform to the stereotypes. Unfortunately, there are too many young people caught up in the criminal justice system to write them all off or to provide for their reentry into the mainstream one or two at a time.[13] In addition, the politics of distinction encourages greater surveillance and harassment of those black citizens who are most vulnerable to unjustified interference because they resemble the lawbreakers in age, gender, and class. Finally, the power of the ideology of individual black advancement, of which the emphasis on role models and race pioneers is but a veneer,[14] is unraveling in the face of collective lower-class decline. To be cynical about it, an alternative form of politics may be necessary if the bourgeoisie is to maintain even a semblance of control over the black masses.

Degenerates, drug addicts, ex-cons, and criminals are not always "the community's" "others." Differences that exist between black lawbreakers and the rest of us are sometimes ignored and even denied in the name of racial justice. "The black community" acknowledges the deviants' membership, links their behavior to "the community's" political agenda, and equates it with race resistance. "The community" chooses to identify itself with its lawbreakers and does so as an act of defiance. Such an approach might be termed the "politics of identification."

In fact, there is not one version of the politics of identification but many. They vary with the class of the identifiers, their familiarity with the modes and mores of black lawbreakers, and the impact that black lawbreaking has on the identifiers' economic, social, and political welfare. In the sections that follow, I will look first at the most romanticized form of identification that prompts emulation among the young and the poor; I will detail the dangers and limitations such identification holds for them. I will briefly describe how in the 1960s segments of the black middle class identified with black criminals as sources of authentic "blackness." I will evaluate the pros and cons of this effort. Next, I will consider black female lawbreakers, with whom there is little identification, and suggest why there ought to be more. Finally, I will look at the folks who are situated somewhere between the middle class and the lawbreakers. In leading their everyday lives, these bridge people draw a sensible line between the laws that may be broken and the laws that must be obeyed. Their informal, illegal economic behavior could provide the basis for a praxis for an integrated politics of identification.[15] . . . It is a politics that demands recognition of the material importance of lawbreaking to blacks of different socioeconomic strata, however damaging such recognition may be to illusions of black moral superiority. Moreover, the politics of identification described herein would have as an explicit goal the restoration of some (but not all) lawbreakers to good standing in the community by treating them like resources, providing them with opportunities for redemption, and fighting for their entitlement to a fair share of the riches of this society.

There is an enormous comfort that comes from being able to think and talk about "the black community" without doing much more than thinking and talking to insure its continued existence. Many of us treat "the black community" like a capital investment made long ago; we feel entitled to sit back and live off the interest. The only problem is that the criminals are opting out of "the community" faster than we can jettison them. . . . There is much evidence that the "'quintessential' black community" no longer exists. A new politics of identification, fueled by critically confronting the question of the positive significance of black lawbreaking, might restore some vitality to what has become a mere figure of speech.

II. "NOT HARDLY SOCIAL BANDITS": IDENTIFICATION AND THE ROMANCE AND THE REALITY OF BLACK LAWBREAKING

In the black vernacular, a "bad" person may be a potent and respected force for good rather than a despised source of evil.[17] In the culture of "the community," there has historically been a subtle admiration of criminals who are bold and brazen in their defiance of the legal regime of the external enemy. Tricksters who used their wits to get the better of the master and badmen, such as Stackolee, who thwarted white law enforcement are the black folklore antecedents[18] of modern outlaw heroes like New Yorker Larry Davis, who allegedly killed drug dealers and eluded capture in a shoot-out with police.[19] A further reflection of this phenomenon is the respect shown to drug dealers by their neighbors and the beneficiaries of their philanthropic largess. Blacks, of course, are hardly unique in idolizing the criminal element of their ethnic group or race as social critics and resisters of oppression.[22] It is possible to mount a substantial and quite coherent case for the appreciation of the black male lawbreaker.[23]

Those who identify with black male lawbreakers accept the validity of the justifications the lawbreakers offer to rationalize their behavior. For some blacks who commit crimes, it makes economic sense to engage in such conduct. It is the best job available.[24] The rewards to be gained by young urban males from the drug trade—for example, money ("paper"), fancy cars ("Benzo's," "Beemers," and "'vettes"), and fine females—seem worth the risk, given the alternatives of unemployment or a dead-end job.[25] The willingness to risk incarceration and physical harm, together with the high demand for drugs, can make drug dealing quite remunerative.[27] Jail may be delayed or avoided even if one is caught because the criminal justice system is overburdened and should one wind up serving time, the harshness of prison life may be cushioned by access to liquor, drugs, friends, and some of the comforts of home.[29] Furthermore, death and injury from violence are constants in some urban areas whatever one does. Where one's physical survival is always in jeopardy, the line between offensive and defensive toughness and aggression wears thin.

Crime provides lawbreakers "a social and occupational identity that has meaning beyond its monetary returns."[32] As Mercer Sullivan reports in *"Getting Paid": Youth Crime and Work in the Inner City*, a ethnography comparing the criminal careers of teenage lawbreakers from three racially and ethnically distinct neighborhoods of New York City:

> They call success in crime "getting paid" and "getting over," terms that convey a sense of triumph and of irony. . . . When they talk of "getting paid," they are not equating crime and work with utter seriousness, as if they do not know the difference. . . . What they "get over on" is the system, a series of odds rigged against people like themselves. Both phrases are spoken in a tone of defiant pride.[33]

The refusal to surrender to the stranglehold of material deprivation and social constraints has a heroic quality, as is suggested by John Edgar Wideman's brother Robert in *Brothers and Keepers*.[34] The resistance he and others see in black lawbreaking produced in Robert Wideman such feelings of admiration that he was inspired to pursue the street life himself. (He is presently serving a life term for felony murder.):

> [W]e can't help but feel some satisfaction seeing a brother, a black man, get over on these people, on these people, on their system without playing by their rules. No matter how much we have incorporated these rules as our own, we know that they were forced on us by people who did not have our best interests at heart. So this hip guy, this gangster or player or whatever label you give these brothers that we like to shun because of the poison they spread, we, black people, still look at them with some sense of pride and admiration, our children openly, us adults somewhere deep inside. We know they represent rebellion—what little is left in us.[35]

Similar sentiments are shared by many blacks who, unlike Robert Wideman, do not act on them. For example, Martín Sánchez Jankowski reports that "a significant number of adults from low-income areas identify with the 'resistance component' of gangs."[36] Some blacks follow the exploits of deviants with interest and sympathy because their criminal behavior generates tangible and intangible benefits. Through the antisocial acts of others, the law-abiding experience a vicarious release of the hostility and anger they cannot express themselves without jeopardizing their own respectability. Moreover, criminals whose illegal behavior brings additional resources into economically marginal neighborhoods achieve a greater degree of acceptance than criminals whose conduct simply recycles the wealth that is already there.[39] Additionally, local gang members and lawbreakers have been known to provide a community with such services as protection from more dangerous malefactors and unscrupulous entrepreneurs.[40] Finally, the lawbreakers' presence justifies the existence of anticrime or antigang social programs that employ community residents and otherwise benefit the law-abiding population.[41]

All in all, then, identification with lawbreakers seems justified to some. It is based on a recognition of the need for critical assessments of the dominant society's laws and for some kind of resistance against material and cultural subjugation.

But so much for the romance. Ordinary lawbreaking is a lame manifestation of revolt. Most lawbreakers are not social bandits. Even the majority of their admirers are ambivalent about their activities and have good reasons for refusing to join their campaign of the streets. A praxis based on a literal association of lawbreakers with race-war guerrillas could be justified only by a gross magnification of the damage black criminals actually inflict on white supremacy and a gross minimization of the injuries the criminals cause themselves and other blacks.

Excluded from a fair share of society's bounty, the most economically and socially vulnerable young black people resort to violence and aggression as if it were a matter of choice. They succeed only in having their behavior indicted not as a symptom of their marginalization but as its cause. Psychologist Timothy Simone's reading of minority adolescent deviant behavior highlights its counterproductivity. According to Simone, the requirement that blacks present themselves as the abject objects of white sympathy in order to get a bit of attention provokes a rebellious response from poor young blacks.[43] Because the public's concern does not go very far in an era where casualties of oppression abound, "[y]oung kids of color, by announcing their intention to victimize those perceived as making it in the larger society, attempt to recoup their own status as victims. . . ."[45] Simone continues, "If they hunt and prowl, rather than subject themselves to the paltry manifestations of a receding interest in their situations, they are no longer the victims, even if, in the larger scheme of their capacities to function and thrive, this particular strategy intensifies their victimage."[47] The behavior that the young people see as their "only way of guaranteeing the accordance of respect"[49] is then "cited as evidence for [their] *de jure* or *de facto* exclusion from mainstream economic and political life."[50]

These young people's lawless resistance also misfires because more often than not their targets are similarly situated minority folks. Either for lack of access to or identification of more suitable marks, the anger and alienation poor blacks feel are displaced upon those close at hand: family, peers, and neighbors. Though those who resort to violent lawlessness may cite self-preservation as their justification, an element of self-destruction is operating as well. The killings of young blacks by other young blacks are mass suicide disguised as murder. In his seminal work *The Wretched of the Earth*,[52] Frantz Fanon maintains that "a community of victims, unaware of its history and unable to control its destiny, tends to victimize itself viciously."[53] So-called black-on-black crime "constitute[s] expressions of misdirected rebellion and collective autodestruction" that "cannot be explained apart from the prevailing structural and institutional violence in society."[54] Unfortunately, Fanon's insights are rarely invoked in analyses of contemporary black urban violence.

Black lawbreaking is in addition a form of collective *economic* suicide. Gauging the winners and losers of the underground economy is a complicated matter. To be sure, blacks are included among the realtors, clothiers (including purveyors of athletic shoes), car dealers (including the sellers of fancy foreign cars and popular cheap jeeps), and other business and professional persons (including lawyers) who are profiting from criminal enterprises in minority neighborhoods.[56] Sales to white, middle-class suburban customers who frequent inner-city drug markets probably do contribute to the economies of the surrounding neighborhoods. But black drug dealers have few qualms about who their customers are. Women and older persons, segments of the population never before involved in drug usage, smoke crack; this means that profits are now being extracted from a broader base than ever before.[57] Crack dealing to other poor folks depletes the resources of the community; the money travels out of the neighborhood, out of the state, and out of the country.

The law plays an integral but somewhat obscure role in structuring opportunities in the underground economy and facilitating the depletion of the resources of poor black enclaves. For example, once upon a time poor young black children worked in shops and stores in the neighborhood or at jobs they made for themselves, like carrying groceries from the supermarket, delivering papers, or running errands for a small fee.[59] Labor laws, economic disinvestment, and changing demographic patterns have narrowed employment opportunities for poor black children. Drug dealing is filling the void. Children are natural replacements for adults, who face harsher criminal penalties for drug dealing. "To a drug dealer, [children] can seem the perfect employee: inconspicuous, loyal and—perhaps their chief attraction—almost immune from the law."[60] The law's response has been to increase the stigma attached to juvenile participation in the drug trade and the sanctions meted out to juvenile offenders.[61] Whatever the ethic or values these enterprising children espouse as they go about their work, their involvement in behavior that is now considered a serious crime reflects an alteration in the legal environment that first structures the means by which the children's needs and aspirations can be satisfied and then judges the propriety of their conduct as if it had occurred in a vacuum. Moreover, concentrating the resources of the criminal justice system on the actors at the most localized distribution points—the crack corners in woebegone urban neighborhoods—deflects attention away from the real profiteers and the master exploiters who operate in the comfort and anonymity of distant offices.[62]

The affirmative exploitation of black lawbreakers by the dominant society is not solely material; furthermore, the ideological response to black lawbreakers is not solely vilification and negative stereotyping. To some extent, the dominant society itself participates in elevating the black lawbreaker to the status of hero. Misogyny plays a substantial role in defining the persona of the black male outlaw. In the mythology of black banditry, women—like cars, clothing, and jewelry—are prized possessions. . . . Sociologist Anthony Lemelle contends that "black masculinity is hustled by the white patriarchy. The relationship transforms the black male role into that of a prostitute to masculine institutional systems—athletics, [the] military, and prisons—where macho is the dress needed to pass through the forms; the more the better."[66] As a result of this glorification of black males as "macho heroes," unacceptable attitudes about women are increasingly being displaced upon and associated with them so as to create the illusion that sexism has been contained by a form of ghettoization.

• • •

The values that even bona fide black delinquents are thought to exemplify are not necessarily the values by which they actually live. Consider the youngsters employed in the urban crack trade. They are hardly shiftless and lazy leisure seekers. . . . Their commitment to the work ethic is incredible; they endure miserable working conditions, including long hours, exposure to the elements, beatings and shootings, mandatory abstinence from drugs, and low pay relative to their superiors.[72] Indeed, their rejection of the dominant ideology is quite selective. They have been called "irrational materialists. Their rebellion is part of their conformism to the larger culture. They spurn the injunctions of parents, police, teachers and other authorities, but they embrace the entrepreneurial and consumption cultures of mainstream America."[73] Because they do not subscribe to the entire materialist program, however, they get no credit for being at least half right.

But closer analysis suggests that young black lawbreakers may not be conspiring in their own subordination to the full extent imagined. There are a multitude of reasons why young black lawbreakers spend their hard-earned money so conspicuously.[75] Conspicuous consumption may be less an affirmation of the self or an expression of generalized materialism than a conscious defense mechanism that uses armor, camouflage, and artifice to protect a fragile self from exposure and annihilation. For example, sociologist Elijah Anderson describes the way young mothers compete with one another by dressing up their children in expensive outfits that common sense suggests the kids will soon outgrow and will never wear out.[76] . . . Having lost status along conventional lines, the mothers try to make it up in another way. "'Looking good' negates the generalized notion that a teenage mother has 'messed up' her life, and in this sea of destitution nothing is more important than to show others you are doing all right."[78] The responses mask the mothers' true economic situation but do little to challenge the societal put-down that makes the charade necessary in the first place. . . .

Young lawbreakers wind up with little control over their images and less control than they imagine over their lives and their own world views. Far from being self-conscious political insurrection, most ordinary black male criminal behavior may not even be progressive. The lawbreakers' rebellion is limited because it is not based on a thoroughgoing critique that attacks the systemic sources of their material deprivation. Nor is it likely to generate or exploit the sort of material and ideological dislocations that lead to economic and political reform.

Destructive at home and ineffective abroad, ordinary black criminals typically do not live up to the mantle of race-war guerrillas. But tempered identification persists among those with whom they live and work and among blacks who observe them from afar. This is partly because so much hypocrisy is entailed in labeling some activities illegal and other equally dangerous, detrimental, and larcenous activities not. There is also no other overtly political alternative that constitutes as provocative, creative, crass, hard-nosed, and daring an assault on the status quo as does the culture of young black male criminals. Blacks who would never think of emulating the risky entrepreneurial activities of lawbreakers nonetheless ambivalently admire them and point to their example when the subject turns to resistance.

III. IN VOGUE: BOURGEOIS IDENTIFICATION AS MILITANT STYLE

The urban poor are not the only segment of "the community" that can be seduced by the elan of black male lawbreakers. At times the black middle class has also bought into the quixotic view of the black criminal as race rebel. During the late 1960s, black male lower-class and deviant cultures provided a source of up-to-date signs and symbols for the antiassimilationists. Leather jackets, big Afros, and "talking trash" were de rigueur for upwardly mobile yet nationalistic black college students. It is not clear what prompted this wave of identification.[80] . . .

This is not the place for a full-blown critique of the black nationalism movement of the 1960s.[81] Some of its aspects undoubtedly ought not be repeated if a similar surge of lawbreaker identification should overtake the middle class anytime soon. The movement was fiercely misogynistic.[82] The predominant leadership style was marked by masculine bravado and self-aggrandizement.

• • •

The movement did not maximize opportunities for lower-status blacks to speak and act on their own behalf. . . . The middle class . . . identification temporarily lent an aura of respectability to those who earned their deviant status by virtue of actually breaking the law. But when the movement died, or was killed, the real lawbreakers and others on the bottom of the status hierarchy found themselves outsiders again.[85]

In general, the "newly materializing" black militant bourgeoisie of the 1960s did not go very far in incorporating the concerns of lawbreakers into their demands or in adopting the more aggressive practices of criminals as the praxis of their movement. Others did. The Black Panthers, for example, employed black turtlenecks, leather jackets, berets, dark glasses, and shotguns as the accoutrements of militancy and attracted the attention of young northern urban blacks with their "belligerence and pride" and their outspokenness on issues of relevance to ghetto residents.[86] The Panthers specifically addressed the role white police officers played in black neighborhoods as well as the status of black criminal defendants and prisoners.[87] They called for the release of "all black men held in federal, state, county and city prisons and jails" on the ground that "they had not received a fair and impartial trial."[88] (No mention was made of incarcerated women.) Their close observation of white cops as they arrested black citizens on the street highlighted the problem of police brutality. The Panthers' posturing and head-on clashes with the authorities, however, provoked repression[89] and government-instigated internal warfare. This in turn caused the Panthers to squander resources on bail and attorneys that might have been better spent on "Serve the People" medical clinics and free break-fasts for children. Such service activities stood a better chance of mobilizing grassroots support among ordinary blacks and overcoming neighborhood problems than did the Panthers' attempts at militaristic self-defense and socialist indoctrination.[90]

Despite the shortcomings of the black militancy of the 1960s, identification with black lawbreakers still has something to contribute to political fashion and discourse. That blacks are once again fascinated with the outspoken national-ist leader Malcolm X illustrates this.[91] Even the most bourgeois form of iden-tification represents an opening, an opportunity, to press for a form of politics that could restore life to the ideal of "the black community" by putting the in-terests of lawbreakers and their kin first. Drawing on lawbreaker culture would add a bit of toughness, resilience, bluntness, and defiance to contemporary mainstream black political discourse, which evidences a marked preoccupation with civility, respectability, sentimentality, and decorum. Lawbreaker culture supports the use of direct words and direct action that more refined segments of society would find distasteful. It might also support a bit of middle-class law-breaking.

There is nothing that requires militant black male leaders to be selfish, stu-pid, shortsighted, or sexist. There is certainly nothing that requires militant black leaders to be men. As sources of militant style, women lawbreakers set a somewhat different example from the men. Furthermore, it is impossible to understand what lawbreakers can contribute to the substance of a politics of identification without considering women who break the law.

IV. JUSTIFYING IDENTIFICATION WHERE THERE IS NONE NOW: FEMALE LAWBREAKERS AND THE LESSONS OF STREET LIFE

Black men do not have a monopoly on lawbreaking. Black women too are en-gaged in a range of aggressive, antisocial, and criminal conduct that includes prostitution, shoplifting, credit card fraud, check forgery, petty larceny, and drug dealing.[93] But unlike her male counterpart, the black female offender has little or no chance of being considered a rebel against racial, sexual, or class in-justice. There is seemingly no basis in history or folklore for such an honor. The quiet rebellions slave women executed in the bedrooms of their masters and the kitchens of their mistresses are not well known today. Thus, the con-temporary black female lawbreaker does not benefit from an association be-tween herself and her defiant ancestors who resorted to arson, poisoning, and theft in the fight against white enslavement.[94]

Aggressive and antisocial behavior on the part of black male lawbreakers is deemed compatible with mainstream masculine gender roles and is treated like race resistance, but the same sort of conduct on the part of black females is scorned as being unfeminine. Women are not supposed to engage in violent actions or leave their families to pursue a life of crime. Women who do such things may be breaking out of traditional female patterns of behavior, but their departures from the dictates of femininity are attributed to insanity or les-bianism without any basis in psychology or sociology.[95] No consideration is given to the structural conditions that make violence a significant factor in the lives of lower-class women and that suggest that their physical aggression is not pathological. Conversely, forms of deviance associated with feminine traits like passivity and dependency are dismissed as collaboration with the white/male enemy. Black male lawbreaking also backfires, but black female criminals are not given the benefit of the doubt the males enjoy, either because the hole the women dig for themselves is more readily apparent or because their defiance of gender roles is treated as deviance of a higher order.

What most blacks are likely to know about the degradation and exploitation black women suffer in the course of lawbreaking and interacting with other lawbreakers provides no basis for identifying with them. Take the lot of black streetwalkers, for example. Minority women are overrepresented among street prostitutes and as a result are overrepresented among prostitutes arrested and incarcerated.[97] Black and brown women are on the corner rather than in massage parlors or hotel suites in part because of the low value assigned to their sexuality. Many street prostitutes begin their careers addicted to cocaine, heroin, or both or develop addictions thereafter; drug habits damage their health, impair their appearance (and thereby their earnings), and increase their physical and mental vulnerability.[98] Finally, streetwalkers encounter violence and harassment from pimps, johns, police officers, assorted criminals, and even other women in the same line of work.[99]

Other factors work against black identification with black prostitutes. There is some glorification of prostitutes in literature, film, and the media, but not much.[100] The hooker with a heart of gold and the street-walker who needs only the love of a good man to save her are unusual creatures. Typically, though, "the pimps/players [the male actors in the sex trade] are seen as smooth, slick, and smart, [while] the girls [are seen] as stupid and dirty."[101] And "[t]here is no strata [sic] in contemporary society in which females have ever gained positive status from visible promiscuity."[102] Because of this and the reality that the stereotype of the loose black woman, or Jezebel, is so pervasive, black women who consider themselves respectable are especially likely to be inhibited from identifying with black prostitutes.

Prostitution is but one form of criminal activity a woman in street life might be employed in at any particular time. Less is known about lawbreaking of a nonsexual nature. The exploitation, manipulation, and physical jeopardy associated with street prostitution are also experienced by female lawbreakers who are members of male-affiliated female gangs and criminal networks.[103] These networks, which once were quite prevalent, consist of loosely affiliated households or pseudofamilies made up of a male head and one or more females, sometimes referred to as "wives-in-law." In such collectives the male hustlers hustle the females. In return for giving money, assistance in criminal endeavors, affection, and loyalty to "their men," the women get protection, tight controls on their sexual dalliances, and the privilege of competing with other females for attention. Try as they might to break out of traditional gender roles with aggressive criminal or antisocial behavior, the female members of traditional girl gangs and networks sink deeper into the optionlessness of low-status, low-income female existence. That hardly makes them fitting candidates for admiration or emulation.

Life in criminal subcultures is dynamic, and much suggests that, with the ascendancy of crack, the lot of black women who engage in deviant activity has taken a turn for the worse. There is little in the way of systematic research on the impact that crack and the not totally unrelated AIDS epidemic[109] have had on black female deviance. According to news accounts and some scholarly writing, crack usage has driven more black women into lawbreaking, particularly prostitution and violent property offenses. There has been both a decline in the collective and cooperative enterprises associated with networks (which would normally provide women with some protection from violence and exploitation) and a reduction in the remuneration the women receive for their activities.[110] Some females are participating in the entrepreneurial aspects of the crack trade on a nearly equal basis with men, but they are in the minority.

The multigenerational use of crack across gender lines and changing gender roles add to the variety of forms black female deviance takes.[112] For example, some mothers condone the involvement of their children in the crack trade because it increases the mothers' access to drugs or enables their children to give them luxury items as presents.[113] Some drug-abusing females steal from friends and relatives or leave their children with grandmothers and aunts and disappear.[114]

According to Philippe Bourgois,

> [The] greater female involvement in crack reflects in a rather straight-forward manner the growing emancipation of women throughout all aspects of inner-city life, culture and economy. Women—especially the emerging generation, which is most at risk for crack addiction—are no longer as obliged to stay at home and maintain the family as they were a generation ago. They no longer so readily sacrifice public life or forgo independent opportunities to generate personally disposable income. A most visible documentation of this is the frequent visits to the crack houses by pregnant women and by mothers accompanied by toddlers or infant children.[115]

Unfortunately, Bourgois is not very specific about the linkage between his female subjects' increasing independence and their drug usage. Their addictions may be more a cause of their "liberated" behavior than a consequence or symptom. In any event, real emancipation is not to be achieved this way. Still very much restricted by the customary sexual division of labor, addicted women resort to prostitution to support their crack habits. Their very numbers and their desperation earn them the status of the most depreciated sex objects. Bourgois concludes that given their public visibility, they have "a strong negative effect on the community's—and on mainstream society's—perception of Third World women; ultimately it reinforces an ideological domination of females in general."[117] Such stereotyping is unfair and twisted, not the least because many straight black women are put off, if not disgusted, by the exploits of crack prostitutes and do not see any relationship between themselves and such licentious women. It would be asking a lot for them to go beyond that assessment to identify with these women and their life circumstances.

There is accordingly much for which respectable black women can rebuke black females who participate in crime and seemingly little with which respectable women can identify. Hierarchy will not crumble, however, if the wicked do not get a shot at upending the righteous. Where community depends upon challenging the social, economic, and political stratification produced by traditional mainstream values, vice must have some virtue.

In the black vernacular, "the streets" are not just the territory beyond home and work, nor merely the place where deviants ply their trades. More figuratively, they are also a "source of practical experience and knowledge necessary for survival."[118] The notion of a politics of identification suggests that "the streets" might be the wellspring of a valuable pedagogy for a vibrant black female community if straight black women had more contact with and a better understanding of what motivates black women in street life. Black women from the street might teach straight black women a thing or two about "heroine-ism" if straight women let themselves be taught.

I cannot predict what lessons might be learned from an interaction between straight and street black women. Ethnographers report that women engaged in street life typically see more than the negative about their careers. (It is unclear what precise differences there are in this regard between the cultural orientations of black street women and those of white and Latino street women.) In addition to citing economic necessity, street women in general justify their deviant conduct by criticizing straight life. Black street women in particular come from the worst material circumstances. They start life poor and do not acquire the education or skills with which to improve their economic positions. Compared with the "restricted and tedious jobs available to them" in the legitimate market, hustling offers these women "money, excitement, independence, and flexibility."[120] In their view, straight life is "filled with drudgery and disappointment"; it is "the epitome of boredom."[121] Street life, on the other hand, gives women "opportunities to feel a sense of mastery, independence, individual accomplishment, and immediate reward."[122]

. . .

Eleanor Miller reports that street women are more likely to blame their lot on racial and class inequalities than on gender inequality.[127] Moreover, they perceive the criminal justice system as "unjust and unpredictable." This "perception . . . had the . . . effect of making the majority of the women feel that the moral world was somehow out of balance and that they were 'owed' some illegal acts without punishment as result."[128]

. . .

Identification with black street women will be difficult for many in "the community" but not impossible, if we take the women on their own terms as we do the men. What can possibly be wrong with wanting a job that pays well, is controlled by the workers, provides a bit of a thrill, and represents a payback for injustices suffered? To be sure, street women will not accomplish their goals on any sustained basis through lawbreaking. But that does not mean that they should abandon their aspirations, which, after all, are not so very different from those of many straight black women who battle alienation and boredom in their work lives. Street women may be correct in thinking that some kind of risk taking will provide an antidote for a fairly common misery.

Street life is public life. It entails being "Out There," aggressive and brazen, in a realm normally foreclosed to women. Operating on the street takes wisdom, cunning, and conning. The ways of black women should be infused into black political activism, and young black women should be allowed to be militant political leaders, just like their male counterparts. The search for political styles and points of view should extend broadly among different groups and categories of black women, including lesbians, adolescent mothers,[132] rebellious employees,[133] and lawbreakers immersed in street life. In a real black community, everyone would be a resource, *especially* those whom the dominant society would write off as having little or nothing to contribute. That, in essence, is what a politics of identification is all about.

And finally, street women accept the justifiability of engaging in illegal conduct to rectify past injustices and to earn a living. This may prove to be the hardest lesson for straight black women to learn—and the most valuable.

V. NEITHER STREET NOR STRAIGHT: BRIDGE PEOPLE, THE INFORMAL ECONOMY, AND A PRAXIS FOR A POLITICS OF IDENTIFICATION

Melding the virtues of street life with the attractions of straight life may be foreign to some black people, but not to all. "The black community" is not really divided into two distinct segments—one straight, the other street. There are folks in the middle. If blacks who consider themselves totally respectable need role models to help them identify with lawbreakers, the prime candidates are the "bridge people" who straddle both worlds.

Bridge people have a real stake in negotiating the gulf that separates straight and street people and in understanding what constitutes an appropriate balance of the modes and mores of each. Bridge people bear the brunt of the hardship posed by a physical and familial proximity to those heavily engaged in street life. The opportunities of the bridge people for an improved existence are bound up with the life chances of their deviant kin, all of whom cannot be locked up even if we wanted them to be. Bridge people accordingly maintain a critical yet balanced assessment of the deviance of other community members and of the responsibility that the larger society bears for all their troubles.[134]

Oppressed people need to know when to obey the law and when to ignore it. In the way of promulgating an informal, customary jurisprudence, bridge people are involved in a dialogue with the lawbreakers, their most ardent admirers, and each other over the line between legality and illegality, between "getting over" and self-delusion, between collaboration and resistance, and between victimizing one's own and extracting justice from the enemy.[135] . . .

More importantly, the bridge people actualize the distinctions in their own everyday economic activities. Though many of them endure dull and unexciting lives just like straight women and men, bridge people also know how to hustle, in the sense of working aggressively, energetically, and without too much illegality. Hustling is "a way of life" and a "means [of] surviving" for those who must deal with low wages, layoffs, unemployment, and other flaws in the regular job market.[136] It includes "a wide variety of unconventional, sometimes extralegal or illegal activities, often frowned upon by the wider community but widely accepted and practiced in [black urban enclaves]."[137]

Anecdotal evidence suggests that the "hidden," "underground," "irregular," "cash," "off-the-books," or (please excuse the expression) "black market" economy is quite significant in low-income and working-class black neighborhoods.[138]

. . .

Documenting the nature and extent of hustling in black enclaves is difficult. The norms regarding socially acceptable lawbreaking are unwritten, and the activity must be clandestine in order for it to succeed. Scant academic energy has been devoted to investigating how those connected to both the street and straight worlds survive financially. Kathryn Edin's research . . . marks a notable departure from the norm.[140] Edin presents an extended financial profile of a group of twenty-five beneficiaries of Aid to Families with Dependent Children. . . . "[O]nly seven out of these twenty-five families received enough money [from welfare] to cover their rent, food and utilities."[143] . . . Edin catalogues the various ways the women made up the monthly budget deficits that remained after their welfare allotments and food stamps were exhausted.[145] Some of her subjects could rely on help from food pantries and gifts from friends and relatives. All engaged in activities that were illegal because they were not reported to the welfare authorities. This category included doing household chores for neighbors, collecting cans for recycling, mowing lawns, pocketing whatever was left over from an educational grant after books and tuition were paid for, sharing a boyfriend's earnings, and receiving child support directly from the children's fathers. Nearly a third of Edin's informants also did things that were illegal enough to land them in jail. This category included working at a regular job using a false name and social security number, operating a small-scale lottery or raffle, fencing stolen goods, dealing marijuana, dealing cocaine, occasionally engaging in sexual intercourse for money, and shoplifting. A recipient's opportunity structure (her family, friends, neighborhood milieu, and skill level) determined whether her income-generating activity included the unreportable.[147] Edin concludes that "of the welfare clients observed, most work as hard as their middle class counterparts."[148]

By and large, hustling consists of little more than self-sustaining survival mechanisms. The participants in such economic activity lack the wherewithal to increase its productivity and profitability. This is well illustrated by anthropologist Louise Jones's study of black street peddlers in "Riverview," a black enclave of a river-port city of the upper South.[149] . . . The vendors' strengths were their ability to make flexible marketing decisions that took advantage of changing supply and demand and their capacity to capitalize on their personalities and charisma to foster personal relationships with customers. They were handicapped, however, by being "structurally isolated from professional and service-related firms which functioned to provide a variety of managerial and financial assistance to business enterprises."[151] . . . Moreover, they used only cash, and no credit, in transactions with distributors and customers. Finally, Jones maintains, "they lacked control over their marketing niches, as well as those political and economic arenas which were fixed on transforming the economic landscape into an environment conducive to the profitability of the large-scale firms of the formal market sector."[152]

Whatever its limitations, hustling may nonetheless be an important factor in the development of more self-reliant black urban communities. Social scientists would classify much of the hustling described above under the rubric of "the informal economy." There is no single definition of the term. For the purposes of the discussion here, the informal economy encompasses "the range of overlapping subeconomies that are not taken into account by formal measures of economic activity."[153] Moreover, whether the activities are considered illegal or extralegal, the informal economy tends to escape direct regulation by the institutions of society, although other similar activities are not so immune.[154] At the same time, the informal economy is responsive to the regulatory environment whose actual jurisdiction it seeks to avoid or evade. Finally, the informal economy is characterized by operations that are "small scale," "labor intensive, requiring little capital," and "locally based," with business transacted "through face-to-face relationships between friends, relatives, or acquaintances in a limited geographical area."[156]

The informal economy has social and entrepreneurial aspects. It may manifest itself largely as a social undertaking, fueled not by money exchanges but by reciprocal gift giving and bartering. Informal activities assure social cohesion and protect folks "from total and abject economic failure" by providing a community with "its own informal safety net."[157] The informal economy also encompasses entrepreneurial market operations whose connection to the dominant economy may be close or distant. In some instances, the informal activity reflects the community's isolation from the formal economy.[158] . . . Alternatively, a community's informal sector may be highly connected to the formal economy in that it produces goods and services for external markets, competes for business with firms in the formal economy, and generates substantial income.[159]

• • •

In assessing a broad range of informal economic activity in Europe, Central and South America, and Asia, one group of scholars has concluded that the informal economy has experienced growth under the following circumstances: (1) the informal sector took advantage of technological advancement and "capture[d] a niche in upscale segments of the market"; (2) there was a strong "export orientation" that generated goods and services not exclusively for the local market; and (3) the enterprises were relatively autonomous and were not vertically connected to other, larger businesses via multiple layers of subcontracting.[165] Moreover, sociocultural factors played a role. In the most successful informal economies, there existed an "unusual receptivity to technological innovation and entrepreneurial opportunities,"[166] "a concentration of entrepreneurial abilities in a given location" . . . and a common culture that created "overarching solidarity that facilitate[d] . . . cooperation . . . rules of conduct, and obligations . . ."[167] Finally, the state also made a contribution. "[E]very successful instance register[ed] evidence of an official attitude that downplays the lack of observance of certain rules and actively supports the growth of entrepreneurial ventures through training programs, credit facilities, marketing assistance, and similar policies."[168]

This list of what are in essence the preconditions for optimal growth of the informal sector strongly suggests that the informal economy is not a "generalizable solution to [the problems of] economic underdevelopment."[169] Nonetheless, given high levels of poverty and unemployment in poor black urban enclaves, "the possibility of semiformal neighborhood subeconomies should be regarded with interest."[170] Poor black communities will unquestionably have difficulties strengthening and enlarging their informal economies because their inhabitants lack technical skills, business expertise, start-up capital, access to credit, and links to external markets. Yet there may be ways to overcome these obstacles.

Poor and working-class enclaves have an abundance of workers unskilled except in the hard work of hustling. They need on-the-job training. Both the politics of identification and the processes of the informal economy teach the same lesson: Start with people where they are and work with what you get! Grounded in communal kinship and altruism, the informal economy is one in which the son who just got out of jail and the niece who is in a drug rehabilitation program can find employment. It should remain that way. The importance attached to social ties ensures that deviants will have a role in the economic life of the community. . . . The social aspects of the informal economy should be infused into as much economic activity as possible.[171] A politics of identification should fight against the extension of market operations into relationships that are now quite adequately governed by social considerations.

The black middle class might provide the expertise that informal entrepreneurs and the poor and poorly trained labor force presently lack. Historically, members of the black middle class were not simply role models for their less-well-off neighbors. They also served as conduits through which family, friends, and young folks from the neighborhood found jobs with mainstream employers. Through employment in the larger society, they generated income that they spent in the community and, as professionals and entrepreneurs, aided in the recycling of income earned by their patients, clients, customers, and parishioners.[172] Members of the black middle class could be substantial generators and recyclers of income, suppliers of technical expertise, and links to the formal economy for individuals and businesses ready to cross over—if the black middle class were willing to accept the entrepreneurial and juridical risks associated with participation in the informal economy.

This call for the bourgeoisie to assist poorer black communities through informal enterprises should not be taken as an invitation to economic abuse. Their incursion should be limited in scope and duration.[173] Members of the middle class who are motivated by racial solidarity and a desire to sustain "the black community" might contribute through nonprofit or cooperative ventures. In any event, being a black person employed in an informal black-owned enterprise located in a black neighborhood is not the ideal situation, but it may be better than the next best alternative. . . .

The state might be urged to provide the training programs and credit and marketing assistance other governments have accorded successful informal economies. Social welfare benefits that are not wage-based, such as income guarantees or universal health insurance, would also protect workers from some of the exploitation and abuse that accompany jobs in the informal sector.[174] In addition, the state might support new forms of communal or cooperative ownership that break down the distinction between capital and labor.[175] Unfortunately, the prospects for government assistance do not look particularly bright. Programs that require substantial expenditures have very little chance of being enacted in today's reactionary and recessionary political climate. Furthermore, black capitalism and minority self-help tend to be oversold as panaceas for the structural ills of poverty and limited employment opportunities in regular labor markets.[176] The ideological utility to the government of measures to assist the informal economy in black communities may far exceed their actual monetary payout.

Nonetheless, any liberal politics of economic reform should push for governmental support of black informal entrepreneurship. A politics of identification, however, would take a somewhat different, more deviant tack toward the role of the state. Informal enterprises shrink from the light; their operations are aided by their invisibility and covertness. Legal regulation is what they avoid and undermine, not necessarily what they require in order to prosper. To facilitate the growth of the informal economy, a politics of identification would, upon occasion, work to keep the law at bay. To this end, a politics of identification might support selective enforcement, rather than total elimination of governmental oversight, so as to better protect the interests of the least-well-off blacks working in the informal sector.

There are several areas in which competition from the informal sector has prompted actors in the formal economy to invoke the law to kill off their rivals. The interests of poorer blacks were on the side of informality in each. For example, squatters who move into and fix up abandoned or unoccupied properties with their sweat equity are informal producers of housing stock. Their lawlessness provokes the ire of the private sector, which has no real interest in taking up the slack of unmet demand but which is put out by the squatters' threat to the concept of private property. Local governments, which cannot supply sufficient decent public housing, respond with evictions or concessions in the form of formal homesteading programs that may co-opt the energy of squatting initiatives. Squatting, which is essentially a form of self-help, is not the answer to the housing shortage in poor black neighborhoods, but it is an informal stopgap measure and a starting point for addressing the larger structural problems.

Sidewalk entrepreneurs compete with more formal purveyors of goods and merchandise whose greater political clout not infrequently translates into regulations and ordinances restricting sidewalk vending. Yet the contributions of many of these fixed-location enterprises to the economies of the surrounding neighborhood are limited because their prices are high, their utilization of local suppliers low, and their track record for hiring community residents virtually nonexistent. Furthermore, vendors' stalls once were loaded down with counterfeit high-status, trademark-bearing watches, handbags, and T-shirts. The industries' efforts to curb the manufacture and sale of such goods seem to be working. The presence of these items on the market had real subversive potential.[182] They made status a commodity within the financial reach of almost everyone. The goods were a tangible critique of the materialism of those who were insecure enough to buy the genuine article. Most purchasers knew from the asking price and the quality that the merchandise was bogus. This should constitute a defense to trademark infringement, but it does not.[183] Here, then, are several instances at the margins between legality and illegality in which a politics of identification could champion the cause of informality. There are surely others.

. . .

Better than anything, rap music illustrates the possibilities for melding the mores of street and straight cultures with the methods of the informal and formal economies. Rap music is the paradigm for the praxis of a politics of identification. The vocal portion of rap—the message, the poetry—reflects the culture and concerns of poor and working-class urban black youth, particularly the b-boys.[190] It invokes such black modes of discourse as toasting, boasting, and signifying. It aims to alienate and challenge white authority. It is misogynistic, self-congratulatory, and very competitive. Whatever else might be said about it, rap does address subjects like guns, gangs, police brutality, racism, nationalism, money, and sex.[191] And it has also generated its own internal debates, with the strongest opposition to the standard fare coming from some female rappers who are making their presence felt with a strong black brand of feminism.[192]

Rap's material appropriation of sound and speech, however, may be more subversive than its ideological message. The background over which the rap artist orates is a synthesis of modern technology and a flouting of the laws of private property. Rap is meant to be danced to, yet it requires no musical instruments and no original notes.[193] At its origin, rap (or hip-hop, as it was first known) . . . was an outgrowth of the same circumstances that produced the street art forms of breakdancing and graffiti.[195] DJs such as the legendary Kool DJ Herc and Grandmaster Flash worked with the equipment they had. "[R]ecords and tapes were the only source of professional-quality sounds available to people unable to buy anything but prerecorded music and the equipment to listen [to it]."[196] These early hip-hop DJs "turned two turntables into a sound system through the technical addition of a beat box, heavy amplification, headphones, and very, very fast hands."[197] The DJs began to broadcast the scratching that results from cuing a record and further developed the technique of moving a record back and forth over the same chord or beat for as long as the "enraptured" crowd could take it."[198]

With time and exposure, rap's focus moved from live performance to recordings and the turntable gave way to the digital synthesizer. The background over which the rappers recite their lines can now be produced by borrowing, editing, and combining digital sound bytes.[200] . . . The technique of "taking a portion (phrase, riff, percussive vamp, etc.) of a known or unknown record (or a video game squawk, a touch-tone telephone medley, a verbal tag from Malcolm X or Martin Luther King) and combining it in the overall mix" is known as "sampling."[201] . . . Rappers didn't pay royalties. Rap was "a domain of the improper, where copyright and 'professional courtesy' are held in contempt. Rappers will take what is 'yours' and turn it into a 'parody' of you—and not even begin to pay you in full."[203]

As rap has crossed the threshold and won a place in the (white, middle-class) mainstream, its production has moved from the subterranean depths of the informal to the limelight of the formal economy. Many of the small inde-pendent labels that first produced rap have been bought up by the major record-ing companies. As a result, rap's message may not be as bold as it once was, and there are concerns that rap will lose its "integrity."[204] More importantly, the samplers are being required to pay royalties. Rap has become a commod-ity that is sold to the very same community that used to get it for free.[206] Some rappers are getting rich. The question is not how many or by how much, but how deep does it go. One hopes that down on the street, among those left out again, the process of innovation and incubation is continuing and that some-thing else is developing to take rap's place.

Rap music is emblematic for a number of reasons of what a politics of iden-tification might accomplish. The rappers capture the drama of street life and serve it up to an audience that is white or middle class or both, an audience both thrilled and chilled to be reminded of the existence of an angry black mass that might someday rise up and take what it will never be given. Someone should be preparing a list of demands. Rap is a political art form that is strength-ened by the clash of viewpoints. It is an arena in which women are coming on strong. Furthermore, the perils of the informal economy—its riskiness, its skirting of the boundaries of legality, its sampling, and its scratching—are ex-plicitly legitimated by rap's appeal and implicitly legitimated by its material success. Rap suggests that for those who want to get ahead and see "the black community" do the same, the bridge, a way station between the street and straight worlds, is an attractive place to be.

VI. "BRINGING IT HOME": A LEGAL AGENDA FOR A POLITICS OF IDENTIFICATION

[A] politics of identification recognizes that blacks from different classes have different talents and strengths to contribute to "a revitalized black commu-nity." In general, this politics of identification would blend the defiance, bold-ness, and risk taking that fuel street life with the sacrifice, perseverance, and solidity of straight life. Taking a leaf from the lawbreakers' style manual, it would confront the status quo with a rhetoric that is hard-nosed, pragmatic, aggressive, streetwise, and spare. In recognition of the struggles of street women, it would foster a public life that is inclusive of deviants and allows both females and males to play an equal role. In order to have an impact on the ma-terial conditions that promote black criminal behavior, it would draw its praxis from the informal economic activity of the bridge people. In this way, a politics of identification would promote a critical engagement between lawbreakers and the middle class in order to move some of the lawbreakers beyond the self-destruction that threatens to bring the rest of us down with them.

The laws of the dominant society are not intended to distinguish between members of "the black community" who are truly deserving of ostracism and those who are not yet beyond help or hope. In addition, it is unlikely that the standards by which "the community" differentiates among lawbreakers can be codified for use by the legal system because of the informal, customary process by which the standards develop. Still, one of the goals of a legal agenda tied to a politics of identification would be to make the legal system more sensitive to the social connection that links "the community" and its lawbreakers and affects black assessments of black criminality.[207]

"The community" acknowledges that some, but not all, lawbreakers act out of a will to survive and an impulse not to be forgotten, and it admires them for this even though it concludes that their acts ought not to be emulated. In recognition of this, the legal program of a politics of identification would advocate changes in the criminal justice system and in other institutions of the dominant society in order to increase the lawbreakers' chances for redemption. "To redeem" is not only "to atone" but also "to rescue," "ransom," "reclaim," "recover," and "release."[208] Thus, redemption may be actively or passively acquired. The lawbreakers need both types of redemption. They need challenging employment that will contribute to the transformation of their neighborhoods and earn them the respect of "the community."[209] They also need to be freed from the material conditions that promote deviance and death. If persuasion, argument, and conflict within the law fail to prompt the dominant society to reallocate resources and reorder priorities, then a jurisprudence that aims to secure redemption for lawbreakers must acknowledge that activity outside the law, against the law, and around the law may be required.

The development of the informal economy in poor black enclaves is crucial to the lawbreakers' redemption and the revitalization of "the black community." The jurisprudential component of a politics of identification would make an issue of the fact that the boundary between legal economic conduct and illegal economic conduct is contingent. It varies with the interests at stake, and the financial self-reliance or self-sufficiency of the minority poor is almost never a top priority. A legal praxis associated with a politics of identification would find its reference points in the "folk law" of those black people who, as a matter of survival, concretely assess what laws must be obeyed and what laws may be justifiably ignored. It would investigate the operations of the informal economy, which is really the illegitimate offspring of legal regulation. It would seek to stifle attempts to criminalize or restrict behavior merely because it competes with enterprises in the formal economy. At the same time, it would push for criminalization or regulation where informal activity destroys communal life or exploits a part of the population that cannot be protected informally. It would seek to legalize both informal activity that must be controlled to ensure its integrity and informal activity that needs the imprimatur of legitimacy in order to attract greater investment or to enter broader markets. Basically, then, a politics of identification requires that its legal adherents work the line between the legal and the illegal, the formal and the informal, the socially (within "the community") acceptable and the socially despised, and the merely different and the truly deviant.

Working the line is one thing. Living on or near the line is another. All blacks do not do that, and some folks who are not black do. Though the ubiquitous experience of racism provides the basis for group solidarity,[210] differences of gender, class, geography, and political affiliations keep blacks apart. These differences may be the best evidence that a single black community no longer exists. Only blacks who are bound by shared economic, social, and political constraints, and who pursue their freedom through affective engagement with each other, live in real black communities. To be a part of a real black community requires that one go Home every once in a while and interact with the folks. To keep up one's membership in such a community requires that one do something on-site. A politics of identification is not a way around this. It just suggests what one might do when one gets there.

NOTES

⋮

3. *See e.g., Developments in the Law—Race and the Criminal Process*, 101 HARV. L. REV. 1472 (1988).

4. *See e.g., A Symposium on Drug Decriminalization*, 18 HOFSTRA L. REV. 457 (1990).

5. *See, e.g.,* MIKE DAVIS, CITY OF QUARTZ: EXCAVATING THE FUTURE IN LOS ANGELES 267–322 (1990); MARTÍN SÁNCHEZ JANKOWSKI, ISLANDS IN THE STREET: GANGS AND AMERICAN URBAN SOCIETY 205–6 (1991).

⋮

9. *See* ELIJAH ANDERSON, STREETWISE: RACE, CLASS, AND CHANGE IN AN URBAN COMMUNITY 66–69 (1990).

10. *See* Philippe Bourgois, *In Search of Horatio Alger: Culture and Ideology in the Crack Economy*, 16 CONTEMP. DRUG PROBS. 619, 631–37 (1989). *See also* CARL S. TAYLOR, DANGEROUS SOCIETY 66–67 (1990) (noting that gangs use violence to discipline members and earn the respect of others).

11. *See* Elijah Anderson, *Race and Neighborhood Transition, in* THE NEW URBAN REALITY 99, 112–16, 123–24 (Paul E. Peterson ed., 1985).

⋮

13. It was estimated that on any given day in mid-1989, 23% of black males between the ages of 20 and 29 were in prison, in jail, or on probation or parole, compared with 10.4% of Hispanic males and 6.2% of white males. MARK MAUER, YOUNG BLACK MEN AND THE CRIMINAL JUSTICE SYSTEM: A GROWING NATIONAL PROBLEM 3 (1990).

14. For a critique of the emphasis on role models, see Regina Austin, *Sapphire Bound!*, 1989 WIS. L. REV. 539, 574–76.

15. *See also* Stuart Hall, *New Ethnicities, in* BLACK FILM, BRITISH CINEMA 27–28 (Lisa Appignanesi ed., 1988).

⋮

17. GENEVA SMITHERMAN, TALKIN AND TESTIFYIN 44, 59–60 (1977) (discussing the usage of the term "bad").

18. *See generally* JOHN W. ROBERTS, FROM TRICKSTER TO BADMEN: THE BLACK FOLK HERO IN SLAVERY AND FREEDOM 44–45, 171–215 (1989).

19. Samuel Freedman, *To Some, Davis Is "Hero" Amid Attacks on Blacks*, N.Y. TIMES, Jan. 2, 1987, at B2.

⋮

22. *See* ERIC HOBSBAWM, BANDITS (1969) (discussing heroic peasant social bandits from Europe, Asia, and the Americas). *See also* Martha G. Duncan, *"A Strange Liking": Our Admiration for Criminals*, 1991 U. ILL. L. REV. 1.

23. The discussion that follows largely pertains to men engaged in crime; black female lawbreakers are the subject of Part IV.

24. *See* TERRY M. WILLIAMS & WILLIAM KORNBLUM, GROWING UP POOR 12, 55–56 (1985).

25. TAYLOR, supra note 10, at 44, 47, 85.

⋮

27. *See* PETER REUTER ET AL., MONEY FROM CRIME: A STUDY OF THE ECONOMICS OF DRUG DEALING IN WASHINGTON, D.C. 94–105 (1990).

⋮

29. Robert Blecker, *Haven or Hell? Inside Lorton Central Prison: Experiences of Punishment Justified*, 42 STAN. L. REV. 1149 (1990).

⋮

32. MERCER L. SULLIVAN, "GETTING PAID": YOUTH CRIME AND WORK IN THE INNER CITY 245 (1989).

33. *Id.*

34. JOHN EDGAR WIDEMAN, BROTHERS AND KEEPERS 132 (1984).

35. *Id.* at 57.

36. JANKOWSKI, *supra* note 5, at 181.

⋮

39. SULLIVAN, *supra* note 32, at 232.

40. JANKOWSKI, *supra* note 5, at 183–93.

41. *Id.* at 239–40, 246–49.

⋮

43. TIMOTHY M. SIMONE, ABOUT FACE: RACE IN POSTMODERN AMERICA 25 (1989).

⋮

45. *Id.* at 159.

⋮

47. SIMONE, *supra* note 43, at 159.

⋮

49. *Id.*

50. *Id.* at 65.

⋮

52. FRANTZ FANON, THE WRETCHED OF THE EARTH (1963).

53. HUSSEIN A. BULHAN, FRANTZ FANON AND THE PSYCHOLOGY OF OPPRESSION 163 (1985).

54. *Id. See also* Bernard D. Headley, *"Black on Black" Crime: The Myth and the Reality*, CRIME & SOC. JUST., Winter 1983, at 50.

⋮

56. *See* TAYLOR, *supra* note 10, at 102–3.

57. Ansley Hamid, *The Political Economy of Crack-Related Violence*, 17 CONTEMP. DRUG PROBS. 31, 71 (1990).

⋮

59. SULLIVAN, *supra* note 32, at 77.

60. *See* JANKOWSKI, *supra* note 5, at 266, 269–70.

61. *See generally* Martin L. Forst & Martha-Elin Blomquist, *Cracking Down on Juveniles: The Changing Ideology of Youth Corrections*, 5 NOTRE DAME J.L. ETHICS & PUB. POL'Y 323 (1991).

62. Jefferson Morley, *Contradictions of Cocaine Capitalism*, THE NATION, Oct. 2, 1989, at 341, 347.

⋮

66. Anthony J. Lemelle, Jr., *Killing the Author of Life, or Decimating "Bad Niggers,"* 19 J. BLACK STUD. 216, 225–26 (1988) (citing Harry Edwards's theory of the black "macho hustle").

⋮

72. *See supra* note 25.

73. Morley, *supra* note 62, at 344.

⋮

75. The emphasis on "fast living" and immediate consumption in lieu of long-term improvement in their economic condition makes sense given that "most low-income dealers know little about the legal banking and credit system, have no legal 'job' to earn credit, and wish to avoid asset seizure in the event of arrest." Bruce D. Johnson et al., *Drug Abuse in the Inner City: Impact on Hard-Drug Users and the Community, in* DRUGS AND CRIME 9, 30 (Michael Tonry & James Q. Wilson eds., 1990).

76. ANDERSON, *supra* note 9, at 124–26.

⋮

78. *Id.* at 124.

⋮

80. *See, e.g.*, Henry Louis Gates, Jr., *"Jungle Fever" Charts Black Middle-Class Angst*, N.Y. TIMES, June 23, 1991, § 2, at 20; Jennifer Jordan, *Cultural Nationalism in the 1960s: Politics and Poetry*, in RACE, POLITICS, AND CULTURE 29, 32–33 (Adolph Reed, Jr. ed., 1986).

81. For an especially critical, class-conscious analysis of black radicalism in the 1960s, see Adolph Reed, Jr., *The "Black Revolution" and the Reconstitution of Domination*, in RACE, POLITICS, AND CULTURE, *supra* note 80, at 61.

82. *See* MICHELE WALLACE, INVISIBILITY BLUES: FROM POP TO THEORY 18–22 (1990); PAULA GIDDINGS, WHEN AND WHERE I ENTER: THE IMPACT OF BLACK WOMEN ON RACE AND SEX IN AMERICA 314–24 (1984).

⋮

85. Barrio gangs underwent a similar elevation of status during the Chicano Movement of the late 1960s and a decline thereafter. *See* Joan W. Moore, *Isolation and Stigmatization in the Development of an Underclass: The Case of Chicano Gangs in East Los Angeles*, 33 SOC. PROBS. 1 (1985).

86. HERBERT H. HAINES, BLACK RADICALS AND THE CIVIL RIGHTS MAINSTREAM, 1954–1970 56–57 (1988). *See generally* OFF THE PIGS! THE HISTORY AND LITERATURE OF THE BLACK PANTHER PARTY (G. Louis Heath ed., 1976).

87. *See generally* HENRY HAMPTON & STEVE FAYER WITH SARAH FLYNN, VOICES OF FREEDOM 348–72 (1990).

88. REGINALD MAJOR, A PANTHER IS A BLACK CAT 292 (1971).

89. *See, e.g.*, HAMPTON & FAYER, *supra* note 87, at 511–38.

90. *See* Gregory Lewis, *He Recalls Panthers' Civic Work*, S.F. EXAMINER, Feb. 17, 1991, at B1 (quoting Ex-Panther Emory Douglas as concluding that the Panthers' "No. 1 threat [to the white establishment] was the breakfast program, not our guns.").

91. *See e.g.*, ABDUL ALKALIMAT, MALCOLM X FOR BEGINNERS (1990); Vern E. Smith, *Rediscovering Malcolm X*, NEWSWEEK, Feb. 26, 1990, at 68; Joe Wood, *Looking for Malcolm: The Man and the Meaning Behind the Icon*, VILLAGE VOICE, May 29, 1990, at 43.

⋮

93. BETTYLOU VALENTINE, HUSTLING AND OTHER HARD WORK 23, 126–27 (1978); ELEANOR M. MILLER, STREET WOMAN 6, 35 (1986).

94. Elizabeth Fox-Genovese, *Strategies and Forms of Resistance: Focus on Slave Women in the United States*, in IN RESISTANCE 143, 149–50, 155–56 (Gary Y. Okihiro ed., 1986). Black women played some role in armed revolts and maroon marauding, but it is not well documented. *Id.* at 146–47, 149–52; Rosalyn Terborg-Penn, *Black Women in Resistance: A Cross-Cultural Perspective*, in IN RESISTANCE, *supra*, at 188, 194, 201–2.

95. Karlene Faith, *Media, Myths and Masculinization: Images of Women in Prison, in* Too Few to Count: Canadian Women in Conflict with the Law 181 (Ellen Adelberg & Claudia Currie eds., 1987).

⋮

97. *See* Priscilla Alexander, *Prostitution: A Difficult Issue for Feminists, in* Sex Work: Writings by Women in the Sex Industry 184, 196–97 (Frédérique Delacoste & Priscilla Alexander eds., 1987) [hereinafter Sex Work]; Gloria Lockett, *Leaving the Streets, in* Sex Work, *supra,* note 96, 96–97.

98. *See* Kathy Dobie, *The Invisible Girls: Homeless and Hooking in the Neighborhood,* Village Voice, Mar. 14, 1989, at 23.

99. *See* Michael Zausner, The Streets: A Factual Portrait of Six Prostitutes as Told in Their Own Words 34–37, 50, 92 (1986).

100. *See* Pierre L. Horn & Mary B. Pringle, *Introduction* to The Image of the Prostitute in Modern Literature 1, 3–5 (Pierre L. Horn & Mary B. Pringle eds., 1984) [hereinafter Image]; James M. Hughes, *The Uncommon Prostitute: The Contemporary Image in an American Age of Pornography, in* Image, *supra* at 101.

101. Williams & Kornblum, *supra* note 24, at 69.

102. Anne Campbell, The Girls in the Gang 16 (1984).

103. *See generally id.:* Kim Romenesko & Eleanor M. Miller, *The Second Step in Double Jeopardy: Appropriating the Labor of Female Street Hustlers,* 35 Crime & Delinq. 109 (1989).

⋮

109. In some parts of the Northeast AIDS is the leading cause of death for black women between the ages of 15 and 44. Susan Y. Chu et al., *Impact of the Human Immunodeficiency Virus Epidemic on Mortality in Women of Reproductive Age, United States,* 264 JAMA 225, 226 (1990).

110. *See* Sally Jacobs, *Captives of Crack,* Boston Globe, Dec. 13, 1989, § 1, at 1; James Kindall, *On Streets to Nowhere,* Newsday Mag., Jan. 21, 1990, at 10; Hamid, *supra* note 57, at 66–67; James A. Inciardi, *Trading Sex for Crack Among Juvenile Drug Users: A Research Note,* 16 Contemp. Drug Probs. 689 (1989).

⋮

112. *See* Gina Kolata, *On Streets Ruled by Crack, Families Die,* N.Y. Times, Aug. 11, 1989, at A1.

113. *Id.* at A13; Taylor, *supra* note 10, at 64.

114. *See* Anderson, *supra* note 9, at 86–90.

115. Bourgois, *supra* note 10, at 643–44.

⋮

117. *Id.* at 645.

118. Edith A. Folb, Runnin' Down Some Lines 256 (1980).

⋮

120. Alexander, *supra* note 97, at 188. *See also* MILLER, *supra* note 93, at 81–82.

121. MILLER, *supra* note 93, at 148.

122. *Id.* at 140.

⋮

127. *Id.* at 161.

128. *Id.* at 168.

⋮

132. *See* Austin, *supra* note 14, at 574–76.

133. *See* Regina Austin, *Employer Abuse, Worker Resistance, and the Tort of Intentional Infliction of Emotional Distress*, 41 STAN. L. REV. 1 (1988).

134. *See* James C. McKinley, Jr., *Friendships and Fear Undermine a Will to Fight Drugs in Brooklyn*, N.Y. TIMES, Sept. 18, 1989, § 1, at 1.

135. *See* VALENTINE, *supra* note 93, at 126–27.

136. WILLIAMS & KORNBLUM, *supra* note 24, at 56.

137. VALENTINE, *supra* note 93, at 23.

138. WILLIAMS & KORNBLUM, *supra* note 24, at 6–7. *See also* Jagna Sharff, *The Underground Economy of a Poor Neighborhood, in* CITIES OF THE UNITED STATES 19 (Leith Mullings ed., 1987).

⋮

140. Kathryn J. Edin, There's a Lot of Month Left at the End of the Money: How Welfare Recipients in Chicago Make Ends Meet (1989) (unpublished Ph.D. dissertation, Northwestern University).

⋮

143. *Id.* at 1.

⋮

145. *Id.* at 9–33, 112–130.

⋮

147. *Id.* at 152–53, 204–20.

148. *Id.* at 70.

149. Yvonne V. Jones, *Street Peddlers as Entrepreneurs: Economic Adaptation to an Urban Area*, 17 URB. ANTHROPOLOGY 143 (1988).

⋮

151. *Id.* at 167.

152. *Id.* at 168.

153. Stuart Henry, *The Political Economy of Informal Economies*, ANNALS, Sept. 1987, at 137, 138–39.

154. *See* Manuel Castells & Alejandro Portes, *World Underneath: The Origins, Dy-*

namics and Effects of the Informal Economy, in THE INFORMAL ECONOMY: STUD-
IES IN ADVANCED AND LESS DEVELOPED COUNTRIES 11 (Alejandro Portes et al. eds.,
1989) [hereinafter THE INFORMAL ECONOMY].

⋮

156. Henry, *supra* note 153, at 140.

157. Joseph P. Gaughan & Louis A. Ferman, *Toward an Understanding of the Informal Economy*, ANNALS, Sept. 1987, at 15, 21.

158. Saskia Sassen-Koob, *New York City's Informal Economy, in* THE INFORMAL ECON-
OMY, *supra* note 154, at 60, 71.

159. *See* Alex Stepick, *Miami's Two Informal Sectors, in* THE INFORMAL ECONOMY, *supra*
note 154, at 111. *See also* M. Patricia Fernandez-Kelly & Anna M. Garcia, *Infor-
malization at the Core: Hispanic Women, Homework, and the Advanced Capitalist
State, in* THE INFORMAL ECONOMY, *supra* note 154, at 247; Kenneth L. Wilson &
W. Allen Martin, *Ethnic Enclaves: A Comparison of the Cuban and Black Economic
Economies in Miami*, 88 AM. J. SOC. 135 (1982).

⋮

165. Alejandro Portes et al., *Conclusion: The Policy Implications of Informality, in* THE
INFORMAL ECONOMY, *supra* note 154, at 302–303.

166. *Id.* at 304.

167. *Id.* at 304–5.

168. *Id.* at 303–4.

169. *Id.* at 302.

170. Sassen-Koob, *supra* note 158, at 74.

171. Louis A. Ferman et al., *Issues and Prospects for the Study of Informal Economies:
Concepts, Research Strategies, and Policy*, ANNALS, Sept. 1987, at 154, 171; Henry,
supra note 153, at 152.

172. *See* WILLIAM JULIUS WILSON, THE TRULY DISADVANTAGED 56, 137–38 (1987).

173. *See* Portes et al., *supra* note 165, at 300–2.

174. *Id.* at 309–10.

175. *See* William H. Simon, *Social-Republican Property*, 38 UCLA L. REV. 1335 (1991).

176. Ferman et al., *supra* note 171, at 169.

⋮

182. *See generally* Susan Willis, *I Shop Therefore I Am: Is There a Place for Afro-
American Culture in Commodity Culture?, in* CHANGING OUR OWN WORDS: ESSAYS
ON CRITICISM, THEORY, AND WRITING BY BLACK WOMEN 173 (Cheryl A. Wall ed.,
1989).

183. *See* Gucci Am. v. Action Activewear, 759 F. Supp. 1060 (S.D.N.Y. 1991).

⋮

190. MARK COSTELLO & DAVID F. WALLACE, SIGNIFYING RAPPERS: RAP AND RACE IN
THE URBAN PRESENT 23 (1990). It is difficult to find a precise definition of the term
"b-boys." The "b" could refer to black, bad, block, or breakdancing. Music critic Nel-

son George says b-boys are "urban males who in style, dress, speech, and attitude exemplified hip-hop culture." NELSON GEORGE, THE DEATH OF RHYTHM & BLUES 193 (1988).

191. *See generally* B. ADLER & JANETTE BECKMAN, RAP: PORTRAITS AND LYRICS OF A GENERATION OF BLACK ROCKERS (1991).

192. *See* Tricia Rose, *Never Trust a Big Butt and a Smile*, CAMERA OBSCURA, May 1990, at 109; Michele Wallace, *When Black Feminism Faces the Music, and the Music Is Rap*, N.Y. TIMES, July 29, 1990, at H20.

193. COSTELLO & WALLACE, *supra* note 190, at 85–86.

⋮

195. David Toop, THE RAP ATTACK (1984) at 12–15. [Ed. note: The complete citation appeared as fn. 194 in the original text.]

196. COSTELLO & WALLACE, *supra* note 190, at 85.

197. Houston A. Baker, Jr., *Hybridity, the Rap Race, and Pedagogy for the 1990s*, *in* TECHNOCULTURE 197, 200 (Constance Penley & Andrew Ross eds., 1991).

198. TOOP, *supra* note 194, at 26, 65.

⋮

200. COSTELLO & WALLACE, *supra* note 190, at 85.

201. Baker, *supra* note 197, at 201.

⋮

203. *Id.* at 204.

204. Tony Van Der Meer, *Introduction to* TOOP, *supra* note 194, at 5–6. *But see* GEORGE, *supra* note 190, at 194 (suggesting that rap's "rebel status and integrity" are not yet lost).

⋮

206. To get exposure, DJs would set up in parks or at block parties and perform for free, TOOP, *supra* note 194, at 60, 71, and give away tapes of their performances to friends and acquaintances. *Id.* at 78.

207. John Griffiths has sketched out a "family model" for the criminal process that would include black people's interest in punishment with the possibility of redemption. John Griffiths, *Ideology in Criminal Procedure or A Third "Model" of the Criminal Process*, 79 YALE L.J. 359 (1970).

208. WEBSTER'S THIRD NEW INTERNATIONAL DICTIONARY 1902 (1981). In black Christian theology, for example, redemption refers to more than repentance and deliverance from one's sins. OLIN P. MOYD, REDEMPTION IN BLACK THEOLOGY 15–59 (1979).

209. Elliott Currie, *Crime, Justice, and the Social Environment*, *in* THE POLITICS OF LAW 294, 307 (David Kairys ed., rev. ed. 1990).

210. *See* DIANA FUSS, ESSENTIALLY SPEAKING: FEMINISM, NATURE AND DIFFERENCE 90–93 (1989).